~ THE OTTOMAN EMPIRE ~
AND THE WORLD AROUND IT

~ For Virginia Aksan
in friendship ~

~ The Ottoman Empire and the World Around It

~ Suraiya Faroqhi ~

I.B. TAURIS
LONDON · NEW YORK

Published for the first time in paperback in 2006 by I.B.Tauris & Co Ltd
6 Salem Road, London W2 4BU
175 Fifth Avenue, New York NY 10010
www.ibtauris.com

In the United States of America and Canada
distributed by Palgrave Macmillan, a division of St Martin's Press
175 Fifth Avenue, New York NY 10010

First published in hardback by I.B.Tauris & Co Ltd in 2004
Copyright © Suraiya Faroqhi 2004

The Library of Ottoman Studies 7

ISBN 1 84511 122 2
EAN 978 1 84511 122 9

A full CIP record for this book is available from the British Library
A full CIP record is available from the Library of Congress

Library of Congress Catalog Card Number: available

Typeset in Times by JCS Publishing Services
Printed and bound in India by Replika Press Pvt. Ltd.

~ Table of contents

List of illustrations   ix

A note on transliteration and dates   x

Acknowledgements   xi

Map of the Ottoman Empire in Asia and Africa   xiii

Map of the Ottoman Empire in Europe   xiv

1 ~ Introduction   1

Islamic law and sultanic pragmatism: 2 ~ Determining the parameters of
Ottoman 'foreign policy': some general considerations: 4 ~ A few ground
rules of Ottoman 'foreign politics': 6 ~ Validity and limits of the 'warfare
state' model: 8 ~ Accommodation, both open and unacknowledged, and the
problem of structural similarities in the early modern world: 10 ~ An
impossible balance between 'east' and 'west'?: 11 ~ Who, in which period,
formed part of the Ottoman elite?: 13 ~ The Ottoman Empire as a world
economy: 14 ~ The abiding centrality of Istanbul: 16 ~ Confronting our
limits: problems of documentation: 18 ~ 'Placing' our topic in geographical
terms: 20 ~ 'Placing' our topic in time: 21 ~ Confronting different
perspectives, or how to justify comparisons: 23 ~ A common world: 25 ~

2 ~ On sovereignty and subjects: expanding and safeguarding
the Empire   27

'Foreign interference' and its limits: 28 ~ A sequence of 'mental images': 30
~ The 1560s/967–77: 32 ~ *Introducing the major 'players' of the 1560s/*
967–77: the Habsburg possessions, France, Venice and Iran: 32 ~ Religious
rivalries of the 1560s/967–77: 34 ~ The mid-sixteenth century: foreign
subjects present on Ottoman territory – and those who were conspicuously
absent: 37 ~ Religious-cum-*political rivalries between the sultans and*
'western' rulers in the 1560s/967–77: 41 ~ How the Ottoman elite did not
organize its relations with the outside world in the 1560s/967–77: 43 ~ Limits
of imperial reach in the 1560s/967–77: Anatolian loyalties to non-Ottoman
princes: 44 ~ Limits of imperial reach: some Rumelian examples: 46 ~ Limits
of imperial reach in the 1560s/967–77, a further example: Yemen as a
frontier province: 47 ~ The Empire in 1639/1048–9: 49 ~ Protecting Ottoman

territories in 1639/1048–9: the eastern frontier: 49 ~ *The northern regions as
a trouble spot in 1639/1048–9:* 50 ~ *Expanding Ottoman territory in 1639/
1048–9: relations with Venice and the imminent conquest of Crete:* 51 ~
*Potential threats to Ottoman control over the western part of the Balkan
peninsula in 1639/1048–9:* 52 ~ *Early links to the seventeenth-century
European world economy?:* 53 ~ Before 1718/1130–1: 55 ~ *Wars on all
fronts:* 55 ~ *'The Empire strikes back': toward a* reprise en main *before
1718/1130–1:* 58 ~ *Extraterritorialities before 1718/1130–1:* 60 ~ *Conquest
and trade as sources of regional instabilities before 1718/1130–1:* 62 ~
*War-induced regional instabilities before 1718/1130–1: Serbs on both sides
of the frontier:* 64 ~ 1774/1187–8: 67 ~ *The Russo-Ottoman war of 1768–74/
1181–8:* 67 ~ *Provincial power magnates and international relations in
1774/1187–8:* 69 ~ *Eighteenth-century prosperity and crisis in the
'economic' field:* 70 ~ *The desert borders in 1774/1187–8:* 72 ~ In
conclusion: the Ottoman rulers within a set of alliances: 73

3 ~ On the margins of empire: clients and dependants   75

The royal road to empire-building: from 'dependent principality' to 'centrally
governed province': 75 ~ 'Dependent principalities' with long life-spans: 77
~ Ottoman methods of conquest and local realities: 78 ~ Old and new local
powers in 'centrally governed provinces': 80 ~ Semi-autonomous provinces
controlled by military corps and 'political households': 82 ~ The case of the
Hijaz: 84 ~ *Subsidising a reticent dependant: the sherifs as autonomous
princes on the desert frontier:* 84 ~ *The sherifs, the Bedouins and the security
of the pilgrimage caravan:* 87 ~ *The sherifs in the international arena:* 88 ~
The case of Dubrovnik: linking Ottoman sultans to the Catholic
Mediterranean: 89 ~ 'Cruel times in Moldavia': 91 ~ In conclusion: 95 ~

4 ~ The strengths and weaknesses of Ottoman warfare   98

Ottoman military preparedness and booty-making: assessing their
significance and limits: 98 ~ Ottoman political advantages in early modern
wars: 102 ~ Financing wars and procuring supplies: the changing weight of
tax assignments and cash disbursals: 104 ~ How to make war without footing
the bill – at least in the short run: 108 ~ Logistics: cases of gunpowder: 110 ~
Societies of frontiersmen: 112 ~ Legitimacy through victory, de-
legitimization through wars on the sultan's territories: 114 ~ In conclusion:
Ottoman society organized to keep up with the military reformation: 116 ~

5 ~ Of prisoners, slaves and the charity of strangers   119

Prisoners in the shadows: 119 ~ Captured: how ordinary people paid the price
of inter-empire conflict and attempts at state formation: 121 ~ From captive

to slave: 124 ~ The miseries of transportation: 126 ~ On galleys and in arsenals: 127 ~ Charity and the tribulations of prisoners: 129 ~ The 'extra-curricular' labours of galley – and other – slaves: 131 ~ Domestic service: 132 ~ The role of local mediation in ransoming a Christian prisoner: 134 ~ In conclusion: 135 ~

6 ~ Trade and foreigners   137

Merchants from remote countries: the Asian world: 138 ~ Merchants from a (not so) remote Christian country: the Venetians: 140 ~ Polish traders and gentlemanly visitors: 142 ~ Merchants from the lands of a (doubtful) ally: France: 144 ~ Subjects of His/Her Majesty, the king/queen of England: 148 ~ Links to the capital of the seventeenth-century world economy: the Dutch case: 150 ~ How Ottoman merchants coped with foreigners and foreign trade: 151 ~ Revisiting an old debate: 'established' and 'new' commercial actors: 154 ~ The Ottoman ruling group and its attitudes to foreign trade: 155 ~

7 ~ Relating to pilgrims and offering mediation   161

The problems of Iranian pilgrims in Iraq and the Hijaz: 162 ~ Jewish visitors to Jerusalem: 164 ~ Christian visitors writing about Palestine and the Sinai peninsula: 165 ~ Ottoman people and places in western accounts of Jerusalem: 167 ~ The Christian pilgrimage to Jerusalem in Muslim eyes: 169 ~ Catholic missionaries in Ottoman lands: 171 ~ Mediations, ambiguities and shifts of identity: 174 ~ An eighteenth-century Istanbul xenophobe: 176 ~ Was friendship between an Ottoman Muslim and a non-Muslim foreigner an impossible proposition?: 177 ~

8 ~ Sources of information on the outside world   179

The knowledge of the ambassadors: some general considerations: 181 ~ Fleeting encounters: a sea captain and diplomat in sixteenth-century India: 183 ~ The knowledge of the envoys: representing Ottoman dignity in Iran: 185 ~ Lying abroad for the good of one's sovereign: obscuring Ottoman intentions in early eighteenth-century Iran: 186 ~ Reporting on European embassies: 187 ~ Old opponents, new allies: 191 ~ In the empire of the tsars: 192 ~ Difficult beginnings: a new type of information-gathering: 193 ~ Framing the world according to Ottoman geographers: 194 ~ Taking notice of the Americas: 197 ~ Kâtib Çelebi and his circle: 199 ~ Non-Muslim Ottoman subjects and their travel writing: 200 ~ Tracking down the knowledge of the educated Muslim townsman: 203 : Evliya Çelebi's stories about Europe: 204 ~ *Holland and the way thither*: 204 ~ *European frontiers: a* quantité négligeable?: 206 ~ *And what about Evliya's intentions in writing?*: 207 ~ In conclusion: 208 ~

9 ~ Conclusion   211

A common world: 211 ~ The integration of foreigners: 212 ~ Imperial
cohesion, 'corruption' and the liberties of foreigners: 213 ~ Coping with the
European world economy: 214 ~ Ottoman rule: between the centre and the
margins: 215 ~ Providing information: what 'respectable people' might or
might not write about: 216 ~ Embassy reports: much maligned but a sign of
changing mentalities: 217 ~

Bibliography   220

Notes   263

Index   283

~ List of illustrations

1. Helmet and armour intended as a diplomatic present from the Habsburg
   Emperor Rudolf II to the Grand Vizier Sinan Paşa.   39
2. View from Semlin towards Belgrade, with the Ottoman fortress beyond the
   Danube, early nineteenth century   66
3. A janissary and his European captive, 1669   124
4. The naval arsenal at Kasımpaşa, Istanbul, after 1784 and before 1800   128
5. The Damascus gate in the walls of Jerusalem   169
6. The parade by which Ahmed Resmi entered Berlin in 1763   189
7. Secretary of the Ottoman embassy to Berlin, carrying the sultan's letter
   (after 1763)   190
8. A visit of the Ottoman ambassador Mehmed efendi, accompanied by his
   son Hüseyin, at the court of King Augustus of Poland in 1731   218

~ A note on transliteration and dates

For Ottoman-Turkish words, modern Turkish spelling according to *Redhouse Yeni Türkçe–İngilizce Sözlük, New Redhouse Turkish–English Dictionary* of 1968 (Istanbul: Redhouse Press) has been used. Only those words denoting places, people and terms of the Islamic realm that never formed part of the Ottoman world have been rendered in the transliteration used in *The Encyclopedia of Islam* (2nd edition, 1960–). ed. by H.A.R. Gibb *et alii* (Leiden: E. J. Brill). Where there exists an accepted English name for a city or region, this has been preferred, i.e. 'Aleppo' as opposed to 'Halep' or Ḥalab', 'Syria' as opposed to 'Şām'.

The present volume contains a good many dates that I have found in sources using only Common Era (CE) datings. This means that the relevant Islamic year normally encompasses two years, and in order to avoid beginning with a 'hyphenated' expression, I have put the CE date first. When giving the birth and death dates of individuals, or the dates between which a given ruler was in power, the first date mentioned is always the first of the two *hicri* years into which his/her birth or accession is known to have fallen. As to the second date, it is the second of the two *hicri* years corresponding to the relevant person's death or dethronement, thus for example: Süleyman the Magnificent (r. 1520–66/926–74). For twentieth- and twenty-first-century dates, there are no *hicri* equivalents.

In the notes only CE dates have been used unless we are dealing with the date of an archival document. Since this is normally in Ottoman, the *hicri* date will be a single year, and its CE equivalent has to be hyphenated. In consequence when giving the date of an archival document the *hicri* date will come first.

~ Acknowledgements

Many colleagues and students have helped in the preparation of this book, and as the Turkish saying goes 'however much I thank them it will be too little'. A large part of the writing was done while I was a fellow at the Wissenschaftskolleg zu Berlin in 2001–2. I owe a great debt to the other fellows, who did much to enlarge my horizons, but particularly to Gesine Bottomley and her team, who obtained books for me whenever I wanted them, and were ever ready to locate outlandish bibliographical information. Mitchell Cohen contributed his expertise as an editor. Barbara Sanders of the secretariat as well as Wiebke Güse and Petra Sonnenberg of the computer department helped to process the correspondence this manuscript occasioned, ironed out word processing problems and upon occasion, patiently listened to the lamentations without which no book apparently gets written. Back in Munich, Yavuz Köse has been a tower of strength; without his efficiency, I do not think I could have written very much, given the university bureaucracy that seems to increase in inverse proportion to the means actually available for historical research. The Library of the American Research Institute in Turkey (ARIT/Istanbul) furnished some books I had not been able to find elsewhere; thanks to Anthony Greenwood and Gülden Güneri. During the weeks that I was based in Istanbul, Pınar Kesen most graciously helped with the editing; and last but not least, I have Christoph Knüttel to thank for his aid with the index, and Yvonne Grossmann for drawing the maps.

Too numerous to list are the colleagues who have supplied me with material and good advice, and I crave the pardon of anyone that I may have forgotten. Virginia Aksan provided me with insights into the problems of war and peace from the Ottoman perspective, particularly by allowing me to read her as yet unpublished manuscript. Stephanos Boulaisikis, Nikolas Pissis and Anna Vlachopoulos introduced me to Greek travel accounts and translated modern Greek texts for me. Penelope Stathe, Marie Elisabeth Mitsou and Albrecht Berger provided further information on this – to me – arcane subject. Many thanks for that and for their overall interest in the emerging work. To Maria Pia Pedani Fabris, I am grateful for sharing her profound knowledge of the documents in the Venetian archives, and above all for a copy of the *relazioni* that she has edited, all but impossible to locate otherwise as the publisher has gone out of business. Without the help of Minna Rozen, I would not have known anything about the Jewish travellers whose silhouettes fleetingly appear on the pages of this book, while Ina Baghdiantz McCabe has provided pointers to the accounts of Armenian travellers available in translation. To Nicolas Vatin, I am much obliged for letting me read his article on illegal enslavement in the Ottoman realm before it actually appeared in print, while Enis Batur has presented me with several publications put out by Yapı ve Kredi Yayınları: my heartiest thanks. Vera Costantini has generously provided information on the Cyprus war, but perhaps more importantly, contributed much through her laughter and love of life.

In addition, there are the people who have read the manuscript and tried very hard to make it into a better book; if I did not take all of their excellent advice, I have no one to blame but myself. Apart from an anonymous reader, whose incisive criticisms I have done my special best to take into account, I extend my warmest thanks to Virginia Aksan, Robert Dankoff, Christopher Hann and Ildikó Béller-Hann, Leslie Peirce, Gilles Veinstein and above all, Christoph Neumann, whose patience has been almost without limits. At I. B. Tauris, Lester Crook has been a most understanding editor, providing tea and endless sympathy when accommodating my intrusions and listening to my follies. All these people have made time in their busy schedules in order to respond to me and my queries, and I can only hope that they will find the results acceptable at least to some degree.

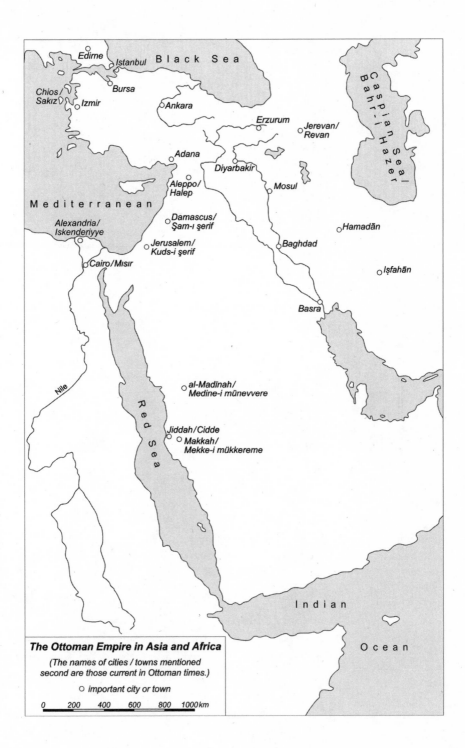

Edirne

Istanbul

B l a c k   S e a

Bursa

Chios /
Sakız

Izmir

Ankara

Erzurum

Jerevan /
Revan

C a s p i a n   S e a /
B a h r - i   H a z e r

Adana

Diyarbakir

Aleppo /
Halep

Mosul

M e d i t e r r a n e a n

Alexandria /
Iskenderiyye

Damascus /
Şam-ı şerif

Hamadān

Jerusalem /
Kuds-i şerif

Baghdad

Cairo / Mısır

İşfahān

Basra

Nile

R e d   S e a

al-Madīnah /
Medine-i münevvere

Jiddah / Cidde
Makkah /
Mekke-i mükkereme

I n d i a n

O c e a n

The Ottoman Empire in Asia and Africa

*(The names of cities / towns mentioned
second are those current in Ottoman times.)*

○ *important city or town*

0   200   400   600   800   1000 km

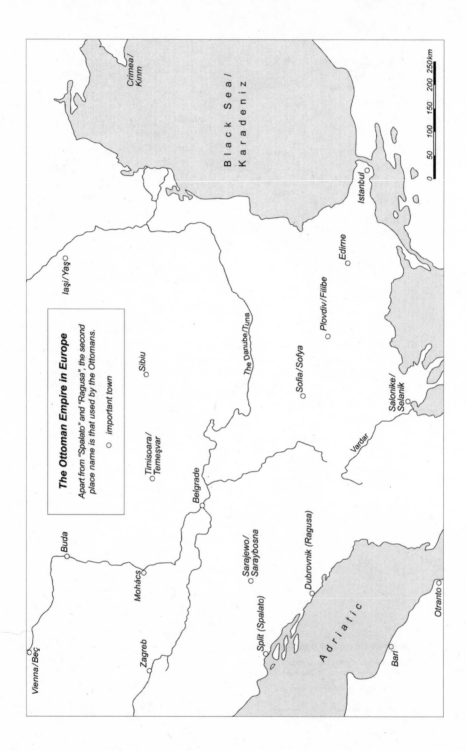

The Ottoman Empire in Europe

Apart from "Spalato" and "Ragusa", the second place name is that used by the Ottomans.

o *important town*

Vienna/Beç

Buda

Mohács

Zagreb

Timisoara/
Temeşvar

Sibiu

Iaşi/Yaş

Belgrade

The Danube/Tuna

Sarajewo/
Saraybosna

Split (Spalato)

Dubrovnik (Ragusa)

Sofia/Sofya

Plovdiv/Filibe

Edirne

Istanbul

Vardar

Salonike/
Selanik

Bari

Otranto

A d r i a t i c

B l a c k   S e a /
K a r a d e n i z

Crimea/
Kırım

0   50   100   150   200 250km

1 ~ Introduction

In a sense, this study deals with one of the oldest and most often studied topics in Ottoman history. From the fifteenth and sixteenth centuries onwards, European ambassadors, merchants and other travellers made it their business to write about their various receptions in the Ottoman lands and, analysed with due caution, these accounts are germane to our topic. On the other hand, Ottoman writers of the sixteenth or seventeenth century, as the perusal of their chronicles shows, certainly focused on Istanbul and the sultans' court, but did not totally ignore the world outside the Empire's frontiers either.[1] After all, the very stuff of such works consisted of campaigns, conquests and the incorporation of foreign territories. But on occasion, these authors also could not avoid including defeats, the losses of provinces and the truces and peace treaties that, provisionally or on a long-term basis, ended inter-state conflicts. All these warlike encounters can be viewed as a way of relating to the outside world: no conquest without something 'out there' that is still unconquered.[2] Certainly the situation at European courts and – albeit to a lesser degree – the institutions characteristic of European societies only became a major topic of Ottoman written texts in the eighteenth century. But given their close concern with war and conquest, it is an exaggeration to claim that the authors of earlier chronicles had no interest at all in what went on outside the borders of the sultans' empire.

Even more obvious is the interest of Ottoman officials in sultanic campaigns in 'infidel' lands, the comings and goings of foreign ambassadors, Central Asian dervish sheiks on their pilgrimages to the holy city of Mecca or traders from Iran bringing raw silk to Bursa. As a result, the sultans' campaigns in Hungary or Iran after the middle 1500s/930s–970s are best followed not by collating the bits and pieces of information provided in chronicles, as is inevitable when dealing with the fifteenth century. Rather the historian will analyse materials produced by Ottoman bureaucrats, in other words, archival sources.[3] Unfortunately the number of spy reports on the internal affairs of Christian unbelievers (*kâfir*) and Shi'ite heretics (*rafizi, mülhid, zındık*) in the Istanbul archives is limited, and those that do survive are not necessarily very informative. But even so, the numerous sultanic commands relating to the goods that foreign traders might or might not export, the safe conducts given to Mecca pilgrims from outside the Empire and other documents of this kind show that leading Ottoman officials had to concern themselves intensively with developments that took place in localities outside the Empire's borders.

~ Islamic law and sultanic pragmatism

In Islamic religious law (şeriat) and also in Ottoman official writing, it was customary to describe the world as being made up of the Darülislam ('the house of Islam') and the Darülharb ('the house of war'). Into the first category belonged not only the domains of the Ottoman sultans themselves, but also those of other Sunni Muslims, such as the Uzbek khans or the Mughuls of India. To what extent the Ottoman elite believed that their sultan was the supreme ruler of the Islamic world, to whom all others were expected to defer, is still in need of further investigation; here we will not attempt to decide this matter. Even more ambiguous was the status of the Shi'ite state of Safavid Iran. In the mid-sixteenth century, a famous Ottoman jurisconsult had refused to recognize the 'Kızılbaş' – one of several terms of opprobrium favoured in Ottoman parlance for Shi'ites both Iranian and Anatolian – as part of the Muslim community. But especially after militant Shi'ism had stopped being a major issue between the Ottoman and Safavid empires, as happened in the late sixteenth century, it is unlikely that this exclusionist view remained the dominant one.[4]

Again in conformity with religious law, non-Muslim rulers who had accepted to pay tribute to the Ottoman sultan were considered part of the Islamic world. One such polity was Dubrovnik, a city-state that due to its size and location was able to avoid most of the conflicts in which the Empire was involved, while the town's wealthier inhabitants devoted themselves exclusively to Mediterranean trade. Other dependencies of the Empire governed by non-Muslim rulers, and by virtue of this relationship part of the Islamic world, that one might mention include the principalities of Moldavia, Transylvania and Walachia in present-day Rumania. Of course, the opposite was true whenever this or that ruler sided with the Habsburgs or the Commonwealth of Poland-Lithuania and thus was at war with the sultan. Thus the category, namely 'the outside world', that we have adopted here cuts across two categories accepted by Ottoman writers themselves. The Ottomans probably would have spoken of the Islamic world that recognized the paramount status of the padişah in Istanbul on the one hand, and the domains of the various rulers of 'the house of war' on the other. High points of inter-empire conflict apart, the 'Iranian question' might have been left diplomatically in abeyance.

In discussing the relationship of the Ottoman elites with the world outside the Empire's borders we have thus intentionally adopted a terminology that is more vague than that employed by the relevant primary sources themselves. While at first glance this seems a clumsy move, some advantages are, or so I think, involved as well. For in reality, there was no 'iron curtain' separating the Ottoman elites and their tax-paying subjects from the world outside the borders of the Empire, while the existence of a neat legal dichotomy between the Islamic and non-Islamic worlds might cause us to think the exact opposite. In the absence of actual war, foreign merchants from India, Iran, Georgia and the various countries of Christian Europe were admitted with few difficulties. In the case of Venice, France, England or the Netherlands, special privileges formally granted by the Ottoman sultans (*ahidname*, or 'capitulations' in European parlance) established what the subjects of the rulers in question were allowed or forbidden to do.[5] Long-term residents from Venice, France or England could be found in Istanbul, Izmir or Aleppo; moreover, during the period that concerns us here, contacts were facilitated by the absence of any war between the Ottoman sultan and the rulers of England or France.

On a different level, inter-communication between the Empire and neighbouring states also extended to culturally valued items: maps, books and, in spite of the Islamic ban on images, even sultans' portraits or pictures showing the exotic animals of the American continent circulated between the Ottoman realm and its western neighbours. One of the major aims of this book is to demonstrate how permeable the frontiers really were in many instances. Of course, this implies that the neat dichotomy between the 'house of Islam' and the 'house of war' is not very useful for the purposes of this study, as it masks the much more complicated relationships existing in the real world.

Moreover, while fully recognizing that wars between the Ottoman Empire and its neighbours were frequent, and relations even in peacetime marred by numerous misunderstandings both intentional and otherwise, we will here be concerned also with many relationships in which military conflict had no role. These include trade, but also the accommodation of pilgrims, gentlemen travelling for pleasure or instruction, and even Christian missionaries. Thus it is one of our major points that, while the dichotomies established by Islamic law were certainly important, the Ottoman elite also governed a far-flung empire that was at least an indirect heir to the administrative lore of the Sasanid, caliphal and Byzantine traditions.[6] More importantly, in my view, the Ottoman ruling group also made a large number of very matter-of-fact decisions, based on expediency and taking into account what was possible under given circumstances.

This emphasis on pragmatism, 'muddling through' to use an expression current among another group of great empire-builders, may appear old-fashioned to some readers today. In the present conjuncture, it has become current to emphasize religion-based oppositions between the Empire and the non-Muslim world, and also the central place of religion in the Ottoman world view. It would certainly be unrealistic to deny the centrality of Islam; but in my perspective, it was exactly because the elites had no doubt about this centrality that they were able to react to the 'people outside the pale' with much more pragmatism than would be possible for an elite whose members felt that the basis of their rule was under constant threat, and therefore in need of permanent defence. As a result the rules of the political game were quite often developed and brought into play without there being a great need for day-to-day references to religious law. In a sense the present volume thus can be read as a plea for the importance of the sultans' prerogative to set the ground rules by promulgating decrees (*kanun*). Moreover, since we are concerned with a period in which some sultans were quite young or for other reasons unable to govern in person, this situation meant that the

Ottoman elite as a whole was able to run its relations with the 'outside world' with a considerable degree of liberty.

Members of the Ottoman ruling group must have been confirmed in their pragmatic attitude by the manner in which the advance of the sultans' power in south-eastern and later in central Europe was in many instances received by local inhabitants. Both minor aristocracies and tax-paying subjects were often quite ready to make their peace with the sultan, and certain would-be or unstable rulers hoped to garner Ottoman support in order to gain power or else hold on to it. Thus the estates of Bohemia in rebellion against the Habsburgs (1618–20/1027–30) tried to obtain Ottoman aid, but the rapid defeat of the movement after the battle of the White Mountain made this a non-issue as far as Istanbul was concerned. On the European side of the great dividing line, the rhetoric of the crusade certainly survived well into the nineteenth century, but as early as the 1450s/854–64, even a dedicated pope such as Pius II was quite unable to transform it into reality. To mention a later example of the same trend, after Lala Mustafa Paşa's conquest of Cyprus in 1570–3/978–81, the Venetian Signoria was prepared to cut its losses and abandon its alliance with the pope and the king of Spain, both for commercial considerations and probably also in order not to facilitate the expansion of Spanish power in Italy. Quite a few Christian rulers thus actively sought accommodation. We do not have a large number of Ottoman comments on this situation on their western borders; in the short run, the permanent disunity of Christian rulers doubtless was viewed as facilitating future conquest. But in the long run, close relations with at least the elites of certain states of Christian Europe must have led to situations in which 'established arrangements to mutual advantage' were preferred over permanent warfare; once again, pragmatism became the order of the day.

~Determining the parameters of Ottoman 'foreign policy': some general considerations

In the course of this study, we will often speak of 'the Ottoman Empire', 'the Ottoman administration', 'Ottoman officials' or 'the authorities in Istanbul'. These are shorthand formulas that need some explanation. Among political historians, it was customary for a long time to assume that states acted in the international arena primarily due to their economic and 'security' interests; in other words, because of considerations involving power struggles with other states. This is the 'primacy of foreign politics' dear to many historians until well after World War II, a theory that regards the political opinions of the relevant elites as reasonably homogeneous. However after World War II, and more vigorously from the 1960s onwards, a school of thought has emerged that emphasizes the fact that major foreign policy decisions may be taken on account of purely domestic power struggles within the ruling elite. Or, at least in the nineteenth and twentieth centuries, members of these elites may act in response to what they perceive as public opinion – and in the Ottoman realm, a comparable tendency went back very far, as high-level officials ignored the wishes and expectations of Istanbul's rank-and-file janissaries and even ordinary craftsmen at their own peril.[7]

It is unnecessary to be dogmatic about these matters and assert that *all* major foreign policy decisions are taken for domestic reasons. But the phenomenon is certainly common enough to be taken seriously, for the early modern period as well as for the twentieth century. Thus we may assume that Ottoman decisions concerning war and peace were often made after struggles between different factions within the elite, struggles which are, in fact, well documented from the second half of the sixteenth century onwards.[8] A certain faction might assume that its interests were best served by war with Iran rather than by another campaign against the Habsburgs, and vice versa. In the case of serious reverses, a different faction might gain the day and initiate a change of policy. Once again, this is a widespread phenomenon in all manner of states, which can be observed in the Ottoman polity.[9]

At the same time, an emphasis upon domestic divisions also serves to place 'geopolitical' claims into perspective; to take but one example, it has sometimes been asserted that the Ottoman Empire was obliged to conquer Crete because the island's geographic situation allowed its possessor to impede communications between Istanbul and Egypt.[10] A glance at the map shows that Crete did, and does, in fact occupy a strategic position. But if holding the island had been as vital to Ottoman state interests as some defendants of geopolitics may claim, then it is hard to understand why neither Süleyman the Magnificent nor his immediate successors made any attempt to conquer it. I would therefore assume that the undoubted strategic value of the island became an issue over which an Ottoman government decided to go to war only during a very specific conjuncture. Once again, factional struggles within the elite during the reign of the mentally unbalanced Sultan Ibrahim surely played a part. But, in addition, a major factor was doubtless the weakness of Venice. For centuries, the Signoria had governed the island, but during the years following 1600/1008–9, Venetian commerce had contracted and its traditional hinterland in central Europe had been lost, due to the devastation caused by the Thirty Years War.[11] Thus the time seemed propitious for annexing yet a further piece of the erstwhile colonial empire of the Signoria. Throughout the present book, we will encounter cases in which momentary expediency of the kind alluded to here inflected long-term policies, and we will have occasion to argue the case of contingency *versus* system-based constraints. Similar struggles among the governing elite are well attested for other major campaigns as well, including the re-conquest of Yemen in the 1560s/967–77 and the war over Cyprus during the early 1570s/978–81.[12] In the present study 'imperatives' of all kinds, religio-legal as well as geopolitical, will be played down; and this means that intra-elite conflicts will be given their due weight, particularly in matters of what we today would call 'foreign policy'.

~ A few ground rules of Ottoman 'foreign politics'

When it comes to Ottoman views of their neighbours, most of our information concerns those living to the west and to the north; but even in this limited sphere, there are serious deficiencies. While numerous envoys/messengers (*çavuş*) visited Venice in the 1500s and early 1600s/X.–early XI. centuries, and one or two of them showed up in France as well, written reports about these missions do not seem to have survived.[13] Only in the early eighteenth century did Ottoman ambassadors begin to write *in extenso* about their experiences in foreign parts, with the well-known Yirmisekiz Mehmed Efendi pioneering the rather novel genre of embassy reports with an account of his visit to Paris in 1720/1132–3.[14] It was at this time too that the authors of Ottoman chronicles made occasional comments about the activities of this or that foreign ambassador present in Istanbul; in earlier periods these men were simply not considered important enough to figure in formal writing. If European ambassadors and their personnel had not written so much about their missions to Istanbul, we would simply have to confess our ignorance and leave it at that; but as these men did write a good deal, and usually had a rather narrow horizon, a book of the kind undertaken here must attempt to redress the balance and highlight the Ottoman viewpoint by means of whatever sources are available.[15]

Matters are complicated by the fact that in some early modern polities, even foreign relations in the narrow sense of the word were not always the exclusive province of the ruler and his closest official advisors. This applied, for instance, to the French monarchy of the seventeenth century. Every reader of Alexandre Dumas' novels knows that a foreign queen, such as Anne d'Autriche (1601–66/ 1009–77), the consort of the French ruler Louis XIII, herself a member of the Habsburg dynasty, was easily suspected of politically disloyal relations with her natal family. Moreover it was not only the queen, who after all possessed some official status, who might be involved in the foreign relations of the kingdom of France; even aristocratic ladies, whose power over this or that minister, or else the king himself, was purely de facto, might extend patronage to noblemen who hoped to be appointed ambassadors.[16]

A similar situation obtained in Istanbul, where, as is well known, members of the sultan's household might use their familial relations in Venice for purposes that were political at least in the wider sense of the word.[17] All this appears strange to us, as we are not accustomed to seeing rulers as the heads of extensive households that in their entirety are active in state politics. We are even less willing to admit that members of these households can have a voice in foreign policy, considered a particularly 'sensitive' domain. If members of a royal household became involved in foreign politics – certainly not an unheard of occurrence at European courts of the later nineteenth century – the ruler and his prime minister would probably be denounced for allowing their camarilla too much 'influence'. However, the role of the sultans in heading households whose bureaucracies formed part of their 'patrimony' has been much studied in the Ottoman case, and we must keep in mind that, at least in the seventeenth century, the royal household in France was not a purely 'domestic' institution either.

This situation has led historians dealing with the Ottoman Empire and the manner in which its ruling class made decisions affecting inter-state relations, to develop rather different views of these processes according to the sources they happen to use. When our sources emanate from European embassies, all manner of intermediaries loom large. After all, the sultan was visible to an ambassador only in the arrival and departure audiences, and often did not speak at all; much less could he be spoken to. Negotiators would see the grand vizier more often, but even these meetings were formal audiences that the ambassadors prepared for by collecting 'local knowledge' from the outgoing ambassador if there was one, from ambassadors of friendly states if available and, most importantly, from Ottoman subjects such as the reviled but indispensable dragomans. In exceptional cases, a foreign ambassador might even seek the mediation of a particularly respected dervish sheik.[18]

An Ottoman dignitary might attempt to 'have a say' in the relations with this or that country, and therefore build relations with an ambassador he considered important for his purposes. After all, we know that a 'war party' and a 'peace party' often contended at the Ottoman court, and the members of the peace party especially might seek information from a foreign ambassador in order to prove their point. Moreover, at least in the seventeenth century, an ecumenical patriarch of the Orthodox Church might also have his own views on the wars in which his sultan should engage. Thus Cyrillos Lucaris (1572–1638/979–1048) attempted to provoke a war between the Ottoman Empire and Poland, which he hoped would lead to the dismemberment of this latter state. For, at the time, the Polish king adhered to the Counter-Reformation and was threatening the survival of the Orthodox Church in his Ukrainian domains.[19] When studied on the basis of European source material, the decision-making process in 'foreign policy' thus appears to be very diffuse, with the input of sultans and grand viziers much less significant than it probably was in reality. And, in so far as this diffuseness was real and not an illusion, we have seen that similar phenomena were observed in early modern France as well.

When our source basis consists of the Ottoman sultans' rescripts to foreign rulers surviving in the original in the recipients' archives, or else as copies in Istanbul, the result will, by contrast, be a very solemn, monolithic and 'official' image. Quite differently from the impression often gained from ambassadors' correspondence, here we see a sultan totally in command of all decisions affecting war and peace. Foreign rulers were treated for the most part as obedient vassals if relations were reasonably good, and as enemies about to be chastised if they were not. However, in the letters of the grand viziers, which for instance in the Venetian archives are often found adjacent to the sultans' rescripts, the tone may already be rather different. Thus we will find appeals to the addressee's self-interest or realistic understanding of worldly affairs, which have no place in more official writings. In this case, it does not make sense to assume that sultan and grand vizier were operating at cross-purposes, but rather that the rescript conveys the official Ottoman understanding of the situation, while the letter of the grand vizier is a move in the process of actual negotiation. In most cases, though, we only possess the rescript, and this makes the Ottomans appear singularly deficient in the fine art of negotiation – which of course, many of them were not. The sultans' rescripts were meant to convey a sense of this ruler's religiously motivated paramount position; and this type of legitimization involved a constantly declared readiness to go to war.

~ Validity and limits of the 'warfare state' model

Viewed from an Ottoman perspective, the ideology of expanding the domain of Islam through warfare against the 'infidel' played a major role in legitimizing the rule of the sultans. While accommodation between Ottoman governors and their Habsburg or Venetian counterparts was certainly not rare in border provinces, in both oral and written culture it was the confrontations that received most publicity. In a parallel fashion, battle against 'the Turk' was also a potent means of asserting the legitimacy of the Habsburg rulers, and the Venetian tendency to place commercial considerations over 'holy war, Catholic style' was quite often the subject of acerbic criticism. Among the major European kings, only François I of France (r. 1514–47/919–54) was willing to brave widespread adverse publicity by entering into an alliance with 'the infidel'. Recent work has shown that sixteenth- and seventeenth-century French policy makers took the 'propagandistic' opposition in a number of European countries to the Franco-Ottoman alliance quite seriously.[20] In order not to 'lose face' among Christian rulers, the kings of France, for instance, were quite willing to allow their noble subjects to enlist in the Order of Malta, and thus have French noblemen engage in the 'battle against the infidel' that the crown itself avoided because of its rivalry with the Habsburgs.

Thus both early modern European states and the Ottoman Empire were organized for war as their principal *raison d'être*. This particular statement is a piece of 'ancient wisdom' that recently has been reasserted.[21] Thanks to a number of patient and sensible studies, both of individual campaigns and of the management of supplies and military personnel, we now know a good deal more about how the sultans' campaigns were prepared. As a result, myths concerning the special, fanatical devotion of Ottoman soldiers to sovereign and religion have been discounted.[22] Regular arrivals of food and war *matériel* as well as a kind of rough fairness in the treatment of soldiers by their commanding officers were just as important for discipline and military performance as they were in other armies. Just as soldiers serving any other ruler, under-supplied Ottoman soldiers tended to desert the battlefield. There is thus no particular reason to claim that the Ottomans were organized for war in a sense that did not apply to their European counterparts.[23]

After all, we also possess a considerable body of studies on the military apparatuses of early modern Europe, and they have demonstrated that a constant preparedness for war was just as characteristic of the Habsburg realm or France as it was of the Ottoman Empire. In most European states of the early modern period, the revenues needed for war-making at some point outran what the limited productivity of the underlying economies was able to provide, leading to economic crises of often considerable severity.[24] Between the Ottoman world and western or central Europe, forms of financing and the political criteria determining the distribution of high commands might differ. Yet the rulers and high officials of all these states saw war and expansion by conquest as their main aims, if not as the very reason for the existence of the states that they governed.[25]

But for a long time, the Ottoman Empire surpassed its rivals in the business of war and, even though the Habsburgs and Safavids could not be finally subdued, the sultan's realm continued to expand well into the late seventeenth century.[26] The relevant campaigns involved the personal participation of sultans and viziers, who throughout Ottoman history led innumerable campaigns. It is well known that at the age of seventy-two Süleyman the Magnificent (r. 1520–66/ 926–74) set out on a last campaign to Hungary, where he died. From the later sixteenth century onwards, the bureaucracy certainly developed routines that enabled it to run the Empire for much of the time without the sultans needing to take major military or even political initiatives.[27] Even so, quite a few rulers, such as Mehmed III (r. 1595–1603/1003–12), Osman II (r. 1618–22/1027–32), Murad IV (r. 1623–40/1032–50) or Mustafa II (r. 1693–1703/1104–15) sought the political prestige that only could be gained by taking the field in person. On the other hand, stay-at-home sultans such as Murad III (r. 1574–95/981–1004) might incur considerable criticism because they had not led any conquering armies.[28]

Moreover, in the eighteenth century, when expansion definitely had ended, Ottoman military effectiveness and sultanic concern for army reform were not totally at an end. To the contrary, certain rulers and their viziers still were quite successful in recovering territories lost during the disastrous war of 1683–99/ 1094–1111. Yet in the later eighteenth century, a period of irreversible territorial contraction, the Ottoman Empire still fought a long rearguard action, whose successes should not be attributed solely to Great Power rivalries, even if the latter were very important. It is thus quite obvious that war and preparation for war formed a major concern of the Ottoman ruling group as long as it occupied the political scene.

However, in this insistence that rulers and high officials should take an active part in the conduct of war, the Ottomans once again were not alone. Henri IV of France (r. 1589–1610/998–1019) was a warlord first and foremost, and his grandson Louis XIV (r. 1643–1715/1052–1127) at least pretended to lead campaigns in person. As for the Habsburg emperor Leopold I (r. 1655–1705/ 1066–1117), though known for his lack of competence in military affairs, his obvious deficiency was not regarded as an excuse for non-participation in warfare; to the contrary, he was roundly criticized for abandoning Vienna just before the siege of 1683/1094–5. Research on the formation of the early modern state in seventeenth-century France has shown how 'war-making' and the 'organized crime' that made its financing possible were central and not marginal activities of the Bourbon dynasty. Similar statements can also be made about the early modern rulers of Spain, the Habsburg territories and Russia.

~ Accommodation, both open and unacknowledged, and the problem of structural similarities in the early modern world[29]

In addition, contrary to certain 'ideological' statements on the part of both Otto-mans and foreigners, it would be simplistic to limit Ottoman 'foreign relations' to wars and their diplomatic preparations and aftermaths. To take a prime example: even though the Venetian colonial empire gradually was conquered by the Ottomans, relations between individual members of the Venetian nobility and high Ottoman dignitaries might be close or even cordial.[30] Thus in the 1530s/ 936–46, just before the beginning of our study, the Istanbul-born son of a Vene-tian doge, who seems to have retained his Catholic religion, was well received at the Ottoman court. Ultimately he was sent to the newly conquered Hungarian territories, where he helped to establish Ottoman control until assassinated by the locals.[31] On the borders of the Empire during those years there seems to have been room for a man with connections to the most prominent families of the Venetian aristocracy, even though it is likely that Ludovico (Alvise) Gritti had lost most of his political support in Istanbul by the time he met his death.[32]

Even better known as an example of Ottoman–European accommodation is the *entente cordiale* between the sultans and the French kings, instituted in the sixteenth century but surviving down to Napoleon's conquest of Egypt (1798/ 1212–13). This special relationship even managed to survive the informal but effective support Louis XIV gave the Venetians during the long war for Crete (1645–69/1055–80).[33] Trade provided further opportunities for peaceful Ottoman encounters with the outside world. Muslim merchants visited Venice in sizeable numbers, while Armenians subject to the sultan established themselves in Amsterdam.[34] As to the French 'commercial diaspora' active in Izmir from the seventeenth century onwards, its members soon established business and familial links to local Greek and Armenian families, to say nothing of the assiduous court that certain French traders paid to Ottoman notables and power magnates.[35] Where the subjects of the shah of Iran were concerned, at least the Armenians of New Djulfa came to Aleppo, Bursa and Izmir in considerable numbers, and some Iranian traders also made their way to the smaller Anatolian towns.[36] 'Peaceful coexistence' between Ottomans and Europeans was thus far more widespread than official ideologies were willing to admit.[37]

Throughout the present study we will have occasion to dwell on the structural similarities between early modern European states and the Ottoman Empire. Certainly it is true that the sultans never recognized a privileged nobility, an estate that formed the backbone of almost all European polities even in the seventeenth and eighteenth centuries. Yet the Ottoman 'great households' that we can observe 'through a glass darkly' in the sixteenth century, and which went from strength to strength in the course of the seventeenth, can be viewed as an aristocracy even if their members lacked the legal guarantees that members of European nobilities possessed at least on parchment or paper.[38] All this is not to deny that the Ottoman state possessed certain special features that we do not find in Christian Europe and vice versa. But in the period to be covered here, that is, down to the last quarter of the eighteenth century, the differences were perhaps not as important as they often have been made out to be.

According to the – doubtless limited – lights of the present author, the activities of the Ottoman elites between about 1540/946–7 and 1774/1187–8 should be placed in a world of states and empires that, for lack of a better term, we may call 'early modern'. In this context technological and organizational constraints made for quite a few structural similarities. I think that one can make a case that serious divergence only began in the second half of the eighteenth century: with the political and military reforms of Maria Theresa and Joseph II in the Habsburg lands, the early industrial revolution in Great Britain, the incipient liberalization of trade in France and, above all, the far-reaching reorganization of Russian governmental and military structure.[39]

~ An impossible balance between 'east' and 'west'?

This study attempts to see the Ottomans as a state and society with both eastern and western neighbours, whose elite maintained more or less extensive relations with both sides. In recent decades, a number of studies have shown that the Ottomans of the sixteenth century maintained a strong presence in the Indian Ocean and the Persian Gulf. In the sixteenth-century Hijaz, there was a degree of rivalry between the Ottomans and the Mughul emperors of India.[40] And even when the Ottoman navy withdrew from the Indian Ocean after top priority had been given to conquests closer to home, Basra continued as an Ottoman port of major significance. From the late seventeenth century onwards, the better-off inhabitants of Istanbul and Cairo became avid consumers of Indian fabrics, and the importation of spices, drugs and cottons formed a mainstay of Cairo's commercial activity.[41] Further south, there was an Ottoman province of Habeş (Ethiopia) on the eastern coast of Africa, even though control of the hinterland often must have been aleatory.[42] Viewed from another angle, political conflict between Iran and the Ottoman Empire did not prevent Ottoman courtly society from modelling itself on Iranian patterns, with the palace of Timur's grandson Ḥusayn Bayḳara the epitome of elegance and refinement. A study of Ottoman ways of relating to the outside world must take these eastern and southern linkages into account, and this has been attempted in the present book.

However, when we search for the relevant primary sources and secondary studies, it soon becomes apparent that the 'east' or the 'south' are much less well documented than the 'west'. To a considerable degree, this has to do with the Ottoman elite's own priorities; after all, the Balkans were a source of foodstuffs for the capital, army and navy, and many migrants from Rumelia lived in Istanbul.[43] Even though Circassians and Georgians were recruited into the governing elite, numerically speaking there was simply no Arab or Caucasian immigration into the Ottoman capital to rival the influx of Albanians, Greeks or Macedonians. Seen from a different perspective, for decades wars against the Habsburg and later the Russian empires loomed large in the decision-making processes of the central authorities, and this fact also must have focused attention on Moldavia, Walachia or Transylvania rather than on Baghdad or Basra. Last but not least, the numerous members of the elite who were themselves of Balkan origin must have furthered the tendency of Ottoman authors to write about this region, rather than about eastern territories and involvements. Seyyidî 'Ali Re'îs, the sixteenth-century naval captain and amateur diplomat who wrote about his travels to India and Iran, unfortunately did not start a tradition, and the very fact that so few copies of his work survive already indicates that Ottoman readers did not accord his observations a high degree of priority.[44]

Our difficulties are compounded by the fact that the works of Iranians or inhabitants of the Caucasus who travelled in Ottoman territories are not numerous either, and those that do exist are only slowly being brought to light. Apparently it was not all uncommon for Iranian literati to travel in India and vice versa, but the merchants from Iran and the Indian subcontinent, whose presence on Ottoman soil is well attested in archival documents, certainly have not left many travelogues. In consequence there is an obvious disproportion between our wish to cover the Ottomans' relations with their eastern neighbours and the primary sources at our disposal. I have seriously thought of circumventing the difficulty by concentrating on the Ottomans' relations with their European neighbours. But this would have involved disregarding some of the most valuable research undertaken in recent decades, and also would have perpetuated the unrealistic image of an Ottoman society without any meaningful ties to its eastern neighbours. It has seemed a better choice to produce a rough sketch with the source materials already available and to leave its 'refining' to the – I hope – not very remote future.

~ Who, in which period, formed part of the Ottoman elite?

In the present context the terms 'Ottoman elite' and 'Ottoman ruling group' will be used interchangeably, although strictly speaking one might regard the elite as broader than the 'hard core' constituted by the ruling group, the men who actually made the decisions. Unfortunately, it is not easy to delineate the contours of this set of people: quite obviously high-level dignitaries such as viziers, finance directors (*defterdars*) or provincial governors of whatever level formed part of it, and so did the often highly educated scribes who manned the bureaux of the central Ottoman chancery. Janissary officers also should be included, especially when we are concerned with a border province, and the same applies to the holders of tax assignments expected to perform military and/or administrative services (*timar, ze'amet*). Quite obviously, kadis were the backbone of local administration, and thus they, along with their hierarchical superiors the army judges (*kadiasker*) and the chief jurisconsult (*şeyhülislam*) figure prominently within the Ottoman elites.[45] Whether dervishes should be considered part of this illustrious group is less easy to determine: an urban sheik of an order esteemed at court, who might even have had the ear of viziers and sultans, obviously had a good claim to form part of the ruling group. But this is not true of the head of a dervish lodge somewhere in the depths of Anatolia or the Balkans, who had trouble defending his modest tax immunities from the demands of provincial governors. In addition there is the problem of those people who qualified for positions within the ruling group by their family backgrounds and upbringing, but who for personal reasons avoided high office. Maybe the overall number of such men was quite small; but it so happened that the authors of two major source texts, namely the 'world traveller' Evliya Çelebi (1611–c. 1684/1019–c. 1096) and the wide-ranging scholar Kâtib Çelebi, (1609–57/1017–68) fell into this category for part of their lifetimes. For the purposes of our study, they will count as fully fledged members of the Ottoman elite.

However, it must be admitted that this study does not deal with the views of high-level *ulema* as extensively as they doubtless deserve. In part this is due to the fact that we do not as yet possess many monographs on these people: if Süleyman the Magnificent's chief jurisconsult Ebusu'ud Efendi has been referred to, this is due to the fact that his legal opinions have been published and analysed in some detail; and the same is true of certain seventeenth- and eighteenth-century Istanbul personages.[46] Many more studies on other people of this stamp are urgently needed. Moreover, the Ottoman archival documents that form an important primary source at least for the section on foreign trade do not highlight the group-specific opinions of the *ulema*, but treat the kadis as state functionaries expected to carry out the sultan's will obediently. Undeniably, this relative downplaying of the *ulema* constitutes a blind spot of the present study. But unfortunately it is difficult to encompass all aspects of our topic within a relatively limited number of pages; 'I crave the reader's indulgence'.

~ The Ottoman Empire as a world economy

Throughout the period under study the Ottoman Empire still was able to function without importing those consumer goods needed by the majority of the population. Grain and other foodstuffs, iron, copper or cloth for everyday use were all manufactured in sufficient quantities within the sultan's territories. In terms of war *matériel* the Ottomans also were largely autarchic, even if English tin, for instance, was appreciated whenever it became available. At the same time, the political elite and the better-off townsmen consumed Indian spices and dyestuffs as well as fine cotton goods in quantity, to say nothing of the Yemeni coffee, which from the 1630s/1039–49 onwards also arrived from an 'eastern' land that the Ottomans no longer controlled. All these Indian and Yemeni imports led to a significant outflow of silver and gold, but precious metals were mined on Ottoman territory only in very moderate quantities. Although by the middle of the sixteenth century, most of Hungary was in the hands of the sultans, the mines that had supplied raw material for the country's famous fifteenth-century gold- and silversmiths remained outside Ottoman control and, moreover, were less productive than they had once been.

If only for that reason, from the perspective of sultans and viziers, it made sense to maintain commercial relations with those states whose merchants had – albeit indirect – access to the silver that both the king of Spain and private traders imported from Mexico and Peru.[47] This need for bullion meant that the Ottoman elite tolerated and even furthered the activities of Venetian, English, French and Dutch traders. This necessity largely explains, in my view, why foreigners were accorded a significant measure of toleration, even though they were doubtless a constant source of disruption in the complicated command economy through which the Ottoman state apparatus attempted to secure the provisioning of the ruler's court, the fighting forces and, last but not least, the inhabitants of the capital.

In addition, the Ottoman elite, and non-elite but reasonably prosperous townsmen, appreciated good-quality woollens from England, Venice or, later, France. There was also the 'real' luxury trade, which quite often shaded off into diplomatic gift exchanges, and concerned items like the Ottoman carpets so appreciated by the nobility and rich merchants of Poland, Italy and even the Netherlands and England. Or on the Ottoman side there was an interest in clocks and watches from central and then from western Europe, and in court circles, in silver tableware, silks and brocades. Of course, the problem of 'luxury' trade and consumption is complicated by the fact that different sections of the Ottoman population would have had differing views of what constituted a 'luxury': for an eighteenth-century Anatolian peasant, a clock or a piece of good Kütahya faience might have been just that, and therefore unattainable, while a prosperous merchant of Bursa or Izmir probably would have considered these items normal household possessions. While not dependent on foreign trade in essentials, the better-off inhabitants of the Empire certainly appreciated its advantages.

Thus, in a world-wide context it is not easy to classify sixteenth- to eighteenth-century Ottoman trade with India or with European countries. It has been assumed that if a macro-region stands on its own as 'world economy', all we will find in terms of foreign trade is a limited exchange, often of luxury goods.[48] By this token, if a very low degree of economic integration had prevailed between the Ottomans and India, or between the former and the 'world economy' of Christian Europe, there should have been an interchange of spices, precious textiles, bullion and not much more. But throughout the period under study, this is not an adequate description of the Ottoman world's commercial links to either 'east' or 'west'. Yet neither can we claim that between the mid-sixteenth and the mid-eighteenth centuries the trade with either India or the various countries of western and central Europe involved 'necessities' as far the Ottoman side was concerned.[49] There was one exception: if the Indian and Yemeni trades were to remain prosperous, Istanbul and Cairo could not live without regular imports of bullion. It was the flow of gold and silver that tied these different economies together.

I would thus agree with Fernand Braudel's characterization of the territory governed by the sultans as a 'world economy' in its own right. This means that these lands were not only a political unit but, in part due to the *pax ottomana*, formed an area in which inter-regional trade was facilitated by relative security on the caravan routes.[50] In spite of internal customs barriers fezzes from Tunis were sold in Istanbul, while Egyptian grain fed the pilgrims and permanent residents of Mecca.[51] Yet in respect of the Ottoman case, I do have some reservations concerning Braudel's remark that trade across the borders of world economies is often not very profitable and therefore little practised.[52] Certainly Braudel, whose analysis of the functioning of a world economy focuses largely on western Europe, implicitly and indirectly admits that this claim did not apply to Europeans of the early modern period. After all, by the 1730s/1142–52 the economic unit controlled by the commercial and banking metropolis of London made great profits from trading with China, at that time still a world economy in its own right. In fact, Braudel's great study of capitalism and material life would scarcely have been written if trade between world economies had been unprofitable for the merchants of Venice, Amsterdam and finally London.[53]

Braudel admits that merchants from other world economies, including the Muslim lands, sometimes succeeded in maintaining a flow of trade across the barriers separating different world economies.[54] But I think that we should go further than he did, and not consider the antennae put out by one Islamic world economy to another as quite so exceptional a case. In the Ottoman instance as well, certain kinds of trade across world-economy boundaries were not unprofitable to local merchants, far from it. Semi-luxuries such as coffee from an independent Yemen and Indian textiles furthered the prosperity of Cairo, while at the same time connecting the Ottoman world economy with its neighbours to the east.

~ The abiding centrality of Istanbul

Braudel's world economies are supposed to possess but one capital and central region; whenever there are two rival centres, the world economy in question is emerging, decaying or else in the process of transition.[55] It is of some interest to try to fit the Ottoman world into this scheme of things. In the 1540s/947–56, when our story begins, Istanbul was doubtless the centre of the Ottoman world economy, and not just the administrative capital from which the Empire was governed. All sectors of economic life under government control were firmly based in this city, where the court resided. Furthermore, the elite corps of the army were stationed in Istanbul, even though a considerable number of the men who fought the Empire's wars in south-eastern Europe came from remote border provinces such as Bosnia.[56] As the Istanbul arsenal easily outclassed all other such establishments on the Mediterranean and Black Sea coasts Ottoman sea power also was centred here. In addition, the capital itself probably was the major conurbation of both Europe and the Middle East. Istanbul derived a consumer's privilege from the fact that, in order to reacquire the gold and silver paid to the central government every year as taxes, the inhabitants of the provinces were obliged to sell their textiles, leathers and copperwares in the markets of the capital.[57]

Moreover, at the end of the period, in the crisis-ridden 1770s/1184–93, Istanbul was still solidly placed at the centre of the Ottoman world economy. Unlike Europe or China, where the central city had moved several times, the Ottoman world economy thus possessed a stable focus. After all, the principal factors making for Istanbul's centrality all remained in place in the second half of the eighteenth century. Even though the army now largely consisted of mercenaries hired for single campaigns and of garrisons stationed in the more important provincial centres, the janissaries and other military corps continued to be present in the capital. The same thing applied to the arsenals, even though the ships manufactured there no longer won major sea battles. The sultan's court continued in residence, and was perhaps more present than ever, as the rulers no longer spent long periods in Edirne, and married princesses were now installed in widely visible palaces along the Bosphorus. The population had not shrunk, and outsiders to the realm continued to find work in the sultan's capital, even if the latter was no longer the wellspring of golden opportunities that it had appeared to be even to many Europeans during the sixteenth century. But the insistence with which Russian tsars and tsarinas aimed at a conquest of Istanbul can be explained, at least in part, by the attraction of the great city even beyond the Empire's borders.

But ever since the conquest of Egypt in 1517/923, Istanbul had acquired a counterweight in the city of Cairo. While a smaller urban centre such as Bursa was one of those 'brilliant seconds' in Braudel's parlance, condemned by its geographic position permanently to serve the needs of the Ottoman capital, Cairo fell into a different category.[58] Certainly, the Egyptian metropolis does not ever seem to have made a bid to take over the leadership of the Ottoman world economy, but researchers have shown that the city more or less monopolized the important trade with India and the Yemen.[59] Moreover, the sultans never control-led the activities of Cairo's merchants as closely as they supervised those exchanges taking place in Istanbul. Cairo thus formed a centre of commercial wealth largely independent of the impulses originating in the Ottoman capital, comparable perhaps to Genoa when Venice formed the centre of the European world economy.

Braudel has said that capitals of world economies are of necessity tolerant of foreigners and their 'strange' practices.[60] Certainly, it has been pointed out, with justification, that from the perspective of an Ottoman subject, sixteenth-century Venice would have appeared as singularly hostile to non-Catholic strangers.[61] But such judgements are unavoidably relative; in the context of a state system in which the ruler could – and did – determine the religious allegiance of his sub-jects, the Venetian Signoria allowed visitors a relative latitude in the practice of their different faiths.

But life in Istanbul was characterized by far more diversity. Apart from occa-sional Muslim merchants from India, whose presence can be inferred although not often formally documented, there were foreign Catholics, Protestants and Jews. Avoidance of non-Muslims was recommended by Muslim religious spe-cialists, while Christian priests and Jewish rabbis made analogous recommendations to their respective congregations. Yet in the marketplace of the Ottoman capital, representatives of the three Abrahamic religions came together: not only did many local guilds encompass members of different religions, mer-chants from Latin Christendom were permitted to trade and reside in the city over lengthy periods of time.

As so much of the disposable income in the hands of Ottoman subjects was concentrated in Istanbul, it is not surprising that foreign importers of woollen cloth and also of luxury goods flocked to the city. But, in addition, by the later 1700s/late XII.–early XIII. century, a lack of indigenous banking services had induced Ottoman tax collectors in the provinces to use the facilities provided by foreign merchants in order to forward money to the central financial offices in Istanbul.[62] As a result of these transactions, by the later eighteenth century Istan-bul had become part of a banking network centred in France, and had thus been turned into one of the commercial nodes linked to the European world economy in a manner that went far beyond the trade connections so typical of other Otto-man cities. Istanbul, but also certain other metropolises such as Aleppo and Izmir thus were turned into the avenues of entry through which, in the closing decades of the eighteenth and the beginning of the nineteenth century, the Ottoman world economy was definitely annexed to the conquering 'high capitalism' centred in London and Paris.

~ Confronting our limits: problems of documentation

'Objective' though they may seem, trade, war and political relations cannot be conceived of without including the views and opinions that the various participants in the 'game' hold of 'the other players'. Perceptions are constructed in the course of relations such as fighting, negotiating and, of course, buying and selling. In turn, the opinions of the participants will at least partly determine the manner in which economic, political and even military relationships develop over time. Every once in a while, if we are lucky, perceptions also may change, with experience a guideline. But often enough the participants manage to avoid the reassessment of preconceived notions that day-to-day contacts seem to demand quite imperiously. Be that as it may, we must never lose sight of this give and take between 'hard' economic, political and military realities on the one hand, and 'soft' perceptions on the other.

Discussing the opinions of Ottoman writers on 'outsiders' to their society also will usually involve at least a passing glance at the ways in which these outsiders themselves viewed their Ottoman interlocutors: tax collectors and business partners in the case of European merchants or, whenever returned captives were involved, the former slave owners in Istanbul or Cairo. As the Ottoman world forms the centre of our story, it would have been ideal to be able to use primary sources written by local Muslims and non-Muslims almost exclusively. But, as materials written by such authors are silent on many issues concerning us here, recourse to the writings of outsiders has *nolens volens* been quite extensive.[63]

Most of the problems related to views and opinions must be discussed on the basis of narrative sources; only in the case of attitudes towards foreign trade and a few other issues of more limited significance has archival documentation been of major help. A problem springs from the fact that inevitably our coverage will be very 'patchy'. First of all, the relevant documentation, if it survives at all, has not necessarily been made accessible through editions and/or translations with any degree of evenness: the Syrian or Hungarian provinces have been studied much more intensively than, for instance, Iraq. Moreover, due to the limited number of languages I am able to read, I have used only a part of what is in fact available. I know very little about the communitarian cultures of Arabs, Armenians, Bulgarians, Greeks or Jews, and in the period under consideration, these people normally did not write in Ottoman Turkish or French, as quite a few of them were to do in the nineteenth century. Yet these authors formed part of the millions ruled by the Ottoman sultans and, as we will see, some of them maintained contacts with the outside world that were quite different in kind or extent from those typical of the Ottoman elite. For both objective and subjective reasons, an even spread of information and analysis over a lengthy period of time and a large geographical area has thus turned out to be impossible.

In a conventional study of foreign relations, this difficulty would not matter so much, as we would start from the premise that the only legitimate contacts with the outside world were those planned and organized by the Ottoman ruling group. But for our purposes 'foreign relations' in the accepted use of the term are only part of a much larger universe, a broader complex of 'political culture' or 'political mentality' vis-à-vis the non-Ottoman world. Understood in this fashion, any subject of the sultan with opinions about the proper way of relating to 'heretics' and 'infidels', foreign trade partners or else slaves imported from outside the Empire theoretically comes within our purview. Unfortunately, we know almost nothing about the ideas of villagers and nomads on these matters. It is a sobering thought that the views of the vast majority of the Ottoman population continue to escape us.

To compound the problem, the present volume attempts a synthesis of a field in which relatively few monographs are as yet available. This means that we are trying to cross a rapidly flowing river not only without a bridge, but also with very few stepping stones. For synthetic works always depend on preceding studies with a more limited focus, and when no such texts are available, the author will have to 'fill in the gaps' from those primary sources with which he/she is familiar. This has happened frequently in the course of the present study. On the other hand, it is impossible for the author of a synthetic work to be as conversant with all the problems to be covered as the writer of a monograph surely would be; after all greater depth often accompanies a more limited focus in temporal or geographical terms. It has not always been possible to find a satisfactory compromise solution.

As a result, readers will note a degree of arbitrariness in the choice of problems treated; they happen to be those with which the present author has had the opportunity to concern herself.[64] Put differently, there is a certain lack of 'order' and 'system'. But in defence of my proceeding, it is worth reminding the reader that the price that would have had to be paid for a more systematic treatment is higher. For this would have meant more extensive recourse to older syntheses, and one of the main reasons for writing this book at all is to highlight the results of *recent* research, and to get away some of the 'ancient wisdom' that often is not particularly valid, and certainly not wise, but has been relayed over generations in works intended for the educated general reader.

In brief: in order to discuss the numerous and varying issues relevant to the relations entertained by subjects of the Empire with the non-Ottoman world, it would be highly desirable to possess a 'flying carpet' or at least the 'seven-mile boots' known to the readers of fairy tales. Since these aids, however, are denied to the historian, it is often necessary to limit discussion to a selection of topics. As we have seen, in some cases the available primary sources and secondary literature determine these choices, but often enough the limits of the present author's knowledge and understanding have been decisive. I can only hope that even with the small selection of issues analysed here, the major points to be made will stand out with a degree of clarity.

~ 'Placing' our topic in geographical terms

Another peculiarity of the present undertaking, to which some readers will surely object, is the fact that it is centred upon Istanbul. Evliya Çelebi, the 'hero' of our tale, during the first part of his life travelled from Hamadan to Vienna, but always returned to the seat of the Ottoman sultanate. We have adopted a perspective that in many ways, resembles that of Evliya during his youth and early maturity.[65] But this traveller at least spent a long life exploring the world outside the Ottoman capital. It was much more common, though, for provincials who hoped to become members of the governing elite to settle in Istanbul at a young age, and to leave the city only if an official appointment made that absolutely necessary. Quite apart from the capital's role in the Ottoman world economy, Istanbul-centredness was part of the elite's way of life.

However, during the last fifteen years or so, much research has been done on provincial life in the Ottoman Empire, with special but by no means exclusive emphasis on the Arab territories.[66] Work on regions that had been popular with researchers for decades has intensified, but even areas previously neglected have come in for a share of attention.[67] In addition, we now possess studies of the Armenian and Jewish diasporas, and of the far-flung activities of some of Cairo's Muslim merchants.[68] All this means that the 'view from Istanbul' adopted here is no longer without rivals. To the contrary, one may well ask oneself whether a Jewish merchant originating from Istanbul, but who did business in Pegu (modern Burma) and Balkh (modern Afghanistan), really thought that the seat of the Ottoman sultanate was the centre of his world, in the way that this was doubtless true of an author of courtly background such as Evliya Çelebi.

In spite of this, I still think that placing the centre in Istanbul makes good sense; for better or worse, most of the primary sources that we study adopt this perspective, consciously or unconsciously. Certainly, we can uncover hitherto unused sources and read long-known ones in new and different ways, but, contrary to what has sometimes been claimed, we cannot invent texts that do not exist. Therefore I submit that we will always know most about the world of Ottoman Muslims and non-Muslims who were based in Istanbul. When all is said and done, while so many things we would like to research remain inaccessible at least for the time being, it would be a shame not to use the chances that we do possess.

Our study will move back and forth between the borderlands and the capital, if only because many contacts with the non-Ottoman world took place in areas close to the frontiers. Thus a city-state such as Dubrovnik, a tributary of the Empire, provided a convenient stopping point for Ottoman envoys on their way to Venice, but also a place where prisoners of war could be unobtrusively exchanged, to say nothing of the goods from Italy and elsewhere that the traders of this town provided to the Ottoman Balkans. Or else Moldavia, with its political and cultural links to Poland-Lithuania, formed a stopping point for travellers on their way to and from the latter state. Here Ottoman merchants found khans in the style to which they were accustomed and any messenger bearing a missive from the sultan or grand vizier could be assured of a highly respectful reception.[69] Thus if the 'movement' inherent in the present study can at all be described in a few words, it would be best to say that we journey from Istanbul to the margins of empire, but ultimately return to our starting point.

However, our understanding of borders and frontiers, as lines that can be drawn on a map, at least in the sixteenth century did not correspond to what educated Ottomans would have meant by their own term of *serhad*. In consonance with the victories of rulers such as Mehmed II (r. 1451–81/855–86) and Süleyman the Magnificent, or even the conquest of Cyprus by Lala Mustafa Paşa on behalf of Selim II (r. 1566–74/973–82), the *serhad* was perceived as advancing ever further into the Darülharb. When truces were negotiated, which according to the stipulations of Islamic religious law had to be strictly temporary, it was usually the possession of individual fortresses that was considered crucial, rather than the course of a line on the map.[70] Recent research, though, has demonstrated that 'line borders' were occasionally negotiated in the sixteenth and perhaps even in the fifteenth century.[71] In the Ottoman–Polish frontier zone in the Ukraine such 'line borders' were agreed upon several times in the 1600s/1009–1111. But the fact that the *sınurname*s documenting such agreements have rarely survived from the period before the seventeenth century, and that the oldest items have come to light not in Ottoman but in Polish archives, may indicate that the administration in Istanbul did not take these 'line borders' very seriously. Probably they were regarded as temporary and soon to be superseded.

The mechanism for establishing such 'line borders' was the same in the early 1600s/after 1008 as that which was to become typical for the late seventeenth century and beyond. An Ottoman official of reasonably high rank came together with a Polish or Habsburg military man of appropriate status, and the two people and their respective suites had to travel through often sparsely inhabited and difficult territories, ensuring that 'landmarks' were erected if no natural features readily presented themselves. However, such agreements did not mean that incursions into the realm of 'the other' were no longer to take place. To the contrary, quite a few truces or 'peace agreements' stipulated that small-scale border violations by either side would not involve the resumption of war. Officially drawn 'line borders' notwithstanding, throughout our period the Ottoman frontiers were still somewhat flexible by our standards.

~ 'Placing' our topic in time

As to the years to be covered, they correspond to the period in which the Ottoman Empire can be said to have achieved a kind of 'stable state'. Ours story begins in the early 1540s/after 946, when the situation in Hungary had been finalized for the next 150 years, as the defunct kingdom of Matthias Corvinus came to be divided up into three different units: the directly ruled territories now known as the Ottoman province of Buda, the dependent principality of Transylvania (in Ottoman: Erdel) and the narrow western strip under Habsburg control (Royal Hungary). While the Empire was to reach its maximum extension only in the late 1600s/1080s, after the conquest of Crete and the Polish fortress of Kamieniec-Podolski, the crucial western frontier was established in the 1540s/ 946–56, even though a few Austrian fortresses were added on in later years. Given the importance of this section of the border, in the eyes not only of modern historians focusing on Habsburg territories, but also of sixteenth- and seventeenth-century Ottoman authors themselves, a good case can be made for letting the period of rapid expansion end here. And surely this 'change of pace' had repercussions on the manner in which members of the Ottoman elites viewed the world without the Empire's borders.

As has long been known, in confronting the Austrian Habsburgs the sultans' armies had to deal not just with a local or at best regional power, but with an empire in its own right.[72] Certainly, after Charles V had divided up his overly large territories, his brother and successor in Vienna, Ferdinand I (r. 1556–64/ 963–72), no longer could draw on the resources of Spain or the Netherlands. Yet the Austrian Habsburgs themselves had extensive holdings all the way to the Rhine and could, moreover, count on some additional financial resources made available by various German princes. In consequence for the sultans' armies, winning even a major battle did not automatically mean winning a war of conquest, as had so often been the case in the past. This novel situation meant that the Ottoman authorities had to adjust to waging long-drawn out wars, the organization and financing of which brought along totally new challenges. Further, this state of affairs meant that certain parts of Hungary remained contested territory over long periods of time, where Ottoman governors and noblemen residing on Habsburg territory taxed luckless peasants twice over. In my view, all these features justify our beginning a new period in the history of Ottoman relations with the outside world in the middle of the sixteenth century, and studying it in the perspective of inter-empire rivalry and a – largely involuntary – stabilization.

Even easier to justify is the decision to end our analysis with the war of 1768–74/1181–8. It was already at the peace of Karlowitz/Karlofça, in 1699/ 1110–11 that the Ottomans in losing Hungary had suffered a major defeat. Yet, in reconquering the Peloponnese from the Venetians, the sultan's armies had been able to make good at least some of the losses involved, and ultimately even to retrieve Belgrade. After a period of several decades, during which the military situation had thus stabilized and in which the economy even experienced substantial growth, the catastrophic defeat by the armies of Catherine II of Russia (r. 1762–96/1175–1211) seems to have come as a surprise to many members of the Ottoman elite. In the peace treaty of Küçük Kaynarca the sultan was obliged to grant Russian ships access to the Black Sea, hitherto a jealously guarded 'Ottoman lake'.[73] Moreover the 'independence' imposed on the Crimean Tatars and the sultan by the Tsarina Catherine II was the first step towards an ultimate annexation of this territory by the Russian Empire in 1783/1197–8. The loss of this territory with its Islamic population, in the eyes of officialdom and the Empire's Muslim subjects in general, added insult to injury. Thus the period of imperial crisis conventionally associated with the reigns of Selim III (r. 1789–1807/1203–22) and Mahmud II (r. 1808–39/1223–55) seems to have already begun in the late 1760s/early 1180s.

~ Confronting different perspectives, or how to justify comparisons

As the discussion following Edward Said's memorable book has shown, the 'orientalist' view of European travel writers, who postulated an immutable and passive 'Orient' that they planned to dominate in the name of 'science and rationality', did not spring forth out of nothingness in the second half of the eighteenth century.[74] To the contrary, this was a long drawn-out process. Thus a tension between the claim to produce empirical knowledge and a de facto continued dependence on texts by ancient authors was typical of Renaissance scholars such as Petrus Gyllius, André Thévet or Pierre Belon.[75] After all, a sixteenth- or seventeenth-century writer with scholarly claims had to demonstrate his familiarity with a corpus of 'classical' authors. It was also common for the writers of travelogues dealing with the Ottoman Empire to work without the slightest knowledge of Ottoman Turkish, a situation that, of course, increased dependence on European predecessors. Crusading rhetoric also served to legitimize the appetite for Ottoman territories. Thus the numerous pilgrimage reports covering visits to Jerusalem and published at the end of the fifteenth and throughout the sixteenth century have as a subtext the unwillingness to accept that the Holy Land was no longer in Christian hands.[76] All this has emerged from a variety of studies, and is no longer in doubt.

However, even so, it does not seem realistic to assume that 'orientalism' was immanent in European culture at whatever stage of its history. *Mutatis mutandis*; similar ways of using one's sources can be found in the works of a seventeenth-century Ottoman author as well: Evliya Çelebi often emphasized that he had seen numerous strange and wonderful regions with his own eyes, and yet he depended just as much on oral and literary sources, which he often did not take the trouble to acknowledge.[77] For today's scholar, the same kind of caution is thus appropriate when reading Petrus Gyllius as when reading Evliya Çelebi. Both authors have made a lot of valuable empirical observations, and if Evliya had not written, the present work would simply have been impossible. But in both cases, the claim to have collected empirical knowledge 'in the raw' often may not stand up under closer investigation.

Similarly the concern with a 'symbolic appropriation' of foreign territory, which was a common feature especially in European pilgrimage accounts of the Holy Land, was not foreign to Evliya Çelebi either. When describing Vienna, it was at least one subtext of his story that here were potentially useful subjects of the sultan, 'infidels' though they might be.[78] As to the city's buildings, they were interesting architecturally and well kept; in short, the place was a worthwhile future acquisition. That Evliya thought in these terms becomes quite clear when one reads the numerous sentences he devoted to the places in and around Vienna linked in one way or another to Süleyman the Magnificent's siege of 1529/ 935–6. In a similar vein, one might interpret his account of the adventures of the semi-mythical Kasım Voyvoda whose heroic death, supposedly within Vienna itself, might be also be viewed as a kind of symbolic appropriation. I would therefore submit that the tendency to view foreign lands in the hands of 'unbe-lievers' as possible objects of conquest in the sixteenth and seventeenth centuries was common to certain Ottoman and European authors.

In Sultan Süleyman's time the Ottoman Empire had been recognized, albeit grudgingly, by European humanist authors such as Ogier Ghiselin de Busbecq (1522–92/928–1001) because of its superior military power, and the absolute rule of the sultans admired as an ideal that the Habsburg emperor, confronted with fractious nobilities, had been unable to emulate.[79] While Busbecq's account certainly is full of polemics, the 'superiority complex' that makes many travel writers of the years after 1750/1163 such stultifying reading had not as yet come into being.[80] Or to be more exact, this latter-day manner of viewing the world only began to emerge in the seventeenth century and became all-pervasive in the course of the later eighteenth. As Lucette Valensi has shown, the vision of the Ottoman polity relayed by the Venetian ambassadors, whose views were to become crucial for European political thinking down to – in some cases – the twentieth century, began to change from admiration to abhorrence only around 1600/1008–9.[81]

In this context it seems reasonable to take our brief from some recent work on the genesis of European Renaissance artwork that stresses the numerous connec-tions with the Middle East and the use of Middle Eastern models in architecture, metalwork, textiles, majolica and other media.[82] As late as the sixteenth century there was a remarkably close relationship on the artistic level between Renais-sance Europe and the Ottomans. Jerry Brotton has a point in contradicting the often-made claim that the rediscovery of the Greco-Roman world in the course of the Renaissance resulted in an unbridgeable chasm between European and Ottoman cultures.[83] Certainly I would think that he exaggerates for polemical purposes when claiming that the reception of Greco-Roman texts and artefacts had no impact at all on the genesis of Renaissance culture. Yet his point concern-ing the importance of 'the Ottoman connection' is well taken. When it comes to architecture, it has been pointed out that there is something resembling a sublim-inal relationship between Sinan the Architect (c. 1497–1588/902–97) and his contemporary Andrea Palladio (1508–80/913–88), although we can be certain that there was no direct contact between the two masters.[84]

Was there even an indirect one? Certainly in the fifteenth and sixteenth centuries, artistic ideas travelled from the Ottoman realm to Renaissance Italy as well as vice versa, and there may have been linkages about which we know nothing. But if we assume that the intellectual worlds of Sinan and Palladio had something in common, they also may have developed similar architectural ideas independently from one another. If this assumption is at all realistic, such an artistic commonality would indicate that the cultural worlds of mid-sixteenth-century Istanbul and the contemporary Veneto were less remote from one another than is usually believed. And when it comes to written texts, it does appear that Busbecq and Mustafa Âlî (1541–1600/947–1009), Luigi Fernando Marsigli (1658–1730/1068–1143) and Hüseyin Hezarfenn (probably d. 1678–9/1089), or Evliya Çelebi and Antoine Galland (1646–1715/1055–1128) in certain respects inhabited rather similar worlds.[85]

~ A common world

I would claim that, in the sixteenth and seventeenth centuries, Ottomans and Frenchmen, or subjects of the Habsburg emperors for that matter, were less remote from one another than the people under study themselves would have thought. This statement invites discussion from several angles. The first has to do with a statement by Marc Bloch, who made the comparative approach 'respectable' among historians dealing with medieval and early modern Europe.[86] Bloch was especially interested in comparing phenomena that he considered 'close' to one another, such as the English and French varieties of feudalism. Many historians in later years have tended to agree with him, so that those scholars who use this methodology on, for instance, Ottoman and European histories have always felt the need to justify their procedures. Obviously, if we are willing to view Ottomans, Frenchmen and Venetians of the sixteenth and – with some qualifications – even the seventeenth and earlier eighteenth centuries as still belonging to one and the same world, further justification is unnecessary.[87] If, on the other hand, we choose to regard the Ottomans as inhabiting a world apart from their early modern neighbours in Europe, it is certainly not impossible to legitimize our procedures. But our task would be a good deal harder, and I choose to take the easy way out.

Secondly, we must keep in mind the common material environment in which all these people found themselves, and which allows us sometimes to view them as – albeit inimical – cousins. Surely the answer is linked to the basic fact that both Ottomans and Europeans were then all living in societies in which agriculture was the ultimate source of all wealth, even if the peasants themselves did not get to see much of the riches that their labour had generated. Moreover, all the civilizations involved depended as yet on similar technologies. Thus the vagaries of the weather determined whether the harvest would be good or bad, in most

cases with little flexibility to compensate for the loss of one crop by quickly sow-
ing another. Armies could only be supplied if the roads were passable, and the
Danube and its affluent rivers defied all efforts to reliably map them, as the late
seventeenth-century Habsburg general Luigi Fernando Marsigli found out to his
cost.[88]

While the present volume in no way deals with peasant society and elemen-
tary technology, we cannot afford to ignore these basic commonalities of the
early modern world in constructing our study. I will try to present an account of
the manner in which members of the Ottoman ruling group interacted with – and
regarded – denizens of the non-Ottoman world. But, differently from conventional studies of political ideology or international relations, I will try to keep the
constraints of commercial exchange, natural conditions and technology constantly in the picture. The opinions of a person drenched with rain in a leaky tent
will differ from those of a man or woman comfortably ensconced behind his/her
computer; and as historians of World War I know very well, the shared miseries
of a military campaign tend to make even the soldiers of opposing armies voice
rather similar views.

2 ~ On sovereignty and subjects: expanding and safeguarding the Empire

In the present chapter, we will discuss some of the major problems in the realm of what we today would call 'foreign policy'. Of course, as we have seen, the Ottoman elite had a conception of these matters that differed greatly from ours, yet throughout the approximately two and half centuries covered by our study, sultans, viziers and provincial governors still needed to confront whatever power imbalances occurred in the world that they inhabited, be it through war or through negotiation. We will set the scene for later discussions by briefly survey-ing the numerous and varying conflicts between the governmental apparatus in Istanbul on the one hand and, on the other, foreign powers such as the Safavids, the Habsburgs or the Signoria of Venice. Through this overview it should become clear that the mature Ottoman Empire was confronted with a staggering multitude of political problems, some of which were linked to religious conflicts. Many others belonged to the 'nitty gritty' of political competition between rulers or else stemmed from the imperfect control, on the part of the sultan's bureau-cracy, of provincial forces such as fortress commanders or farmers of customs dues. After all, such personages might precipitate inter-state conflict by raiding the territories of neighbouring states or overcharging foreign merchants. More-over these different categories of political conflict are not always easy to disentangle, not for us denizens of the twenty-first century and certainly not for contemporaries.

Prominent – and sometimes intractable – is the problem of central control over the management of inter-state conflicts. The surviving archival documentation emphasizes the fact that numerous matters of but moderate intrinsic importance were referred to Istanbul even from an outlying province such as Hungary. But when we look more closely at day-to-day events in the borderlands it soon becomes clear that central regulation was only part of the story. Admittedly our understanding of the Ottoman viewpoint concerning the centre's prerogatives and the latitude allowed to local officials at different time periods is rather lim-ited. Writing about the 'problems of the state' in the tradition of the 'advice books' addressed to sultans and viziers (*nasihatname*) certainly was common practice from the late sixteenth century onwards. Yet the limitations of the cen-tral power's prerogatives did not form a favoured issue, if only because it was part of 'political correctness' to assume that the sultan, the Ottoman centre, that is, possessed absolute power, which – as we will see – was not exactly realistic.[1]

Moreover, given the sultan's 'ideological role' as the ruler who constantly expanded the borders of the Islamic world by victorious campaigns, Ottoman authors writing on the affairs of the Empire rarely debated decisions affecting war and peace. For these were strictly reserved to the ruler and his viziers, and thus must have formed part of the *arcana imperii*. Only in the second half of the eighteenth century did a few senior Ottoman officials come to discuss and defend their own political choices in a less coded fashion than had hitherto been current and, at least in the case of Ahmed Resmi, openly question the wisdom of certain sultanic campaigns.[2] As a result of this reticence we are usually limited to occasional remarks in chronicles and 'advice literature' concerning the prudence or imprudence of this or that vizier; and the conclusions we can draw concerning Ottoman 'foreign policy' often remain speculative.[3]

In discussions of the Ottoman elites and their relationships to Muslim and non-Muslim neighbours it is often assumed that Islamic religious law determined practice until the second half of the eighteenth century, when the Ottoman elites began to adopt numerous assumptions and institutions from their European neighbours. However, it is a basic contention of the present study that, while religious law certainly set the parameters, sultanic/bureaucratic pragmatism was by no means an invention of the late eighteenth century. Furthermore, in spite of the relative conservatism of the interpreters of Islamic law, it does not make sense to assume that relations between foreign rulers and their subjects were conducted in the same fashion in 1540/946–7, when expansion in central Europe was still a major concern, and in 1730/1142–3, when it was more a question of maintaining the western frontiers and temporarily seeking aggrandizement only in Iran.

~ 'Foreign interference' and its limits

At least to a certain degree, the manner in which the Empire was run permitted the interference of non-Ottoman subjects in Ottoman affairs. Seen from a distance, it is remarkable that all frontiers were relatively permeable; by the middle of the sixteenth century, Venetian bailos, Habsburg internuncios and French ambassadors were residing in Galata, today part of downtown Istanbul, or in the khans of the capital itself. Merchants from Venice, France, and later England or the Netherlands were not restricted to special quarters in this or that port town, but travelled to the capital, or to provincial trading centres, with the tolerance of the Ottoman administration. Thus sultanic policy differed significantly from what was practised in China or Japan, or even in sixteenth- and seventeenth-century Russia, where it was common practice to turn away travellers considered undesirable by the government.[4] Numerous international trade routes passing through the Empire's territory resulted in frequent comings and goings of all manner of foreigners, which, apart from sixteenth-century Iranians, the Ottoman government almost never tried to impede. Throughout its existence the latter's bureaucracy seems to have regarded a minute control of these people as unnecessary.

Of course, no absolute standard exists for the evaluation of such matters. Rather, judgement will depend on the perspective adopted either by contemporaries or else by modern historians. Foreigners resident in places such as Istanbul, Izmir or Aleppo certainly socialized mainly among themselves, and hardly ever met Ottoman Muslims except in certain highly formalized settings. Yet some of these foreign sojourners, especially from the eighteenth century onwards, might live in the Empire for several generations, and this could not have been possible without both the knowledge of local authorities and a good deal of daily contact with Muslim and non-Muslim subjects of the sultans.[5] And while traders coming from states with which the Ottomans were at war were supposed to leave the sultan's territory at the declaration of hostilities, even that command was not always strictly obeyed.

In consequence, it was possible, though certainly not common, for a high-level Ottoman dignitary to maintain close contacts with, for instance, a given foreign envoy. This latter personage in turn would try to induce his ally in the Ottoman ruling group to follow a policy which the envoy himself, and the ruler whom he served, considered advantageous. This was doubtless the reason why, in the early eighteenth century, the French ambassador marquis de Bonnac cultivated his relationship with the Grand Vizier Damad Ibrahim Paşa.[6] Such attempts at 'influencing' often might be successful in minor matters but usually not in major ones. Or at least this was the pattern before the crisis of the 1683–99/ 1094–1111 war seems to have made it imperative to strengthen the alliance with France, even if a heavy price had to be paid in terms of political concessions.

Unofficial political 'influence' by foreigners was rarer in the 1560s/967–77 than in later periods, but it certainly existed, albeit to a limited extent, even during the reign of Murad IV (r. 1623–40/1032–50). In the eighteenth century, such outside involvement certainly increased. Now it was not only French, English, Dutch or even Bohemian envoys who tried to involve the sultans in their various political projects.[7] In addition, the Ottomans themselves now also at times sought informal understandings or even alliances with European rulers, as demonstrated by the embassy of Yirmisekiz Mehmed Efendi to Paris in 1720/1132–3.[8] Especially after Russian expansion in the Balkans had become an imminent possibility, links to other powers capable of opposing the empire-building of Catherine II (r. 1762–96/1175–1211) seemed indispensable.

However, in spite of the divisiveness that this form of decision-making must have engendered, Ottoman administrations remained remarkably cohesive. This aspect was usually not noticed by European observers, who only saw the factionalism but understood very little of the forces making for agreement.[9] Yet these were of considerable strength. To begin with, there was the well-known but often underrated fact that the Ottoman sultan gained a high degree of legitimacy from his role as *Padişah-ı İslam*. In addition, the existence of a professional bureaucracy, which had experienced one major spate of growth during the sixteenth century and another in the mid-eighteenth, made a significant contribution toward holding the Empire together. Given the high degree of integration of

Ottoman specialists in Islamic religious law and divinity (*ulema*) into the state apparatus, it makes sense to view them as part of the bureaucracy in the meaning intended here.[10] Moreover, the scribal and financial officials, connected by ties of collegiality and patronage wherever they might be posted, also constituted a powerful factor strengthening the Empire's cohesion.

Outside the bureaucracy, but within the governing apparatus, the lifetime tax farmers (*malikâneci*), whose material interests were intimately linked to the survival of the Ottoman state, also often acted in favour of unity.[11] After all, once the Ottoman Empire had collapsed, there was no guarantee that the *malikânecis* would continue to profit from the tax farms that they had acquired at considerable expense. This consideration is of special significance as the provincial power magnates so characteristic of the eighteenth-century political scene derived much of their power from their roles in lifetime tax-farming and the assessment of dues upon townsmen and villagers.[12] In consequence, individual high office holders and provincial power magnates might derive some profit and power from their association with European consuls and traders. But what really counted was their allegiance to the Ottoman state.

These observations evoke the concept of power-sharing, which historians of China and Central Asia have been using for a long time, but which Ottomanists have mostly ignored.[13] It would seem that, by the seventeenth century, the theoretically absolute power of the sultans in real life was shared with coteries of dignitaries, often organized in 'political households', who struggled for control over the decision-making process. Indirectly, due to the alliances with resident foreign envoys that certain dignitaries might forge, the French or Dutch ambassadors of the seventeenth or eighteenth century might become involved in certain aspects of Ottoman politics.[14] But it would be a mistake to make too much of this situation; in the end, such relationships of power-sharing – widespread though they might be – with rare exceptions were subordinate to the loyalty of the officeholders to their religion and to the Ottoman state.

~ A sequence of 'mental images'

To make such long-term changes more visible, we will draw a sequence of 'mental pictures' that proceeds from 1560/967–8 by way of 1639/1048–9 and 1718/1130–1 to 1774/1187–8. As our first period, we have selected the early 1560s/967–77 instead of the 1540s/946–56, when our overall study begins. The Registers of Important Affairs (Mühimme Defterleri), one of the principal sources for sixteenth-century history, and also for the activities which we might call Ottoman 'foreign policy', survive mainly from 1560/967–8 onwards.[15] It simply makes more sense to discuss a period about which we can say something coherent on the basis of Ottoman archival sources that can be consulted more or less as a series. If the 1540s/946–56 had been chosen, we would have had to focus on a timespan from which we possess only scattered documents, chronicles and European sources.

As to the year 1639/1048–9, it is the date of the treaty of Ḳaṣr-i S̲h̲īrīn, which inaugurated a lengthy period of peace between the Ottoman and Safavid Empires. Moreover, between 1606/1014–15 and 1663/1073–4 the Ottomans did not wage war with the Austrian Habsburgs either, so that 1639/1048–9 can stand quite conveniently for a period of stable and relatively uncontested frontiers in both east and west. After the upheavals of the 'Long War' with the Habsburgs (1593–1606/1001–15), the military rebellions known as the Celali uprisings and the wars with Iran involving the loss (1623/1032–3) and ultimate reconquest of Baghdad (1638/1047–8), the 1640s/1049–59, in spite of continuing unrest at the centre, were a period of relative calm.

Things were different in 1718/1130–1; in a long series of wars that had begun in 1683/1094–5 with the failed siege of Vienna by Kara Mustafa Paşa, the Ottomans had lost Hungary for good. Also, by the treaty of Passarowitz/Pasarofça (1718/1130–1), the Ottomans no longer controlled parts of Walachia and Serbia, including the important fortress of Belgrade. But other provinces and towns conquered by Habsburgs or Venetians between 1684/1095–6 and 1699/1110–11 ultimately were regained by the sultans' armies; this included the Peloponnese in 1715/1126–8 and Belgrade in 1739/1151–2.[16] Following the collapse of the Safavid dynasty, the Ottomans engaged in a series of campaigns on Iranian territory, which resulted in the temporary acquisition of Tabrīz (1725–30/1137–43); however, in the end, the frontier as it had existed since 1639/1048–9 was more or less reestablished. Thus, at least the 1730s/1142–52 and to a degree even the 1720s/1132–42, once again can be regarded as a period of consolidation.

By contrast, 1774/1187–8, as the cut-off point adopted for our study, stands for something quite different, namely the – for the Ottomans – disastrous peace treaty of Küçük Kaynarca. Nor did the series of political and military misfortunes end here. By the late eighteenth century, Egypt had slipped out of Ottoman control; this was true even before Napoleon, albeit for a very few years, conquered the province in 1798/1212–13.[17] This sequence of losses was of a different quality from those that had occurred about eighty years earlier, in 1699/1110–11. For Hungary had functioned mainly as a frontier province that, as most territories of this kind, did not generate revenue for the central treasury, but only financed – in part – its own local defence. By contrast, Egypt had been an important source of sultanic revenue well into the eighteenth century.[18] As to the Crimea, while also a border province producing a limited amount of revenue, it had for centuries been governed by the Girays, a princely family, which in terms of political prestige ranked second only to the Ottoman dynasty itself.[19]

Given these historical changes, at the four dates under study political, military and cultural relations with the outside world took on rather different forms. Unfortunately it is impossible to make 'surgically neat' cross-sections dating exactly from the years under investigation. Especially where the 1560s/967–77 are concerned, but also when dealing with the seventeenth and eighteenth centuries, it will at times be necessary to refer to studies covering a slightly earlier or else a somewhat later decade. Available research does not always provide the best possible coverage for those years most convenient for our purposes, and more importantly, there are major gaps in the surviving primary sources. Particularly where the middle of the sixteenth century is concerned, but elsewhere as well, the 'mental pictures' proposed here pertain to a decade or two rather than to a single year. Last but not least, events from the years selected here often can only be explained if the period under discussion is extended to a greater or lesser degree.

~ The 1560s/967–77

Introducing the major 'players' of the 1560s/967–77: the Habsburg possessions, France, Venice and Iran

As is well known, the Ottomans expanded in the Balkans from the mid-fourteenth century onwards. By this time, the 'Latins', that is, the various Roman Catholics of western European background, had already been present in the peninsula, and especially in the territories of what is today Greece, for hundreds of years. By the fifteenth century, a number of European states, including France, Hungary, Poland, Venice and Genoa, had significant political interests in the Balkan peninsula.[20] However, by the mid-1500s, Genoa had withdrawn to the western Mediterranean, and the time in which the Polish kings actively attempted expansion into the Black Sea region also was long past. Between 1526/932–3 and 1541/947–8, Hungary had been largely conquered by Ottoman armies. As a last remnant of medieval Hungary, a strip of territory in the west was governed by the Habsburgs, which included Poszony/Pressburg, today's Bratislava; the dynasty paid tribute to Istanbul for this possession, and the Ottoman–Hungarian frontier was situated only a few miles east of Vienna.[21]

Within the European context as a whole, by the mid-sixteenth century the Habsburg royal family had come to constitute a major power. This was a dynasty of Swiss-Austrian origin whose members since the later thirteenth century had occasionally been elected 'emperor' in the Germanies, a title which by this time implied prestige but only limited power. By the second half of the fifteenth century, the head of the Habsburg family had acquired a traditional claim to the 'Holy Roman Empire of the German nation'. This same dynasty also controlled the Netherlands (present-day Belgium and Holland). Moreover, by a sequence of cleverly organized dynastic marriages, Charles V, of Spanish, Habsburg and Burgundian descent (r. as emperor 1519–55/924–63), had been crowned king of a but recently unified Spain. Throughout the period concerning us here, both Austrian and Spanish Habsburgs, tied together by a – from the medical standpoint – excessive number of marriages, were to form the major opponents of the Ottomans in south-eastern Europe and the Mediterranean.

Yet Spain's interests in the Mediterranean world were only partly due to the Habsburg connection. The Aragon dynasty had long possessed important dominions in southern Italy and in addition, the Reconquista – the conquest of the Muslim kingdoms on the Iberian peninsula mainly by the kingdoms of Portugal, Castile and Aragon – had been completed in 1492/897–8. At the end of the fifteenth and the beginning of the sixteenth century, both the Spanish and Portuguese kings further attempted to expand their domains by conquests in the coastlands of northern Africa. Furthermore, as a result of the Franco-Spanish contest for hegemony in Italy, by the mid-sixteenth century the king of Spain had acquired significant territories both in the northern and the southern part of the Italian peninsula. Thus, by the 1540s/946–56, while the Ottomans confronted the Austrian Habsburgs on their Hungarian border, their major opponent on the north African coast and on the waters of the Mediterranean was the Spanish branch of this same dynasty.[22]

Given this geographical distribution of Habsburg power, the kingdom of France was surrounded by territories controlled by the Spanish king Philip II (r. 1556–98/963–1007) and the Austrian ruler Ferdinand I (r. as emperor 1556–64/963–72) with the Netherlands at its northern, Spain at its southern and the 'Holy Roman Empire' at its eastern borders. François I, the first king of France belonging to the Valois dynasty (r. 1515–47/920–54) attempted to limit and balance this power by a series of wars and strategic alliances. Not all his anti-Habsburg wars were successful, far from it; in 1525/931–2, at the battle of Pavia, the French king was in fact taken prisoner and only liberated after substantial political concessions and the payment of a princely ransom. This difficult position made François I willing to conclude agreements with Sultan Süleyman several times during the 1530s/936–46 and 1540s/946–56. For a brief period, the two allies together campaigned against the duke of Savoy, an ally of the Habsburgs; in 1543/949–50, Nice was besieged, and during the following winter an Ottoman fleet commanded by the admiral Hayreddin Barbarossa spent time in Toulon. But this initiative was not followed up, partly because François I came to an agreement with Charles V and partly because the negative reaction of most European courts, noblemen and publicists against an alliance with the 'infidel' to the detriment of another Christian ruler placed French royal policy in the defensive.[23] However, an *entente* between the king of France and the Ottoman sultan remained a constant possibility, and was revived now and then, especially during the war years of the 1680s/1090–1101 and 1690s/1101–11.

While not possessing a large territory, Venice was a significant 'player' on the political chessboard of the mid-sixteenth century because of its financial, commercial and naval resources. Due to the conquest of Byzantium by a Venetian fleet supported by knights from western Europe (1204/600–1), this Adriatic city-state had acquired the island of Crete and the Peloponnesian ports of Modon and Monemvasia. Crete remained Venetian until the war of 1645–69/1054–80, when it was conquered by the Ottoman navy, while the Signoria had lost Modon already in 1500/905–6, when Bayezid II annexed this port town to his empire.

Monemvasia fell into Ottoman hands in 1540/946–7. Further north, separated from Athens by a narrow stretch of sea, the island of Euboa also had been Venetian until its conquest by the Ottomans. But these losses on the Greek peninsula were compensated for during the closing years of the fifteenth century: after the Lusignan dynasty, established in Cyprus after the 1204/600–1 partition of the Byzantine Empire, had died out in 1489/894–5, Venice acquired the island after having 'adopted' its current queen, and held on to it until the Ottoman conquest of 1570–73/977–81. Thus the Signoria still controlled important positions in the otherwise Ottoman-dominated eastern Mediterranean and, given its commercial prosperity in the second half of the sixteenth century, continued to be of some importance to the Ottomans on the level of inter-state relations as well.[24]

On the eastern border, the situation had changed considerably from the mid-fifteenth to the mid-sixteenth century. In the later fifteenth century, the dominant state in that area, founded by the Aḳ-ḳoyunlu dynasty, had controlled a sizeable part of Iran from a capital located in the ancient eastern Anatolian city of Diyarbakır.[25] By contrast, the establishment of the newly powerful Safavid dynasty meant that the political centre of gravity shifted to Iranian territory proper. This mutation resulted from the fact that Shah Ismāʻīl, the founder of the Safavid dynasty, had been defeated by Sultan Selim I in battle (1514/918–19). In consequence, the border between the Ottoman and Safavid Empires was moved east; during the early phase of Safavid expansion, the frontier separating the two realms had been situated as far west as Erzincan. In the reign of Süleyman the Magnificent, the northern section of the border zone, located in Anatolia, remained relatively stable. On the other hand, a major Ottoman conquest from the Safavids did occur in the south-east during this period. For, in a series of campaigns between 1534/940–1 and 1546/952–3, Iraq, with the ancient Abbasid centre of Baghdad and, ultimately, the lively port city of Basra, became an Ottoman province.[26]

Religious rivalries of the 1560s/967–77

In the middle of the sixteenth century, political tensions frequently possessed a significant religious dimension. Yet it would be completely unrealistic to assume the existence of either Christian or Islamic 'united fronts'. The Ottoman and Safavid empires were at war over much of the sixteenth century. On the Christian side, Catholic rulers occasionally cooperated in ventures that, even in the early modern period, they still liked to call 'crusades'. But the normal state of affairs was all-out and very worldly rivalry for crowns and territories. This was true even before 1517/923–4, while all of western Europe still adhered to the Roman Church. Conflicts were exacerbated when, in the first half of the sixteenth century, England and the Scandinavian states, in addition to a sizeable share of the German princes and some French and Hungarian noblemen, adopted the Reformation either in its Lutheran or its Calvinist variety. For now political tensions often were overlaid with bellicosity legitimized by the other side's supposedly 'heretical' views.[27] Equally tension-ridden were the relations of the kingdoms and republics of western and central Europe with those Christian states whose rulers and populations adhered to the Orthodox creed. But as we are looking at the 1560s/967–77, these later conflicts will not concern us here, for, by the time our study begins, the territories of the former Balkan states all had been absorbed by the Ottomans. Only in the far north was the grand duke of Muscovy, who in 1547/953–4 was to declare himself the tsar, able to retain his independence.[28]

It is well known that even before the conquest of Istanbul, and more specifically after 1453/857, the Ottoman sultans had recognized the Orthodox Church as an organization, and supported that faction within it that was adamantly opposed to union with the Catholics. Given this situation, attempts by the papacy to promote 'unity of the Christian church' under the auspices of Rome – to eliminate Protestantism and secure the recognition of papal supremacy on the part of the Orthodox – had significant repercussions in the Ottoman realm. For, in accordance with the decisions of the Council of Trent (1546–63/952–71) numerous missions were sent out, usually consisting of Jesuits, Capuchins or Franciscans. The teaching and preaching of these ecclesiastics were meant to persuade the Empire's Gregorian Armenians, Orthodox, or Lebanese Maronite subjects to convert to Catholicism, or at the least, recognize the pope as the head of the Christian churches while retaining their accustomed ecclesiastical rites.

These priests and friars, who were able to attract a following among Ottoman Christians not least because they established schools, normally operated under the auspices of the French ambassador, who could most effectively promote their interests because before 1798/1212–13, the Ottoman Empire and France were never at war. Often enough, the French ambassador also was involved in the attempts of the Franciscans to gain – or retain, as the ever unstable circumstances of the moment might dictate – control of the holy sites in Jerusalem and Bethlehem. The Church of the Holy Sepulchre ('Kumame' in Ottoman parlance) in particular was continually disputed between Catholics and Orthodox.[29] But in addition, it was not rare for the missionaries to pursue policies of their own, which might not coincide at all with the wishes of the French ambassador. For our purposes, the missionaries are of some importance because of their physical presence in certain remote Ottoman provinces, in places where foreign merchants or diplomats would rarely, if ever, venture. Moreover, they could establish contacts with Ottoman Christians in a way impossible to other Europeans, because they had learned the relevant languages at school in colleges especially founded for this purpose in Rome. Even if in the 1560s/967–77, their presence was minor compared to what it was to become in later centuries, it still added to the variety of religious persuasions active on Ottoman soil.

In the early and mid-sixteenth century, religious problems also were an issue in the Muslim world, namely between the Ottoman and Safavid Empires. Around 1500/905–6 the young Sheik Ismāʿīl, from the western Iranian town of Ardabīl, had made use of the devotion of the local Turkish-speaking tribesmen to his person and ancestors, particularly the thirteenth-century holy man Sheik Ṣafī, to declare himself ruler (shah) of Iran.[30] Shah Ismā'īl adopted the Shi'a as a state religion, and quite a few Sunni Muslims were forced to emigrate. On the other hand, certain Turkophone tribesmen of Anatolia, among whom the charismatic figure of Shah Ismā'īl soon became highly popular, moved eastwards to join the armies of the sheik turned shah. But not everybody convinced of Shah Ismā'īl's special sanctity was willing to emigrate from the Ottoman domains. Anatolian adherents of the Safavid sheiks, who had received the headdress (*tac*) of the dervish order bearing the name of Sheik Ṣafī through emissaries from Ardabīl, inducted adherents into their lodges, in spite of the mortal danger incurred if recruiters or recruited were detected by the Ottoman authorities.[30]

Throughout the sixteenth century, the Ottoman and Safavid rulers fought out long and bitter wars. While the dynasty of Shah Ismā'īl identified as Shi'ite, it comes as no great surprise that the Ottoman sultans, particularly Selim I and Süleyman the Magnificent, legitimized themselves as champions of Sunni 'right belief'.[32] This insistence on Sunnism was quite a novelty; for early Ottoman sultans had often sympathized with heterodox dervish sheiks following their armies in battle. Even when, from the fifteenth century onwards, they came to favour Sunni Islam explicitly, rulers such as Bayeyid II (r. 1481–1512/885–918) had at the very most, attempted to convert their subjects by supporting those dervish orders that, such as the Halvetis, possessed impeccable Sunni credentials.[33] But by the middle of the sixteenth century, Ottoman official propaganda described wars against the Safavids as directed at the extirpation of heresy. Whenever treaties were concluded from a position of strength, such as the peace of Amasya (1555/962–3), it was usually demanded that the Iranians cease the ritual cursing of the early caliphs Abū Bakir, 'Omar and 'Othmān, whom the Shi'ites considered usurpers and the Sunnis, by contrast, as 'rightly guided'.[34]

Certainly the religious propaganda of the dervish order of Sheik Ṣafī continued to be sponsored by the Iranian shahs until the later sixteenth century. As a result, there has been some debate among twentieth-century Ottomanist historians concerning the degree to which Safavid interference in Anatolian affairs actually constituted a threat to the sultan's control of certain regions of this peninsula.[35] Yet when trying to answer this question it is necessary to distinguish carefully between different times and places, always taking into account that, due to the destruction of the Safavid archives in the wars of the eighteenth century, we have much more information on Ottoman than on Safavid attitudes and policies. And as a matter of ordinary prudence, claims of 'subversion' on the part of any established power should, of course, be viewed with a degree of scepticism. Thus it would seem that Safavid propaganda added to the political and religious dissent already present in mid-sixteenth-century Anatolia, but it is unrealistic to assume that Ottoman power in the region would have remained uncontested had it not been for Safavid-sponsored religious unrest.

The mid-sixteenth century: foreign subjects present on Ottoman territory – and those who were conspicuously absent

Probably the middle years of the sixteenth century, when our story begins, are the time at which 'Ottoman centralism' was at its height. These years also form a period during which many of the later European 'players' in the contest for commercial supremacy, and who in the eighteenth century developed political ambitions as well, were not as yet present on the Ottoman scene. Or at the very least, these states and merchants were still comparatively weak. The interest of English and Dutch merchants in the eastern Mediterranean lands lay in the future. In consequence, there was no involvement in Ottoman affairs on the part of the young Queen Elizabeth I, who ascended the English throne in 1558/965–6. As to the Northern Netherlands, popularly called Holland, they had only just begun their long struggle for separation from Philip II's Spanish Empire.

Even the one ally of the sultans in the world of western Europe, namely the kingdom of France, had as yet only very limited concerns in the eastern Mediterranean. By the 1560s/967–77, it had become obvious to high-ranking Ottoman officials, including the current Grand Vizier Sokollu Mehmed Paşa, that the successors of King François I were neither able nor willing to go through with the commitments that the founder of the Valois dynasty had made to Sultan Süleyman with respect to the common struggle against the Habsburgs.[36] Due to intermittent civil war between Catholic and Reformed nobilities, Catherine de Medici, first as regent for – and later as advisor to – her sons, most of the time allowed the French embassy in Istanbul to languish because of insufficient funds. Or rather adventurous projects were suggested: in 1566/973–4, the ambassador Grantrie de Grandchamp attempted to gain Ottoman consent for the establishment of a large number of Huguenots, as well as French and German Lutherans, in Moldavia. These families were supposed to form a military colony against the Habsburgs, while removing a source of contention from the French kingdom. Grantrie de Grandchamp even took a personal interest in this scheme, attempting to marry the sister of the *voyvoda* of Moldavia, and at one time offered to fill the position of *voyvoda* himself, paying an annual tribute of 20,000 ducats. Apparently these projects resulted from the queen mother's and Charles IX's (r. 1560–74/967–82) desperate attempts to retain control of the volatile situation in France, and were not taken very seriously at the Ottoman court.[37]

As far as the Habsburgs themselves were concerned, the activities of merchants from their territories in the Ottoman lands were mostly limited to border trade. That commercial contacts did not expand was due to the frequency and destructiveness of war. After 1526/932–3, when the Ottomans swept away the army of the Hungarian King Lajos II, and the young ruler himself was killed in battle, the Habsburgs attempted to take over Hungary on the basis of a previously concluded treaty of inheritance with the but recently established Hungarian royal house, now extinct in the male line. This ambition resulted in a spate of

Ottoman–Habsburg warfare, which was terminated only after Ferdinand I had accepted to pay tribute for his rather circumscribed domains in Hungary. At first a five-year agreement was concluded in 1547/953–4, the so-called peace of Edirne, and in 1555/962–3, the ambassador Ogier Ghiselin de Busbecq arrived in Istanbul to negotiate another treaty, which was finalized only in 1562/969–70.[38] While Busbecq was sometimes admitted to Süleyman the Magnificent's court and sometimes confined to an Istanbul khan, the Ottomans engaged in major attacks on Croatia, to which Ferdinand I reacted by organizing a centralized border defence under a single commander. This measure, which from hindsight can be regarded as the founding of the *Militärgrenze* (military frontier), was to play a significant role in impeding further Ottoman advances.[39]

Thus the Habsburgs largely had lost the battle for Hungary. If we adopt the Ottoman viewpoint, in the 1560s/967–77 it was not at all clear that the first siege of Vienna (1529/935–6) would not be repeated with better success in the future. This remains true even though the sanguine hopes of imminent major conquests in Italy and the Germanies, which seem to have been entertained at Süleyman the Magnificent's court during the 1530s/936–46, had by now been given up.[40] Protection of Ottoman territories from the Vienna-based Habsburgs (in Ottoman parlance, the 'kings of Beç') thus involved small-scale border warfare, which occurred every now and then, even in times of peace.[41]

As to the Spanish branch of the Habsburgs, these were the initial years of Philip II's reign, who had taken over from his father Charles V only in 1556/ 963–4. Hispano-Ottoman rivalry concerned the Mediterranean coastlands of northern Africa. A starting point of this conflict was the expulsion of Arab Muslims from Spain after 1492/897–8; for from north African bases, some of the expellees engaged in sustained corsair attacks against Spanish coasts and shipping. In a series of counter-attacks, the Spanish kings took several north African ports, including Tripolis in 1510/915–16; this town they held until they were dislodged by the Ottomans in 1551/957–9. Newcomers from the eastern Mediterranean, namely Hayreddin Barbarossa and his brother, organized Muslim resistance against the invaders, ultimately accepting the suzerainty of the Ottoman sultans, whose chief admiral Hayreddin Paşa was to become.[42] More or less precariously, the Spaniards now held on to merely a few seaside fortresses without any hinterlands, the so-called *presidios* (Melilla, Mers-el-kebir, Oran). In addition there was a major naval contest on the high seas, of which the battle of İnebahtı/Lepanto (1572/979–80) was merely a single episode, well publicized but in no way decisive.[43] On a day-to-day level, the defence of the Ottomans' Mediterranean domain mainly aimed at an – often imperfect – protection of ships and inhabitants of coastal settlements against corsairs and pirates. As for Spain proper, Selim II, shortly after ascending the throne in 1566/973–4, decided to give the conquest of Cyprus from the Venetians priority over the support of the Morisco uprising against the king of Spain. Requests for military support from Philip II's Muslim subjects were accordingly answered by assurances that the governor of Algiers would help out with arms and supplies. But in practical

1. Helmet and armour intended as a diplomatic present from the Habsburg Emperor Rudolf II to the Grand Vizier Sinan Paşa, manufactured in a style that was hoped would please a high-ranking Ottoman. Due to the beginning of the 'Long War', it was never sent. Augsburg about 1590.

Source: Vienna, Kunsthistorisches Museum, Hofjagd- und Rüstkammer, inventory no. A609; reproduced by permission. The photograph has been taken from the exhibition catalogue *Im Lichte des Halbmonds, Das Abendland und der türkische Orient* (Dresden and Bonn: Staatliche Kunstsammlungen and Kunst- und Ausstellungshalle der Bundesrepublik Deutschland, 1995): 98.

terms, the Moriscos were left to fight their losing battles without anything more tangible than the Ottoman sultan's moral support.[44]

Prominent among the corsairs threatening Ottoman coastlands were the Maltese Knights, who claimed religious sanction for their attacks upon Ottoman subjects.[45] In response to this threat, during the last years of his reign, Süleyman the Magnificent had his admiral Turgut Re'is undertake the siege of Malta; but even though the fort of San Elmo was captured for a while, the conquest of the island itself failed.[46] It is worth noting that among the Knights of Malta there were not only the subjects of rulers frequently at war with the Ottoman Empire, such as Spaniards or gentlemen from the Spanish-controlled sections of the Italian peninsula, but also those of an ostensibly friendly ruler such as the king of France. By tolerating the anti-Ottoman moves of their noblemen, French rulers apparently tried to mitigate the negative reactions of emergent 'public opinion' both in France and in western Europe as a whole, against the alliance of the 'most Christian king' with the 'enemy of Christendom'.[47]

Apart from Hungarians living under the rule of Ferdinand I (r. as king of 'royal' Hungary, 1526–64/932–72), few Habsburg subjects seem to have visited Ottoman territory in the 1560s/967–77, at least if we discount the numerous prisoners of war who became slaves of Sultan Süleyman himself, or else served his soldiers and subjects in a servile capacity. As far as the 'westerners' sojourning on their territories were concerned, the Ottomans were confronted mainly with merchants from various cities in Italy, and more particularly with the Venetians. In addition the Signoria maintained resident ambassadors in Istanbul, at a time when this practice was only just coming into fashion among European rulers. Apart from the official duties discharged by these ambassadors, the latter doubled as purveyors of intelligence to the Signoria, and even to those states, such as Spain, that had no official representation on Ottoman territory.[48] Venetian merchants and diplomats often also provided the Ottoman government with useful information on European politics.

On the northern frontier, direct involvement on the part of the Ottoman government remained relatively limited. The raids against what is today Ukrainian and Russian territory constituted a significant element in the economy of the Crimean Tatars, mainly because of the booty and captives that these campaigns normally produced. Captives made by the Tatars were often sold into Ottoman territory as slaves, which explains why the so-called Rus (Süleyman the Magnificent's consort Hurrem Sultan came from this region) by the second half of the sixteenth century constituted an appreciable share of the slaves documented in the kadi records of Bursa.[49] Direct involvement in the northern borderlands on the part of the Ottoman sultans was limited to a very few instances. Among the latter, the campaign undertaken in reaction to the Muscovite conquest of Astrakhan was the most spectacular, due to the failed project of a Don–Volga canal, which was to have facilitated sultanic conquests in the area.[50] Whether the Ottomans had developed a coherent 'northern policy' by this early date, in respect of the emerging state of the tsars remains a subject of debate.[51]

Among its eastern neighbours, the Ottoman state apparatus maintained relations with Iran, and to a much lesser degree, with the Muslim polities of India, especially the Mughul Empire.[52] Around 1560/967–8, the latter state was recovering from a major crisis as in the recent past its ruler Humāyūn, son of the empire-builder Bābur, had been chased from his throne, forced to take refuge at the court of Shah Ṭahmāsp in Iṣfahān and then died in 1556/963–4, shortly after recovering Delhi (1555/962–3). In the early 1560s/967–77 his son and successor Akbar was as yet reconsolidating Mughul control of northern India.[53] Thus among the Muslim states it was mainly Safavid Iran that, in the Ottoman perspective, was considered a threat both in religious and in political terms. As a result it was the Iranian presence in Anatolia and on the Arabian peninsula that the administration in Istanbul tried, not always successfully, to limit and supervise.[54] Matters were complicated by the fact that in times of peace the Ottoman sultan could not refuse Iranian pilgrims access to the holy sites of Mecca and Medina. Nor could he deny them access to the tombs of members of the Prophet's family situated in what, after the 1530s/936–46, had become Ottoman Iraq.[55] In addition, quite a few Iranian Sunnis, particularly those originating from the Caucasian borderlands, had immigrated to the Ottoman Empire, and some of them managed to find employment in the bureaux of the central administration. There thus existed an Iranian-speaking group of Ottoman officials, esteemed for their command of the Persian literary tradition but often enough, suspected by their colleagues and rivals as unreliable outsiders.[56]

Religious-*cum*-political rivalries between the sultans and 'western' rulers in the 1560s/967–77

We have already encountered, albeit briefly, the conflicts between Christian rulers of rival denominations. In this branch of historical studies specialists of the early modern period have attempted for many years to disentangle purely religious concerns from struggles for economic advantage and territorial aggrandizement, and a certain – admittedly limited – degree of success has been achieved. On the one hand, it is obvious that religion often enough was used to cover very mundane power plays with the mantle of respectability. Antagonisms between ethnic groups, political factions and social classes in early modern Europe were sometimes expressed by quarrels between rival churches and sects.[57] Some historians, often but not always of a Marxian persuasion, may have overworked this theme; but that does not mean that they were wrong in principle. On the other hand, it has been pointed out that Christians of the sixteenth century not only were convinced that their respective churches represented right belief, but also held that violence was justified to bring any 'misbelievers' back into the fold. In consequence, opponents often found it very difficult to compromise when religious matters were at stake, even when, from our present-day perspective, it would have been in their mutual interest to do so.[58] At least down to about 1700/1111–12, and sometimes even much later, rivalries between Catholic,

Orthodox and less frequently, Protestant churches formed the backdrop of the policies that different Christian states pursued towards the Ottoman sultan. Thus, when the Orthodox patriarch Cyrillos Lucaris became a Calvinist in the late 1620s/1029–39, he was supported by the Dutch and English ambassadors, both Protestants, while encountering sharp opposition from the French envoy, who saw Catholic interests in danger.[59]

However, these rivalries did not always prevent Christians from both western and south-eastern Europe from seeing themselves as belonging to one and the same religion, and this sentiment was especially strong when they were confronted with a Muslim ruler. During the second half of the sixteenth and the beginning years of the seventeenth century, this sentiment, such as it was, was more often shared between certain Catholics and Orthodox, than between Catholics and Protestants. This was due partly to reasons of dogma and partly to the fact that, with the exception of warfare between Muscovy and Poland, Catholic and Orthodox rulers had not in the recent past had much occasion for armed conflict. Religious communalities between Christians, so it was often assumed, might induce Orthodox subjects to rise against their Muslim overlords whenever the presence of a strong 'western' army or navy would make this a viable option. While this assumption was frequently made by advisors to various Christian rulers, at least where the sixteenth century was concerned, there was in fact plenty of evidence to the contrary. For such uprisings were really rather rare, and occurred with some frequency only if there were established native Christian rulers to lead them; this condition existed in Moldavia and Walachia until 1716/ 1028–9. Or in other cases, such rebellions occurred in poor and outlying regions such as Montenegro, where an Ottoman army could only be sent at great expense, a move that the authorities in Istanbul might well consider as 'not worth the trouble'. All this was in principle well known to many contemporaries but, especially in times of war, such knowledge did not prevent the emergence of personages who claimed that they could bring about an anti-Ottoman rebellion.[60]

Projects involving the subversion of Ottoman Christians were entertained at European courts of the early modern period with some frequency because the relevant rulers, often including ostensible allies of the sultan, assumed the Ottoman Empire to be much less stable as a state than we today, with the benefit of hindsight, know it to have been. Thus for example the financial, economic and political crisis of the late sixteenth century was viewed by many European authors as an indication that the Ottoman Empire had started to 'decline', and would 'fall' in the near future. In such an eventuality, many states of western and southern Europe had hopes of territorial acquisitions; in this sense, 'dividing up the Ottoman Empire' was not entirely an invention of nineteenth-century diplomats.[61] But as long as the Empire did remain in existence, these self-same rulers, with the French king an obvious example, might have no particular objection to forming political alliances with the Ottoman sultans.[62]

These expectations and assumptions permeate many European archival sources dealing with the history of the sultanic domains. Since these materials usually became accessible to researchers long before their counterparts in the Ottoman archives, it is not surprising that they have left profound traces in the relevant historiography. This impact was reinforced by the fact that early republican historiography in Turkey also was much inclined to dwell on Ottoman 'corruption' and 'decline'.[63] In the nineteenth century, most European historians strongly identified with the empire or nation-state of which they were subjects/ citizens. Ottoman historians, on their part, tried to explain the internal and external developments that had first halted the Ottoman advance and then led to the loss of ever more territories.[64] In this endeavour, after about 1850/1266–7 the more prominent authors, to a greater or lesser degree, adopted the methodologies current among European and American historians of their time; Fuat Köprülü's interest in frontier zones and their inhabitants is a well-known case in point.[65]

How the Ottoman elite *did not* organize its relations with the outside world in the 1560s/967–77

Yet interestingly enough, this emergence of a common methodology did not, for a considerable time, result in a perspective on Ottoman history shared by Ottomanists and Europeanists. In part, language barriers may have been responsible; as long as Turkish scholars published all but exclusively in Turkish and Europeanist historians did not normally know this language, scholarly interchange remained difficult. But this cannot be the whole story, because even Europeanists who were admirable linguists might write about the Ottoman Empire using only a minimum of Ottomanist secondary literature, even if it was available in English. This situation ensured that topoi such as 'Ottoman decline', which many Ottomanists came to consider increasingly dubious as explanatory devices, continued to be widely used, for instance, by scholars dealing with Balkan history.

On the other hand, Ottomanists have rarely addressed themselves to certain issues crucial, for instance, to anyone attempting to place 'corruption' into a historical context. We still possess all too few studies dealing with the purchase of offices in an Ottoman context, a topic germane to the 'corruption problem' and well studied for early modern France or Florence. Given the frequent sales and purchases of Ottoman offices from the late sixteenth century onwards, this constitutes a serious omission, even if the growing number of studies on lifetime tax-farming and provincial power-holding are beginning to fill this gap at least in part.[66] Only when we understand the historical context of what some contemporaries and many authors of later periods regarded as corruption, will we able to assess the extent to which such practices impinged on Ottoman relationships with foreign rulers and their subjects.

As a result of these historiographical traditions, perspectives have become seriously distorted. Studies dealing with matters pertaining to both Ottoman and European history, including the diverse religious and political rivalries fought out between Europeans in Istanbul, or else the supra-state contacts of the Orthodox Church, are very often treated as if Ottoman officials had no interest in these issues, apart from the 'bribes' that powerful individuals might derive from supporting one side or the other.[67] The Ottoman administration, which down to the 1660s/1070–80 had still been expanding its domain, thus is pictured as if it were merely a congeries of individuals pursuing their private financial interests, and occasionally their desires for bloodthirsty revenge.[68] If this image had in fact been realistic, the Ottoman Empire should have collapsed after the very first serious military setback, which was very far from being the case. To the contrary, if we compare Ottoman history of the eighteenth century to the precipitous decline of certain formerly powerful states such as Sweden or Poland, the tenacity of the Ottoman ruling group in defending its polity rather strikes the eye.[69]

Recent studies have shown that, beginning with the seventeenth century, the Ottoman elite was held together not only by factional ties, but also by the loyalty of the heads of 'political households' to the most important 'household head' of them all, namely the sultan.[70] But, in addition, there was an increasingly intricate organization of bureaux, financial and other, constituting a 'ladder of success' that, with a bit of good fortune and political *savoir-faire*, might lead a former scribe to high office. It is difficult to believe that in such a group, there was no consensus on general policy issues, even if, due to the gaps in the accessible documentation, we sometimes have to hypothesize about these opinions, rather than simply piecing them together from the relevant state documents.[71] In my view, it is an 'orientalist' assumption of the most outmoded variety to postulate an atomized Ottoman elite unable to formulate even a loose consensual framework, within which its individual members might pursue the interests of the state, that alone could guarantee their positions and – as was true also of other polities – their personal financial concerns as well.

Limits of imperial reach in the 1560s/967–77: Anatolian loyalties to non-Ottoman princes

Even though it makes some sense to regard the Ottoman state of the later Süleymanic years as strongly centralized by the standards of the early modern period, it would be unrealistic to assume that this situation implied a standardized level of control on the part of the Ottoman authorities over their entire territory. After all, such uniformity was a desideratum not always realized even in twentieth-century states. Coastlands were particularly at risk. Similar to what has been observed concerning Spain and Italy during this period, locations close to the sea were not much favoured by the inhabitants of western Anatolia. While the malaria problem was largely responsible for this choice, the constant danger from corsairs and pirates, some of them Ottoman subjects although many of them were not, constituted an additional deterrent. Only at their own risks and perils might peasants from inland settlements periodically come down from the hills, in order to cultivate the fields of abandoned seashore villages.[72]

In the interior of the Anatolian peninsula, there existed other reasons for a less than perfect control of Ottoman territory by the central government. We will neglect purely domestic reasons for this state of affairs, such as the intermittent warfare between the sons of Süleyman the Magnificent contending for the imperial throne. It must, however, be kept in mind that a major uprising in favour of the Dulkadir, an eastern Anatolian dynasty with links to Mamluk Egypt, took place as late as the 1520s/926–36, and was repressed with a good deal of bloodshed.[73] Was this really the last rebellion attempted by adherents of a dynasty that had controlled this or that province prior to the Ottoman takeover? Unfortunately our knowledge of Anatolian provincial history during the 1560s/967–77 is quite limited, and probably will remain so due to a persistent lack of primary sources. As a result, we do not know whether certain movements that the Ottoman central authorities loosely described by the term *eşkiyalık* (robbery, rebellion) were not really gestures of support for deposed non-Ottoman dynasties. Unbeknown to officials in Istanbul, loyalties to such figures may have continued for a long time among the nomads inhabiting the dry steppes of central Anatolia.

Even more complicated was the role of the 'Kızılbaş' tribesmen who lived in more or less compact groups throughout Anatolia, but were especially concentrated in the south-western section of the peninsula. There were also many adherents of this heterodox brand of Islam in the province of Rum, that is the area around Amasya, Tokat and Sivas, and as we have seen, quite a few of them showed a pronounced attachment to the Safavid dynasty emerging in Iran at the beginning of the sixteenth century. Throughout, the Ottoman government continued to be wary of religiously motivated discontent in these isolated regions of Anatolia. Moreover, it appears that under Süleyman the Lawgiver Safavid and non-Safavid dervishes deemed heterodox by the authorities were persecuted with equal relish. This common peril may have induced the two groups to form connections that they would not otherwise have established. Thus the Bektashi order of dervishes, with its central lodge in what is today the town of Hacıbektaş, received all manner of adherents who thus attempted to escape persecution. Given the paucity of sources we can surmise, but cannot claim with any certainty, that some desperate or disillusioned former adherents of the Safavid order also figured among the Bektashi recruits. In any event, Pir Sultan Abdal, a religious poet who may have lived in the sixteenth or seventeenth century and whose poems were transmitted among both Bektashis and the adherents of an Anatolian variety of 'folk' Islam known today as Alevis, was also an ardent follower of the shahs of Iran. If his poetry adequately reflects the state of mind characteristic of certain Anatolian heterodox circles, there were people in this region willing to lay down their lives for the sake of the shah.[74]

Dervishes were not necessarily unarmed, and sometimes could mobilize adherents among professional soldiers such as active and candidate janissaries. Complaints about the sheiks of dervish lodges making common cause with known *eşkiya* are not at all rare in the Registers of Important Affairs. Often it is unclear whether the *eşkiya* in question were 'ordinary' robbers or whether, at least in certain cases, they were religious dissenters of one kind or another.[75] Deciding this question is made even more difficult by the fact that so many people regarded as heterodox by the authorities were nomads or semi-nomads, who, given access to horses and arms, might turn to robbery in order to supplement a meagre livelihood. Separating the quest for booty from a degree of insurgency for religious and political reasons is not easy for the present-day historian, and presumably was even less so for people of the sixteenth century.

Limits of imperial reach: some Rumelian examples

Nor was central control at all absolute in the often mountainous territories of the Balkans. Where the Muslim population was concerned, the sources of unrest were, however, but marginally linked with forces outside the Ottoman Empire. Heterodox dervishes faced repression like their Anatolian colleagues, but there were no claims that they maintained links with the Safavids. When considering possible 'security risks', the central authorities were rather more suspicious of the sympathies of Orthodox monks in rural areas. Given the often remote places in which such monasteries were located, many monks maintained stores of arms in order to protect themselves against marauders. In some instances, such as the famed Meteora, the monasteries in question, located high up on rocky mountains, could only be reached by means of baskets and ladders. During the war over Cyprus (1570–73/977–81) these monasteries were regarded as possible sources of aid and comfort to the enemy, although many of the monks in question, as devout Orthodox, may not have been very partial to the Catholic rulers of the Holy League. Local administrators accordingly were ordered to confiscate horses and weaponry. In part, this may have been due to the rule, enshrined in religious law, that non-Muslims were not to carry arms. At least as important was probably the overall policy of disarming the subjects, Muslims and non-Muslims alike, which the Ottoman authorities pursued at least where firearms were concerned.[76] In more peaceful circumstances, monasteries located close to the seashore were considered hotbeds of smuggling, the monks being accused of illegally selling grain to 'Frankish' merchants.[77] In one instance, dating from the 1580s/987–98, we also learn of the nuns of what was to become the St Philothei convent of Athens, who provided refuge to escaped slaves and especially slave women wishing to return to 'Frengistan'.[78] Apparently the nuns were willing to disregard the tensions between Catholics and Orthodox for the time being.

On a higher level of the hierarchy, there were contacts between the Serbian Orthodox Church and the grand dukes of Muscovy, later to become the tsars of Russia, the earliest records going back to the sixteenth century. Visits of church dignitaries, as well as correspondence, continued with increased intensity after 1600/1008–9. However, the published documents, mainly letters from Serbian churchmen asking the Russian rulers for material and moral support, show a gap between 1509/914–15 and the seventeenth century. As for the oecumenical patriarchate in Istanbul, its contacts to the grand dukes of Muscovy and later to the Russian tsars were quite intensive, especially during and immediately after the patriarchate of the staunchly anti-Catholic Cyrillos Lucaris.[79] After the latter's execution, several of his adherents continued to furnish a good deal of information on the political situation in Istanbul; apparently the intelligence-gathering of the tsars through dignitaries of the seventeenth-century Orthodox Church was almost comparable with that of the Venetian Signoria, whose activities in this field are much better known.[80]

Other threats to Ottoman territory might come from the rather numerous projects to subvert the sultan's domain with help from foreign rulers, especially those of Counter-Reformation Italy. These are amply documented in European sources; however, Ottoman official correspondence tells us very little about them.[81] This poses the question whether the authorities in Istanbul were informed of such projected uprisings, and if so, whether they were willing to have the documents relevant to such delicate concerns copied into the ordinary Registers of Important Affairs. Possibly there existed a special chancery for such matters directly relevant to the security of the state, with an archive of its own that has not been preserved. But it is also conceivable that in the relatively settled conditions of the 1560s/967–77, projects with little chance of realization were not taken too seriously. Once again, matters were different during the war of the Holy League over Cyprus, when Philip II of Spain received several offers from Balkan Christians who claimed that they were able to raise armies against the sultan if given logistical support. Here the Ottoman administration did follow such movements with great care; however *le roi prudent* was not really willing to engage himself in a war on Ottoman territory, and these attempts all came to nought.[82]

Limits of imperial reach in the 1560s/967–77, a further example: Yemen as a frontier province

By the 1560s/967–77, Ottoman rule had been established in the formerly Mamluk territories for over forty years, and rebellions by military men hoping to reestablish the defunct state also had receded into the past. However, the Portuguese threat to the Ottoman possessions in the Red Sea had by no means disappeared. There was a raid on Jiddah in 1542/948–9, and for their cooperation in repulsing it, the sherifs of Mecca were awarded half the local customs dues. Now Jiddah constituted not just the port of disembarkation and embarkation of Mecca pilgrims, but also an entrepôt of some significance for the trade with India. Thus at least in the 1570s/977–87, the customs revenues accruing to the sherifs apparently amounted to sizeable sums.[83] We may therefore surmise that the military contribution of the sherifs of Mecca had been substantial, and the Portuguese threat serious in proportion.

Protecting the Hijaz from further Portuguese attacks also seems to have formed one of the considerations prompting the Ottoman reconquest of Yemen in 1568–71/975–9.[84] Taxing the trade in spices from southern Asia and procuring these condiments for the palace kitchen also must have been an attraction. As to taxes and customs dues, provincial budgets of Ottoman Yemen show that the

Indian Ocean ports produced a substantial share of the revenues remitted to Istanbul.[85] Moreover, during the closing years of Süleyman the Lawgiver's reign, and until his successor Selim II opted for the conquest of Cyprus in preference to the assertion of Ottoman power in the Indian Ocean, the Empire maintained a political interest in the southern seas. This included a favourable response to the petition of the sultan of Atjeh in northern Sumatra, who requested cannons and gunners to be used against the Portuguese.[86] As long as an active Indian Ocean policy remained an option at the Ottoman court, control of the Yemeni ports was of considerable strategic interest.

Preparations for the campaign to conquer the Yemen were long delayed due to the rivalry of Sinan Paşa and Lala Mustafa Paşa, the two commanders in charge, as each of the two viziers was trying to prevent his rival from achieving a major conquest and thus becoming a serious candidate for the position of grand vizier.[87] This observation is of interest for our purposes, since it shows that in the Ottoman realm as elsewhere, decisions pertaining to what we would call 'foreign policy' might be taken, not on the basis of abstract notions of the state's best interests and the welfare of the Muslim community, but due to very mundane factional tensions within the ruling group. The contest was ultimately won by Sinan Paşa, who waged a successful campaign in 1569–70/976–8.[88] However, it is difficult to judge how far Ottoman control extended beyond the hinterlands of Sana'a and the Indian Ocean ports; and local powers continued to be strong. While the conquest of the Yemen certainly prevented further Portuguese incursions into the Red Sea, it did not lessen the dependence of the Holy Cities upon Egyptian foodstuffs. In any case, Yemeni grain does not appear to have played a major role as a source of nourishment for pilgrims and residents of the Hijaz. Thus from this viewpoint, the Yemen should be regarded as a typical frontier province, valuable not so much for what it produced but for the protection it gave to regions further inland.

All these examples show that Ottoman central control, while substantial in certain aspects of life and also in some geographical regions, in no way covered the entire surface of the Empire in an even and regular fashion. Unsupervised contacts with the non-Ottoman world thus were much more frequent than might appear at first glance. Even in the Ottoman heartlands certain groups, such as the hill- and steppe-dwelling heterodox nomads that the authorities liked to call the Kızılbaş, might manage to keep a distance between themselves and local administrators, under certain circumstances even hiding emissaries from Iran. Orthodox monasteries in outlying places also might be difficult to control, and the links of church dignitaries to their 'patron' the Russian tsar must have added to the opacity of the Orthodox Church from the government's point of view. Moreover in remote locations such as Yemen, control could only be secured if the centre was willing to send a major expedition every few decades or so. Early modern centralization of the kind practised by the Ottomans should thus not be confused with the kind of control that only became possible after railways and telegraph lines had been instituted. However, we must also keep in mind that

Ottoman bureaucrats were attuned to the social and technological limits of their control and that as a result, well into the eighteenth century, the Empire could be governed quite satisfactorily even if vast stretches of the subjects' lives remained outside the purview of the imperial bureaucracy.

~ The Empire in 1639/1048–9

Protecting Ottoman territories in 1639/1048–9: the eastern frontier

An Ottoman official who considered the situation of the state he served as it appeared in 1639/1048–9, had some reason for guarded optimism, for it seemed that Murad IV (r. 1623–40/1032–50) had stabilized the Empire both domestically and in the international arena. Presumably members of the governing class were most appreciative of the fact that the sultan had succeeded in retaking Baghdad from the Iranians (1638/1047–8). This is a likely conclusion even though the conquest of Eriwan (Revan), celebrated with some fanfare, and the construction of a handsome pavillion in the Topkapı Palace, proved to be quite short-lived. Military successes also would explain why Evliya Çelebi (1611–1684/1019–96), who was related to court circles even though not personally a high Ottoman official, was appreciative of Murad IV, whose campaigns had dominated the writer's youth and young adulthood. Where members of the subject population, such as the Serres Greek Orthodox priest Papa Synadinos were concerned, they presumably were more impressed by the fact that this sultan had thoroughly intimidated janissaries and other would-be rebels, who so often robbed 'ordinary' taxpayers, both Muslim and non-Muslim.[89] Given these points in the ruler's favour, the bloodshed involved, which was considerable, apparently was regarded as tolerable by quite a few contemporaries, or at least by those who put down their thoughts in writing.[90]

Concluding the peace of Ḳaṣr-i Shīrīn involved the Ottomans' renouncing control over the Caucasus, which had seemed so important during the sixteenth century.[91] But then the Ottoman occupations of this area, where numerous principalities and ethnic groups coexisted, always had been short-lived. By the late 1630s/1039–49, the 'buffer zone' that separated Ottoman from Iranian territory at least had become thoroughly stabilized. A special bureau in the central government was responsible for relations with the Kurdish princes of eastern Anatolia, and one of its senior officials had even produced a manual of advice concerning the manner in which these local potentates were to be treated. Aziz Efendi impressed upon his readers, presumably for the most part his colleagues and future successors, that these princes, due to their staunch Sunni loyalties, were of great importance in Ottoman border control, and should therefore be treated with forbearance.[92] Unfortunately we do not know whether Shah 'Abbās' policy of reducing the Kızılbaş tribesmen to a subordinate position, and balancing their power by means of a soldiery loosely patterned on the janissary model, was perceived in Istanbul as a measure limiting the danger of heterodox subversion. If that was indeed the case, as is probable, the stabilization of the Iranian frontier should have been linked to a 'de-ideologization' of the Ottoman–Safavid conflict.

The northern regions as a trouble spot in 1639/1048–9

In 1639, the northern borders of the Ottoman world crossed a region contested between the Crimean Tatars and the Cossacks; the latter formed a group of border warriors owing loose allegiance to the kings of Poland. Small-scale warfare was endemic, but did not normally involve the major states beyond exchanges of diplomatic protests.[93] However, there were exceptions to this rule: in 1621/ 1030–1, conflicts of this kind escalated into full-scale war, and the young Sultan Osman II personally participated in a campaign against Poland, fighting a pitched battle near Chotin/Hotin. The subsequent peace treaty stipulated that Osman II would restrain the Tatars, while King Sigismund accepted the same responsibility with respect to the Cossacks. Sigismund's successor King Władislaw made a variety of plans for war against the Ottomans in the course of his reign, hoping to gain a foothold in Moldavia and Walachia and also to strike a blow at the Crimean Tatars. But in 1648/1057–8 the Cossacks, exasperated by the behaviour of certain Polish magnates and their agents, allied themselves with their old opponents the Tatars. Poland thus became embroiled once again with the Ottoman Empire, while lacking the support of its most experienced border troops.[94]

From the mid-seventeenth century onwards, in consequence, this area was to enter into the *grande histoire*. In 1637/1046–7 a band of Cossacks took the fortress of Azov on the Black Sea and for several years defended it with a small force against both Ottoman and Tatar armies.[95] When unable to hold out any longer, the Cossacks offered Azov to Tsar Mikhail, of the newly enthroned Romanow dynasty. However, in the early seventeenth century the tsars, in spite of conflicts over Astrakhan and Tatar or Cossack depredations, were very much concerned about maintaining reasonably good relations with the sultans. In Moscow, the struggle against Poland-Lithuania was generally accorded priority. After all, Azov was located at an enormous distance from the Russian frontiers of that time and had been much damaged by recent warfare. Experts who had surveyed the fortifications were of the opinion that a long time would be needed to rebuild them, while the fortress could not withstand another Ottoman siege in its current condition. Furthermore, the Ottoman envoy Vasile Lupu, the hospodar of Moldavia, argued that a war between the sultan and the tsar would be very dangerous to the Empire's Orthodox population, who would probably suffer the wrath of the unpredictable Sultan Ibrahim. It would be interesting to know whether this line of reasoning had been thought out in Istanbul in advance, or was Vasile Lupu's own ad hoc contribution to the success of his mission. As a result, Tsar Mikhail

in 1642/1051–2 not only refused the offer of Azov but, in line with previous policies, disclaimed all responsibility for the actions of the Cossacks. His
ambassadors even stated that the tsar would not object to an Ottoman punitive
campaign against these freebooters. It was also in accordance with accepted
Muscovite practice that, all these disclaimers notwithstanding, Tsar Mikhail had
provided the Cossacks with some financial support as long as they actually held
on to Azov.

Expanding Ottoman territory in 1639/1048–9: relations with Venice and the imminent conquest of Crete

Where the Mediterranean coastlands were concerned, the attention of Ottoman
ruling circles focused on Venice, whose only remaining possession in the eastern
Mediterranean was Crete, strategically located on the route from Istanbul to
Egypt. We do not know exactly to what extent high officials in Istanbul were
aware of the fact that by the mid-seventeenth century the Venetian economy was
in profound crisis.[96] The city had lost its role in the European spice trade and in
addition the southern German market, once so important for Venice's commercial prosperity, had severely diminished due to the Thirty Years War.[97] But, given
the numerous comings and goings between the territories of the Signoria and the
Ottoman Empire, it is hard to imagine that knowledge of the troubled economic
situation, with its negative consequences for Venetian naval armament, had not
reached the sultan's council. Once again we may repeat our hypothesis that some
such information concerning Venetian weakness ultimately prompted the attack
on Crete.

At the same time we must keep in mind that data on customs and dues levied
upon the trade in spices and woollen textiles, which to the modern historian provide irrefutable arguments demonstrating the seventeenth-century decline of
Venice, were not available to contemporaries.[98] In the early 1600s, numerous
merchants still travelled between Ottoman and Venetian territories. Daniele Rod-
riga's offer of investment in the port of Spalato in order to provide a secure link
between the two Adriatic coasts seems, if anything, to have encouraged Ottoman
merchants to do business in the lagoon. After all, it was only in the early seventeenth century that an old palazzo on the Grand Canal, in the very heart of the
city, was revamped to form the Fondaco dei Turchi. Moreover, the efficient
organization of Venetian representatives abroad, including a far-flung network of
consuls, was not dismantled from one day to the next.[99] Quite to the contrary, in
the early seventeenth century, both consuls and the *bailo* were actively promoting the interests of Venetian traders, and the Spanish crown considered
information on Ottoman state matters arriving by way of Venice more reliable
even than that procured by its own viceroys of Naples.[100]

All this activity was observed by Ottoman dignitaries and merchants, and it is
quite possible that in the 1630s/1039–49, the Ottoman government regarded Venice as more important than, for example, the contemporary advisors of the

English king Charles I would have done had they been members of the sultan's council. It has recently been pointed out that, in spite of the many wars fought out over the course of the centuries, the Ottoman Empire and Venice during the middle and later 1600s both represented an '*ancien régime*' now being superseded by the 'new style' trading of the British or French.[101] As the Ottoman–Iranian (1578–90/985–99, 1603–19/1011–29, 1623–4/1032–4, 1629–39/1038–49) and Ottoman–Habsburg wars (1593–1606/1001–15) had amply demonstrated, on these two main fronts the sultans' armies were no longer able to secure permanent acquisitions of territory on any major scale. If, however, significant conquest was necessary in order to legitimize the sultanate in the eyes of both the ruling group and the wider military establishment, then it made good sense to turn against Venice, still an important state in Ottoman eyes but currently in serious difficulties.

Potential threats to Ottoman control over the western part of the Balkan peninsula in 1639/1048–9

During the 'Long War' (1593–1606/1001–15), when Ottoman armies were fighting the Austrian Habsburgs in Hungary, the Spanish monarchy toyed with the idea of conquests on the eastern Adriatic coast. But the war against the northern Netherlands (until 1609/1017–18), financial support of the Austrians (until 1606/ 1014–15) and, wherever possible, aggrandizement in Italy had priority. As a result once again no direct participation in a Balkan campaign was ever envisaged. In some cases, however, arms and small amounts of financial aid were supplied to would-be insurgents, without producing any concrete results.

Some credit for the failure of Spanish-inspired uprisings certainly was due to Venice and Dubrovnik, whose elites were opposed in principle to the Balkan projects of Philip II and his descendants. Where the Venetians were concerned, tensions with Spanish governors in Italy were so serious that the Serenissima opposed any further expansion of the Habsburg domain. In addition, both the Venetian and Dubrovnik governments were much worried that if they came to be viewed in Istanbul as supporting anti-Ottoman intrigues, they would endanger some of their most significant political and economic assets. Control over large parts of Dalmatia constituted the major issue in the Venetian case while, for Dubrovnik, the town's cherished autonomy under the Ottoman 'umbrella' was at stake. Admittedly, anti-Ottoman movements of the 1630s/1039–49 have not been studied as throroughly as those of the late sixteenth and early seventeenth centuries, with their spate of Ottoman–Venetian wars. But it does seem that after 1630/ 1039–40, it had become relatively clear to would-be Balkan insurgents that the Spanish government was not seriously interested in supporting them. Only the so-called Sultan Yahya (who had become a Catholic), an alleged son of Mehmed III and a brother of Ahmed I, was still travelling through Europe and the lands of the steppe frontier. At one point he managed to win the support of the Tatar Khan Şahin, and of the Cossacks as well. But by the 1630s/1039–49 even Sultan

Yahya's activity was ebbing, and he finally entered Venetian service, dying in 1648/1057–8.[102]

Early links to the seventeenth-century European world economy?

Perhaps to its disadvantage, Venice constituted a highly visible 'player' in the Mediterranean power game of the times. But structural changes in certain Otto- man territories, which had been brought about by some less obvious participants in the politico-economic contest, were more important in the long run. While our discussion of the limits of Ottoman control in the 1560s/967–77 has revolved entirely around politcal questions, by the 1630s/1039–49 and 1640s/1049–59, changes in the international 'economic balance of power' entered the picture as well. However, these latter mutations presumably were not as apparent to con- temporaries as they are to us, arguing on the basis of the always ambiguous benefits of hindsight.

To mention but one example, by the 1630s/1039–49 and 1640s/1049–59, Izmir had become a significant mart for foreign trade; this had not been true in the 1560s/967–77, when the Ottoman tax registers show us a minute settlement which could barely claim urban status.[103] Sixteenth-century Izmir had formed part of the extensive coastlands that, in the calculations of Ottoman officials, were intended to supply the capital with foodstuffs and raw materials.[104] With its Mediterranean climate, the western coast of Anatolia constituted a significant source of raisins – that sixteenth-century equivalent of sugar – and also of cotton, essential for the sails of the sultan's navy. Beyond the subsistence needs of the local inhabitants, other uses for grains, cotton and fruit from the Izmir region were but rarely envisaged. Export of these goods was either forbidden or at the very least closely controlled. Moreover local urban development in Izmir or Aya- soluğ (Selçuk, Efes), which could only have created competitors for Istanbul's food supply, was probably discouraged by the Ottoman authorities for just that reason.[105]

However, by the 1630s/1039–49 and 1640s/1049–59, this situation was begin- ning to change. Apparently foreign merchants, Venetians, Englishmen, Frenchmen and some traders from the newly established Dutch republic, were at first attracted to the region by its local resources and, stringent Ottoman prohibi- tions notwithstanding, in some cases the foreigners also smuggled out some grain. Yet the authorities in Istanbul never attempted to remove all foreign trad- ers from the Aegean; to the contrary, around 1600/1008–9 the export of cotton was permitted at least during certain years.[106] In all likelihood this willingness to allow long-established rules to be occasionally broken was motivated by the pressing need for silver, which European merchants regularly supplied because the Ottoman balance of trade at this time was positive. In spite of mercantilist pressures to keep precious metals at home, European traders could continue to supply bullion to the lands of the eastern Mediterranean because by indirect routes, they all had access to the large quantities of Latin-American silver that the Spaniards were bringing in from Mexico and Peru. That naval warfare between Spaniards and Ottomans declined after the 1580s/987–98, turning the Mediterranean into a secondary venue of inter-empire confrontation, must have increased Ottoman inclinations to exchange cotton for silver.[107]

Furthermore, once the foreign traders had become established in Izmir, their presence encouraged the Armenian merchants who marketed the Iranian raw silk, which Shah 'Abbās had declared a royal monopoly, to bring some of this silk not to Aleppo or Bursa, but rather to Izmir.[108] Or as an alternative, one may hypothesize that the trade in raw silk had been an important factor in Izmir's commerce from the very beginning.[109] There has been some speculation concerning the reasons for this drastic change in trade routes. Certainly there were grave security problems on the Aleppo route – but we do not really know that they were more serious here than on the way between Iran and Izmir. We also may surmise that one of the attractions of Izmir in the eyes of European merchants was its relative proximity to their ports of origin. In addition, the distance between Bursa and the Aegean is not very great; thus it is also possible that the shah's Armenian merchants, who found the demand in Bursa flagging, sought and found a new outlet in Izmir.[110] We can also imagine that in the merchant councils of New Djulfa near Iṣfahān – where, by the mid-seventeenth century, many of the more important decisions concerning Armenian commercial policy were being taken – it was considered advantageous to have not one, but several outlets. When all is said and done, competition between purchasers does boost prices.

However, the seventeenth-century growth of Izmir into a major commercial centre did not mean that the silk trade through Aleppo was being phased out. If the construction of new khans is a reliable guide to the city's commercial potency, it appears that the sixteenth century constituted the major period of florescence. But even in the second half of the seventeenth century, a newly built establishment of this type added a large amount of commercial real estate to the supply already available in Aleppo. It must, though, be admitted that this was one of the few major projects to be realized after 1600/1008–9, and before the renewed expansion of trade in the nineteenth century. Like what has happened in the historiography of Izmir, specialists on Aleppo also have debated to what extent long-distance trade was really the cause of the city's sixteenth- and seventeenth-century expansion. It has been suggested that Aleppo's hinterland, with its numerous towns and populous villages producing soap or cotton cloth, was the real source of urban prosperity, with the silk trade no more than 'icing on the cake'.[111]

These discussions obviously complicate the problem of the 'incorporation' of Ottoman regions into the European-dominated world economy. Due to the shift away from economic and toward cultural history during the last two decades or so, and also due to the discovery that 'incorporation' is not the answer to all the historian's problems, this question in recent years has been rather neglected. But

in my view, we have not as yet determined the exact chronology of the 'incorporation' process on Ottoman territory; this means that a major problem, once
posed by Immanuel Wallerstein and his associates, has not been solved but
merely pushed aside.[112] But neither has it been proved insoluble or irrelevant. We
still need to discuss whether, by the mid-seventeenth century, a region of the kind
that then surrounded Izmir can be regarded as having become part of a European-
dominated 'world economy'.[113] By the standards once proposed by Wallerstein,
separate 'world economies' are supposed to exchange but a limited amount of
goods, mainly luxuries. But if we accept this definition, the Ottoman Empire
even in the mid-sixteenth century should have been 'incorporated', a claim
which to my knowledge, has never been made by any Ottomanist historian. Yet
Venice in this period was undeniably able to obtain numerous special permissions to import wheat from Ottoman territories, and the survival of its population
depended to an appreciable degree on grains purchased in the Balkan
coastlands.[114]

To avoid this difficulty, I would suggest a different criterion for 'incorporation': namely we might consider a region as 'incorporated' if its products for the
most part were destined for the European-dominated 'world market'. This was
not true of any Ottoman region in the sixteenth century, and as far as we can tell
from the limited number of primary sources and secondary studies currently
available, no such regions as yet existed in the 1630s/1039–49 or 1640s/1049–59
either. Aleppo certainly, and Izmir probably, were at this time still firmly
anchored in the Ottoman economic system. But at least in the case of Izmir, by
the later seventeenth century we encounter some indications that this situation
was about to change.

~ Before 1718/1130–1

Wars on all fronts

By the 1720s/1132–42, the Ottoman position on the map of world politics had
changed appreciably. On the eastern frontier, the most dramatic event was the
collapse of the Safavid dynasty: a relatively small Ghalzay force took Işfahān
after a terrifying siege, and forced the current shah Sulţān Ḥusayn to abdicate in
favour of their leader (1722/1134–5). Central government by the Safavids thus
came to an end, even though princes from this dynasty, with varying degrees of
success, continued to rule greater or lesser portions of the country for several further decades. Ottoman troups occupied Georgia and Tabrīz in 1723/1135–6,
replacing the Safavid prince Ţahmāsp II, who had been pushed northwards by
the Afghan invaders. However, when the Ottoman and Russian empires divided
up northern Iran into 'spheres of influence' (1724/1136–7), Ţahmāsp II was able
to ingratiate himself with both sides, and the Ottoman commander now justified
his campaign by claiming to defend the rights of the legitimate Safavid ruler. The

Ottomans held Tabrīz until 1729/1141–2, when they were driven out by Nādir Shah. By this time their administration had produced an impressive number of archival records, which still constitute one of our major stocks of primary sources concerning pre-nineteenth-century Tabrīz. Ottoman reconquests during the 1730s/1142–52 proved ephemeral and in 1736/1148–9 the border decided upon a century earlier, in the treaty of Ḳaṣr-i S̲h̲īrīn, was reestablished.[115]

The confusion engendered by the disintegration of the Safavid state also encouraged Peter the Great of Russia (1675–1728/1085–1141) to attempt an incursion into the Caucasus. In 1722/1134–5 an army, some of the time commanded by Tsar Peter in person, conquered Derbend, Baku and, in a naval expedition across the Caspian, Res̲h̲d in Gilān. In a peace treaty concluded a year later, the tsar was able to hold on to these conquests. Moreover he tried to ensure that, in the troubled situation obtaining in Iran at that time, the Ottoman sultan did not place his own candidate on the throne in Iṣfahān.[116] Thus the Russian state, with its newly revamped military machine, had begun to make claims for territory in a region where the Ottoman Empire previously had been the only competitor of the shahs. Even if the conquests of 1722–3/1134–6 did not remain in the hands of the tsars for very long, the fact that they had taken place at all indicated a major change in the balance of power in the Caucasus and Caspian regions.[117]

At an earlier point in Tsar Peter's reign, in 1711/1122–3, there had been direct conflict between the Ottoman and Russian empires to the north of the Black Sea, which had ended very badly for Peter I's army. Only the hesitations of the Ottoman commander Baltacı Mehmed Paşa prevented a total defeat by the river Prut. This success may well have induced Ottoman sultans and viziers to take the emerging power to the north less seriously than they might otherwise have done. However, indications of future Ottoman difficulties are visible at least to historians with the benefit of hindsight. Thus the power of attraction that the Russian state had developed with respect to the Empire's Orthodox subjects became visible when the Moldavian hospodar Dimitrie Cantemir (1673–1723/1083–1136), one of the more important southeastern European intellectuals of his time, threw in his lot with Tsar Peter. After all, Cantemir had lived in Istanbul for decades, spoke and read Ottoman and had been in contact with many educated Istanbullus. Cantemir, whose history of the Ottoman Empire, while conventional in itself, was enriched by copious notes reflecting the Istanbul folklore of his time, ultimately followed Tsar Peter's armies into Russian territory (1711/1122–3). In so doing, he was to precede a long line of Ottoman-born Orthodox merchants, intellectuals and even military men who in the eighteenth and nineteenth centuries, gave up their allegiance to the sultans for careers in the Russian state.[118]

On the western border, 1718/1130–1 marked the date of the treaty of Passarowitz/Pasarofça, which closed a series of wars that had gone badly for the Ottoman Empire. In a sense military difficulties on the western front had first become obvious during the short war of 1663–4/1073–5. However, the Habsburgs had been so preoccupied on their own western borders that they were unable to derive any concrete advantage from their victory at St Gotthard an der Raab (peace of Vasvar 1664/1074–5).[119] This experience may well have induced Mehmed IV (r. 1648–87/1057–99) and his Grand Vizier Kara Mustafa Paşa to believe that after the election of a French-supported candidate to the Polish throne, the Austrian Habsburgs were completely isolated and unable to count on any kind of foreign support even when their capital of Vienna was under siege. In any case, this seems a plausible explanation for Kara Mustafa Paşa's otherwise inexplicable neglect of his army's rear, which allowed a relief force to approach the city and dislodge the besiegers after a major battle near the Kahlenberg (1683/1094–5). Unfortunately where Ottoman strategic thinking is concerned, we often are reduced to guesswork because the relevant correspondence has not survived or, in any event, not as yet come to light.

Apparently the Ottoman 'information service' – the names and specializations of late seventeenth-century agents seem to be less well known than those of their colleagues active a century earlier – had not found out in time that King Jan Sobieski, once safely on the Polish throne, had passed into the opposite camp and now supported the Habsburgs.[120] Or if informers did transmit a warning to that effect, Mehmed IV and his entourage did not take it seriously enough. A significant source of Ottoman misinformation was probably the Hungarian nobleman Imre Thököly who for a brief period was installed as an Ottoman client ruler in an area which previously had belonged to Habsburg Hungary, and was known to the Ottomans as Orta Macar. Thököly only could maintain himself if the Ottomans won. In consequence, he may well have provided unrealistic information which the grand vizier neglected to check.[121]

In itself, a failure before Vienna need not have constituted a great disaster for the Ottoman state; in 1529/935–6, this reverse had simply meant that further campaigns in central Europe or Italy were given up, while the still very recent Ottoman acquisitions in Hungary remained in the sultan's hands. Unlike Charles V in his over-extended empire, the Habsburgs of the late seventeenth century were able to maintain major armies on a war footing for over a decade. This was due in part to an alliance that, in addition to Sobieski's Poland, included the Russian Tsar Peter the Great, Pope Innocent XI and the Venetian Signoria. Moreover, several minor princes from the southern Germanies actively participated in the war, mainly in order to enhance their international stature by military success. But at least in the Bavarian case, the Wittelsbach duke also must have taken into consideration that the fall of Vienna would expose his own territory to Ottoman raiders. Four years later, this army of Habsburg allies was able to take Buda with a great deal of bloodshed (1687/1098–9). During the next few years of campaigning, the Ottoman armies lost control over Hungary. While Mustafa II and his Şeyhülislam Feyzullah Efendi attempted to reverse the situation by taking the field in person, the battle of Zenta (1697/1108–9), at which the Grand Vizier Mustafa Paşa was killed, turned into another military disaster.[122] As late as 1687/ 1098–9, the Ottomans still had offered merely a peace similar to that concluded after St Gotthard an der Raab, that is, they felt strong enough to demand the restitution of Hungary, but the peace of Karlowitz/Karlofça in 1699/1110–11 made the loss of the Hungarian provinces official.[123]

The movements of the Habsburg armies in the Balkans resulted in large-scale migrations: in 1690/1101–2, several thousand households followed the Serbian Patriarch Arsenius Crnojevic III who had sworn allegiance to the Emperor Leopold I, when the Habsburg troops were obliged to beat a hasty retreat.[124] Those immigrants who settled in the immediate vicinity of the new Habsburg–Ottoman frontier were granted the status of military colonists, the so-called *Grenzer*. At a time when serfdom was the 'normal' peasant status in the Habsburg lands, the soldier-colonists were freemen subject to the military administration and in spite of numerous protests on the part of the Croatian and Hungarian nobilities, were never subjected to the land-holding aristocracies of the Habsburg Empire. By this arrangement, Leopold I was able to expand the size of his border troops considerably. At limited cost to the imperial finances, the immigrants from Ottoman territory provided the Habsburg ruler with a rela-tively efficient border defence, whose existence made it much more difficult for the armies of the sultan to recoup their losses on this particular frontier.[125] Even though it was not rare for the *Grenzer* to rebel when they felt that their rights had been violated, the frontier troops never made common cause with the emperor's enemies.

Ottoman reverses on the western front resulted in a rapid turnover at the top echelons of government: Kara Mustafa Paşa had been executed upon the sultan's orders shortly after the retreat from Vienna, and Mehmed IV himself was deposed in 1687/1098–9. It is quite likely that the fall of both Mustafa II and his *şeyhülislam* in 1703/1114–15 was also due to their failure in guarding the Otto-man frontiers; after all, a loss of the kind incurred at Karlowitz was totally unprecedented in Ottoman history.[126] This situation may have convinced highly placed Ottomans, including Sultan Ahmed III, on the throne since 1703/1114–15, of the need to show some important military success as soon as possible. How-ever the war of 1716–18/1128–31 was a failure, and even resulted in the loss of the important fortress of Belgrade, which had formed part of Ottoman territory ever since the beginning of Süleyman the Magnificent's reign (1521/927–8).[127]

'The Empire strikes back': toward a *reprise en main* before 1718/1130–1

Yet the treaty of Passarowitz also brought the Ottoman government certain advantages, namely with respect to certain provinces which today form part of the state of Greece. For, when Venice joined the Holy League in 1684/1095–6, the Signoria was hoping for some compensation for its recent loss of Crete. In 1685/1096–7 Venetian troops first conquered the Peloponnese, and then pro-ceeded to besiege Athens, which was occupied but could not be held against an approaching Ottoman army.[128] The treaty of Karlowitz conceded the Peloponnese to the Venetians, where the Signoria's officials proceeded to prepare an elaborate count of people and settlements.[129] After Sultan Ahmed III had reconquered the province in 1715/1126–8, he ordered a similar description to be compiled, and a comparison between the two documents allows us to appreciate the impact of war on a population literally caught between two fires.[130] Thus the official confirmation of the conquest of the Peloponnese, for it was as a novel acquisition, and not as a reconquest, that the Ottoman authorities chose to view the matter, constituted *the* major gain achieved in Passarowitz. Presumably this success contributed toward the legitimization of Sultan Ahmed III.

Once peace had been concluded and Ahmed III's rule thus stabilized, the Ottoman government was free to attempt a certain reorganization of its territory. As a first step, towns such as Vidin, which long had been located deep in the Ottoman lands but in 1689/1100–1 had temporarily been occupied by the Habsburgs, were revamped as fortress towns. Garrisons of janissaries were established; at least in part these men must have come from the lost Hungarian provinces.[131] Reorganization was an urgent matter as, during the wars, all resources had been channelled into the army and navy, and even important matters such as the security of the roads had been neglected. Attacks on the pilgrimage caravans had become much more frequent, and as the Ottoman sultans made much of their role as protectors of the pilgrimage to Mecca, this matter demanded immediate attention.

Apart from the pilgrimage, minimal security on the roads was also of prime importance to traders, to say nothing of the peasants who were liable to flee when exposed to too many marauders. In consequence the interests of the Ottoman ruling group too were affected by pervasive banditry. Many office holders in the capital supported their households out of the revenue provided by lifetime tax farms (*malikâne*), but the subaltern tax farmers responsible for selling the grain or cotton they had collected from the tax payers, were unable to remit much revenue under conditions of rampant insecurity. Last but not least, customs payments and taxes constituted a revenue item of some significance to the central administration itself, so that securing the trade routes constituted a basic precondition for political and economic recovery.[132]

This explains why, in the years following Passarowitz, the construction of fortified khans was undertaken along the major routes. With their windowless walls and single solid gate, such buildings could function as minor fortresses in case of need, and seem to have attracted settlement because of the protection they provided. Equally, along the Syrian hajj route, such khans were built in appreciable numbers. Moreover, the old institution of the passguards (*derbendci*) was revamped. It is certainly not a matter of chance that while the sixteenth-century tax registers contain scattered references to villages responsible for the security of travellers, documents describing the passguard organization in detail normally date from the 1700s. Now the villages in charge of road security were placed under the authority of officially appointed commanders and their obligations, which in earlier centuries must have been defined largely by custom, were now formalized by means of sultanic commands.[133]

How did this *reprise en main* affect the activities of foreigners in the Ottoman Empire? It would seem that, in times of war, the subjects of rulers in armed conflict with the sultans were expected to leave Ottoman territory. This becomes apparent from the complaint of an Iranian subject directed at the central administration, dated 1760–1/1173–5 but referring to events which had occurred in the past. Unfortunately, we are not able to date exactly the details of the complainant's story.[134] The person in question was a trader who had not left Ottoman territory when he should have done so, but had remained in the northern Anatolian town of Kastamonu under the protection of a local notable. However, at one point, the latter threatened to sell his protégé as a slave, and in order to avoid this fate, the hapless Iranian preferred to confess his breach of the rules to the authorities in Istanbul.

Whether the prohibition to remain on Ottoman territory in wartime was enforced in earlier periods as well is a problem which needs closer investigation: when Selim I (r. 1512–20/917–27), was at war with Shah Ismā'īl, Iranian merchants had been imprisoned and their wares confiscated, an act later considered illegal by Selim's successor Süleyman.[135] This means that either the traders in question had not thought it necessary to leave Ottoman territory as soon as they heard that war was probable, or else that in doing so they had not been quick enough. But although a formal sultanic command to subjects of the shah of Iran, informing them of the imminence of hostilities and ordering them to vacate Ottoman territory within a specific time limit, has not so far been located, Iranian subjects were probably already being expelled in wartime in the sixteenth century. For there survive, admittedly from a period when the Ottomans still considered the Kızılbaş heterodoxy a major threat, elaborate rules concerning Mecca pilgrims from Iran who, in peacetime, wished to traverse Ottoman territory. When war was expected or in progress, travellers from Iran apparently were not admitted at all; and what applied to pilgrims must have been true of merchants as well. But given the sparseness of our documentation, the length of the border and the general inaccessibility of much of the frontier zone, it is hard to know to what extent the rules, whatever they were at any given time, actually could be enforced.

Extraterritorialities before 1718/1130–1

Iranian subjects – during the period we are concerned with here, these were for the most part Armenians from New Djulfa – had the disadvantage of not being protected by inter-state agreements. This is probably the reason why they were at times subject to vexations, and the relevant complaints mean that we have some documentation concerning their plight. However, it is hard to say whether even inter-state agreements would have been helpful in the early eighteenth century, when the Safavid dynasty was in a state of collapse. Things were different where European merchants were concerned. By the eighteenth century, the so-called capitulations (*ahidname*) that – mostly in the shape of unilateral sultanic grants –

had regulated the presence of many European merchants from the fifteenth or sixteenth century onwards, were increasingly turned into a source of privilege particularly by French and English consuls or ambassadors. Given the increased political impact of the latter, moreover, many Ottoman non-Muslim subjects tended to use ambassadorial protection in order to acquire tax-exemptions. This was usually achieved by claiming a position as a translator (dragoman) to a European consulate, even though in quite a few instances, the 'translators' did not even reside in the place where they were supposedly officiating.[136]

In all probability, the advantage enjoyed by non-Muslim merchants was resented by Muslim traders and craftsmen, as the latter did not have access to outside protectors. To what extent this tension became politically relevant before the end of the eighteenth century is not easy to tell. However, the Izmir pogrom against non-Muslims of 1770/1183–4, after the Ottoman naval defeat at Çeşme, does seem to point to resentments that may have begun to accumulate even in the period under investigation here.[137] From the Ottoman government's point of view, this abuse of ambassadorial and consular privileges cancelled out the gains from dues and taxes which non-Muslim traders would otherwise have paid. In addition, having its subjects 'slip away' in this fashion involved a galling loss of prestige to the Ottoman administration.

Official protests were therefore numerous, yet of limited effectiveness. For, from the viewpoint of the European ambassadors and consuls, it was a long-standing custom to surround oneself with a substantial number of protégés; a numerous retinue enhanced the status of a consul or ambassador, above all among his European competitors.[138] Furthermore the payments made to the embassies and consulates in exchange for 'protection' formed a significant source of financial gain.[139] Considerations of this kind seem to have outweighed the constant friction with the Ottoman authorities which this practice necessarily entailed.

An 'ideological' factor also was of some importance; while in the sixteenth or even the early seventeenth century, the power of the sultans had been respected and even feared, this was no longer true after the numerous Ottoman defeats in the wars of 1683–1718/1094–1131. Thus in the eighteenth century, although there was as yet no nationalism among the Muslim and non-Muslim subjects of the Ottoman Empire, a discourse concerning the latter's 'despotic character' and, perhaps more pertinently, its 'decline' was gaining in importance.[140] Outside intervention could comfortably be legitimized in this fashion. In addition, old-style discourses concerning the sultans as threats to Christendom, common enough in the fifteenth or sixteenth century, had by no means disappeared in the 1720s/1132–42 or even the 1730s/1142–52. To the contrary, in the thinking of the staunchly Catholic governing class of the Habsburg Empire, and also in the ruling group of the expanding Russian state of Tsar Peter I, religiously motivated opposition to the Ottomans was now being overlaid with the 'decline' discourse, which was to assume such an overwhelming dominance in the nineteenth and twentieth centuries.[141]

As to the interests of the non-Muslim traders themselves, which often have received rather short shrift, it must not be forgotten that limited central control over the provinces tended to make traders and artisans, Muslim as well as non-Muslim, vulnerable to overcharging by notables and tax farmers. Given these conditions of *sauve qui peut*, it made sense for Ottoman Christians to protect the family fortunes by changing their religious denominations from Orthodox or Gregorian to Catholic, by becoming a foreign protégé, and if possible, by forming marriage alliances with foreign merchants long established on Ottoman territory.

Conquest and trade as sources of regional instabilities before 1718/1130–1

Due to the unsettled situation on the western and eastern frontiers, controlling the involvement of foreigners in eighteenth-century Ottoman provincial life evidently became much more difficult than it had been in the sixteenth or early seventeenth century. This was partly due to the fact that certain areas, such as the Peloponnese or the region of Belgrade became Venetian or else Habsburg territory for one or two decades. Thereafter, it was not possible to govern these regions as if nothing had intervened. Reintegration into the Ottoman state might only be possible at the price of considerable socio-political tensions on the local level.

But in addition we will see that in certain regions – such as, for instance, the Izmir area – where European merchants had long been active, this presence became more intrusive in the course of the eighteenth century. As the Aegean seaboard of Anatolia or coastal Macedonia became more and more export-oriented, the traders engaged in this business came to exercise at least indirect political influence through the connections they established with local grandees offering agricultural products for sale.[142] This was true especially of French merchants, who not only exported but also carried in their ships a substantial amount of the goods transported within the Empire proper. However, this economic and political impact did not necessarily mean that the French or English merchants active on Ottoman territory were doing well commercially. For the competition offered by traders subject to the sultans, particularly seafaring Greeks and Serbian or Bulgarian organizers of mule caravans, might be rather effective, especially in wartime.[143] In addition, although French exchanges with the Levant had grown in absolute figures throughout the period following 1740/1152–3, by the time our story ends, the relative share of this branch of trade within French commerce as a whole was no more than 5 per cent.[144] The Mediterranean clearly had lost its dominant position in world trade, and French merchants still active in this region had good reason to worry about their Atlantic competitors.

These overall developments will become more intelligible when discussed on the basis of three examples we have already encountered in other contexts, namely Morea, the Izmir region and the borderland Serbs. As we have seen, in 1718/1130–1 the Ottomans reorganized the Peloponnese as a 'new' conquest.[145]

This move may well have resulted in some disaffection, as it meant that pious foundations dating back to the sixteenth or even the fifteenth century were now abolished. As a result Muslim families long established in the Peloponnese, who previously had received income from this source, now were deprived of it. Ottoman government largely depended on the garrisons placed in a number of small towns. There were the customs farmers too, who collected the dues paid by merchants, many of them French, who bought up the local olive crop for use in the soap manufacture of Marseilles. Otherwise the countryside, mountainous and difficult of access, was run by Muslim notables (*ayan*) or their Christian counterparts *(kocabaşı)*. Given the amount of local discontent that must have resulted from a double change of regime within less than twenty years, this loosely structured administration probably was not a very effective guarantor of Ottoman control.

Olives apart, the Peloponnese, with its small plains and numerous infertile hills, was known for 'orchard' products such as grapes or silk, not for field crops. When discussing eighteenth-century commercial agriculture, however, what first comes to mind are products such as grain or cotton, for which there existed a mass market. Until about twenty years ago, it was assumed that by the eighteenth century, the so-called *çiftlik*s, large landholdings cultivated by practically – if not legally – enserfed labour and producing largely for export, had become a major feature of Ottoman agriculture. More recent studies have shown that *çiftlik*s were less widespread than had previously been thought and, additionally, that the link of this phenomenon to export trade had been vastly overestimated: some *çiftlik* owners produced not for the market at all, but simply appropriated the limited quantities of food which the 'classical' Ottoman taxation system had left to the peasant family over and above immediate survival needs.[146] In other cases, such as the Black Sea coast of what is today Rumania and Bulgaria, before 1774/ 1187–8 production was not for export, but merely supplied the needs of Istanbul. In addition, many *çiftlik*s did not rely on 'enserfed' peasants, but on sharecroppers, easier to supervise because such peasants could be counted upon to 'exploit themselves' in order to feed their children.[147] However even if the link of *çiftlik* agriculture to export was thus weaker than had originally been supposed, in certain places it did exist. A recent study has shown that the notable family known as the Kara Osmanoğulları possessed large landholdings in the commercially active Izmir area, and as population density was quite low, they brought in Greek immigrants from the Aegean islands to work these lands.[148] The same family also marketed cotton produced by the local peasantry. As typical notables of their times, the Kara Osmanoğulları collected dues on behalf of absent governors, or else farmed taxes themselves. They often served as middlemen too, between peasant sellers and exporting merchants, many of the latter being Frenchmen.[149] These varied links made it possible especially for subjects of the French king to establish a strong presence on the Aegean coasts of the early eighteenth century.

War-induced regional instabilities before 1718/1130–1: Serbs on both sides of the frontier

In a previous section of this chapter, we have briefly referred to the late seventeenth-century emigration of a sizeable number of Serbs into the Habsburg borderlands, and their replacement by Albanians, developments whose consequences, particularly in Kosovo, are still very much with us. If our topic is interpreted restrictively, the Serbs on Habsburg territory should not concern us here. But at times it is useful to pay some attention to events occurring beyond the Ottoman border; for contacts between the two groups of Serbs were continuous throughout the eighteenth and nineteenth centuries. As a result we will need to ask ourselves whether the fate of the emigrants prompted those who had stayed behind to view their lives in a different perspective. Moreover, the Ottoman reconquest of necessity brought soldiers from outside the region into the province of Belgrade on a long-term basis; and this novel cohabitation presented problems of its own, as we shall see.

Ecclesiastical matters occupy centre stage, for it was largely through their church organization that the Orthodox immigrants asserted their separate identity. Between 1718/1130–1 and 1739/1151–2, the Serbs present on Habsburg territory were at first organized in two distinct ecclesiastical units, governed by the archbishops of Karlowitz and Belgrade respectively. Yet the archbishop of Belgrade, Moise Petrovich, made strenuous efforts to have himself recognized as sole metropolitan; upon the death of the Karlowitz incumbent, Petrovich had himself elected to this latter position as well. For a long time, the authorities in Vienna refused to recognize this double incumbency, and explicitly stated that they were not willing to deal with any 'Serbian nation', but merely, on a separate basis, with the two church dignitaries and their respective charges. However after Moise Petrovich's death in 1730/1142–3, his successor was able to secure official confirmation to the two archbishoprics simultaneously, as the office in Vienna governing the territories newly acquired from the Ottomans did not wish to further alienate the numerous Serbian peasant-soldiers serving on an ever critical frontier.[150]

Conflicts between the Serbian immigrants and the Habsburg administration become more easily explicable when we take note of the wording of the privilege issued by Leopold I to Arsenius Crnojevich upon the latter's migration into Habsburg territory (1690/1101–2). For in this constitutive text, the metropolitan was recognized as both the religious and secular head of the Serbs. However, during the following years, the Habsburg bureaucracy developed the ambition to directly control the border militias. Ultimately the peasant-soldiers were either to be incorporated into the regular army, or else the administration planned to satisfy the long-term demands of the Croatian and Hungarian nobilities for the reduction of the *Grenzers* to 'ordinary' peasant servitude. In addition, the powerful Catholic establishment attempted to persuade the Serbs to accept union with Rome, which the vast majority utterly refused – in some instances, the ecclesiastical dispute even induced *Grenzers* to return to Ottoman territory.

More significantly, the disillusionment of many Serbs with the Habsburgs led them to seek aid from the Russian tsar as the one major Orthodox ruler. This occurred, for instance, when, in the mid-1740s/around 1158, certain sections of the military frontier were ceded by the Habsburg government to the Hungarian nobility. Several thousand Serbian *Grenzers* regarded this as a breach of their privileges: they emigrated to Russian territory.[151] Even earlier, when Peter the Great was still on the throne, the Serbs currently resident in the Habsburg lands had encountered petty vexations by an imperial administration that had still not given up its ambition to make the newcomers recognize the authority of the pope. When the Austrian authorities prevented the *Grenzer* Serbs from setting up a printing press, the latter asked Tsar Peter for help, and a small number of books, along with two teachers, were in fact supplied by the Russian government.[152] These events tended to increase the links of the Serbian Orthodox with Russia, a phenomenon we have encounted, albeit on a smaller scale, in the seventeenth century as well.

Concerning those Serbs remaining on Ottoman territory, our information is less ample; quite possibly the Istanbul archives may still contain much unexploited material relating to their status. Belgrade was besieged and conquered several times before finally reverting to Ottoman control in 1739/1151–2. Severe population losses and the destruction of numerous buildings left the town much diminished in comparison to the high point it had reached in the late sixteenth and early seventeenth centuries, when there had been between 60,000 and 100,000 inhabitants. By the later eighteenth century, defence of this now neglected border town was entrusted to a garrison of janissaries, who caused endless trouble not merely to the civilian inhabitants, but also to the Ottoman central government. In fact, shortly after the end of the period treated in this book, Sultan Selim III (r. 1789–1807/1203–22) made strenuous but ultimately unsuccessful efforts to dislodge the janissaries from Belgrade.[153]

To summarize the situation in which the Ottoman state found itself following 1718/1130–1, we encounter contradictory tendencies: on the one hand, the central government made a real effort to regain control of its territory, a policy which included the reorganization and surveillance of the land routes. On the other hand, even though quite a few territorial losses were not final, and ultimately could be compensated for, we observe an increasing impact of usually European outsiders on the economy and socio-political arrangements of certain regions. These phenomena were most visible in outlying border territories such as the Peloponnese. But as the Empire-wide problem of the protégés demonstrates, in quite a few instances, the same tendency also affected the central regions of the Empire. Certainly, increasing links with foreign traders and diplomatic representatives did not mean that Ottoman regions were becoming politically detached from the Empire. Whenever territorial losses occurred, they were simply due to war and not to commercial or diplomatic activity. But even so, we do observe a gradual 'loosening' of the structures which had seemed so much more solid in the second half of the sixteenth century.

~1774/1187–8

The Russo-Ottoman war of 1768–74/1181–8

This solidity was nowhere in evidence at the end of the Russo-Ottoman war of 1768–74/1181–8, which the government in Istanbul had begun because it considered the impending first partition of Poland an intolerable disruption of the 'balance of power' in eastern Europe. Possibly the military successes obtained against Tsar Peter in 1711/1122–3, and later in 1737–9/1149–52 against the Austrians, had misled high-level Ottoman officials in respect of the limits of their own armies. As yet the real might of Russia under Catherine II was not appreciated. This is all the more probable since, in the war of 1768–74/1181–8, an important element of the tsarina's success was the appearance of the Russian navy in the eastern Mediterranean; their overwhelming victory before Çeşme was partly due to British support and partly to the element of surprise.[154]

However, the major battles were fought not on the sea but on land, and it was the Ottoman defeats on the bords of the Dniestr (1769/1182–3), the Larga (1770/1183–4) and the Kagul (1770/1183–4), as well as the Russian conquest of the Crimea, that encouraged Catherine II to proffer major demands before she was willing to make peace. Apart from the right of navigation on the Black Sea, and the 'independence' of the Crimea, Russian diplomats also demanded, and obtained, control of a broad sweep of hitherto sparsely inhabited territory on the Black Sea coast.[155] With the foundation of Odessa, and the establishment of commercial wheat-growing, this region was to become a major asset to the Russian Empire.

The tsarina's demand for the right to have her ships sail the Black Sea was motivated both by commercial and by political considerations. In the second half of the eighteenth century, men-of-war were constructed differently from ships used for trade; but it was still possible to adapt vessels originally built for commercial purposes for use in warfare. These considerations were important for Catherine II and her ministers. Whatever Russian diplomats claimed to the contrary at certain stages of the negotiations, Russian ships in the Black Sea always implied a military threat to the Ottoman heartlands.

(facing page) **2.** View from Semlin towards Belgrade, with the Ottoman fortress beyond the Danube, early nineteenth century; both Ottoman and central European costumes represented among the men. This lithograph, published in 1824–6, was part of a promotional venture by Adolph Kunike (Vienna) and intended to acquaint prospective customers with the newly invented technique of lithography. The entire course of the Danube was covered, from its source in Donaueschingen to the Black Sea.

Source: Jacob Alt, Ludwig Ermini, Adolph Kunike and Franz Sartori, *Donau-Ansichten vom Ursprunge bis zum Ausflusse ins Meer, nach der Natur und auf Stein gezeichnet* (Vienna: Adolph Kunike, 1824–6): no. 176.

'Independence' for the Tatars also constituted a demand to which the Ottoman government only acquiesced under grave duress. In previous wars, the Tatars always had provided the sultans' armies with formidable raiding forces, weakening the enemy by the enslavement of the local peasantry and the removal of livestock. These activities greatly facilitated the advance of the Ottoman armies, even if the manner of fighting employed by the Tatars made them all but useless in the siege of fortress towns that constituted the major wartime activity on the Habsburg–Ottoman frontier. Moreover, the Tatar political establishment did not at all wish to be independent, and even less did its members desire to accept a Russian protectorate. In consequence, the Ottoman government almost went to war in order to retain the Crimea in 1778–9/1191–3; but in the long run, it proved impossible to prevent Russian annexation of the peninsula (1783/ 1197–8).[156]

Peace negotiations that ultimately resulted in the treaty of Küçük Kaynarca (1774/1187–8) were complicated, rather than facilitated, by the fact that Prussia and Austria, whose governments had just joined the tsarina in the first partition of Poland (1773/1186–7), acted as mediators between the two warring parties.[157] But even though, in this period of royal absolutism, friendly personal relations between rulers sometimes eased negotiations – this applied particularly to Frederick II of Prussia and the tsarina – the Austro-Prussian mediation should in no way be regarded as disinterested.[158] Frederick II was concerned that the Russo-Ottoman conflict might escalate into a European war. For such an eventuality his small and poor kingdom, which in the recent Seven Years War (1756–63/ 1169–77) had barely survived the overblown military ambitions of its king, was ill prepared. As to the Habsburg rulers Maria Theresa and Joseph II, they saw their own 'sphere of interest' in Walachia and elsewhere in the Balkans threatened by the expansion of tsarist Russia: Viennese diplomats felt that a greatly weakened Ottoman Empire was less problematic as a neighbour than the dynamic state of Catherine II. In consequence, peace negotiations involved not only balancing the interests of the two actual belligerents, but also, the concerns of the four other states (England, France, the Austrian Habsburg territories and Prussia) that, in the second half of the eighteenth century, determined the 'European balance of powers'.[159]

It is of some interest that in the course of the peace negotiations, Austrian diplomats proposed to include the Ottoman Empire as a member in this European balance. Such an inclusion would have implied the understanding that the realm governed by the sultans was no longer the territory of a power considered hostile 'on principle', but rather a 'legitimate' state on a par with the other members of the European 'club'.[160] As such, the Ottoman Empire, in the case of territorial losses or gains made by its partners, would have been entitled to compensation elsewhere, an arrangement common enough in eighteenth-century peace conferences. However, Catherine II, who in the 1780s/1193–1204 was to go to war with the explicit ambition of dismantling the Ottoman Empire in Europe for the benefit of two yet-to-be-founded Russian vassal states, did not consent to this expansion of the list of 'legitimate' polities.[161] Her invocation of the interests of Balkan Christians, whom suppposedly she could not abandon to the Ottomans, was merely a polite way of expressing her own designs for territorial aggrandizement.

Even so, we must take into account the disaffection of the Ottoman Empire's Orthodox subjects in the later eighteenth century, which made far more people inclined to throw in their lot with the tsarina's armies than had been true in earlier periods. One of the major reasons for discontent was the behaviour of poorly disciplined and supplied Ottoman soldiers on their marches to the front, especially of the irregulars who formed a sizeable contingent of the sultan's field armies. These considerations are made explicit in an important primary source, one of the first secular works to have been published in Bulgarian, namely the 'Life story and tribulations of the sinful Sofroni', bishop of Vratsa (1739–1813/ 1151–1229).[162] Sofroni was born as Stoiko in the proto-industrial settlement of Kotel. His father and uncle were both livestock traders (*celeb*) supplying Istanbul, and as an aide to his uncle the young and inexperienced Stoiko saw the capital and had some narrow escapes in his encounters with low-level officials and urban criminals. In later life, the former *celeb* became a priest and finally a bishop. But while originally his family seems to have been quite prosperous, the author was bankrupted by the robberies of assorted mercenaries, and also by the back taxes due from his war-ruined bishopric. The local peasantry and townspeople during the 1768–74/1181–8 war, and during the following years as well, apparently spent much of their time fleeing from bandits and soldiers, and production must have been disrupted accordingly. In the end Sofroni was forced to leave Vratsa and take refuge in a Walachian monastery. In 1810/1224–5, when another Russo-Turkish war was in progress, the elderly ex-bishop published a declaration encouraging his fellow Orthodox to side with the Russians.[163] As a government unable to protect the people it taxed, the Ottoman administration had lost the legitimacy it previously had possessed in the eyes of many of its non-Muslim subjects.

Provincial power magnates and international relations in 1774/1187–8

By the standards of the late fifteenth and sixteenth centuries, when a strongly centralized government had attempted to control closely the administration of the provinces, movements toward decentralization became noticeable, at the very latest, from the seventeenth century onwards. However, if we disregard the rather unusual cases of Canbuladoğlu Ali Paşa in northern Syria and of Fahreddin Ma'n in present-day Lebanon, these local potentates of the years before 1750/1163–4 but rarely maintained links to foreign powers. Moreover, Fahreddin Ma'n, one of the major exceptions to this rule, established connections not to one of the major states of the day, but to minor Italian princes such as the grand duke of Tuscany.[164] From this viewpoint the threat to Ottoman control remained slight.

In the second half of the eighteenth century, though, this situation had begun to change. To mention one example among many, the Kara Osmanoğulları, whom we have already encountered as powerholders in the productive region of Izmir and Manisa, were on cordial terms with the local French consuls. Given the centralized set-up of trade in the Levant, these latter officials possessed considerable authority over those merchants active in the region who were subject to King Louis XV of France (r. 1715–74/1127–88).[165] As the Kara Osmanoğulları sold agricultural products to French exporters, it made sense for them to keep open a channel of communication to the consuls who could significantly hurt or facilitate their trade.[166] Certainly, the Kara Osmanoğulları never showed an ambition to found a state of their own. But after 1800/1214–15 figures such as Ali Paşa of Janina (c. 1750–1822/1163–1238), to say nothing of Mehmed Ali Paşa of Egypt (1770–1849/1183–1266), did harbour such projects, at least during certain periods of their careers. Once these men had begun to develop intentions of state-building, they often regarded their special links to foreign consuls and traders as important assets. Correspondingly, these connections were liabilities from the central administration's point of view.[167]

Another reason why provincial power magnates might wish to develop their relations with one or several European consuls was financial. Due to insecurity on the roads, it had become very risky to send tax monies to Istanbul by caravan, and banks that could have handled such transfers did not as yet exist. At the same time, French traders, who were the most active of the eighteenth-century European commercial communities established in the eastern Mediterranean, sold much more in Istanbul, the Empire's *capitale et ventre*, than they could ever buy.[168] The opposite was true in provincial port cities such as Izmir, where cotton purchases could not have been financed only by the – rather limited – sale of imported goods to local people. In principle, there was thus considerable incentive for financial cooperation. French merchants could pay the debts owed by a given magnate to the authorities in Istanbul, and get their money back when they needed to make purchases in Izmir or elsewhere. However, there obviously was room for bad faith on both sides, and strident complaints caused the practice to be prohibited every now and then – with only limited effectiveness.[169] It is probably not unfair to say that, as a result of such arrangements, foreign traders had already come to be the bankers of the Ottoman state by the eighteenth century, long before the 'official' financial dependence which followed the mid-nineteenth-century Crimean War. In addition, these 'banking services' also permitted many foreign merchants to engage in financial speculation, much to the detriment of the Ottoman Empire's 'economic independence'.[170]

Eighteenth-century prosperity and crisis in the 'economic' field

Mid-eighteenth-century military successes apart, another factor which may have led the Ottoman government to overestimate its own forces prior to 1768/1181–2 was the commercial and industrial upswing that began after 1718/1130–1 and lasted well into the 1760s/1173–83. In regions such as Egypt and northern Syria, and in the central Anatolian manufacturing town of Tokat, not merely commercial activities but also textile and metal crafts showed a remarkable spate of growth.[171] A relative florescence of craft production may well have convinced the responsible officials that the production of war *matériel* could now be handled effectively.

However, if the hypothesis of one of the foremost connoisseurs of Ottoman eighteenth-century economic history is correct, it was the war of 1768–74/ 1181–8, or more exactly the manner in which it was financed, that ended the mid-eighteenth-century period of economic growth.[172] For, throughout the centuries, the Ottoman government continued to hold that low price levels increased the feasibility of all manner of projects, and facilitated the conduct of war in particular. As a result, administrative fiats decreed that little was to be paid to the producers of all manner of goods, and when the state was the 'purchaser', prices sank even below the level applicable to ordinary customers. In quite a few instances the pay was indeed largely symbolic. In addition, there was a tendency to demand higher deliveries from the more efficient – and presumably better capitalized – producers, thereby pushing them down to the level of the poorer ones. Such a solution was convenient for bureaucrats who could collect more effectively from a limited number of important producers than from numerous minuscule ones. But the widespread assumption in guild circles, that no artisan should be more prosperous than his fellows, also may have been of some significance in making this policy seem acceptable.[173]

This practice of 'selectively bankrupting' the more efficient producers must have aggravated the deficiency in capital formation, which had been a trouble spot in the Ottoman economy even in the sixteenth century.[174] As the producers of war *matériel* were paid very little, they could not generate the 'war booms' typical of capitalist societies by the second half of the eighteenth century. But without such a boom, the likelihood that producers would invest in inventory and implements was slim indeed. In consequence, the war meant that the crafts sector producing arms, tents or uniform material, which expanded production in wartime, suffered from the same weakness as the 'civilian' sector, which normally contracted (and still contracts) in time of war. Possibly the long period of economic depression from which Ottoman crafts and trade seemed unable to recover before the middle of the nineteenth century was at least in part caused by the crisis of the 1770s/1183–93 and 1780s/1193–1204.[175] Thus it is not surprising that the Ottoman armies could no longer be properly supplied, and under the circumstances of the eighteenth century, training and equipment constituted the *conditiones sine qua non* of military success.

The desert borders in 1774/1187–8

Up to this point, the region in which Ottoman territories bordered on the Syrian and Arabian deserts, where major states did not exist before the second half of the eighteenth century, has interested us mainly because it had to be be traversed by the hajj caravans. Certainly these dry steppe and desert regions did not produce any revenue for the Ottoman treasury – quite to the contrary, in order to ensure the safe passage of the pilgrimage caravans to Mecca, the government every year provided the Bedouins with substantial subsidies in the shape of money and supplies. But given the fact that protection of the Holy Cities and the pilgrimage caravans was viewed as an important means of legitimizing the sultans, keeping this region under some kind of control did form a major concern for the Ottoman administration.

Yet by the 1770s/1183–93 certain developments came to jeopardize Ottoman ascendancy in the region. From the mid-eighteenth century onwards, the contribution of the 'political households' governing Egypt to the fund that financed the Ottoman presence in the Hijaz became increasingly aleatory. With much less money to spend on appeasing the Bedouins, the risk of attacks on the pilgrimage caravans increased. There was, however, another factor, this time internal to desert society, which augmented the dangers incurred by the pilgrims. For in the central Arabian peninsula, the important tribal confederacy of the 'Anaza was on the move, and in changing its accustomed pasture grounds, displaced a number of smaller, often semi-sedentary tribes.[176] These, though, were more dependent on sultanic largesse than was true of the larger and wealthier ones, and a decline in payments thus increased the likelihood of attacks upon the pilgrimage caravan. A major disaster of this kind, in which a sister of the reigning sultan perished, had occurrred as early as 1757/1170–1.[177]

Moreover, by the mid-eighteenth century, state formation was under way in the centre of the Arabian peninsula. Close to what is today Riyāḍ, the founder of the Bedouin dynasty of Ibn Su'ūd had established a capital outside the area effectively controlled by the Ottoman sultans. As a political and spiritual advisor, he had received into his entourage the scholar Ibn 'Abd al-Wahhāb (1703–92/1114–1207), who in the Ḥanbalī tradition preached a return to the purity of Islam as it had been at the time of the Prophet Muhammad. 'Abd al-'Azīz Ibn Su'ūd (r. 1765–1803/1178–1218) consolidated the rule of his family in northern Arabia, attacking both the Shi'ism of Iraq and the, in his opinion, 'lax' Sunnism represented by the Ottoman authorities. In the 1770s/1183–93, these changes, though visible, were probably not as yet viewed as major problems by the administration in Istanbul. However, this was to change a few decades later, when, in the early nineteenth century, Mecca and Medina were occupied and plundered by 'Abd al-'Azīz's Bedouins, and the pilgrimage caravans were prevented from reaching their destinations.[178]

~ In conclusion: the Ottoman rulers within a set of alliances

As this brief survey will have shown, the Ottoman Empire from the mid-sixteenth century onwards, and arguably even earlier, formed part of a network of European alliances, and these political connections were considerably intensified around 1700/1111–12. Such an imbrication in the European political system did not contradict the intention of the sultans, and of the Ottoman political class as a whole, to expand and protect the realm of Islam against the unbelievers. For as Islamic religious law prescribed, in the Ottoman perspective such alliances were always viewed as temporary.[179] As we have seen, in these matters the governing class in Istanbul thought no differently from the rulers of European states during the early modern period. When in a time of Ottoman strength, the French kings did form alliances with the sultans, they did not consider these ties as permanent either, but rather as a necessary – and indeed temporary – evil in the face of Habsburg power.

However, alliances originally concluded for short periods of time might well develop a dynamic of their own; for the kingdoms and empires involved, be they Ottoman, French, Russian or Austrian Habsburg, were highly structured polities that existed over many centuries, in spite of sometimes significant modifications along their frontiers. Given the length of the common borders and 'ideological' conceptions of what it meant to be an Islamic sultan or a Catholic emperor, hostilities between Ottomans and Austrian Habsburgs were very much a phenomenon of the *longue durée*. As a result, after more or less lengthy periods of abeyance, the Franco-Ottoman alliance was revived several times in the course of the sixteenth and seventeenth centuries. In the mid-1500s, its *raison d'être* from the French point of view had been the 'encirclement' of Valois France by Habsburg possessions, and to facilitate the expansionist policies of Louis XIV, the alliance was resuscitated in the late seventeenth century. And after 1750/1163–4, when Russian expansion had come to threaten Austrian concerns in Walachia and elsewhere, Ottoman–Habsburg alliances might even be formed, although such a community of interests would have been unthinkable as late as beginning of the 1700s.[180]

In the area of inter-state relations, no matter whether we adopt the Ottoman, French or Habsburg viewpoint, the discrepancy between ideology and practice was often considerable. Certainly the Ottoman ruling group, as well as the majority of its Muslim subjects, regarded the sultan as the ever-victorious champion of Islam against the unbelievers, and as the power that alone could expand Muslim rule. But in practice the defeats of 1683–99/1094–1111, and *a fortiori* those of the later eighteenth century, made it necessary for Ottoman goverments to develop a defensive strategy. Moreover even before that period, the need to secure the frontiers once obtained and the impossibility of dealing with all 'infidel' states at one and the same time, had induced the ever-pragmatic Ottoman administration to establish alliances and 'understandings' with individual European rulers. As to the perspective of the latter, eighteenth-century balance-of-power concerns have been studied quite often; but the tendency of certain rulers to include the Ottomans in these calculations and by contrast, the unwillingness of others to do so, have received rather less than their due attention.

Matters were further complicated by the fact that this or that alliance might be promoted by coteries of high Ottoman officials as part of their respective political agendas. It was quite frequent that a given vizier or prominent official was considered a representative of either the 'war' or the 'peace' party. In 1683/1094–5 Kara Mustafa Paşa formed a well-known example of these Ottoman 'hawks', while in the 1770s/1183–93, Ahmed Resmi stood for the 'doves'.[181] In addition, Ottoman dignitaries who did not themselves form part of the circle of people that officially made decisions on war and peace might still form projects, and attempt to convince the sultans of their value and feasibility.[182] It would thus be an unrealistic view of Ottoman politics to assume that the tenets of Islamic religious law, or even the opinions of respected jurists with regard to war and peace, suffice as explanations of Ottoman attitudes to foreign alliances.[183]

We may concede that the Ottoman political elites of the seventeenth and eighteenth centuries were probably more open to interventions by outsiders than had been true of their sixteenth-century predecessors. Yet the phenomenon of 'porous borders' had been familiar from earlier periods as well. In many localities, the Empire was bordered by vassal principalities of greater or lesser importance, where local rulers might attempt to maintain themselves by playing off the Ottomans against some of their Muslim or Christian neighbours. Cases of this type will occupy us in the following chapter.

3 ~ At the margins of empire: clients and dependants

~ The royal road to empire-building: from 'dependent principality' to 'centrally governed province'

Fifty years ago, Halil Inalcik, when discussing Ottoman methods of conquest in a still fundamental article, emphasized that in newly conquered territories the Ottomans often appointed as governors personages from among the previously established elite, who had been willing to throw in their lot with the new regime.[1] Thus recently acquired territories might at first be constituted as dependent principalities, of the type rather frequent on the margins of the earlier Seljuk sultanate in Anatolia, but also in medieval Europe.[2] Such a solution had the advantage of neutralizing aristocrats long established in the region, who continued to possess prestige in their respective homelands, and who were familiar with the specific local arrangements governing the collection of taxes.[3] From a different viewpoint, by instituting a 'local man' as governor it was possible to reward someone whose cooperation had been important in establishing Ottoman control in the first place.

Only after a certain lapse of time were the sons of former dynasts-turned-Ottoman-dignitaries appointed to serve in faraway provinces, while the territories once held by their fathers or grandfathers were integrated into the Ottoman imperial structure, and now administered by people with no previous links to the localities concerned. In late sixteenth-century south-eastern Europe, some people apparently assumed that a different, but still somewhat related, procedure was often followed. When a dependent but hitherto autonomous prince was to be deprived of his territory, the sultan seems to have sent his soldiers into the lands now scheduled for conversion to a directly governed province. This army typically included the contingents of princes who for the time being still retained their subordinate but autonomous status. These troops then proceeded to occupy certain strategic fortresses as a preamble to the establishment of direct Ottoman rule. Unfortunately we do not know on what experiences this piece of 'princely folklore' had originally been based.[4]

Examples for the transition from dependent principality to directly administered province are numerous. To cite one that occurred shortly before our study begins, Ali b Şehsuvar, a member of the east-central Anatolian dynasty of the Dulkadir, after the Ottoman takeover in the beginning years of the sixteenth century accepted sultanic appointments to high office. He was, however, killed on

the orders of Sultan Süleyman in 1521–2/927–9, when his loyalty to the Ottomans had been called into question by a personal enemy.[5] Another story of
formerly independent princes functioning as Ottoman governors could be told
about the Ramazan-oğulları, a minor dynasty of southern Anatolia whose representatives continued to govern the town of Adana for decades after their
submission to the Ottomans.[6]

Where south-eastern Europe was concerned, after the defeat of the Hungarian
forces under Lajos II near Mohács (1526/932–3), John Zapolya, elected to the
throne of Hungary by magnates in opposition to the Habsburgs, was at first supported by Sultan Süleyman as well.[7] Only after a lengthy war between Zapolya
and Ferdinand I, followed by a treaty according to which the Habsburg ruler was
recognized by Zapolya as his eventual heir (1538/944–5), was central Hungary
transformed into a centrally ruled province (*beylerbeylik*). After all, the agreement placed Ottoman interests in serious jeopardy. From now onwards, this area
was divided up into a large number of tax assignments (*timar, ze'amet*), so characteristic of sixteenth-century Ottoman administrative practice, whose holders
owed military service as cavalrymen and doubled as low-level administrators.
Hungarian scholars have for a long time debated whether the local aristocracy
might have devised a policy inducing Sultan Süleyman to convert the entire
kingdom of Hungary into an Ottoman vassal state that would have been granted
domestic autonomy and permitted to retain its socio-political structures intact.
Apparently a consensus among historians has now emerged that deems such a
compromise solution to have been impossible, given the fact that two large-scale
empires, namely the Ottomans and the Habsburgs, after 1526/932–3 confronted
each other on the territory of the now defunct state of King Lajos II.[8] But caution
is in order; for by the same logic, Moldavia, Walachia and Transylvania also
should have been made into *beylerbeyliks*. In any case, the sheer fact that such a
debate was conducted at all, in itself demonstrates the important role that Ottoman vassal principalities might play in the political calculations of local
aristocracies, foreign rulers and, last but not least, nineteenth- and twentieth-
century historians searching for the antecedents of national states.[9]

By contrast, the views of the Ottoman central authorities concerning their vassals are less easy to discern as, in official correspondence, the fiction was
preserved that the sultan only needed to command for all lesser powers to obey.
Differences between Ottoman governors, semi-independent rulers such as the
Tatar khan, and independent powers such as Venice and the Habsburgs, which,
however, paid tribute for one or another of their possessions, were not much
emphasized in sultanic parlance. According to Ottoman diplomatic fiction, differences between independent rulers and dependent princes, which appear so
crucial to the modern historian, were only expressed in a very muted fashion, for
instance through the ceremonial with which the ambassador of a given ruler was
received at the sultan's court. It was only in correspondence emanating from the
office of the grand vizier, which has been much less well preserved than rescripts
emitted in the name of the sultan, that acknowledgement might be made of the

fact that, for example, the doge of Venice was a more powerful figure than the *voyvoda* of Moldavia.[10] Chroniclers, however, might take a more realistic view. Thus the seventeenth-century author Hüseyin Hezarfenn distinguishes between the tribute paid by areas 'veritably conquered' and that due from rulers living at peace with the sultan, such as Moldavia, Walachia and Transylvania.[11]

~ 'Dependent principalities' with long life-spans

While the central Hungarian provinces were thus rapidly transformed into Otto-man *vilayet*s under provincial governors (*beylerbeyi*), Sultan Süleyman and his successors preferred to recognize a vassal principality in the eastern sections of the defeated Hungarian state; this new entity was known to the Ottomans as Erdel and to English speakers as Transylvania. Located on an important route linking Istanbul with Lvov (Lwiw) in the modern Ukraine by way of the towns of Brašov and Sibiu, which both constituted active commercial centres, Transylvania had no significant Muslim population. Local princes as well as the noble and urban vassals of the latter rulers, also known as estates, were largely autonomous in their internal affairs. On certain occasions, Transylvania even came to play a role of some significance in seventeenth-century inter-state politics. Although possession of this territory was hotly contested by the Habsburgs, Transylvania never became a centrally governed Ottoman province, as so many other acquisi-tions of the sultans had done, but remained in the orbit of Istanbul as a dependent principality until finally conquered by the Habsburgs in the war of 1683–99/ 1094–1111.[12]

Among dependent princes who were Muslims, both the Crimean khans and the sherifs of Mecca also retained their positions over many centuries. The khans had become vassals of the Ottoman sultans after 1475/879–80, the sherifs in 1517/922–23. Given the dependence of the Hijaz on Egyptian grain, the sherifal dynasty had submitted voluntarily, without any confrontation in the field, after Selim I's conquest of the Mamluk sultanate of Egypt and Syria. Neither the exist-ence of the khanate nor the dignity of the sherif as a subordinate but autonomous ruler was ever called into question by the Ottoman government. In both cases, individual khans or sherifs were quite often deposed, but their successors always appointed from the same ruling families. In this manner, the khans of the Crimea held office until Catherine II annexed their lands to the Russian Empire in 1783/ 1197–8, and the sherifs as rulers of the Hijaz even survived the end of Ottoman government in the Arabian peninsula (1918), albeit only for a very short time. It was thus common enough for a principality to maintain its vassal status over many centuries.

～ Ottoman methods of conquest and local realities

At first glance, one might assume that relatively 'late', that is post-1500/905–6, Ottoman conquests were normally transformed into vassal states, while older acquisitions, where the established methods of conquest had had time to play themselves out, became ordinary provinces governed by *beylerbeyi*s. But this was not always true. Thus Syria, conquered in 1516/921–2, became a set of centrally administered Ottoman provinces, without an intervening transition period during which a dependent ruler held sway. Moreover, even later conquests might be turned into centrally administered provinces. A glance at the sixteenth- or early seventeenth-century map of the Ottoman Empire shows that in this very period, a sizeable number of new *vilayet*s was formed on the Iranian frontier and elsewhere, such as the Iraqi provinces of Mosul, Baghdad and, later, Basra.[13] Factors other than the date of conquest clearly were decisive here.

Rather, it appears that local conditions, and also international power relations, determined whether a newly conquered territory remained a principality whose ruler recognized the Ottoman sultan as his suzerain, or else became a full-fledged Ottoman province. Thus when territories such as Cyprus or Crete had been conquered from Venice (1573/980–1, 1669/1079–80) – a long-term rival of the Ottomans in the Mediterranean – there was no 'intermediate stage' in which an Orthodox dignitary willing to serve the Ottomans was permitted to act as a vassal ruler. Not that some members of the local Cypriot or Cretan aristocracies might not have been willing to undertake such a task: Venetian rule was not popular, due both to economic exploitation and the difficult conditions that the staunchly Catholic Signoria imposed on the Orthodox Church.[14] But probably because both of these islands had been colonial territories, administered by officials taking orders directly from Venice, the sultan's government was not motivated to establish an autonomous power that, in the long run, might prove a challenge to Ottoman control.

Given these data, the only generalization possible concerns the fact that vassal principalities normally maintained themselves for any length of time only at the margins of the Ottoman Empire. This contradicts the hypothesis that assumes that, as a matter of principle, Hungary was not viable as a vassal state because it was the main venue of Ottoman–Habsburg rivalry; even though this may have been true in the specific case of Hungary, there were other territories in a similar location that did manage to hold out as vassal principalities.[15] The Kurdish princes governing parts of eastern Anatolia down to the reign of Mahmud II (r. 1808–39/1222–55) were situated on the border to Iran. As to the khanate of the Crimea, it was located on the steppe frontier separating Ottoman territory from that of the commonwealth of Poland-Lithuania, as well as from the lands controlled by the grand princes of Muscovy, later to become the tsars of Russia. Transylvania, as we have seen, formed part of the Habsburg–Ottoman borderlands. One might debate whether the vassal states of Moldavia and Walachia really were located in a frontier zone, as they had long common borders with both the Ottomans and the Crimean khans. But as the border with the Crimea ran through steppe lands – which in the sixteenth and seventeenth centuries were almost devoid of permanent habitation – these territories also may be regarded as border zones. And the janissaries, sea captains and local rulers who held sway in seventeenth- or eighteenth-century Algiers and Tunis certainly were located in a border area far away from the imperial centre.

Something similar can be claimed for the sherifs of Mecca even for the period between 1568/975–6 and 1632/1041–2, when the Ottomans held the province of Yemen to the south.[16] For, between the oases and port towns of the Hijaz and the Red Sea coast, or even the Ottoman provincial capital of Sana'a itself, lay broad stretches of desert. Thus one might almost consider the province of Yemen as an 'island', separated from the Hijaz by a desert 'sea'; in this perspective, the lands ruled by the sherifs can be viewed as a remote borderland of the Ottoman-controlled 'continent'.[17] Moreover, Ottoman control of Yemen in the end proved quite ephemeral, and the transitory character of the sultans' rule in this outlying territory must have further stabilized the semi-independent position of the Meccan sherifs.

Thus it makes sense to amend the model proposed by Inalcik in the following fashion. While the sequence described in his seminal article was in fact characteristic of many early Ottoman conquests, there also existed cases in which a dependent but more or less autonomous principality was never instituted, but direct Ottoman control established immediately after the conquest. By contrast, in other instances a principality of this kind, once recognized by the sultans, never was turned into a centrally administered province, but remained a dependent but autonomous entity over many centuries. This was likely to happen whenever a – within limits – stable frontier with a major state, such as the Safavids or Habsburgs, was established in a given region, or if the territory in question bordered on the desert, where the control of any early modern state was limited at best.

More surprisingly, the process by which centralized government was established in newly conquered areas quite often turned out to be easily reversible. At least in the Muslim territories, centrally controlled administrations might well be replaced by 'dependent principalities' informally recognized by the central government; this occurred not only in outlying territories such as western and central North Africa, but even in a province such as Egypt, essential both as a supplier of foods and fabrics for Istanbul, and as a source of monetary revenues for the Empire as a whole. Along the entire northern coast of Africa, military forces established in these territories after the Ottoman conquest were able to subvert central rule within a few decades, and establish what might be called 'dependent principalities' of a novel type. Moreover, in certain provinces quite close to the centre, government on the part of the authorities in Istanbul might even in the sixteenth century be something of a façade, behind which locally powerful families governed almost as if they had been dependent but autonomous rulers. And once, by the late seventeenth or early eighteenth century, 'power magnates' had established their rule in many parts of the Ottoman Empire, the dividing line between 'centrally governed provinces' and 'dependent but autonomous principalities' became even more blurred.[18]

As to the permanence of dependencies under Orthodox, Catholic or Protestant princes, we may place in a distinct category those that were useful to the Ottoman centre as links to the Christian world. At least at certain times, such dependencies served as the venues of diplomatic and/or commercial exchanges that the authorities in Istanbul certainly had approved of, but did not wish to carry out in full view of everyone. One manner of dealing with such sites was to keep them outside the regular Ottoman administrative system altogether, or to at least have the central power represented only by low-level dignitaries.[19] Dubrovnik (in Italian: Ragusa) constitutes the best documented instance of this type; when the military threat was limited, apparently there was little motivation to dignify relations with 'the infidel' by managing them under the auspices of a high-ranking provincial governor.

~ Old and new local powers in 'centrally governed provinces'

Ottoman policies aiming at the integration of new conquests were further complicated by the fact that even in provinces governed by a *beylerbeyi*, under the umbrella of central control, the rule of local lords might continue to a greater or lesser extent. This has amply been demonstrated in the instance of 'Greater Syria'.[20] While the *vilayet*s of Aleppo (Haleb) and Damascus (Şam) were instituted immediately after the Ottoman conquest, especially on the borders of the Syrian desert, there existed lordly families, resident in fortified dwellings that sometimes were veritable castles, whose prominence frequently reached back into Mamluk times. After 1517/922–3, some of these dynasts were regularly nominated to minor governorships (*sancakbeyi*), but also to highly coveted offices such as the command of the Damascus pilgrimage caravan.[21] Thus, while Syria presented a façade of centralized government, in real life the 'first stage' of Inalcik's model continued, not for a single generation, but for over a hundred years. This fact is all the more remarkable as the Syrian provinces were strategically located on the eastern littoral of the Mediterranean, where one would thus expect a great deal of centralized control. Moreover, one of the major pilgrimage routes leading to Mecca began in Damascus. From the viewpoint of the Ottoman sultans, whose legitimization to a considerable extent depended on their successful protection of the pilgrimage, this made the province of Damascus into a most sensitive area. Yet it was only after the local magnate Fahreddin Ma'n had attempted to aggrandize his territory to the point of challenging Ottoman control, that the central government re-entered the region in force; after the defeat of Fahreddin in 1633/1042–3, central control over the Syrian provinces was finally instituted. Yet if we consider that in Damascus, from the early 1700s onwards, a local family known as the 'Azms succeeded in controlling the province for over fifty years, it becomes clear that, at least in Greater Syria, the heyday of Ottoman centralism was rather brief, and the limits between a 'dependent principality' and a 'centrally governed province' less clear-cut than might appear at first glance.

Another territory where central control and local lordships coexisted uneasily is the *beylerbeylik* of Buda in Hungary. Here, Islamization was relatively limited, even though the hierarchy of the Catholic Church was much disrupted in its functioning: but then, as Protestantism, with its decentralized structure, was widespread in Hungary at the time, the practice of Christianity was not dependent upon the maintenance of close ties to Rome. Possibly because of the limited number of Muslims resident, apart from in a few fortress towns and some strategically located villages, the seventeenth-century Ottoman authorities do not seem to have covered their territory with a dense net of kadi-administered districts. This gap permitted Hungarian lords resident in the Habsburg-controlled section of the former kingdom, the so-called Royal Hungary, to send out judges and even collect taxes in Ottoman territory – the unfortunate villagers being obliged to pay their dues twice over.[22]

As this brief introduction has demonstrated, the status of a dependent prince within the Ottoman system varied considerably from one lordship to the next. Due to considerations of space and also because of the limitations, linguistic and otherwise, of the present author, not all varieties of dependent statehood can be explored here. We will confine ourselves to a small sampling, which does, however, reflect some of the very real diversity existing on the Empire's borders. As we are mainly concerned with the Ottoman perspective, to a very considerable extent the choice has been governed by the availability or otherwise of Ottoman sources, written by both Muslims and Christians. Experience has shown that dependent principalities in the Ottoman orbit are by no means equally covered by the available documentation. Where archival materials are concerned, it remains an open question to what extent this variability can be explained by a greater or lesser concern on the part of the central government. According to the documents preserved in the Istanbul archives, it would appear that the central administration of the sixteenth or seventeenth century, at least in normal years, was more concerned with the Hijaz than with Trablusgarb (Tripolis in Africa) or the remote border principalities of eastern Anatolia. *Nolens volens*, this perspective is reflected in the present study.

We will begin with the 'constitutional oddity' of provinces that at first were centrally governed and then turned by local ruling groups into 'dependent principalities', namely the *beylerbeylik*s of Algiers, Tunis and Tripoli. Our next concern will be with a territory that, throughout the existence of the Ottoman Empire, possessed a special, privileged status, namely the Hijaz, where the pilgrimage cities of Mecca and Medina were governed by rulers who traced their descent from the Prophet Muhammad himself. Turning from dependent rulers who were Muslims to those who were Christians, we will study the cases of Dubrovnik and Moldavia. Dubrovnik, an Adriatic port town with close links to

Italy, has been selected because its rich archives, which contain numerous sul-tanic rescripts, permit the historian to see things that remain in the shadow where other, less well-documented cities are concerned. As to Moldavia, the writings of the seventeenth-century nobleman Miron Costin and especially those of his younger contemporary Prince Demetrius Cantemir, the scholarly prince elected a member of the Prussian Academy of Sciences, open a fascinating perspective on a borderland wedged in between Poland, the Tatars and the Ottoman sultans.[23]

Algiers, Tunis and Tripolis were governed by military and corsair elites, who dominated merchants, craftsmen and a rural population partly sedentary and partly nomadic. In the Hijaz, Mecca and Medina had almost no agricultural hinterlands and largely lived off the pilgrims, with the provision of lodgings and food supplies a major source of income. Beyond the oases, there was a small population of camel-breeding Bedouins. Dubrovnik was a city-state and a Catho-lic merchant republic, while Moldavia formed an Orthodox territorial principality with limited urban development outside Yaş/Iassy, the capital city. This diversity will permit us to see how Ottoman rule, certain overarching princi-ples notwithstanding, flexibly adapted itself to a wide variety of socio-political conditions.

Our choice of cases also allows us to analyse the functioning of the Ottoman administration of frontier territories, given vastly different geographical settings. The North African *beylerbeylik*s and Dubrovnik were oriented towards the Med-iterranean, while Moldavia was accessible from the non-Ottoman world only by overland routes, as the Black Sea was an Ottoman lake. Located on the Empire's northern borders, this territory with its cold winters also formed a vivid contrast to the Hijaz, a desert land in which an orientation towards the Red Sea coexisted with dependence on long, dangerous but indispensable caravan routes. In all cases, distance and the conditions of early modern transport technology placed limits on what could be achieved by armed force alone, and often enough obliged the central authorities to devise what, with a modern expression, we might call 'political' rather than 'military' solutions.

~ Semi-autonomous provinces controlled by military corps and 'political households'

Local aristocrats apart, military or paramilitary corps stationed in the towns and cities of certain Ottoman provinces also might establish a form of rule compara-ble to that of dependent princes. This type of military takeover is particularly obvious in the case of Algiers, Tunis and Tripolis. In Algiers, until the end of the sixteenth century, governors officiated who owed their appointments directly to the sultans in Istanbul. In fact, it had been Hayreddin Barbarossa, the most nota-ble among these early governors, who had given up a very precarious independence in exchange for Ottoman support against Spanish power. He was rewarded by a governorship and later by the position of chief admiral (*kapudan paşa*).[24] But after 1600/1008–9, the *beylerbeyi*s of Algiers were eclipsed by a council (*divan*), in which both the local janissaries (*ocak*) and corsair captains were represented. From 1659/1069–70 onwards, the head of this body, known first as the *ağa* and later as the *dey*, constituted the supreme dignitary of the province – as long as he was able to maintain himself in power.[25] Variant but comparable arrangements existed in Tripolis, where the militia known as the *kuloğlu* dominated the political scene, with the Ottoman navy appearing only in the case of major local uprisings.[26] In Tunis, the system of government by councils consisting of sea captains and military men only continued until 1705/ 1116–17, when Husayn b 'Ali, a local commander, established a dynasty of *bey*s. This development also may be viewed as an example of the rule by provincial power magnates, so frequent in the eighteenth-century Empire.[27]

But from a different perspective, we might also consider the political trajectories of the three north-western African provinces as examples of a little-studied but extremely interesting development. For Algiers, Tunis and Tripolis, which had at least for a brief period been governed directly from Istanbul, rapidly reverted to the status of vassal principalities. As an indicator of this development, we may regard the fact that in the seventeenth and eighteenth centuries the governing bodies of these three provinces refused to adhere to peace treaties with European rulers entered upon by the sultans, and only considered such agreements valid if they themselves had negotiated them.[28] While the authorities in Istanbul never entirely accepted this situation, and every now and then commanded their North African subjects to adhere to the agreements that the sultan had concluded, 'pragmatic' European governments, with a view towards the safety of their shipping, typically signed the separate treaties demanded by the governing bodies of Algiers, Tunis and Tripolis. This demand for a 'voice' in what we would call 'foreign policy decisions' – at least in so far as they directly affected the livelihoods of the corsair captains – did not, however, preclude a strong sense of loyalty to the sultan, which in Algiers was further strengthened by the fact that recruits for the local regiments continued to come from Anatolia.[29] As a further indicator of the 'vassal principality' status of the three North African provinces after 1600/1008–9, we might, moreover, regard the fact that they occasionally went to war among themselves. Thus in 1705/1116–17 an attack was made by the Algerian military corps on the important commercial mart of Tunis, and this was by no means the only case on record.

While earlier historians have tended to emphasize that the ruling groups of Algiers, Tunis and Tripolis were 'outsiders' of one kind or another, with few links to local society, this claim has been strongly modified by recent researchers.[30] At least in the sixteenth century, it was quite possible for the more prominent inhabitants of a province to get rid of an unpopular governor by complaining about the latter's misdeeds to the sultan. Therefore members of the ruling groups, be they military men or corsairs, often found it expedient to strengthen their positions through judicious marriage alliances with local families. Such connections also might come in handy when there occurred a conflict between the heads of different 'political households', large and sometimes powerful organizations consisting of relatives, sons of family friends and also slaves, especially those taken prisoner in corsair raids and converted to Islam. For, just as in the Ottoman central provinces from the seventeenth century onwards, such a well-endowed household (*mükemmel kapı*) enabled its head to achieve high office, struggles between 'political households' also often decided who would accede to important positions in Algiers, Tunis and Tripolis.[31] Ties to prominent figures among the local subject class, as well as to families powerful in the nearby sultanate of Morocco, thus counted among the 'immaterial resources' which the most fortunate among the 'political households' of Ottoman north-western Africa might mobilize.[32]

~ The case of the Hijaz

Subsidising a reticent dependant: the sherifs as autonomous princes on the desert frontier

In the perspective of the Ottoman central administration, the importance of the sherifs of Mecca lay not in the number of people and/or the extent of the agriculturally usable lands that they controlled. In all these respects they had little to offer, but it was of significance that, from the tenth century onwards, members of this family had ruled the pilgrimage cities of Mecca and Medina.[33] As descendants of the Prophet Muhammad, they were, moreover, strongly legitimized in a religious sense, which did not apply in the case of the Ottoman dynasty itself. It is also worth noting that, while quite a few successful Islamic rulers had promulgated genealogies purporting to show their descent from the Kuraysh, the tribal unit to which the Prophet had also belonged, the Ottoman sultans never made claims of this type.[34] Rather than descent, these rulers in their legitimizing discourse emphasized the concrete services they had rendered, and were still rendering, to the Muslim community, among other roles, as 'servitors of the two Holy Places'. Such service involved facilitating the pilgrimage to Mecca for Muslims from both within and without the Ottoman Empire.

Obviously this endeavour could only succeed if a local government was established in the Hijaz that was cognisant of the needs of the pilgrims. Theoretically speaking, the Ottoman sultans had the choice of maintaining the sherifal dynasty in power – this did not preclude a degree of supervision – or else of establishing a centrally controlled administration in the far-off Hijaz. We do not know whether Selim I and his viziers ever seriously considered the second alternative. Given the paucity of documents relating to the early sixteenth century, it is quite possible that they did take this option into consideration, but rejected it in the end. Or else the ruling sherif's voluntary submission to Selim I may have made such deliberations unnecessary. After all, direct control of the Hijaz would have been impossible without stationing regular garrisons in the port cities, and in Mecca and Medina themselves. Given the paucity, and in some places, the near-absence of taxable resources, this would have meant the transfer of large amounts of cash merely to pay the soldiery. Not that costly solutions of border defence problems were never resorted to by Ottoman rulers: in the desert to the south of the Nile's First Cataract, such border garrisons were, in fact, maintained over the centuries. But direct intervention in eastern Africa may well have been linked to the fact that in the Nilotic region there was no local figure of power and inherited prestige on which the sultans could have conferred the responsibility of guarding the southern borders of Egypt.[35]

Far from paying taxes to the Ottoman rulers, as was normal in the case of 'dependent princes', the sherifs were in fact subsidized by annual payments remitted from both Istanbul and Cairo. This was not the least of their privileges. Here the Ottomans once again followed a tradition inherited from previous rulers over Egypt, namely the late Ayyubids and their successors, the Mamluks. For, by the late twelfth century, if not earlier, the better-off pilgrims seem to have been regarded by the sherifs as appropriate candidates for spoliation through forced loans, with scant probability of repayment. This kind of extortion was only averted if the sultan of Egypt regularly sent money and supplies to the Hijaz. Or at least this appears to be the implication of a story told by the wealthy Andalu-sian Ibn Djubayr who, indignant though he might be, was quite unable to defend himself against the sherif's demands for money.[36] In the Mamluk period (1250–1517/647–923), aid to the Holy Cities was set on an institutional footing by the Egyptian rulers' establishing pious foundations expressly intended to serve the needs of Mecca and Medina. Apparently these were augmented from time to time, particularly when, due to the crisis which shook Egyptian agricul-ture in the fifteenth century, the revenues of the original foundation villages no longer sufficed.

Immediately after the Ottoman conquest of Egypt, Sultan Selim I regularized these services, ordering a count of the inhabitants of the Holy Cities as a basis for future payments. Egyptian pious foundations in the service of the Hijazis were augmented under Sultan Süleyman the Magnificent, and once again under Murad III. Yet the chronicler Kutbeddin of Mecca, who was originally from India but had permanently settled in the pilgrimage city, considered that by the later six-teenth century, many of these foundation lands had become unproductive through neglect and maladministration.[37]

Out of the Ottoman subsidies paid to the Hijaz, the sherifs themselves appar-ently collected a significant share, which they used, among other matters, to retain the armed support of certain Bedouins with whom they had formed alli-ances. These tribesmen the sherifs could call upon in order to defend Mecca against a possible Portuguese threat, but also against their own enemies among the Bedouin tribesmen, or marauding Ottoman deserters from the Yemen garri-sons.[38] It is impossible to specify the exact number of these retainers, as lists documenting their pay do not survive; however one sherif claimed that there were between twenty and thirty thousand, and the Ottoman central administration did not dispute this figure.[39] At least some of these Bedouins were also available should the ruling sherif decide on a headlong confrontation with the sultan, as happened, for instance, in the later seventeenth century. Unfortunately we do not know very much about the antecedents of a dispute whose last stage has been vividly described by Evliya Çelebi, who was himself an eyewitness.[40] Matters escalated to the point that, in 1671/1081–2, the sherif apparently placed his soldiers on the minarets of the main mosque of Mecca, from where they shot into the crowd of pilgrims. This attack led to the deposition of the sherif a year later; of these calamities, Evliya has given an indignant and sometimes ironic account.[41]

In addition to the revenues annually sent to the Hijaz from Cairo, or else from Istanbul, the sherifs also possessed local sources of income, which had been granted to them by the Ottoman sultans. Among these revenues, the most important were probably the customs duties collected in the port of Jiddah, of which the sherifs retained one half. For Jiddah was not only the port at which pilgrims from India, Africa and the Yemen disembarked; it was also a commercial centre of some significance.[42] The revenues derived from customs duties and port taxes must thus have been substantial, even though in the late sixteenth century, they were known to have suffered a – probably temporary – eclipse, as excessive tax demands induced Indian traders to carry their goods to the northern port of Suez instead.

The direct and indirect subsidies paid to the sherifs, and to the inhabitants of Mecca and Medina in general, were intended as an indemnity for their cooperation in ensuring the success of the pilgrimage. Given the minimal agricultural productivity of the Hijaz, if grains had not arrived on a regular basis, in part free of charge, all the food available locally would have been consumed by the permanent inhabitants, and the pilgrims would not have been able to purchase what they needed at affordable prices.[43] In addition, it would not have been possible to succour those pilgrims who, for one reason or another, arrived in the Holy City more or less destitute; and given the hazards of the desert routes and the fact that some pilgrims set out for Mecca who could not really afford the journey, this was a consideration of some significance.[44] In exchange for their services to the pilgrims, and also because the poor of Mecca were regarded as especially worthy of charitable aid, by the late sixteenth century most of the permanent inhabitants of Mecca throughout the year lived on the grains remitted by the sultans.[45] At the same time, the Ottoman administration attempted to discourage the locals from overcharging the pilgrims, and the payment of regular subsidies legitimized official intervention in the market process, for instance where the provision of camels to prospective pilgrims was concerned.[46] The system appears to have worked rather well; not that pilgrims were not charged 'what the market would bear', for that remained a common occurrence.[47] But we do not hear of major famines or the holding to ransom of wealthy pilgrims, comparable to the case of which Ibn Djubayr has left such a dramatic testimony.

The sherifs, the Bedouins and the security of the pilgrimage caravan

However, worries concerning the pilgrims' food and water supplies did not form the only reason why the Ottoman rulers considered it necessary to send relatively large sums of money into the Hijaz every year, quite apart from numerous ship-loads of Egyptian grain. The sherif's Bedouin forces were also made responsible for the security of the desert routes. First and foremost, this meant that they themselves had to refrain from attacking the pilgrims; in addition, the recipients of subsidies were to come to the aid of the pilgrimage caravans if the latter were attacked by third parties. For Bedouins loyal to the sherif this obligation must have been especially binding, as by the gifts they had received through the lat-ter's agency they were at least loosely attached to the Ottoman sultan and thus expected to share the latter's commitment to the safety and well-being of the pilgrims.

Arrangements of this kind did not, however, constitute a full guarantee of car-avan security, so that apart from the weapons carried especially by Maghribī pilgrims, the caravan commander had a force of armed men at his disposal. On the Damascus route, this contingent consisted of Syrian *timar*-holders, who were excused from normal campaign duties, and a contingent of often somewhat eld-erly janissaries. Moreover, the caravan carried small cannons that could be transported on the backs of camels, and which usually sufficed to secure the camp sites.[48] But especially when subsidies had not been paid in full, which probably happened during the long Ottoman–Habsburg wars of 1683–99/ 1094–1111, and certainly several times during the 1700s, major attacks might ensue, and as we have seen, in 1757/1170–1 a Damascus caravan was virtually annihilated on its return journey.[49]

As to official Ottoman parlance, it was common enough to regard Bedouins who attacked pilgrimage caravans not as 'ordinary' highway robbers, even though as such they would have merited execution according to Islamic law.[50] Rather, such marauders were often equated with unbelievers, which meant, among other things, that their date palms might be uprooted, an act otherwise considered highly reprehensible in desert warfare.[51] Yet this punishment did not necessarily deter those tribes that, because they seemed of scant political impor-tance and/or lived in the middle of the Arabian desert, were in any case excluded from the distribution of the sultans' bounty. Evliya Çelebi narrates not only the troubles of his own caravan travelling to Mecca from Damascus, which only passed through areas where the Ottoman writ was supposed to run, but he also mentions the plight of the pious travellers from Lahsa (al-Ḥasā) and Basra, who, having to pass through the uncontrolled deserts of the Arabian peninsula, almost missed the central rites of the pilgrimage because they had been held up by Bedouins.[52]

The sherifs in the international arena

Thus the sherifs who, along with 'their' Bedouins, were subsidized by the sultans instead of themselves paying tribute, occupied a rather special place in the Ottoman imperial structure.[53] In the perspective of the central government, this privileged position doubtless was justified by the need to protect and supply the pilgrimage caravans, and did not impede officials in the central administration from regarding the sherifs as subordinate rulers. However, at least in the sixteenth and seventeenth centuries, the sherifs did not see themselves as mere dependants of the Ottoman sultan, but attempted to play a role in 'international politics'. This was made possible by the ambition of the Mughul emperors of India to maintain a foothold in the Holy Cities, a place to which disgraced courtiers and princes could conveniently be banished.[54] At least this was true as long as Akbar (r. 1556–1605/963–1014) had not yet changed his allegiance from the Muslim religion of his ancestors to the syncretistic *dīn-i ilāhī* that he had himself created and, well into the middle years of his reign, the Mughul emperor tried to institute a charitable and even a 'diplomatic' presence in Mecca. In this latter perspective, we can point to the long stay of Akbar's aunt Gulbadan Bēgam and consort Salīma in the Hijaz, a presence that caused certain representatives of the Ottoman central government considerable uneasiness.[55] As indications of Akbar's charitable concern with the Holy Cities, we may regard the fact that at one point, he financed the pilgrimages of many poor Indians, and also founded a Kadiri dervish lodge which became popular among Indian visitors.[56]

Due to this attempt to build a Mughul presence in Mecca, the sherifs could thus count on financial support from Delhi and Agra, which lessened their dependence upon Ottoman bounty. Moreover, in the seventeenth century further support was forthcoming from as yet independent rulers of southern Indian principalities, whose territories were, however, gradually incorporated into the empire of the Mughuls. Subsidies from southern India often took the form of large consignments of rice, which were either directly distributed as alms, or else sold and the proceeds spent on charity.[57] It is hard to say, though, whether the donations of southern Indian princes sufficed to compensate the sherifs for a decidedly diminished interest on the part of the Mughuls themselves. For although Awrangzīb (1618–1707/1027–1119) presented himself as a strictly Muslim ruler who was much less willing to accommodate Hindus within his state than had been true of his predecessors, his concern with the Hijaz was negligible. The paucity of sources does not at present permit us to judge whether the eighteenth-century collapse of the Mughul Empire and the growing power of the British in India forced the sherifs to fall back exclusively on such Ottoman support as was available in those difficult times, and cut back their international ambitions. This does, however, appear a likely hypothesis.

It also is hard to say how sultans and viziers in Istanbul regarded the ambitions of the sherifs in the international arena; for this is a matter on which the documents in the Registers of Important Affairs, our only surviving official source, remain all but mute. Nevertheless, when designing the administrative structure of the region, some concession was made to the status of the sherifs as rulers, albeit dependent ones. At least under normal conditions, there were no soldiers under the command of a provincial governor stationed in Mecca or Medina. Furthermore, at least in the sixteenth century, there was no full-fledged *beylerbeyi* at all officiating to the south of the *vilayet* of Damascus, and to the north of Yemen. As to the official who did represent the Ottoman central government in the eastern Red Sea region, he bore the unassuming title of an *emin* ('trustee', 'in charge of') of Jiddah, and ranked as a *sancakbeyi*.[58] We may surmise that this unusual arrangement was due to official Ottoman concern for the position of the sherifs as rulers; after all, the latter could be expected to share in the responsibility for the pilgrimage only if their authority was not too obviously called into question.

~ The case of Dubrovnik: linking Ottoman sultans to the Catholic Mediterranean

While the Hijaz thus cost money, Dubrovnik, which in some sources is called Ragusa, retained the status of a 'dependent principality' over the centuries because this was financially advantageous to the Ottoman sultans. For Dubrovnik paid a very substantial tribute, which at the end of the sixteenth century had reached the level of 12,500 gold pieces a year. This sum was rather higher than what could be obtained even from the more prosperous port towns directly governed by the sultans.[59] Dubrovnik thus fell into a category that has been noted already in the case of proto-historical empires: against payment of the appropriate tribute, these major states often seem to have refrained from intervening in the affairs of inter-regional trade centres located right on their borders.[60] A comparable behaviour on the part of the Ottoman sultans can be interpreted as a symptom of a 'pre-capitalist mindset'; by contrast, in European states of the early modern period, a different policy commonly prevailed. In sixteenth-century France for example, Lyons had been able to take the place of Geneva as a site of major international fairs because the French kings wanted a commercial centre situated on their own territory, and had taken the appropriate measures to foster Lyons' development at the expense of a foreign city.[61]

Dubrovnik's case, in which a commercial town was allowed autonomy or even independence of a sort against payment of a significant tribute, was rare but not unique within the Ottoman world; until 1566, the Maona, a commercial company based in Genoa, had been allowed to administer the island of Chios under similar conditions. It was only when the decline of Chios' position in international trade made these payments appear less certain, that the island was occupied by an Ottoman force.[62] Dubrovnik's trade certainly was more prosperous in the fifteenth and sixteenth centuries than after 1600/1008–9, when the – to use a present-day term – Indonesian spice trade to northern Europe no longer passed through the Mediterranean, and, perhaps more importantly, when Bosnian traders had expanded their activities so as to severely limit the commercial radius of Dubrovnik.[63] But the town's merchants still made enough money to pay the tribute, and thus stave off an Ottoman occupation. Moreover, just to be on the safe side, even after the catastrophic earthquake of 1667/1077–8, when much of the town was ruined and only could be rebuilt in a greatly reduced style, the governing bodies of Dubrovnik did not neglect to repair the – even today rather impressive – city walls. Presumably the latter were meant not so much to keep away an Ottoman army or naval detachment sent out directly from Istanbul, as to discourage pirates, and especially the military ambitions of provincial governors and local fortress commanders.

The 'classic city-state' of Dubrovnik was able to pay such substantial sums because on the one hand, its status as an Ottoman vassal allowed the town's merchants to trade in the Balkan peninsula, where they specialized in the purchase of raw wool, wax, skins and hides.[64] While these goods found takers in Italy, the townsmen and peasants – especially of what is today Bulgaria – purchased from the Dubrovnik merchants rough kerseys and also the better qualities of Venetian and Florentine woollen cloths. Salt was also in demand, because in the highlands bordering the narrow coastal strip on which Dubrovnik is situated, livestock breeding was a major activity.[65]

From the political point of view, the local mercantile patriciate had been able to maintain its autonomy because it had long followed a policy of what its governing circles regarded as neutrality. This involved seeking protection from Venetian ambitions by submitting to the Ottoman Empire. In addition the 'lords' (beyler) of Dubrovnik succeeded in gaining Spanish consent to their demand that Dubrovnik ships should not be confiscated for use in battles against the Ottomans – this would indicate that the governing bodies of the Spanish Empire also saw some benefits in Dubrovnik's mediation.[66] As to the Venetian threat, it was very real for, in the eyes of the Signoria, Dubrovnik had long formed a dangerous competitor, one of the obstacles that prevented Venetian claims to control of the Adriatic from being fully realized. Thus, in the early seventeenth century, Venice developed its own eastern Adriatic port of Split (Spalato) in order to discourage Ottoman traders in particular from using the services of Dubrovnik merchants as intermediaries. In the 1620s/1029–39 and 1630s/1039–49, these Venetian-imposed impediments resulted in a period of commercial stagnation, and even decline, in the port of Dubrovnik. Yet, when the Ottoman Empire and Venice were at war, for instance during the long struggle over Candia (1645–69/1054–80), the Venetians themselves found it necessary to fall back on Dubrovnik, using the city as a conduit for whatever textile exports Venice was still capable of transacting at this time.[67]

As far as the Ottoman side was concerned, apart from the annual tribute, Dubrovnik's importance lay in the goods – and also the political information – of European provenance that its merchants could provide.[68] At the same time, the city's power obviously was too small to ever constitute a threat to Ottoman political aims.[69] This latter consideration was graphically expressed in the letter of an Ottoman vizier to the Venetian Signoria, in which the author described Dubrovnik as an infertile rock that, due to its poverty, the sultan had not seen fit to conquer.[70] Yet it appears that the Ottoman authorities also appreciated the existence of a small 'neutral ground' on the edge of their far-flung territories. Here messengers with letters to and from Venice could rest before and after crossing the Adriatic, and last-minute directives from Istanbul might still reach them. Moreover, in this place on the margins of empire, delicate diplomatic procedures, such as the exchange of prisoners, could take place without fanfare.[71]

~ 'Cruel times in Moldavia'[72]

Moldavia was a late Ottoman acquisition, and attempts on the part of Polish kings to bring the principality back into their own sphere of influence recurred every now and then until the late 1600s. As the seventeenth-century Moldavian historian Miron Costin so graphically expressed it, due to the small size of their territory, any step the Moldavian rulers and boyars might undertake immediately affected the interests and ambitions of other states.[73] Formal tribute payments may have begun in 1455–6/859–61.[74] During the first years, 15,000 Hungarian florins were demanded anually, but payments all but quadrupled in the less than forty years separating the final Ottoman conquest from the uprising of Prince Ion the Terrible in 1574/981–2, and the enthronement of Murad III later the same year. This augmentation, which carried the tribute to the level of 53,389 Venetian sequins, was not due to any particular economic development or population expansion, but was largely an outcome of the bitter rivalries between local princes, who offered constantly increasing amounts of tribute in order to rule with Ottoman support.[75] In addition, there were factors that operated quite inde-pendently of the situation in Moldavia itself, such as the pressing financial needs of certain Ottoman sultans, especially after the battle of Lepanto/İnebahtı (1572/979–80), or whenever large payments were due to the janissaries, for instance at the enthronement of a new sultan.

Moldavia's political position certainly was not improved by the attempts of Prince Tomşa, who ruled for but a few months in 1564/971–2, to formally seek aid at the Polish court.[76] Admittedly in this particular instance, the king could be prevailed upon by the Ottoman authorities to order the execution of the trouble-some *voyvoda*. Yet since the rulers of Poland-Lithuania often had attempted to assert suzerainty over Moldavia, in the Ottoman perspective, requesting Polish aid must have been regarded as tantamount to high treason on the *voyvoda*'s part. However, at this time, the international situation apparently precluded the Otto-man administration from augmenting its financial demands in response to Prince

Tomşa's flight. This augmentation only occurred in 1566–7/973–5, when Selim II had newly ascended the throne, and needed to pay the janissaries their customary gratifications.[77] Generally speaking, the treasures amassed by certain princes also must have encouraged the Ottoman central government in the belief that Moldavia could well afford to pay an increased tribute.[78]

Moldavian socio-political structures in certain respects were comparable to those of the late Byzantine world, while affinities of the boyars to the Polish nobility were not absent either.[79] The politically dominant group were the nobles or barons. From these people, down to the defection of the famous scholar Prince Demetrius Cantemir to Tsar Peter in 1711/1122–3, the Ottoman sultans chose the ruling princes; afterwards, the appointments went to members of Istanbul's prominent Greek families, the so-called Phanariots.[80] According to Cantemir, Moldavian nobles were divided into four ranks. The lowest, in the author's perhaps jaundiced view, consisted of people who should have been regarded as freemen rather than as nobles, who cultivated their lands either in person or else by employing hired servants. Above them ranked the knights, who had been given lands by the prince, in exchange for which they owed military service. By contrast the members of the lower-level nobility had inherited their property – Cantemir speaks of 'this or that village' – from their ancestors. The most elevated rank, which Cantemir compares to that of the Russian boyars, consisted of men who had held or were actually holding public offices, in addition to the descendants of former high office-holders. The number of families thus distinguished was quite limited, the author listing seventy-five including his own.[81]

Certain Moldavian princes, while residing in Istanbul as candidates to the throne, had acquired Circassian or Abaza slaves whom they took with them to Moldavia when elevated to the princely dignity. These slaves must have become Orthodox Christians, as some of them were manumitted, appointed to high court office and later accorded noble rank.[82] This practice may explain why among the noble Moldavian families listed by Cantemir, we find names such as 'Karabaschestij' or 'Tscherkiesestij'. Here we are confronted with a rare example of what one might call 'civilian Mamluks': that is, slaves purchased young, educated and later manumitted for employment in government positions. A similar arrangement was found in the eighteenth-century Ottoman provinces of Egypt, Iraq and Tunis, but in these places it usually involved Islamized military men.[83] But the most probable model was the Ottoman court itself where, from the seventeenth century onwards, ex-slaves of Caucasian, especially Abkhazian backgrounds often rose to high rank.[84] Even so it is remarkable that Christian princes thus attempted to check the power of local aristocrats by importing freedmen (*homines novi*) from outside their own domains, and that the Ottoman sultans condoned this practice.[85]

In his guide to the political landscape of late seventeenth- and early eighteenth-century Moldavia, Demetrius Cantemir does not much emphasize the significance of wealth in acquiring and maintaining high rank. In fact, he minimizes this factor in stressing that some families were considered noble even though they might have lost the 'five thousand' peasant holdings they had originally possessed, and retained no more than 'five'. But we may assume that under normal circumstances, wealth did form an important criterion in determining who came to exercise power, and as a corollary obtained high rank.[86] Cantemir would have liked to govern Moldavia as an absolute ruler, and therefore tended to consider all the properties owned by Moldavian noblemen as gracious gifts from previous princes.[87] He also tended to exaggerate the degree of deference that the boyars showed towards the prince. In actual life, as the author himself admitted in a moment of realistic observation, it was not rare for great boyars to plot among themselves, or even form links with foreign rulers without the permission of their princes.[88]

Among the offices that in Cantemir's perspective imparted real distinction, the highest was that of the great chancellor, followed by the governors of the two main provinces into which Moldavia was divided.[89] According to a rule also typical of central European feudal lordships, Moldavian barons presided over provincial or local courts of law; there was no equivalent to the hierarchy of Ottoman kadis who reported to Istanbul independently of the governors. However, in some of the principal towns judges officiated who do not seem to have necessarily been barons. The highest court in the land was presided over by the prince himself and accessible to all his subjects. Within certain limits, it also functioned as a court of appeals, to which litigants could apply if they were dissatisfied with the decision of a given baron.[90] The court of appeals did not reopen the case in its entirety, though, but only checked whether the earlier decision conformed to the law of the land. This ruling in itself confirms the primordial role of Moldavian noblemen as judges, which the prince himself was forced to recognize.

Although adherents of non-Orthodox religions, Jews included, were granted a degree of toleration, and quite a number of Tatar merchants and agriculturalists had established themselves in Moldavia, Orthodoxy was the state religion professed by both nobility and commoners.[91] In this sense, Moldavia differed quite sharply from neighbouring Transylvania where, by the second half of the sixteenth century, five different varieties of Christianity were espoused by major groups of the population. As in other Orthodox societies, monasteries were significant landowners.[92] But in Moldavia, and also in the nearby principality of Walachia, it was possible for religious houses located outside the territories in question to claim the dues of local taxpayers. For, in order to ensure the permanence of their foundations, princes and other aristocrats often dedicated them to famous foreign monasteries. Thus one or another of the Athos houses, or else the ancient foundation of St Catherine's on the Sinai, laid claim to shares of the revenue collected by Moldavian monks. Church ceremonies played a significant role in legitimizing the princely family, as is apparent even from the writings of Cantemir who, in quite a few other respects, viewed the world through the eyes of an adherent of the early Enlightenment, and saw himself as something of an enlightened despot.[93]

Folklore apart, Cantemir as the prime nobleman of his realm was not much interested in his non-noble subjects, nor in their manner of making a living. Thus he makes no attempt to estimate their number: in the early 1800s, it was said that Moldavia held half a million people.[94] In the early nineteenth century, the major product of both Moldavia and Walachia was grain, which was reserved for the needs of Istanbul and the Ottoman armies, and we can assume that this had been true during the preceding one hundred years as well. Timber was of high quality and much used by the Ottoman navy. As to Moldavia's trade in other products, such as beeswax or honey, it also was strictly controlled by the Ottoman state. Local demand being low, the price level does not seem to have encouraged land-holders to increase production, and there was much unused land.[95]

Taxes were paid by the commoners, mainly consisting of peasants and herds-men. Throughout the seventeenth and eighteenth centuries, all manner of dues demanded from the villagers tended to increase substantially. Thus in the early 1700s, un-free peasants owed their lords three days of unpaid labour per year, but by the end of the century, this burden had increased to twelve days, and was to be augmented yet further in the nineteenth century.[96] Moreover these 'labour days' from 1776/1189–90 onwards became much more burdensome than they had been in earlier times. For in this year, Prince Grigore Ghica fixed the amount of work to be done in one 'labour day' at such a high level that two or even three 'real days' had to be devoted to the tasks set for a single 'labour day'. And, while in 1749/1162–3 the peasants were officially given the right to leave the farms of the nobility, this right was nullified in practice by demanding that the departing vil-lagers pay their dues in advance. Even worse off were the approximately 80,000 gypsies, who were officially classified as slaves, either of the state or of noble proprietors, serving in households or exercising certain crafts, but incapable of leaving the country legally.[97]

In good years, the revenues that a careful administrator could derive from Moldavian villagers were considerable. However, in the seventeenth century, the country frequently found itself in a war zone, always a special disaster in regions where herding forms a major source of livelihood. In the mid-seventeenth cen-tury Miron Costin witnessed the battles between the Moldavian prince Vasile Lupu and his Walachian and Transylvanian rivals, which brought foreign merce-naries, including Germans and Poles, into the country.[98] In addition, Vasile Lupu had courted Cossack support by marrying off his daughter to the Cossack leader Tymis. Tymis was a son of the well-known Ukrainian hetman Bogdan Chmeln-itzkij, who had been instrumental in switching the allegiance of a large number of Cossacks from the king of Poland, first to the Ottoman sultan and ultimately to the Russian tsar. Even if we discount the hostility of Miron Costin, a partisan of the Polish king, towards a man whom he probably regarded as a turncoat and a traitor, it is still obvious that these battles resulted in the destruction of numerous villages and towns. The hapless subjects were also hopelessly overtaxed, as princes and boyars amassed treasure in order to prepare for warfare. In 1711/ 1122–3, when Cantemir deserted his Ottoman suzerain for Tsar Peter I, Moldavia was once again a theatre of war and, in part, the Ottoman–Habsburg conflict of 1735–9/1147–52 also was fought out on this territory. Then there was the disastrous Russo-Ottoman conflagration of 1768–74/1181–8, when both sides devastated the Moldavian countryside. As during this war, the soldiers were more often than not underpaid and undersupplied, their depredations were especially serious. Writing in the 1660s/1070–80, Miron Costin had worried whether the spate of warfare that his generation had suffered through would continue in the decades to come.[99] With hindsight it would seem that the author's worst fears came true.

From the viewpoint of the Ottoman court, the role of these appointees, whether sixteenth- or seventeenth-century native princes or later Phanariots, consisted in the payment of tribute and, in times of war, in participation in the sultans' campaigns. In addition, both Moldavia and Walachia functioned as sources of foods and raw materials needed in the Ottoman capital. Wax and honey were much in demand in Istanbul, in addition to salt and fish. By contrast, grain deliveries seem to have become important mainly after the end of the period discussed here, namely during the last quarter of the eighteenth century.[100] Maize was cultivated since the 1600s and replaced millet; that it was not much consumed in the Ottoman capital appears to have increased its attractiveness to Moldavian cultivators.

In the period under discussion, cattle- and sheep-breeders still predominated among Moldavian villagers and, in consequence, supplying Istanbul with meat on the hoof at low, officially controlled prices constituted a further important obligation of the Moldavian rulers and taxpayers. A sizeable number of animals every year was sold to *celeb,* officially recognized livestock traders responsible for delivering sheep to Istanbul butchers. In good years, a profit could be made from this trade, as the mid-seventeenth-century account of Evliya Çelebi indicates.[101] But things were different in times of war, when ordinarily prosperous traders could be ruined because soldiers requisitioned their flocks. Beyond the payment of tribute, Moldavia, with its easy access to the Black Sea, thus formed an integral part of the gigantic area in which the demands of the Ottoman central administration for food and raw materials made themselves felt on a day-to-day basis.

~ In conclusion

Our circuit through the Ottoman borderlands, where the life-chances of dependent principalities were much better than in the territories closer to the central power, has shown that these territories were yet linked to the centre in a multitude of ways. Such a polity might provide occasional reinforcements to the sultans' armies in wartime and, in peace and war, serve as a source of foodstuffs both for the army and the capital; this was the role of Moldavia. The city-state of

Dubrovnik had its utility as a source of tribute and as a 'door left slightly ajar' through which goods from 'Frengistan' could be acquired and diplomatic problems solved in an unobtrusive fashion. As to the Hijaz, while draining a substantial quantity of resources every year, it permitted the sultans to enhance their legitimacy as protectors of the pilgrimage to Mecca, a basic obligation of all Muslims with the necessary means. And where the North African provinces were concerned, remote from the centre and difficult to control though they might be, they permitted the Ottomans to remain a strong presence in the western Mediterranean even when, after the 1590s/998–1008, the 'hot' phase of Hispano-Ottoman conflict was definitely a thing of the past. Doubtless a lengthier survey of the dependent principalities would permit us to discern yet other benefits that the Ottoman centre derived from its various princely dependants; but for the present this sampling must suffice.

As we have seen, incorporation in certain instances conformed to the model developed by Inalcik, however, reality was much more complicated than this model indicates. In those acquisitions that were old Islamic lands, such as Greater Syria, local elites might be permitted to govern under the umbrella of Ottoman control for a century or more; and, given the prevalence of local notables appointed as governors from the early eighteenth century onwards, the period of maximum imperial centralization might be less than a hundred years. In northern Africa, provinces governed by a *beylerbeyi* were allowed to revert to indirect rule after only a few decades. On the eastern frontier, throughout the period under study, Kurdish princes were allowed to govern their territories with minimal interference, though sometimes glorified by the title of *sancakbeyi*. In the cases analysed, there was no general course leading stage by stage towards increasing centralization. Rather, local contingencies determined how a given province would be run. Moreover, it now seems rather artificial to discuss sixteenth-century centralism and the relative decentralization characteristic of the seventeenth and eighteenth centuries as if they belonged to different worlds. In many provinces, certain parts of Greater Syria forming a prime example, local families remained powerful throughout the Ottoman period. Thus it seems more realistic to think of a relatively brief time-span of – often incomplete – centralization in the sixteenth or, in the Syrian instance, the seventeenth century, bordered by centuries of comparatively decentralized rule. Of course this was especially true in the borderlands; and given the distances and communication technologies involved, it could not well have been otherwise.

Rather different considerations applied in the case of the principalities in the Ottoman–Habsburg–Polish borderlands, and at a later stage, on the Russo-Ottoman frontier as well. Here the proximity of competing 'Great Powers' might have induced the Ottoman administration to establish direct rule, as had been done in central Hungary. Especially after the spectacular defection of Demetrius Cantemir to Tsar Peter I, such a solution must have offered itself, and we know that members of the local elites of the three principalities occasionally worried about such a possibility.[102] Yet the Ottoman authorities continued to prefer indirect rule by Christian governors. Possibly one factor in this decision was the near-absence of a Muslim population in these territories, so that establishing *bey-lerbeyi*s would have necessitated the implantation of Muslims from the Ottoman core provinces. Moreover, given the experiences that the Ottoman upper class had, by the late seventeenth century, made with the discipline problems posed by garrisons in outlying provinces, this costly operation may well have been regarded as unnecessary and even counterproductive.

However, it would be a great mistake to regard this accommodation of vassal princes and heads of 'political households' as an early indicator of 'Ottoman decline', or even worse, to view the princes involved as the 'predecessors' or 'ancestors' of twentieth-century nation-states. As we have seen (see Chapter 2), decentralization was not equivalent to disintegration. To the contrary, the *aga*s, *dey*s and *bey*s of western and central North Africa maintained their links to Istanbul well into the nineteenth century and, when these connections were finally cut, it was not due to the will of the dignitaries involved, but to French military conquest. Given the enormous distances and heterogeneous political structures involved, a judicious measure of decentralization allowed local elites both old and new to acquire a stake in the Ottoman enterprise, and may well have strengthened the Empire's coherence rather than weakening it.[103]

Frontier principalities, with the exception of trading centres such as Dubrovnik, were rarely peaceful for any length of time. Not only were their rulers expected to furnish troops to the Ottoman army, and that entailed the passage of soldiers through villages and towns, but a larger state in the vicinity might compete for 'influence' with the Ottomans. Last but not least, the rulers of these lands, however petty when viewed in a global perspective, might develop political ambitions of their own. A study of life in the borderlands therefore necessitates some understanding of the finances, supplies and soldiers indispensable for Ottoman warfare, and these issues will form the topic of the following chapter.

4 ~ The strengths and weaknesses of Ottoman warfare

~ Ottoman military preparedness and booty-making: assessing their significance and limits

In the military sense, the Ottomans' reputation for invincibility among their mid-sixteenth-century European opponents was due to a judicious combination of cavalrymen and foot soldiers, in addition to a great deal of discipline on the battlefield.[1] But strategy and tactics, although important, were only part of the story. It has often been written, and a recent study has confirmed, that the Ottoman state and Ottoman society in its entirety, at least to the very end of the seventeenth century, was effectively organized for war.[2] This was due to the unchallenged authority of the sultans, as well as to a central administration unconditionally devoted to the ruler and capable of mobilizing the enormous resources of a territory reaching from Budapest to Van, and from the northern shores of the Black Sea all the way to Yemen.

However, a statement of this type should not be taken to mean – as it has sometimes been – that everything Ottoman subjects undertook beyond securing their subsistence was geared to a direct or indirect preparedness for military confrontation, and that a whole society was animated by the spirit of 'holy war'. Certainly this latter ideology was significant among those Ottomans who put down their thoughts in writing. But it has been argued, in my view with justification, that at least for sixteenth- or seventeenth-century soldiers, issues of rough justice and equality among the different categories of military men were more important motivating forces than the idea of 'holy war'.[3]

Wars certainly took their toll on Ottoman society. During the exhausting conflicts of the seventeenth century on the Habsburg, Iranian and Venetian fronts, the concerns of the civilian population took but a very poor second place compared to the needs of warfare. Internal security in the provinces often was badly neglected and, particularly during the mid-seventeenth-century Venetian blockade of the Dardanelles, the very food supplies of Istanbul were threatened.[4] Even worse, in border areas and regions through which armies frequently passed, destruction might be so total that human habitation, for the time being, virtually came to an end (compare Chapters 1 and 2). In war years Ottoman subjects unfortunate enough to inhabit these regions must have lost much of what they had produced in less disastrous times. Moreover, in the second half of the eighteenth century, warfare and the evacuation of populations that it often entailed, did ruin some previously prosperous regions of the Ottoman interior as well, as we shall see. In these contexts, but in these alone, is it possible to speak of an economy totally dominated by the dictates of war.

Information on such disasters is available mainly for the regions behind the western and northern fronts; little comparable evidence survives about warfare against the Safavids. This in turn has resulted in an unfortunate imbalance in our understanding of an empire whose rulers, as is often forgotten, also waged numerous wars in the Caucasus and western Iran.[5] Conducting wars on these two remote frontiers at the same time was obviously beset with many difficulties for the populations involved, yet we do know that at certain times the Ottomans took up this challenge with a degree of success. But in spite of the expenditure of men and resources that such wars entailed, this was not 'total war' in the modern sense, conceivable only in societies with at least a modicum of industrialization. During both World Wars the mobilization of civilians to supply moloch-like war-machines did occur, and stimulated scholarly interest in polities that appeared to have solved similar problems in the past. Yet it is not very helpful to view sixteenth- or even eighteenth-century warfare as consuming the resources of an entire empire. In Ottoman provinces relatively remote from the fighting, life in most war years must have gone on much as usual, apart of course from a greatly increased tax load.

There is yet another reason why it does not, in the view of the present author, make much sense to construct a model of an Ottoman economy totally geared to war. There is no denying that attempts of this kind have been undertaken in the past: some scholars have indeed assumed that Ottoman prosperity could only be sustained if new resources constantly entered circulation in the shape of booty. Once this was no longer possible, because the conquest of further rich lands proved unfeasible, the Ottoman economy supposedly entered into a period of crisis.[6] Certainly, the Ottoman politico-economic system of the period under discussion did not exactly facilitate the formation of capital that could be put to economically productive uses.[7] Yet in spite of such a handicap – whose importance, as some recent studies have shown, must not be exaggerated – Ottoman crafts adapted reasonably well to changes in the market. Artisans produced an increasing variety of goods, even and particularly when, as happened in the eighteenth and nineteenth centuries, the booty to be gained from foreign wars was no longer of any importance whatsoever.[8]

On the other hand, it is undeniable that soldiers in many if not most political or cultural systems fight because they hope for material rewards, and Ottoman military men were no exception to this rule.[9] In seventeenth- and eighteenth-century western and central Europe, it was also regarded as normal that a town taken by assault would be left to the soldiers to plunder.[10] Commanders considered that this was one of the major incentives that induced the soldiers to accept the formidable risks inherent in the storming of a fortified place. All the property of any prisoners taken was also regarded as forfeit to their captors and, at a later stage, to the command of the army of which the unit that had brought in the captives formed a part. The only limitation on plundering was the consideration that discipline broke down during these scrambles for booty, and had to be laboriously restored afterwards.[11] Thus, in spite of the different political and religious legitimization involved, Ottoman attitudes towards plunder were not so fundamentally different from those that have been documented with respect to war among Christian princes. In the Ottoman instance, to be sure, booty gained in battle with the infidel (gaza malı) was a source of social prestige. To cite but one example, the seventeenth-century travel writer Evliya Çelebi took pains to emphasize that his family's home had been built with such resources, brought back by one of his ancestors.[12] But quite apart from the 'Türkenbeute' proudly displayed by eighteenth-century German princes and sometimes simply acquired through purchase, a 'military entrepreneur' such as Albrecht von Wallenstein (or Waldstein, 1583–1634/990–1044) also had no scruples about displaying the wealth he had gained through the successful practice of war. Today the palace he built himself in Prague forms an impressive background to the deliberations of the Czech parliament.[13]

However important booty may thus have been for an individual border warrior and his family, it would be a serious mistake to view Ottoman society as a larger version of the Tatar khanate in the steppes to the north of the Black Sea, where booty in slaves and livestock really constituted an important contribution to the well-being of tribal society at large.[14] To begin with, the population of the Empire was much too large for booty to have an overall impact: around 1520/926–7, the Ottoman population probably amounted to about fifteen million, and it increased substantially until about 1580/987–8. Most of these people lived in places where gaza malı was of no importance whatsoever.[15] All this means that while Ottoman soldiers were concerned about booty-making, in this they were not very different from their central European opposite numbers. As far as Ottoman society as a whole was concerned, in the period we are studying, gaza malı was important for its social connotations but, apart from very short periods, not for the quantity of wealth it brought into circulation. Matters might have been different had the Ottomans been able to take Vienna, Venice or Rome …

In addition, one of the major gains of Ottomanist history during the last forty years has been the understanding that far from being, in its overall character, 'military and agrarian' in orientation, the Ottoman elite was quite intent on profiting from trade. We have understood that Muslim and Ottoman merchants, especially those operating outside the perhaps over-administered capital of Istanbul, were far more dynamic than had been believed forty or fifty years ago.[16] From this viewpoint as well, we should discard the notion that booty played more than a localized role in Ottoman economic life. If a simple formula is needed, it makes more sense to adopt that proposed by Fernand Braudel during his later years. In Braudel's perspective, the Ottoman Empire greatly profited from the fact that, well into the eighteenth century, it managed to retain control over the western Asian trade routes.[17] Moreover, as scholars working after Braudel have demonstrated, down to the later 1700s these routes were eclipsed by their oceanic competitors to a much lesser degree than had previously been assumed.[18]

In a somewhat different vein, there are good reasons for stressing the limitations that political structures in the Balkans, Anatolia and the Arab lands placed on sixteenth-, seventeenth- or eighteenth-century military preparedness. If we construct an image of Ottoman society as 'totally mobilized' for war, we also imply that no resources were left over for other purposes. This is in fact the impression that certain visitors to the sixteenth-century Ottoman Empire have conveyed to their readers. When Ogier Ghiselin de Busbecq emphasized the frugality of Ottoman soldiers and the 'virtues' of slave labour, he wished to praise the political organization of the realm governed by the sultans with an eye towards conditions at home. For, in Busbecq's view, in Rumelia and Anatolia the resources of an entire society had been placed at the beck and call of the sultan.[19] On the other hand, Busbecq's employers the Habsburgs, given the strengths of the nobilities of their variegated territories, were in a much weaker position.

However, there were limits to the authority of the Ottoman ruler as well, and thus to the things that he could induce his army to do or refrain from doing. In another context, Busbecq claimed to have heard from Grand Vizier Rüstem Paşa himself that in times of war the janissaries were inclined to do whatever they liked, and could not always be controlled even by Sultan Süleyman himself.[20] Certainly this statement may have been part of a diplomatic bargaining process, but this does not mean that it was wrong in itself. Thus, although the sultans enjoyed a high level of legitimacy, there were clearly visible limits to their authority even in the mid-sixteenth century, normally considered the high point of sultanic centralism.[21]

Of course, warfare did indeed impose serious sacrifices on Ottoman populations, especially since the limited productivity of agriculture in a largely semi-arid environment did not leave much room for manoeuvre. Yet it is highly doubtful whether, apart from a few catastrophic years, all available resources were normally devoted to war. After all, the wealth of certain merchants in Cairo, or the presence of better-quality consumer goods in the houses of wealthier Bursalıs of the eighteenth century, do demonstrate that among Ottoman subjects money was spent on peaceful pursuits as well. The economic expansion of the sixteenth century and, in some regions, its less obvious counterpart that took place during the mid-1700s, did allow some scope for the enrichment of at least a certain group of urban taxpayers. It would seem that one can overdo the emphasis on war-related impoverishment and 'total mobilization' of the Ottoman subject class.

Given our concern with the relations that both the state apparatus and Ottoman society as a whole entertained with the 'outside world', the present chapter will deal not with military affairs per se, but with the social and economic effects of warfare. Geographically speaking, we will discuss events taking place on the Habsburg–Ottoman frontiers in the west, and the Polish–Ottoman and Russo-Ottoman borderlands in the north. To obtain a complete picture, it would be desirable to also include the Caucasus and Anatolian–Azeri borderlands in the east and, last but not least, the African desert frontier in the south. But given the relatively limited number of primary sources and secondary studies available, this is not at present a realistic option.

~ Ottoman political advantages in early modern wars

Such an account must include a brief summary of the research that has been undertaken on the overall context of Ottoman warfare during the last twenty years or so. Just before the beginning of the period covered by our study, in the 1520s/926–36 and 1530s/936–46, Ottoman effectiveness on the battlefield was such that the conquest by the sultans of central Europe in its entirety, and even of Italy, appeared as a distinct possibility.[22] Some of the great advantages of the Ottoman sultans lay in the political deficiencies of their opponents. Thus Balkan or Cypriot peasants overburdened by taxes were often not sorry to see their rulers destroyed, and avoided participating in the defensive efforts of these princes.[23] Some discontented subjects even might provide information about the movements of the military detachments commanded by their lords, if indeed they did not themselves go over to the Ottoman side. On a higher socio-political level, official attempts to convert local aristocracies, townsmen and peasants to the religious denomination favoured by their rulers of the moment might have similar effects. As we have seen (Chapter 2), Hungarian noblemen in particular quite often rose against their Habsburg overlords with open or tacit Ottoman support. Here the attempts of the government in Vienna to build a centralized state with a militant Counter-Reformation ideology proved highly counterproductive when it came to stabilizing Habsburg control over Hungarian territories, where Calvinism was widespread.[24]

While state-building and centralizing efforts on the part of the Habsburgs could thus work in favour of their Ottoman opponents, the exact opposite – namely the incomplete success of such centralization – could also result in an advantage for the sultan's commanders. For in the first half of the seventeenth century, Habsburg armies were still not fully state-controlled, but had been organized largely by military entrepreneurs. These commanders-*cum*-businessmen supplied soldiers to a variety of rulers with the hope of profiting from their investments, in terms of money and also of political power.[25] By the second half of the century this form of recruitment certainly had, to a large extent, been superseded by direct military service to the ruler and the payment of war-related costs by the exchequer. But numerous vestiges of the older arrangement persisted well into the eighteenth century. Thus the highly successful field commander Prince Eugene of Savoy, in his identity as the head of the Habsburg military administration, struggled, with indifferent results, to curtail the rights of the noble 'proprietors' of regiments.[26] Even though it was not unknown for Ottoman commanders in the field to make moves without orders from the centre, the command structure as a whole was much more strongly centralized.[27]

In addition, most European battles against the Ottomans were fought by coalitions of rulers. Even if at times there existed a great disparity in power between the allies, the leaders were not necessarily capable of influencing the decisions of their coalition partners. Thus, even though the late sixteenth-century Spanish Empire constituted the principal political force in Italy, Philip II was not in a position to prevent the Venetians from abandoning the 'Holy League' and concluding a separate peace with Selim II in 1573/980–1.[28] Inducing the German states, loosely confederated in the 'Holy Roman Empire', to pay subsidies and/or send contingents to help in the fight against the Ottomans was always a complicated endeavour. The Habsburgs succeeded best in securing such cooperation when territories governed by southern German princes – that is, situated outside the Habsburgs' 'hereditary lands' – appeared to be threatened as well.[29] Furthermore, when such auxiliary contingents did arrive, it might be necessary to appoint as a commander a prince manifestly unsuited for his task, for otherwise the offended ally might choose to withdraw his armed forces.

On the other hand, Ottoman sultans depended much less on coalitions with foreign rulers than was true of their European opponents. If we disregard the unique episode of Süleyman the Magnificent's alliance with François I of France, it is only in the eighteenth century that we encounter sultanic coalitions with rulers who could claim 'great power status' in their own right. Ottoman requests for the mediation of such a sovereign in order to make peace with a third party also occurred for the most part after 1700/1111–12.[30] Certainly even earlier, the sultans had needed to take the wishes of some of their allies into account. Thus the khan of the Tatars played an important role in Caucasus warfare, and even more so in steppe or Balkan campaigns, and his support had to be bargained for.[31] At the same time, on some occasions the alliance with the khans also might constitute a liability: in the sixteenth and seventeenth centuries, Tatar raids on the Poland-Lithuanian or Russian frontiers might draw the Ottoman sultans into conflicts that the latter apparently would have preferred to avoid.[32] But given the great difference in power between the sultans and the Crimean rulers, it was usually possible to depose a recalcitrant khan and replace him by a relative more amenable to Ottoman wishes. To an even greater degree this applied to minor Caucasus potentates or Hungarian magnates, who brought a few contingents to do battle on the Ottoman side.

There was yet another wartime problem which early modern European sovereigns needed to confront, but which was unknown to the Ottoman sultans: throughout the period under study: local aristocrats saw themselves as possessing the right to take service with whatever ruler would employ them. In principle, if the new employer was not identical with the 'natural sovereign', he was at least expected to be a Christian, but there were exceptions even to this rule.[33] The Habsburgs took advantage of the situation, and hired talented commanders from outside their own domains. Among these aristocratic immigrants, the most famous was Prince Eugene of Savoy (1663–1736/1073–1149), who had been slighted at the French court where he had first attempted to build a career. Into the same category fell the scholarly general Luigi Fernando de Marsigli (1658–1730/1068–1143), who, as a Bolognese, was in secular terms a subject of the pope.[34] But this privilege of the European nobility to seek honours and employment at courts other than those of their own rulers also made it difficult to secure military discipline. Not all commanders were willing to set aside their previous loyalties, and in some instances their status as petty but sovereign princes, when entering the service of the Habsburgs. In consequence, Habsburg war councils in the field, and also the interventions of the Aulic War Council in Vienna, often aimed mainly at hammering out political compromises, with single-minded devotion to military success an ideal rather than a reality.[35]

However, the Ottomans of the seventeenth century sometimes were judged by contemporaries to have suffered from the opposite problem: in view of the difficulty of the terrain, and also because the adversaries often were equally matched, it was inevitable that even talented commanders on occasion suffered serious reverses. In the Habsburg armies such defeats did not necessarily bring about negative consequences for the generals in question, unless the ruler decided to 'set an example'; ultimately Luigi Fernando de Marsigli was a victim of such a – perhaps overdrawn – attempt to ensure discipline.[36] But in the Ottoman instance, failure often was tantamount to execution; and as military talent and experience were scarce resources, similar to cannons or soldiers, the sultans may well have deprived themselves, to their long-term detriment, of the services of potentially very successful commanders.

~ Financing wars and procuring supplies: the changing weight of tax assignments and cash disbursals

Another Ottoman advantage was doubtless financial. To the middle of the sixteenth century, decision in battle still was often due to the actions of the cavalry armed with swords and lances. Given this situation, and a society where cash was at a premium, it was certainly a major advantage that a large number of cavalrymen did not cost the sultan's treasury anything in cash; for they had been assigned 'livings' (*dirliks*), the famed *timars* and *zeamets*, which allowed the grantees to collect their revenues directly from the taxpayers. On the other hand, all office holders could be – and were – frequently reassigned to distant provinces, and these mutations made it impossible for the beneficiaries to develop independent local power and thus threaten the central administration's control.[37] It is perhaps instructive that, in the village disputes recorded in the provincial kadi registers, the role of *timar*-holders was but moderately prominent.

However, by the second half of the sixteenth century, cavalrymen using swords and lances, and for whom firearms were at best an auxiliary weapon, were no longer the decisive force when it came to winning battles. This consti-tuted a momentous change, even though throughout the seventeenth and eighteenth centuries cavalrymen, now outfitted with firearms, remained indis-pensable because of their speed. To this strategic situation, the Ottoman government reacted with a 'phasing out' of the *dirlik*s and an increasing stress on the cash nexus. Thenceforward, revenue sources were administered by the cen-tral treasury, which farmed them out to the highest bidders, at first for short terms of up to three years. Towards the end of the seventeenth century, however, the deleterious effects of this practice had become obvious. Due to the brevity of their tenures, tax farmers attempted to make maximum profits as quickly as pos-sible, without much concern for the long-term productivity of the tradesmen or peasants from whom they collected taxes and dues.[38] More importantly, the Otto-man government, embroiled in a losing war with the Habsburgs, urgently needed large sums of cash, which only contractors sure of long-term tenure were willing to provide. Thus in 1695/1106–7, against the payment of sizeable entry fines, which were determined by competitive bidding, many tax farms were assigned for the lifetime of the grantees. As to the importance of the cash-down payment, it was compensated for by allowing the holders to pay relatively low and, above all, fixed annual dues for the remainder of their lives.[39] This abolition of the *dir-lik*s in favour of tax farms was a gradual process, which continued throughout the 1700s, yet in some regions, quite a few *timar*s managed to survive to the middle of the nineteenth century.

To phrase it differently, from the second half of the sixteenth century onwards, ready money was needed in much larger amounts than ever before, because the new-style foot soldiers wielding muskets, who increasingly constituted the back-bone of the Ottoman army, were not assigned 'livings', but paid in cash.[40] We do not yet know why the Ottoman administration did not try to 'modernize' the *timar*-holders, for instance by assigning them to elite corps of musketeers, and thus extend the useful life of the *dirlik* system. This is all the more remarkable as both Ottomans and Ottomanists usually have believed, and still believe, that the *timar* as an institution was central to the functioning of the entire state apparatus.[41]

We do not know what arguments prevailed in the sultan's councils when the Ottoman authorities decided to get rid of the *dirlik*s. Yet we can, with hindsight, hypothesize why no attempt was made to pay the new-style musketeers hired, for instance, during the Long War (1593–1606/1001–15) with the Habsburgs, by issuing them rural tax assignments as had been customary around 1500/905–6. For while the *timar*s were, at least in principle, granted for several years, by now the Ottoman authorities were trying to save money by hiring soldiers for the duration of a single campaign only. Moreover, the central government had come to rely on the contingents that high-level administrators furnished on their own initiative, and that therefore were not the state's responsibility at all.[42] We thus encounter the formation of a two-class system in the army: on the one hand, there were the servitors of the sultan (*kul*), who had the right to a 'living' or else received monthly pay. Outside this privileged circle, there remained the musket-wielding soldiers recruited from the subject population, who possessed no 'job security' and whose frequent rebellions during the seventeenth century were motivated in part by their desire to achieve parity with the established military corps.[43]

In addition to this concern with saving money, the Ottoman government in the second half of the sixteenth century seems to have doubted the military value of all infantrymen who did not live in barracks as full-time soldiers, but were, in peacetime, stationed in the countryside. For in this period the central administration abolished the ancient corps of foot soldiers paid by the assignment of agricultural holdings (*yaya, müsellem*), and relegated these men to the status of ordinary peasants.[44] At the same time, the nomad contingents (*yürük*) that had played a significant role in the Ottoman conquest of the Balkans and possessed a well-developed military organization, were largely stripped of their soldierly functions and limited to non-combatant roles, such as guarding and transporting supplies.[45] And while official documents tell us a good deal about the practical procedures involved in the abolition of these corps, the present author has not to date seen a text in which the reasons for this measure are explained. 'Ideological' considerations – that is, a firmer separation of tax-paying subjects (*reaya*) and tax-collecting servitors of the state (*askeri*) – may have had something to do with this decision. If this is indeed true, there should have been little motivation to create a new corps of military men provided with landholdings whose status was 'intermediate' between these two basic socio-political categories of the sixteenth-century Ottoman Empire.[46] Also, from a practical point of view, the tax or land assignments that could have been granted to individual musketeers would have been so small and so numerous as to make accounting virtually impossible.

Once commercial or agricultural taxes were less frequently assigned to military men, it became imperative to increase the monetary revenues accruing to the Ottoman administration. The central treasury was obliged to pay large quantities of cash to the soldiers permanently stationed in Istanbul and provincial capitals, even though the amounts received by individuals were often not very important. Moreover, high-level dignitaries needed extra income in order to augment the number of armed men on whose services in wartime the government had come to rely. Often the money needed was simply unavailable, and several times during the seventeenth and eighteenth centuries precious items in the palace treasury were melted down in order to pay the soldiers. Even so, military men were paid irregularly in any early modern state, and especially so in the Ottoman case, given the need to bring large numbers of men, and enormous quantities of money, to the remote frontiers of Hungary, eastern Anatolia or Iraq.[47]

Loans from its own subjects were available to the Ottoman government only to quite a limited extent. Tax farmers were often asked to pay for goods needed by the army and produced in the localities for which they were responsible. In these cases, the debt was repaid by allowing the tax farmers turned state creditors to subtract the appropriate amounts from their remittances to the central treasury when the next instalment fell due.[48] As to the funds of pious foundations, they were not much mobilized by the Ottoman administration before the eighteenth century, and when this finally did happen, money was more often collected as dues than as loans.[49] Banks in the narrow sense of the word did not exist, even though, in the late sixteenth century, a pious foundation had been established in Istanbul with the express aim of providing credit to solvent merchants; this institution did not, however, survive for very long.[50] Some eighteenth-century moneylenders were so active that we might class them as small-scale bankers, but they acted as providers of credit to village communities and private persons, not to the Ottoman government. And while in the eighteenth century money changers (*sarrafs*) serving high-level administrators and tax farmers were in the business of facilitating financial transactions, once again, they did not channel funds held by the public into government loans.[51]

Instead, the Ottoman administration relied on a plethora of deliveries, often unpaid. Or else the peasants and craftsmen who provided goods and services received a remuneration less than the 'administratively determined' price (*narh*) so often recorded in the kadi registers, and sometimes in separate booklets (*narh defteri*) as well.[52] The obligation to deliver such goods, usually grain stockpiled along the routes that the Ottoman armies could be expected to use, was known as the *nüzul* and *sürsat*. *Nüzul* constituted an unpaid delivery, one aspect of the *avarız* taxes that, as early as the fifteenth century, could be demanded of the sultan's subjects in times of war; by the 1600s the *avarız* had been turned into an annual payment. By contrast, goods delivered under the heading of *sürsat* were paid for, even though the prices were often minimal. Thus even those taxpayers fortunate enough to have gained exemptions from the *avarız* could not avoid this particular sacrifice.[53] But even if the deliveries in question were remunerated according to the *narh*, the taxpayers still might end up with a loss, as the price paid did not include the very considerable expense of transporting grain by land over long distances. If in the case of outlying districts, it proved impractical to require deliveries in kind, a sum of money might be substituted (*bedel-i nüzul*). Villagers who for one reason of another were late in delivering might also be asked to pay a large amount of money in compensation. More typical of the eighteenth century was the requirement that a certain percentage of the grain produced in a given region be bought up by state officials at a very low price; this was the so-called *mübayaa*, intended to feed both the city of Istanbul and the men serving in the Ottoman armies.[54]

In addition to grain, textiles needed by the soldiery might be demanded from certain categories of taxpayers in lieu of dues. The most famous case is probably that of the Sephardic Jews of Salonica, who had been settled in this town after their expulsion from Spain in 1492/897–8, and had been assigned the job of manufacturing the woollen cloth needed for janissary uniforms.[55] In the sixteenth century, the government paid for these deliveries, but the sums of money disbursed were not sufficient for the survival of the producing artisans. Yet, down to about 1650/1060, the latter succeeded in making ends meet by selling part of their production on the open market. But the number of customers declined more and more during the seventeenth century. On the other hand, the Ottoman government found itself increasingly short of cash, and began to demand woollen cloth in lieu of taxes, causing great hardship to the producers. Moreover, in Thessaly, where cotton production was significant, producers were ordered to furnish underwear for the janissaries, while on the Aegean seaboard of Anatolia, we often encounter demands for sailcloth.[56]

Craftsmen were also required to accompany the Ottoman armed forces on campaign. The artisans thus drafted set up shop within the camps: there they baked bread, manufactured shoes, swords, pistols or muskets as needed and undertook repair jobs.[57] This had the advantage of keeping the army on the march away from the towns, where soldiers normally caused a good deal of disturbance, and also of minimizing the disruption of military discipline. The initial expenses that a craftsman on campaign needed to undertake included such things as a tent and a stock of raw materials; these were paid for by the fellow guildsmen of the departing artisans. Sometimes smaller and less influential guilds were appointed 'aides' (yamak) to those formed by their more prosperous fellow craftsmen; in this capacity, the 'aides' had to help the larger guilds finance those artisans who were to participate in a campaign. In addition, as long as galleys were in use, and they were only phased out in the course of the seventeenth century, the boatmen of Istanbul and 'despised' guilds such as those of the wine merchants and inn owners, had to supply rowers to man the navy. In view of the conditions prevailing on the galleys, this obligation must have given rise to some dissatisfaction.[58] Yet before 1730/1142–3 we do not hear that goods and services demanded from Ottoman artisans led to urban uprisings. It was only in this year that discontent, caused by a mobilization of guildsmen for an Iranian campaign, contributed materially to the rebellion which brought down Sultan Ahmed III. The administration seems to have been incapable of moving the army out of Üsküdar.[59]

~ How to make war without footing the bill – at least in the short run

All this meant that wars could be financed with a relatively limited disbursal of cash, and when peace was finally concluded, there was no mountain of debt to be paid off. It is worth recalling that in 1789–92/1203–7, the French monarchy largely fell from power because the burden of past wars obliged Louis XVI (r. 1774–92/1187–1207) to seek the cooperation of nobles and commoners in order to service the state debt. Therefore terminating a war without major sums falling due constituted an inestimable advantage to the Ottoman side.

This arrangement, however, also had its problematic aspects. For since little cash entered the hands of the taxpaying subjects as remunerations for the sailcloth, woollen coats or muskets that they delivered to the Ottoman armed forces, there was no possibility of generating a war-induced boom in the armaments sector. This failure could become the source of numerous difficulties. As is well known, wars result in a decline of demand for manufactured goods used by civilians. Men are taken away from home to serve in the armies and navies, often leaving their families in straitened circumstances. At the same time, the civilian population frequently will suffer food scarcities, due to the priority accorded to the needs of the armed forces, and due to the destruction of harvests in the course of fighting. High prices for food will, of course, further decrease the demand for civilian manufactured goods, and thus hasten the decline of this sector. In consequence, the war-related boom in armaments and army supplies, as it generates employment for artisans, comes to form an important 'anti-cyclical factor'. When peace is concluded, obviously reconversion to a civilian-dominated market will be necessary, a process often accompanied by a serious economic disruption.

It has been suggested that, in the Ottoman setting, this model did not operate, or at least operated only in part. War-related losses to the civilian population did occur, and these must have resulted in a declining demand for manufactured goods. But there was no sectorial boom to counterbalance this war-induced slump, because craftsmen working for the military were paid too little to generate extra investment capital or even increase their consumption of food. To the contrary, a lengthy war tended to result in overall economic exhaustion, exacerbated by the inclination of the Ottoman bureaucracy to collect the largest amounts of dues from the most efficient producers.[60] This meant that, at the war's end, virtually all artisans were starved of working capital, and thus unable to procure the raw materials that they would have needed to make the transition to production for a civilian market. Moreover, presumably there was little demand for their products, at least if we disregard a few high-quality items purchased by the Ottoman court and high-level officials. It is likely that under these conditions the better-off townsmen, normally the purchasers of craft products, lost so much in wartime that, even after peace had finally been brought about, they no longer generated much demand (compare Chapter 2).

This line of argument has been developed to explain the situation observed in the late eighteenth century, when the Ottoman armies in fact were being so badly supplied that they were no longer in a position to win victories. However, there is an important difficulty involved: for Ottoman methods of war financing did not change substantially from the sixteenth to the eighteenth century, even though it is possible that the load placed on the backs of Ottoman subjects was less heavy in the earlier period. Unfortunately, at our present level of information, we are not able to provide quantitative data. Further, as has been stressed in a recent study, in the sixteenth and partly even in the seventeenth century, artisans were not overtaxed to the extent that universal exhaustion was the result.[61] These considerations may at first glance cast some doubt on the explanatory value of the 'war financing model' in explaining Ottoman economic crisis and military failure.

Yet when using this model in order to explain eighteenth-century defeats, we must keep in mind that the overall conditions under which Ottoman war financing had to prove itself had now changed dramatically in comparison to the years around 1600/1008–9. Therefore practices which had not been economically ruinous in the sixteenth or seventeenth centuries may well have become so after 1768/1181–2. Most importantly, the principal opponent of the Ottomans was now Russia, with its enormous resources in metals and timber. Due to a series of measures, often quite brutal, aiming at economic and political 'modernization', these had been made available to the armies of the tsars and tsarinas. An empire based largely on semi-arid zones with limited ore deposits would have been hard put to match this performance under almost any conditions. In addition, by the late seventeenth century the Habsburg opponents of the Ottoman sultans also had established centralized rule over many of their territories. They thus developed the means to mobilize more effectively resources for war than had been true in the sixteenth century, when in Bohemia, Austria or royal Hungary, the construction of absolutism was as yet under way.[62]

Ottoman commanders attempted to match these superior material resources by fielding armies much larger than those of their opponents, and this practice must have increased the load that peasants and artisans had to bear.[63] In an effort to keep up with the Habsburg and Russian challenges, the Ottoman government of the eighteenth century may well have carried the exploitation of its subjects to lengths that caused the malfunctioning of the whole system. Such a mistake, after all, would not in any way have been an Ottoman peculiarity: Historians of early modern Europe today are of the opinion that seventeenth- and eighteenth-century states to the west of the Ottoman frontier also were constantly 'living beyond their means' when it came to the conduct of war. If the guideline of their rulers had been economic rationality, which evidently it was not, these potentates should have shunned armed conflict altogether. It is quite possible that similar considerations applied to the Ottoman ruling group.[64]

~ Logistics: cases of gunpowder

Ottoman wars have not exactly constituted a favourite subject for recent and present-day historians. This may well something to do with the fact that the Turkish Republic has managed to steer clear of most international conflicts since its foundation in 1923. While Ottoman prowess in war has become significant for the identity that a certain segment of Turkish society has fashioned for itself, it is not an issue that professional historians have felt greatly inclined to stress. Highlighting the state-building talents of Ottoman viziers and sultans, the professional skills of architects and miniaturists, or even the commercial acumen of foundation administrators and merchants fits much better into the self-image of most modern Turkish intellectuals, and also into the concerns of many Ottomanists, including the present author.

Furthermore, now that Ottoman warfare has become a topic of serious study, research tends to focus on conflicts between the established army corps and mercenaries hired ad hoc, or else on the difficult relationship between the military on the one hand, and the taxpaying population on the other. Thus Ottomanist studies of warfare fit rather well into the 'war and society' problematic which first became popular in England during the 1960s. And as logistics constitutes an obvious interface between the army/navy and society at large, it is easy to explain why this branch of the military enterprise is the best-known aspect of Ottoman campaigns.[65]

After all, Ottoman archival sources on logistics are relatively rich, particularly for the late sixteenth and early seventeenth centuries, when tax assignments (*timar*) were still significant, yet *timar*-holders were increasingly being supplanted by mercenaries. This latter transition must have occasioned a good deal of additional record-keeping. *Timar*-holders had been expected to bring their own servitors, horses and arms, so that their demands for centrally procured supplies were more modest than those of mercenaries. Moreover, gunpowder, one the major items that had to be centrally procured at all times, was not needed by cavalrymen fighting with swords and lances. In fact, by the close of the sixteenth century, some *timar*-holders, now deemed superfluous on campaign, were offered the continuation of their military privileges on the condition that they supplied the central administration with fixed quantities of saltpetre.[66]

In the sixteenth and seventeenth centuries, the Ottomans did not suffer from a lack of gunpowder. Even in the later 1600s the experienced Habsburg commander Montecuccoli observed that Ottoman gunners wasted a lot of gunpowder, but that this lack of skill did not result in any bottlenecks.[67] According to the same source, Ottoman gunpowder was of superior quality. Saltpetre was in relatively ample supply, and the *timar*-holders responsible for collecting supplies did not make themselves odious among the population by intruding into private houses and churches, as was often reported from contemporary England.[68] This should probably be taken to mean that manufacturing gunpowder by horse-drawn mills, and not by waterpower, was as yet of no major disadvantage to the Ottoman side. Only in the late eighteenth century did this manner of producing gunpowder come to be regarded as a major drawback.

Gunpowder was not only used in shooting but, perhaps even more devastatingly, in the blowing up of fortifications. While powerful earthworks made the destruction of fortress walls by artillery alone increasingly difficult, Ottoman explosive experts became masters in the digging of tunnels in which gunpowder was ignited, thus causing the collapse of bastions and curtain walls. This technique had been perfected during the long siege of Venetian Candia, and came close to succeeding in the 1683/1094–5 battle over Vienna, when the relieving army arrived just before the city, with its defences breached, was to have been stormed.[69] At least in this sector, even in the late seventeenth century, the technical changes in European warfare did not yet cause major problems to Ottoman armies.

~ Societies of frontiersmen

Even a good supply system cannot easily make up for problems of manpower and in this field the Ottomans had also developed tactics which resembled those of their western opponents.[70] Ottoman wars were only in part fought out by regular soldiers paid by the central government, or by the musket-wielding mercenaries who made up the household forces of a typical seventeenth- or eighteenth-century provincial governor. In addition, like the Uskoks and free peasants of the Austrian *Militärgrenze* (see Chapter 2), the Ottomans also employed forces whose job it was to secure the borders while at the same time their members eked out their incomes by raiding. As we have seen, on both sides of the Ottoman–Habsburg frontier, there was a tacit agreement that minor violations of this kind would not be regarded as breaches of the peace. However, there always existed a 'grey zone' of major raids that might be regarded as 'ordinary' border fighting that had got out of hand, or else as the beginning of 'real' war. Thus the Long War (1593–1606/1001–15), according to some authors, actually began in 1591/999–1000, because of the unusually large Ottoman raids taking place in that year.

On the Ottoman–Habsburg frontier, offence and defence alike were based on sites fortified by wooden palisades (*palanka*s), castles built of stone-faced earth and more populous walled towns. Hungarian archaeologists have excavated several such Ottoman fortifications and brought to light evidence concerning the way of life of the soldiers manning them.[71] Officers could afford some 'Ottoman-style' luxuries, which accounts for the fragments of Iznik pottery that have come to light in some of these places. Many of the frontiersmen manning fortresses in Hungary were Bosnians, that is Muslim Slavs. Apart from the limited cultural resources available in any border province, this fact helps to explain why the material culture of Istanbul's upper classes made only a timid appearance in Hungary's castle towns.[72] Moreover, many fortresses changed hands several times during the wars following 1526/932–3, the Long War, and/or the 1683–99/1094–1111 confrontation. This must have resulted in the loss of many items of material culture. Due to the military character of the Hungarian–Ottoman border provinces, high-quality arms formed one of the more coveted luxury goods, and such items are in fact documented in significant numbers.[73]

While the Ottoman–Habsburg frontier thus was characterized by a soldiery inhabiting fortified points, the situation was quite different in the territories to the north of the Black Sea. Here the Cossacks and Tatars confronted one another in a wide-open steppe land crossed by major rivers; on both sides of the border, livestock-breeding was much more important than crop-growing.[74] Towns were weakly developed on both the Cossack and the Tatar territories, with the exception of the khans' capital of Bahçesaray. By contrast, the other northern Black Sea towns of some importance, such as Kefe (Feodosiya), Akkerman and Kilia were under direct Ottoman control.

This steppe economy was quite fragile; in the 1550s/957–67 and 1560s/ 967–77, for example, a major famine occurred, which even resulted in some Tatars selling their children into slavery on Ottoman territory. As this was totally inadmissible in terms of Muslim religious law, it is not surprising that a horrified central government intervened to stop this practice, even threatening the purchasers of such illegally enslaved persons with execution.[75] However, apart from such extraordinary crisis situations, it is quite possible that this economic weakness of the Tatar state was regarded as a political advantage in Istanbul. For, as a result, Tatar soldiers hoping for booty were more easily available when needed for Ottoman campaigns. If this was in fact a consideration, we can easily explain why, in the late sixteenth century, Khan Gazi Giray's energetic attempt to secure for himself the governorship of Moldavia came to nought.[76]

Given the weakness of both border economies, raiding for slaves, livestock, food and money formed an important ingredient of both the Cossack and the Tatar way of life. Where the Tatars were concerned, raids were directed at the villages and towns of Muscovy, but also at the territories of Poland-Lithuania. In addition, when the khans participated in Ottoman campaigns against the Habsburgs, their soldiers also raided the villages of Moldavia, Walachia and Transylvania. If the prince ruling one or another of these territories happened to sympathize with the Habsburg or Polish side, such attacks were licit according to the Ottoman understanding of just war.[77] But, of course, under wartime and postwar conditions, the dividing line between licit and illicit raiding was not clearly drawn, and very often crossed by soldiers of both sides.[78]

While some Tatar leaders and especially certain khans, including the late sixteenth-century figure of Gazi Giray, were highly educated Ottoman gentlemen, frontier society as a whole was not very conducive to the production of written texts. In addition, a good deal of what had previously existed was probably destroyed in the course of the Russian takeover in the late eighteenth century, and the subsequent emigration of Tatar grandees into the Ottoman realm. At least relations with the Crimean khanate were sufficiently important for the administration in Istanbul to justify careful record-keeping, so that it is possible to elucidate certain aspects of Crimean Tatar society on the basis of Ottoman records.[79] Even so, however, we know much less about the internal workings of the town of Bahçesaray than about the functioning of Bursa, Salonica or Izmir.

Yet less evidence is available on the Kurdish principalities of eastern Anatolia, although one of their rulers, namely Idris-i Bitlisi, in the early sixteenth century had produced an important chronicle.[80] For the middle of the seventeenth century/1039–81, most of our information comes, once again, from the travel account of Evliya Çelebi, who visited the court of Bitlis in order to deliver an official letter and was detained by the khan, partly as a hostage, and partly as an *arbiter elegantiarum* and courtly entertainer.[81] Evliya describes a highly sophisticated court society, where both exotic foods and fine books were highly esteemed. But once we move outside Bitlis into the smaller territories controlled by minor princely families, including the principality of Hakkâri, our information is often limited to occasional references in the Ottoman Registers of Important Affairs.[82] In addition, tax registers of the type well known from the Ottoman central provinces were put together in certain places, often apparently for the first time, towards the end of the sixteenth century.[83] Their reliability, however, is difficult to determine in the absence of continuous series within which individual registers can be securely 'placed' and evaluated. Much of what is known about eastern Anatolia beyond those cities directly controlled by the central government, such as Mardin or Van, thus dates only from the nineteenth century.[84]

~ Legitimacy through victory, de-legitimization through wars on the sultan's territories

It is perhaps unnecessary to review once again the many references to the Otto-man sultans of the sixteenth and later centuries as warriors for Sunni Islam (*gazis*) against both Christian 'unbelievers' and Shi'ite 'heretics', and to the legitimacy these rulers derived from successful wars. However, it is of interest to note how, in the frontier territories, the legitimacy of Ottoman rule could be enhanced by border warfare. In Bosnia for instance, the rugged terrain severely limited the possibilities of making a living from the land, and many young men were forced to migrate; as we have noted, quite a few of the Ottoman troops deployed in Hungary were of Bosnian extraction.

As long as war with the Habsburgs continued, these mountaineers could thus be integrated into the framework of the Ottoman state as doughty warriors, even though a representative of Istanbul's high culture such as Mustafa Âlî might note with chagrin that it was not possible to enforce the ground rules of the Ottoman state (*kanun-ı osmani*) in such remote border territory.[85] Moreover, even if the nationalist historiography of the nineteenth, twentieth and – regrettably – twenty-first centuries has tended to exaggerate the 'special status' of Bosnia, it still remains true that border warfare and the concession of an often far-reaching de facto autonomy provided a 'place' for Bosnians within the imperial system. In the second half of the sixteenth century, the Bosnian recruits drafted into the Ottoman administration, sometimes allied with and sometimes in opposition to their Albanian counterparts, managed to form one of the dominant factions among the sultan's servitors who vied for high office in Istanbul.[86] Beyond such opportunities for advancement at the Ottoman centre, march warfare against the Habsburgs offered the province of Bosnia a political status that it would not otherwise have possessed. Thus, when Mustafa Âlî decided that he would weather out a semi-disgrace as the holder of a tax assignment in this province, he could console himself with the reflection that now he had come close to the well-spring of Ottoman martial virtue. For, stationed in Banyaluka and elsewhere, he was at 'the source of the trusty warriors for the faith of [all] the climes'.[87] Thus border warfare permitted the political integration of a poor and remote province into the Ottoman imperial structure, secured employment of sorts for a number of its young men and even gave it prestige in the eyes of sophisticated Istanbul literati.[88]

By contrast, once warfare could no longer be carried into the lands controlled by the sultan's enemies, trouble was in store for the inhabitants of the Empire's more central regions. With some justification, historical scholarship has dwelt on the privilege of strong states, situated at the core of a given world economy, to wage war on the territories of their opponents without ever allowing the attendant destruction to approach their own lands.[89] After all, in the pre-modern context it was always difficult to control the behaviour of troops on the march, and they might wreak as much damage on the subjects of their own rulers as on those of the enemy. Strategically speaking, it thus made sense to get all military men onto foreign territory as speedily as possible. But a receding frontier could also have a de-legitimizing effect because irregular troops, no longer needed to harass the opponent, usually cut loose and terrorized the local population instead. The entire phenomenon of Balkan banditry, an endemic disaster during much of the eighteenth and early nineteenth centuries, has even been explained as a consequence of the dislodging of former border warriors from their previous habitats on the frontier.[90] Moreover, during the Russo-Ottoman war of 1768–74/1181–8, soldier-bandits, deserters and other robbers created such havoc in the Bulgarian provinces that previously loyal subjects reacted to this failure of sultanic protection by throwing in their lot with the Russian tsarina. Thus while the Ottomans in their conflicts with the Habsburgs had often been able to carry the war into enemy territory, or at least limit the fighting to the unfortunate Hungarian provinces, they failed to do the same in their 1768–74/1181–8 conflict with Catherine II. The result was a catastrophic de-legitimization of the sultan's rule.

Another case in which prolonged warfare on the territory of a border province undermined the Ottoman position concerns the eighteenth-century Morea (Peloponnese). This province had been marginal in some ways even during the seventeenth century, when we encounter the otherwise unprecedented case of an Englishman taking up a local tax farm.[91] In the war of the Holy League (1683–99/1094–1111), the province was conquered by the Venetians, who hoped to find here a substitute for their recently lost colony of Crete.[92] As a result, the Signoria so badly overtaxed the inhabitants that the latter received the Ottoman re-conquest of 1714–15/1126–8 with some relief.[93]

However, the reestablishment of sultanic power produced problems of its own. As we have seen, the authorities decided to consider the Morea as a newly acquired province (see Chapter 2). This policy allowed them to reassign taxation rights and even the holdings of pious foundations. But it must have created a degree of discontent among those people who had held these rights in the past, and probably had counted on reestablishing themselves in the manner to which they had become accustomed. On the other hand, the Ottoman government permitted local notables, Christians included, a considerable share in the

administration of the province, which included the right to make direct represen-
tations to the authorities in Istanbul. There was even a body, unprecedented in
other territories governed by the sultans, known as the Peloponnesian senate.

These concessions did not prevent certain Orthodox notables from conspiring
with the agents of Catherine II in view of a Russian takeover. By the 1760s/
1173–84, the Ottoman hold on the province had loosened considerably, for even
the landing of just a few hundred Russian soldiers in 1770/1183–4 sufficed to
create complete anarchy in the province.[94] Moreover, the Albanian troops
ordered to repress the rebellion could not be regularly paid, and this resulted in a
total breakdown of military discipline as soldiers grabbed the local tax farms in
order to secure their pay 'at source'. In the end a second campaign was necessary
to dislodge the Albanian troops, and these extensive spates of fighting, along
with the concomitant rapine, must have significantly contributed to the de-
legitimization of Ottoman rule. Put differently, the concessions made to the local
notables did not make up for the disruption that the inhabitants of a marginal
province had suffered due to the fact that the Ottoman central authorities had not
succeeded in keeping Venetian, Russian and Albanian invaders at bay.

~ In conclusion: Ottoman society organized to keep up with the military reformation

Ottoman wars have been frequently studied by people with a primary interest in
other topics, especially the fate of Austria and more particularly of Vienna.[95]
Other historians with a passing interest in the Ottomans have concentrated on
central and western European warfare, in particular the set of developments
sometimes called the early modern 'military revolution', and for which more
cautious observers prefer the term 'military reformation'.[96] In this case, the question to be answered has been to what extent the Ottomans participated in these
developments, or else remained attached to an *ancien régime*-type warfare which
put them at a disadvantage vis-à-vis their European opponents.

The military reformation of the sixteenth and seventeenth centuries was characterized by a set of closely connected phenomena, the most important feature
being an increasing use of firearms, especially of artillery. Among other things,
this latter development necessitated a redesigning of fortifications in order to
make them resistant to artillery attacks. Improved fortifications in their turn gave
rise to the use of explosives in subterranean mines. Of course, the defenders of a
besieged fortress resorted to countermining, in order to destroy the attackers'
mines before explosives could be ignited.[97] A veritable underground war was the
result, of which Hungary, with its numerous fortifications, formed a principal
theatre.

All these techniques were in use in wars among Christian princes of the early
modern period. But in many instances, the wars studied by historians of the 'mili-

tary reformation' did in fact pit Spaniards, Venetians or Austrian Habsburgs against the Ottomans. Apart from the loss of Hungary in 1683–99/1094–1111, the commanders of the sultans were able to hold their own reasonably well until the disastrous second half of the eighteenth century. This must mean that, similarly to their opponents, the Ottomans adapted to the new technologies. Given the numerous confrontations between armies of comparable strengths, it would been impossible to reject new military techniques merely because they had been pioneered by an adversary.[98] Military innovations thus spread rather quickly in both directions. A recent study has pointed out that sixteenth- and seventeenth-century Russian military reforms – that is, organizational change in the pre-Petrine period – owed a good deal to Ottoman models.[99] Given this constant interchange, quite a few studies of early modern warfare in Europe now include the Ottomans, even though most historians writing about the 'military revolution/reformation' know much less about the armies and supply systems of the sultans than about those of their Christian opponents.

Moreover, a successful war was the most highly valued element in the panoply of policies intended to legitimize the ruler in the eyes of the ruling group, and thus a conquering sultan greatly added to his prestige. In this the Ottomans were in no way unique, and recent research on France has shown that French kings also emphasized this aspect of their rule, both by actually going to war and by having their propagandists write about it.[100] On the other hand, the fate of Mehmed IV, deposed in 1687/1098–9, shows that major defeats, such as those sustained before Vienna and Buda during the preceding years, could cost the ruler his throne. This same point was demonstrated once again when Mustafa II was deposed in 1703/1114–15, shortly after the peace of Karlowitz.[101] Beyond military gains and losses, political chances and risks were always involved in the decision to go to war.

Ottomanist historians, however, have viewed Ottoman warfare less as a question of military professionalism or political legitimacy than as an aspect of the 'war and society' problematic. As we have seen, most scholarly work has been done on Ottoman military recruitment, logistics and war financing, all of which involve the – voluntary or involuntary – participation of the subjects. For the present study this emphasis on societal factors has been an advantage, for we are here concerned with warfare as simply one way among others of relating to the outside world. At the same time, research on the societal ramifications of Ottoman warfare has not, at least in the present author's opinion, yet gone far enough. Given the sometimes rather full documentation, for instance in the kadi registers, on wartime taxation and coerced services, it should be possible to study in considerable detail the reactions of Ottoman townsmen in the face of the state's wartime demands.[102] Research is more difficult where the peasantry is concerned, but possibly some information can ultimately be teased out of the surviving archival material, at least with respect to the eighteenth century.[103]

In addition, the study of civilian reactions to warfare must be supplemented by a closer investigation of what happened to those people who actually went on campaign. That we still know so little about the fates of Ottoman prisoners of war in the hands of the Habsburgs, and almost nothing about those who ended up in Russia, forms but one aspect of a much more general ignorance. A concerted effort will be needed to close these gaps in the future, and the following chapter will set out what little we know at present and suggest possible avenues of research.

5 ~ Of prisoners, slaves and the charity of strangers

~ Prisoners in the shadows

After this analysis of the overall conditions determining the fates of men and women captured in war, we finally can turn to the histories of these unfortunate people themselves. The study of war captives in the period before 1850/1266–7 is a much neglected field, not only in the Ottoman context, but also where the early modern history of Europe is involved.[1] A recent collection of articles on prisoners of war in general, supplemented by a wide-ranging bibliography, highlights the fate of captives in the War of the American Secession (1861–5/ 1277–82), the Boer War in South Africa (1899–1902/1316–20) and, mainly, the two World Wars.[2] In addition, the volume also contains a few studies on Greco-Roman antiquity, the European middle ages and the early modern period. When discussing the inclusion of such pre-1850s material, the editor considers this broadening of the field as quite a novel departure on the part of his own research team.[3] Doubtless his claim is justified: if one analyses the copious appended bibliography, it soon becomes apparent that studies on earlier prisoners of war amount to but a minute share of the total of captivity-related research publications. It has been calculated at no more than 2 per cent.[4] This neglect is partly due to the treatment of captives in the sixteenth, seventeenth or eighteenth centuries. On the Habsburg–Ottoman front, or in the Mediterranean theatre of war, those captives who had not been killed in the immediate aftermath of the fighting were soon ransomed, exchanged or enslaved, so that the transitional status of the prisoner of war did not normally last very long.

By contrast, during the wars of the later nineteenth century, and even more during the following period, captivity in war became a mass phenomenon of a dimension unknown in earlier confrontations. Especially after the two World Wars, many people recounted stories and published memoirs about imprisonment in German stalags during World War II, or on the German/Austrian side, the experience of captivity in the US or in the Siberian camps of the Soviet Union. These statements could not possibly be neglected by the agencies that attempted to facilitate the reintegration of former POWs after their return. Thus a large medical literature emerged, dealing with captivity-related traumas, and social scientists studied problems such as the delinquency of former POWs. From the 1980s onwards, moreover, the understanding that the mistreatment of Soviet prisoners by the Wehrmacht had reached genocidal proportions further encouraged historians to concern themselves with the fates of war captives in extreme situations.[5]

On the other hand, military history of the early modern period had been developed and reached the peak of its prestige and popularity during the processes of 'nation formation' in the nineteenth century, when this discipline was taught, at least in part, with the aim of training future (reserve) officers. Prisoners of war were of no use to the armies to which they had once belonged, and some suspicion was frequently attached to the motives of those who allowed themselves to be captured if they were not seriously wounded. While it was possible to dwell on the heroic deaths of the many soldiers who failed to return, prisoners of war – who might have made a contribution to the war effort of the opposing side by their labours in agriculture – seem to have been an embarrassment to their own governments and military men. Thus there was a perfectly good 'pedagogical' reason for avoiding war captivity as a serious subject of military history.

Only with the development of 'war and society' studies from the 1960s onwards has this situation changed.[6] Throughout Europe these studies can be regarded as part of the movement towards democratization and valorization of 'ordinary people', not only of 'mainstream' urban and rural workers, but also of marginals of one sort or another, a social category of which prisoners of war also can be said to form a part. Moreover, the widespread public realization in many European countries that little glory can be gained in late twentieth-century warfare has legitimized studies of people who, by virtue of their captivity, could not be concerned with the gaining of military advantages, but merely with material and moral survival. When dealing with the recent past, 'war and society' studies also have formed links to what in the German-speaking lands is known as *Alltagsgeschichte* ('history of everyday life'), typically concerned with the Nazi period and World War II. In the works of researchers belonging to these schools, the social structure of armies as well as the fate of ordinary people in wartime, combatants and non-combatants alike, has become a principal topic, as opposed to war itself. Throughout, this shift of focus has permitted historians to formulate an intellectual (or emotional) justification for focusing on the fates of early modern prisoners of war.

Given this late and difficult emergence of interest in war captives, even where intra-European history is concerned, it is not altogether surprising that even those few synthetic studies on early modern war captives that do exist disregard the fates of those taken in wars involving the Ottomans. In most cases, secondary sources only tell us that the elaborate exchange agreements concluded between the French, Habsburg and Prussian states in the eighteenth century formed part and parcel of a strategy that aimed at reducing but not really destroying the opponent. In consequence, such arrangements supposedly were not possible when non-Christian rulers such as the sultans were involved.[7] Viewed from a different angle it is worth noting that, from the early fifteenth century onwards, the number of reports by European captives on Ottoman territory who managed to return to their respective homelands was not huge but still quite substantial. Yet, once again, the lack of interest in our problem has been remarkable and these books have not often been studied with the specific purpose of investigating the fates of war captives, but have been treated as ordinary travelogues.[8]

Where the situation of Ottoman captives in the Habsburg lands, Venice or the Papal States is concerned, there are very few studies by Turkish historians, in part certainly because of the language barriers involved. But another reason is doubtless the relatively marginal status of military history on the Turkish historiographical scene. Military history is sponsored by the Turkish General Staff, as happens elsewhere, but the number of publications in this field directed at professional historians is relatively limited, especially where the pre-1850s/ pre-1270s period is concerned; and, in any case, military history as sponsored by army authorities is, for the reasons described above, not very much interested in the fate of war captives. But I think that reasons for this neglect go rather deeper: there is typically very little inclination to study the fates of 'Ottomans abroad' at least as long as the travellers in question were not official envoys.[9] As a result, prisoners of war have tended to fall into a 'black hole', and our knowledge concerning Ottoman captives in early modern Europe is very partial and provisional. The present overview cannot avoid reflecting this situation.

~ Captured: how ordinary people paid the price of inter-empire conflict and attempts at state formation

To a significant extent, information on European captives in Ottoman hands concerns those taken at sea, or else in corsair attacks on villages and small offshore islands. Lands belonging to the Spanish crown were most at risk. Not only were they situated at a convenient distance from Algiers, Tunis and Tripolis, but the Spanish monarchs made their first formal treaty with the Ottoman Empire only in the later eighteenth century and did not deal directly with the local governments of the three North African provinces. The latter thus regarded the inhabitants of Spain proper, and those of the Italian possessions of the Spanish Empire as legitimate prizes. Moreover, not a few corsair captains and sailors had originated from the Italian coastlands; and while many were unwilling to attack their former fellow villagers, perspectives might change if, for instance, a vendetta was involved. Thus, as late as 1798/1212–13, the town of Carloforte on the island of San Pietro was attacked by Tunisian corsairs with the aid of former inhabitants of the place; several hundred prisoners were taken, whose liberation was the subject of arduous negotiations lasting for several years.[10]

But corsairs from North Africa also operated further afield: some of them might make agreements with the commanders of Ottoman fortresses on the Adriatic coasts. The latter would provide the protection of their guns if the corsairs were pursued, and also the facilities for selling slaves and valuables. In exchange they probably received presents, and various dues from the booty marketed. It is also likely, but cannot be proved in the absence of sources, that some governors saw themselves as upholding the cause of the Muslim religion against 'unbelievers', never mind the agreements made by the authorities in far-off Istanbul.

On the other hand, arrangements between corsairs and provincial administrators were not necessarily approved of by sultans and grand viziers. Firstly, the Ottoman version of the *pacta sunt servanda* principle precluded attacks on shipping belonging to the subjects of rulers to whom the sultans had granted capitulations.[11] Secondly, the Ottoman central government viewed itself as the arbiter of war and peace. In consequence, activities initiated by the governors of outlying maritime provinces, which might lead to the formation of yet more semi-independent small-scale states, presumably were not regarded in a favourable light (compare Chapter 3). A third consideration must have been that such attacks could give rise to major international complications. Thus a Venetian captain pursuing a freebooter subject to the sultan might in retaliation bombard the Ottoman fortress that sheltered the corsair/pirate – whether the captain in question was regarded as one or the other would, of course, depend on the perspective adopted. From the mid-sixteenth century onwards, the Ottoman sultans held Venice responsible for the security of shipping in the northern section of the Adriatic and, in principle, conceded the Signoria the right to pursue pirates of whatever allegiance.[12] Thus when viewed from Istanbul, the activities of certain freebooters of Ottoman allegiance might not be viewed with a great deal of indulgence: when recounting the adventures of such people, a seventeenth-century anonymous novella tells us that the latter might need to protect themselves against an Ottoman governor quite as much as against the unbelievers.[13]

Corsairs/pirates were also common on the Christian side of the Mediterranean. As a result, Ottoman seamen and travelling traders, as well as the inhabitants of the Anatolian coasts or the Aegean and Ionian islands, lived under the permanent threat of such people. In the late sixteenth and seventeenth centuries, one of the major dangers for Ottoman shipping in the Adriatic came from the Uskoks. Ensconced in the coastal fortress of Senj (Segna), which is perched high on an inaccessible rock, these frontiersmen mostly had come from Ottoman territories, but also, quite frequently, from Venetian or Habsburg domains.[14] While these men often presented themselves as 'defenders of Christianity', their activities were directed just as much against Ottoman Christians as against Muslims and, occasionally, even against Venetian subjects. When challenged on this issue, Uskok spokesmen often replied that Christians who had accepted the protection of the sultans deserved no better, or else that 'bad Christians' of whatever state, who collaborated with the 'enemy' should be considered fair game.[15] Officially the Uskoks figured as subjects of the Habsburgs. But since they also attacked shipping belonging to states not at war with their overlords, it is justified to regard them as pirates acting on their own account, rather than as corsairs serving their sovereign against his enemies only.

If, of course, the Uskoks had managed to found a stable semi-dependent or even independent state, which they did not succeed in doing, our perspective might be different, and we would today view them as a parallel to the corsairs of

North Africa or the Knights of Malta. But as it was, Uskok attacks on Ottoman shipping did not result in resource accumulation that could have enabled some particularly successful captain to set himself up as a minor prince.[16] In part such a development was prevented by the strong reaction of the Ottoman sultans, who frequently sent out their messengers (*çavuş*) in order to put pressure upon the Venetian Signoria. If the latter was unable or unwilling to honour its commitment to protect peaceful shipping, so the Ottoman argument went, it would become necessary to send a naval force from Istanbul to deal with the problem. But this was an eventuality the authorities in Venice wished to avoid at all costs; for it was unclear whether the Ottoman navy, once it had come so close to the rich and almost unfortified city, would limit itself to reducing the infertile rock of Senj. In addition, allowing the Ottomans into the northern Adriatic would greatly lower Venetian prestige, not very high even under normal circumstances, in the eyes of the powerful Spanish viceroys of Milan and Naples. It was even feared that such a situation might give rise to a Spanish attack on Venetian territories. In consequence, as we have seen, Venice went so far as to fight a brief war with the Habsburgs (1615–17/1023–7) in order to ensure that Senj did *not* become the centre of a small but aggressive semi-independent border state.

Other pirates who viewed themselves as defenders of Christianity were the Cossacks of the Ottoman–Polish–Russian borderlands, whom we have already encountered in their steppe conflicts with the Tatars. But at present it is their activity at sea that will concern us. In the years before and after 1600/1008–9, the Cossacks built small but sturdy ships able to weather the dangerous storms of the Black Sea, and began to attack Ottoman port towns and villages. Thus they surprised Sinop, whose inhabitants, guardsmen included, had left the fortified settlement to attend a fair in the vicinity (1615/1023–4).[17] They also briefly occupied Trabzon, the most important town on the Black Sea coast, famous for its gold- and silversmiths. There was even a Cossack attack on Beykoz, a Bosphorus village on the outskirts of Istanbul (documented 1592–4/1000–3). All this piratical activity forced the Ottomans to maintain a coastguard to protect the Anatolian shores, even though – if official boundaries are considered – at this time the Black Sea constituted an Ottoman lake.[18] Once again, as in the Uskok case, we are confronted with a failed attempt at state formation; the Cossack leaders tried to break loose from the Polish-Lithuanian kingdom, but seem to have realized that they needed resources from outside ventures in order to obtain the funding for such an enterprise. In the long run, however, even the booty gained from Anatolian towns was not sufficient to finance the constitution of an independent state and, as we have seen (Chapter 3), a large section of the Cossacks in the end accepted the suzerainty of the Russian tsar.

~ From captive to slave

Prisoners taken by Muslim corsairs, especially in coastal raids, were often put up for ransom shortly after having been captured, the relevant procedure being known as the *rescate*. In the western Mediterranean, certain small islands were favoured by corsairs as places of safe anchorage, from where the captors would send messengers to negotiate ransoms. If the families of the captives paid up, the latter were released on the spot. For the corsairs/pirates, this proceeding presented the advantage that ransoms were always far higher than the price the same

3. A janissary and his European captive, 1669. The plate is of Iznik fayence of mediocre quality: the colours have run; note the janissary's musket and his characteristic headdress; the inscription is in Greek.

Source: Johannes Kalter and Irene Schönberger, eds, *Der lange Weg der Türken, 1500 Jahre türkische Kultur* (Stuttgart: Linden-Museum, 2003): 129, Illustration no 139. The plate belongs to the Museum für Völkerkunde in Munich and is here reproduced by kind permission.

person would fetch on the slave market. After all, it was predicated on the social standing and wealth of the families of the captives and not on the presumed labour power of the person captured. If, however, the relatives could or did not pay, the prisoners would be taken to Algiers, Tunis, Tripolis or even Istanbul to be sold as slaves to private persons, or else be claimed by the Ottoman state. While ransoming was not impossible even at this later stage, it became less likely once the captives had been removed to far-off localities and sold to masters who, given the distances involved, might be more difficult to convince that a ransom of sufficient magnitude would be forthcoming.

Ransoming and exchanges were also sometimes effected in the case of officers captured in land war. On the seventeenth-century Habsburg–Ottoman frontier such negotiations for exchange, which might succeed or fail, are fairly well documented and were probably not rare. The scholar and Habsburg military officer Luigi Fernando de Marsigli was taken prisoner at an early stage of his career and spent time in Ottoman Bosnia until an exchange could be effected.[19] Claudio Angelo de Martelli, a cavalry officer in the service of the Austrian Habsburgs, captured by the Ottomans at the time of the Vienna siege, finally was ransomed in Istanbul, and has left a fairly detailed description of the negotiations leading up to this event.[20] De Martelli was back in Vienna in time to bring out his book in 1689/1100–1, a full ten years before the war came to an end. This means that, while there were no formal conventions ('cartels' in eighteenth-century parlance) specifying in advance the conditions for ransoming and prisoner exchange between the Ottomans and their Habsburg opponents, the relevant practices were by no means unknown.

We know much less about the fate of Muslim captives sold on the territories of Italian or Habsburg rulers by the Maltese Knights, or the equally piratical Knights of St Stephen, subjects of the grand dukes of Toscana. Moreover, what we do know is owed to a very few recent studies.[21] To some degree, this deficiency may have been caused by the fact that the literary genre of the captivity account, while not unknown in Ottoman literature, was not very widespread, so that researchers have to work mainly with unpublished archival material.[22] But more importantly, European historians, for whom it is much less difficult to access French, Spanish or Italian archives than for their Turkish counterparts, have long tended to view Christian populations as the principal victims of Muslim pirates or corsairs, while the inverse case has largely been ignored. In particular it has seemed convenient to 'forget' that the enslavement of Muslim prisoners in Christian lands was a common enough event. Only in the eighteenth century did all Habsburg–Ottoman treaties contain clauses concerning the exchange or, if that was not feasible, the ransoming of prisoners: as long as the latter had not changed the religions into which they had been born, they were to be sent home, while converts were simply to be liberated. But down to the peace of Karlowitz (1699/1110–11) and sometimes even beyond, prisoners taken in warfare on land were still being enslaved in the Habsburg territories.[23]

In southern Italy, however, the practice of enslaving prisoners continued through the eighteenth century and occasionally even past 1800/1214–15. Admittedly, the numbers of people who suffered this fate after about 1700/ 1111–12 were much lower than those documented for the sixteenth century, when literally tens of thousands of people lived as Muslim or ex-Muslim slaves in different Italian states, especially in Sicily.[24] Only in Venice, whose government, wartime conditions apart, was anxious to maintain passable relations with the sultans, were Ottoman captives often released. However, the Signoria admittedly also possessed a well-deserved reputation for ordering the assassination of captives deemed 'inconvenient'.[25] Further, the likelihood of being released from North African or generally Ottoman captivity seems to have been higher than that of finding one's way home from servitude in the lands of Christian sovereigns.[26] All in all, acknowledging that the enslavement of prisoners was practised not just in the colonies, but right in Europe itself and in the very lifetimes of Newton and Voltaire, has not come easily to many European historians.

~ The miseries of transportation

Anybody who has read captivity accounts of people imprisoned in Nazi Germany or Stalinist Russia knows that transportation to a different camp or prison was a source of special misery for the unfortunates involved. As the reasons for this state of affairs were not significantly different in the early modern period from what they were to be in the mid-twentieth century, it comes as no surprise that former prisoners and eyewitnesses from the sixteenth or seventeenth centuries also have highlighted the traumatic experiences linked to this particular stage of captivity. Due to the confusion attendant upon large numbers of people taking to the roads, the likelihood of flight was not to be gainsaid, especially if the cortege was as yet not too far away from the homelands of the captives. This often resulted in these people's being chained together, an experience as painful as it was humiliating. For the captors, the presence of helpless prisoners might form a convenient outlet for their own frustrations, and insults and beatings were common. When it came to stopping points en route, usually nothing much had been prepared, and the exhausted men and women were fed minimally if at all, while the quality of sleeping quarters was typically abysmal.

Concerning the experiences of an Ottoman captive of the Austrians on the Croatian front in the war of 1683–99/1094–1111, the account of Osman Ağa of Temeşvar/Timisoara forms a most important source.[27] This young officer recounted that after his capture he was able to supply a ransom, but his treacherous captor, an Austrian military man, took the cash and then refused to let him go. The first chapters of Osman's account are full of the miseries of the road: at one point, the prisoner was thrown out of the dwelling in which his captor was housed, because it was assumed that he was close to death, and he survived a major bout of fever lying on a dung heap.

Similar tales can be found in the book by Claudio Angelo de Martelli. However, de Martelli was a prisoner, not of an ordinary officer, but of the Grand Vizier Kara Mustafa Paşa himself, and after the latter's execution, he became the property of the sultan before being returned to Kara Mustafa's heirs. As the Ottomans seem to have considered him a man of some importance, they may have been specially motivated to keep him alive; for de Martelli was a possible candidate for exchange, at least while in the possession of the grand vizier and later of his heirs. This may explain why de Martelli was occasionally given leave to attend mass in Belgrade and other places, where he found people to aid and befriend him. But accommodation in the fortresses of Buda and Belgrade was terrible, and although de Martelli's book, as a piece of war propaganda, highlighted the author's unflinching devotion to the Habsburg cause, it is easy to read between the lines that the author suffered from a profound depression induced by illness and the hardships of prisoner transportation.[28]

~ On galleys and in arsenals

Mediterranean states maintained galleys well into the seventeenth century, and a few ships of this type were in use even after 1700/1111–12. As the overcrowding and overwork on board resulted in high mortality rates, there was a sustained demand for rowers. Where the galleys based in Istanbul were concerned, we have noted that prisoners taken in war had as companions in misfortune both criminals and 'free' rowers furnished by the local craft guilds. In the sixteenth century, it became common also in the Ottoman territories to sentence people to the galleys for a variety of misdeeds. At certain times, the number of Ottoman subjects illegally kidnapped and sold to the naval arsenal may also have been considerable.[29] In the North African provinces, with their much smaller populations, the percentage of slave rowers was probably higher than on the galleys based in Istanbul.

Galley crews consisting largely of prisoners, whether in the service of the Ottoman sultan or else of a Christian ruler, had little reason to feel any loyalty towards the state responsible for their misery.[30] When a galley was under attack, the rowers thus might seize the chance to revolt; and in less extreme situations they were liable to flee if given half a chance. The insecurity generated by this situation in turn was the source of much brutality on the part of officers and guards, which cost the lives of many slaves.[31] When a galley was taken by the ships of a Christian power, the Christian rowers were set free, and the converse was true for Muslim galley slaves if the captor was an Ottoman vessel. On the other hand, rowers with the 'wrong' religion were not included in this gesture of liberation. Thus, when Christian rowers were freed because the galley on which they had served was taken by a Maltese or papal ship, this did not mean that the misfortunes of their Muslim colleagues were at an end, quite to the contrary.[32]

4. The naval arsenal at Kasımpaşa, Istanbul, after 1784 and before 1800, engraving by Antoine-Ignace Melling, who arrived in Istanbul in 1784 and worked for Hatice Sultan, a sister of Selim III (r. 1789–1807). This engraving forms part of a sequence illustrating the shores of the Sea of Marmara, Istanbul proper and the Bosphorus villages that were then turning into places where wealthy residents spent their summers.

Source: *Voyage pittoresque de Constantinople et des rives du Bosphore, d'après les desseins de M. Melling* (reprint Istanbul: Yapı ve Kredi Bankası, 1969): no page numbers. By kind permission of the publishing division of the Yapı ve Kredi Bankası.

Nor were Christian galley slaves normally released when their ship fell into the hands of the Muslims.

To date virtually no memoirs of Ottoman ex-galley slaves have been found, so that we know very little about the way in which these men experienced their captivity. However, the Roman archives do preserve evidence of the acts through which certain slaves serving on the papal galleys attempted to obtain liberation. One way was to flee the port towns where the ships were anchored, and make one's way to Rome as, at least at certain times during the sixteenth century, slaves who reached the Capitol and demanded their freedom were recognized as freedmen. Even after the right to automatic manumission had been abolished, slaves continued to arrive because, if they could provide proof of baptism, they were still able to obtain their freedom.[33] Others attempted to flee to Muslim territory, on a boat that they had found or 'liberated'; unfortunately we only know something about those attempts that miscarried, and often those fugitives who had the misfortune to be recaptured were severely punished.[34] Of course, the successful ones were those who left no trace.

~ Charity and the tribulations of prisoners

In the second half of the sixteenth century, when food prices had greatly increased, captives employed on galleys generally received only the absolute minimum in terms of food.[35] Michael Heberer of the small Neckar town of Bretten, near Heidelberg in today's south-western Germany, who rowed on Ottoman galleys during the 1580s/987–98, described a remarkable scene in which the owner of a galley, a powerful *bey*, demanded that the captain (*re'is*) increase his beatings of the slaves in order to make them row harder.[36] The captain refused, replying that the slaves needed more food, not beatings. When the owner was unwilling to see reason, the captain resigned his post in protest, saying that the slaves were people just as he himself, and that he wanted to treat them as men and as not as animals. According to Heberer, the *bey* was livid, but did not dare to do anything, as both the soldiers and the passengers took the captain's side. Bad though conditions were on Ottoman galleys, they were often even worse on those of the Christian powers, where the bread was frequently inedible and possibly also the moral code which governed the treatment of 'infidel' captives was but weakly developed.[37]

Prisoners in the sultan's territories were thus dependent on charity and, as some of them ultimately made it back to their homelands and wrote about their experiences, we can learn something about Ottoman practices in this respect. The bits and pieces of information provided by returnees are, moreover, of particular interest. Normally, Ottoman sources tell us something about the activities and occasionally the intentions of elite men and women who instituted charities. For their part, foreign visitors such as Rauwolff were not slow to observe that Ottoman Muslims in general took the precepts of their religion seriously, and that in addition to assiduous praying, alms-giving was widely practised.[38] But in all these texts, written by privileged persons either Ottoman or foreign, very little has been said about the strategies and reactions of the recipients.[39] This makes the information relayed by former captives especially precious.[40]

Alms could be solicited from a variety of people. In the case of Christian slaves on Ottoman territory, European embassy personnel, travellers and pilgrims might provide such outside support, especially if they came from the same state or province as the captive. Or else class solidarities might come into play: Michael Heberer tells us that his status as an educated man elicited some sympathy from visitors who had received the same kind of training in Latin and Ancient Greek as he himself.[41] Presumably the fact that – Venice apart – there were so few free Ottomans travelling about western and southern Europe accounts for some of the extra hardship suffered by Ottoman captives in these lands. In addition, in the divided Europe of the Reformation and Counter-Reformation periods, the proper recipients of charity were apparently only the fellow believers of the donor. And if Protestants had little to expect from a devout Catholic and vice versa, the probability that a Muslim would elicit charity was even slimmer.[42]

In the Ottoman context, women were significant as alms givers. When describing his life as an oarsman on an Ottoman galley, Heberer tells us that a royal woman, returning from the hajj and escorted home by the galley belonging to his master, had the brutal owner of the ship upbraided and warned about the consequences of the evil deeds he had perpetrated against his slave rowers. More practically, she also made sure the men were treated, at her own expense, several times during the trip from Alexandria to the Ottoman capital. Bread, cooking oil and some meat were distributed among the unfortunate slaves in the name of the royal lady, whom Heberer did not identify but who, judging from the reception she was given upon disembarking, may well have been a princess.[43]

Less exalted female inhabitants of Istanbul also showed charity towards slaves. Heberer told a remarkable story about women in the company of servants to a powerful man, who were probably of servile status themselves, and who gave out alms when taken by their men-folk to see the galley slaves at work.[44] In another instance, when spending the winter season in the prisons of the sultan's arsenal, he went out to earn some money by doing a job in a private home; he recorded that the wife of the man for whom he worked not only fed him, but admonished her husband to do something for the poor servant as well.[45]

By contrast, Hans Wild (1585–after 1613/992–after 1022), a former Nuremberg soldier and a prisoner of war in Ottoman lands between 1604/1012–13 and 1611/1019–20, who as an Islamized slave had visited both Jerusalem and Mecca, records only charity received from men, above all from the last of his numerous masters. After his manumission in Cairo, Wild pretended to his former owner, a janissary commander, that he wanted to earn his living as a petty trader. If his later claims were true, in actual fact he was trying to make his way home. However, things went wrong almost from the start, and the ship on which he had embarked sank not too far from Cyprus. Wild was picked up by a passing Ottoman craft, where the merchant passengers supplied him with food and clothes, as he had nothing much on him apart from his manumission document. After having proven his freedom in the kadi's court of Limassol/Lemiso, the kadi himself gave him a substantial sum as alms. Wild continued on his way to Antalya, where he fell seriously ill. Penniless and with a high fever, he was kept in food by charitable local Muslims, until his vigorous constitution gained the upper hand. Thus the merchants on the ship, the kadi and the unnamed Muslims of Antalya all were generous towards a poor stranger, whose foreign background must, moreover, have been obvious from his accent.[46]

Heberer and Wild were not the only captives to write about charity dispensed by Ottoman subjects. Claudio Angelo de Martelli's memoirs especially highlight the miseries of a captive in the dungeons of diverse Ottoman fortresses in Hungary and Serbia and, as we have seen, should probably be regarded as a piece of wartime propaganda. Thus it is all the more notable that the author has a good deal to say about the charity he received from inhabitants of the Ottoman Empire. Some of this aid came from fellow Catholics, particularly from the congregations with whom he sometimes attended church.[47] While in Belgrade, he received aid from 'Greeks' (Orthodox) and Catholics alike; aside from money, clean linen and other supplies, this included the conveyance of letters, which much helped the prisoner to keep up his interest in life. In addition to quite a few unnamed individuals, the author mentioned Bishop 'Mattheus Bernakovick' and the pater guardian of a Belgrade convent. Among laymen he was very apprecia-tive of the rich Dubrovnik merchant Francesco Calogero, who not only provided material aid but also psychological support.[48] Furthermore, in spite of war condi-tions, Muslim women sometimes also sent alms to prisoners of war, de Martelli mentioning the wife of the Belgrade fortress commander (*dizdar*), who secretly made a contribution.[49]

~ The 'extra-curricular' labours of galley – and other – slaves

When the galleys were laid up for the winter, some of the prisoners were employed in the naval arsenal as artisans; they might be engaged in shipbuilding itself, but also in the auxiliary crafts, such as blacksmith's work or the installa-tion of masts and sails. In sixteenth-century Algiers, Tunis or Tripolis, such specialists were always in great demand, and if a man was known to be versed in one of the crafts useful to the arsenal, it was notoriously difficult to exchange or ransom him.[50] But on the other hand, specialist skills might also be of help to a prisoner. The English soldier of fortune Edward Webbe, who has left a brief account of his adventures, including a number of years as a slave in the Istanbul arsenal during the 1580s/987–98, records how, as an expert gunner, he was ordered to help with the fireworks display which enlivened the princely circum-cision festivities of 1582/990–1. This enterprise earned him some money, and thereby a chance to alleviate the conditions of his captivity.[51]

The contributions of charitable men and women and what the arsenal – or, in the case of privately owned slaves, the relevant owners – doled out in the way of food, needed to be supplemented by work. Here everything depended upon cir-cumstances. In the Ottoman context, some private owners permitted their slaves to work on their own account and thus ransom themselves. This could take the shape of a binding promise, documented in the kadi's court, that the slave was to be freed after a certain period of service, or else after having performed a given amount of work: weaving a certain number cloths was a popular condition in sixteenth-century Bursa.[52] In other instances, what was earned by work might suffice only for some extra food. Once again, Michael Heberer's account is quite illuminating; he made occasional money by writing congratulatory poems for assorted European dignitaries visiting Istanbul.[53] In this age before copyright, the person so honoured, both in European and Ottoman societies, was expected to reciprocate with a gift. More modestly, Heberer learned from a fellow captive to shear sheepskins, which could be bought cheaply, spin the wool, and knit it into hosiery; this activity made it possible not only to buy better food, but also to give a share to the guards in exchange for more lenient treatment.[54] Last but not least, Heberer's trade as a stocking-seller helped him to establish those all-important contacts that ultimately led to his liberation. But, in addition, even this pious prisoner had no qualms about galley slaves' stealing food or small items that could be sold, whenever the opportunity presented itself.[55]

Conversely, hungry galley slaves of Muslim background were common enough in Christian kingdoms. In the seventeenth-century arsenal of Marseilles there were quite a few unfortunates of this kind. Some of them may have been caught by French captains during attempted raids on the northern Mediterranean shores, but most of them had been purchased from the Maltese, or else from other Christian freebooters active on the North African coast. The latter found a ready market for their captives in the French royal arsenal, and thus were officially encouraged to continue their raids. Living conditions in the Marseilles establishment showed certain features parallel to those observed in the Istanbul arsenal; knitting stockings was also practised as a sideline by galley slaves serving Louis XIV. However, the merchant capitalism characteristic of the seventeenth-century French economy meant that petty entrepreneurs of the kind described by Heberer – indeed, as he portrayed himself – were less widespread in Marseilles: many galley slaves worked for urban masters who thus profited from cheap coerced labour.[56] Moreover, the Sun King being little inclined to let go even those French captives who had served their terms, the likelihood of Muslim slaves being released was even lower.

~ Domestic service

Where Ottoman slaves were concerned, those who were brought to Habsburg territory often enough ended up in domestic service in a more or less well-to-do household; in the early eighteenth century, it was quite fashionable in these circles to have African or Middle Eastern servants. Even though domestic slavery was less dangerous to life and limb than rowing on the galleys, it might still result in hazardous situations. After all, even locally hired and legally free servants had few rights vis-à-vis their employers, and foreigners of slave status were in an even weaker position.[57] Being dependent upon the – possibly non-existent – goodwill of a master or mistress in itself must have been the source of much misery.

Many servants who had reached the Habsburg territories as prisoners of war entered the households in which they served when still quite young. Ultimately many of them were baptized, frequently with one or more local aristocrats acting as godparents. Such connections ensured that at least the ex-Ottoman women after their liberation might well find spouses of the 'middling sort', and in a few cases even among the petty nobility, and thus were not necessarily limited to the servant milieu.[58] But not all Ottoman prisoners, male or female, were willing to accept a permanent separation from their religion, family and home.[59] We have already encountered the young Ottoman officer Osman Ağa, who managed to flee from Vienna in 1699/1110–11 and return to his home province. He recounted that there were women in the group of fugitives he had put together, who risked the dangerous trip over a not yet clearly demarcated border in order to avoid living out their lives in the 'lands of the unbelievers'.[60]

In southern Italy many Muslim captives also wound up as domestic servants. For in this region where, in the sixteenth or seventeenth century, productive activities were not highly developed, what wealth existed was largely monopolized by a class of noblemen, for whom the size of their households constituted a source of social prestige. Once again, slaves were expected to become members of the Roman Catholic Church. And here as well, many, but by no means all, slaves consented when their owners demanded a change of religion, for baptism might well be a precondition for manumission. Moreover, as paid employment was not easy to come by, a freedman who left the household of his former master might secure a roof over his head if he joined a monastery or convent as a lay brother.[61]

Service by Ottoman prisoners at the court of a European ruler or member of a royal family formed a special case. At home in the Ottoman lands these young servitors had normally been commoners. There was, however, at least one case involving girls with connections to the palace milieu. In 1557/964–5, in a battle between Ottoman and Maltese galleys, two young women on their way to Mecca were taken captive and brought to France by a grand prior of the Maltese Knights, who had returned to France in order to take up a position in the French navy. The two girls were baptized, one of them being named Catherine after her presumed godmother Catherine de Medici, and ultimately married off. For over twenty-five years their mother, the Lady Huma in Istanbul, insisted on the return of her daughters; she had received a letter stating that the two girls had been converted by force. Although Huma Hatun was said to be a poor woman, she was able to win powerful champions, which at one time included female members of the Ottoman house and also the Vizier Sokollu Mehmed Paşa. As a result the matter became something of a diplomatic *cause célèbre*. We last hear of the case in 1581/988–9, when the return of the two, now fully grown women, was once again demanded by Murad III, though apparently not with a great deal of conviction. Unfortunately the thoughts and reactions of the two ex-Ottoman ladies to this extraordinary adventure remain altogether unknown.

A little more is known about service performed by slaves of European background in the households of certain great personages of the Ottoman realm and, above all, of the sultan himself. Several former pages have left accounts, among them a Spaniard who later returned home and gave a report of his life story to the Inquisition, to be taken with a grain of salt, as with all 'autobiographies' produced under duress.[62] Gutierre Pantoja entered the sultan's service aged sixteen or shortly afterwards, received the education of a page in the palace chambers, and was later affected to the sultan's suite whenever the latter left the Topkapı precinct, perhaps as a member of the corps of *bostancı* guardsmen. Among his fellow pages there were two ex-Portuguese, and when Pantoja, long since a Muslim, married upon the ruler's orders, his wife was of Russian or Ukrainian extraction; in brief the sultan's household was cosmopolitan, just as, incidentally, the establishment of the high official in Istanbul where de Martelli ultimately awaited his ransoming.

～ The role of local mediation in ransoming a Christian prisoner

In de Martelli's story, most of the aid received doubtless came from fellow Christians; apart from the Belgrade *dizdar*'s wife, the Muslims of whom he spoke with special gratitude mostly were recent converts to Islam, sometimes former prisoners from Habsburg territory. For such men were often enough nostalgic about home and pleased to speak their native language; in some cases, they might even dream of returning to their homelands. De Martelli thus told the story of a certain Abdullah, who was one of the eight formerly Christian servitors of the *kâhya,* the official in charge of the three young sons of the recently executed Grand Vizier Kara Mustafa Paşa. Abdullah, originally a Spaniard from the Canaries who had been sent to Istanbul by the *paşa* of Algiers, cooked up a madcap plan for his own and de Martelli's escape, which, however, was given up before realization had even begun.[63] Other recent converts to Islam cropped up in the course of the tale, among them Mehmed Ağa, treasurer (*hazinedar*) in the *kâhya*'s household, born a Polish nobleman. Mehmed Ağa held a position of trust and was well integrated into Ottoman society, which did not prevent him from supplying the captive with firewood, offering to contribute to his ransom and otherwise befriending him.[64] There was little evidence of the hostility that such people have sometimes been said to harbour against their former coreligionists.

Jews occurred much more rarely in de Martelli's account. But one such person, a certain Davidoğlı Rosales, did play a key role as a mediator negotiating the ransoming of the captive. He was not the only such go-between, as the Habsburg officer, even though he attempted to hide his rank, was soon known to the English and French ambassadors as a figure of some importance. Apparently the Jewish mediator had links to the English diplomat Mountagu (Montagu) North, who asked Rosales both to further de Martelli's release, and to help the latter control both his attacks of melancholy and his impatience. For, in the view of the European diplomats present in Pera, any attempt at escape on the part of the prisoner was likely to create more problems than it solved. The Jewish mediator also contacted the *kâhya* on behalf of de Martelli when it came to negotiating the concrete circumstances of the Habsburg officer's release. This activity was not without its risks, as the sale of de Martelli to a Turk who was a creditor of the executed former grand vizier encountered serious opposition in official quarters, in the course of which Rosales was even threatened with the galleys. In the end

the mediator was successful, but de Martelli never established a personal relationship of the kind he seems to have enjoyed with Mehmed Ağa or even
Abdullah. Thus we do not learn how Rosales was remunerated for his trouble,
what languages he used in these different negotiations, or how he himself saw his
difficult and sometimes dangerous profession. But it is quite clear that the process of ransoming absolutely necessitated the intervention of mediators who
were Ottoman subjects.

~ In conclusion

As these paragraphs have demonstrated, research concerning prisoners of war on
Ottoman territory, and on Ottoman captives abroad is still in its beginning stages:
this accounts for the 'patchiness' of the present chapter. Attempts have been
made to find out what happened to formerly Ottoman captives living out their
lives in central Europe through the study of church records, though in all likelihood, many of these documents are still unexplored.[65] Where prisoners of non-
Ottoman background in the Empire are concerned, a systematic collection of the
rather numerous references to such people in sixteenth- and seventeenth-century
European travel accounts also seems promising. Perhaps it will be possible to
follow the example of the historians of antiquity in scanning the published travel
accounts into a computer and then conducting electronic searches; these data can
then be collated with the growing body of studies of Ottoman slavery based on
Ottoman sources. But at present a major deficiency remains: even though the
study of captives taken in wars between European rulers and the Ottoman sultans
has for the most part been undertaken by Ottomanists, work on the different categories of primary sources has typically been carried out with little coordination
between the different specialists.

However, some preliminary results are important and should be retained. First
of all, the enslavement of prisoners was by no means an Ottoman peculiarity.
Quite to the contrary, until 1699/1110–11 this procedure was officially sanctioned by the Austrian side as well, and even though the numbers had
diminished, there were still enslaved Muslim captives in southern Italy in the
early 1800s. In the Marseilles arsenal there were quite a few Muslim slaves who
had been the victims of raiding by Christian freebooters. Yet this obvious fact did
not help them to obtain their freedom, except for the rare event of a special
agreement by the French kings with one or another of the North African rulers.
Not even a kingdom that normally maintained friendly relations with the Ottomans was willing to forgo Muslim galley slaves. Secondly, agreements to
exchange captives of officer status were common enough at least in the seventeenth century as far as Habsburg–Ottoman wars were concerned. It is thus clear
that such understandings were by no means limited to wars among Christian
potentates, as has often been assumed. In this respect at least, the Ottomans and
their opponents inhabited one and the same world.

Up to this point our concern has been mainly with what might be called political and military 'hard facts', and but rarely with peaceful exchanges of goods and people. Yet there were quite a few foreign merchants, both Muslim and non-Muslim, present on Ottoman soil. This could not have been possible without the toleration of the sultans and their advisors, and we must ask ourselves what advantages the servitors of the Ottoman state hoped to derive from foreign trade. What could these merchant sojourners offer that compensated for the frequent disruptions that their presence caused in the sultan's 'well-guarded domains'?

6 ~ Trade and foreigners

In the early modern world, war and its political results including conquest and subjection, together with trade and pilgrimage, can be identified as the three major modes in which the inhabitants of any principality or empire related to the world outside the frontiers of the relevant polity. In the previous chapters, we have discussed modes of conquest and subjection first, followed by the wars that had brought about these relationships. But while the model of the 'warfare state' (compare Chapter 1) did and perhaps does encourage scholars to think in terms of an Ottoman elite that was unconcerned about trade, research during the last thirty years or so has shown that this is not a realistic notion.[1] To the contrary, customs duties formed a substantial share of state income, and the Ottoman governing apparatus was quite aware of this basic fact. In addition, trade generated rental income from khans and covered markets, and thus contributed to the functioning of the pious foundations that made the reputations of so many members of the Ottoman elite. All these considerations meant that some high-level personages within the governing apparatus were induced to engage in trade themselves. But even those who did not, were in one way or another concerned with the maximization of revenues generated by commerce.[2]

In the present chapter there will be more information on foreign merchants who came to the Empire to do business, than on Ottoman subjects who went abroad for reasons of trade. The reason for this choice is fairly trivial. While there is by now a significant body of research on the activities of foreign merchants in the Empire, 'Ottomans abroad', as we have seen, have generated a much more limited secondary literature.[3] Moreover, to date there is not very much evidence available on the attitudes of the Ottoman elite towards those among their subjects who left the Empire in order to market their goods. However, limited evidence does not mean that there was total indifference: at least in the late 1500s and early 1600s, sultans and viziers went out of their way to protect their Anatolian or Bosnian subjects who had been robbed by Uskoks and other pirates while on their way to Venice.[4] We will have to wait for more research on specific groups at particular points in time before we can draw a comprehensive picture of the Ottoman elite's attitudes on this important issue. But in the meantime it is appropriate to balance our long discussion of war, conquest and modes of political integration by a closer look at the trade nexus.

~ Merchants from remote countries: the Asian world

Whether from Muslim countries or from the 'lands of war', it must have been mainly for reasons of trade that the subjects of foreign rulers appeared on Ottoman soil in person. Indian merchants reached Aleppo through Basra, as in one relatively well-documented case concerning the early seventeenth century.[5] Muslim traders from the coasts of western India equally did business in the Hijaz, after having crossed the ocean in enormous ships which astonished the inhabitants of the timber-starved Red Sea coasts.[6] One of the principal reasons for these commercial links was the importation of Indian cotton prints and painted cotton fabrics into the territories governed by the sultans. After all, these textiles were coveted as much by Ottoman customers of the seventeenth and eighteenth centuries as they were by contemporary western Europeans. As Indian cottons were often distributed through Egypt, the Ottoman market was frequently known to Indian textile producers as Arabian. But customers were also found among the better-off inhabitants of the Turkish-speaking provinces, and numerous terms for different types of cottons entered the Ottoman-Turkish language as loan-words.[7]

Egyptian distributors of Indian goods did not often venture south of Jiddah, and thus a significant number of Indians must have spent some time on Ottoman territory.[8] In 1564–5/971–3, a letter from Süleyman the Magnificent to Don Sebastian, king of Portugal, explained that the latter's recently expressed desire for peaceful relations was incompatible with Portuguese attacks on pilgrims and merchants. King Sebastian would have to make up his mind whether he desired peace or war, 'and what else is there to say'.[9] Some of these Indian traders did business in the Yemen, at that time recently reconquered by the Ottomans; a command to the governor of Sana'a forbade these merchants to acquire arms and items made of silver.[10] However, while something is known about the commercial organization of Indians on Russian territory, particularly in Moscow and Astrakhan, their counterparts in the Ottoman lands are very poorly documented, and these people's commercial organization continues to escape us.[11]

Iranian merchants were in a special position, and often enough in a peculiarly uncomfortable one. Among Indian visitors to the Ottoman lands, Shi'ites probably were not absent, but since there was no major conflict between Indian rulers and the Ottoman sultans, and a fortiori none involving religion, the convictions of these businessmen were of no concern of the authorities in Istanbul. Matters were different in the case of Iran. In the fifteenth century, traders from Azerbaijan and other Iranian provinces had frequented Bursa. But then the war between Selim I and Ismā'īl I (1514/919–20) induced the Ottoman ruler to prohibit the importation of Iranian silk, confiscate those silks already on his territory and even imprison importing merchants.[12] For a number of years, Iranian traders must have all but disappeared from the Ottoman scene. Moreover, even though Sultan Süleyman, shortly after ascending the throne in 1520/926–7, once again permitted trade with Iran, Muslim Iranians seem to have found the Bursa trade increasingly problematic.

In the course of the sixteenth century, the place of the Muslim merchants was taken over by an expanding network of Armenian traders who, in the long run, came to dominate the importation of Iranian silk into Ottoman territories.[13] Quite possibly this was due not only to the policy of Shah 'Abbās and his successors, who entrusted the Armenians with this enterprise, but also to Ottoman preferences. After all, non-Muslims could not be suspected of being sheiks of the Safavid order in disguise, a persistent worry of sixteenth-century Ottoman officials.

Even so, however, the formation of the Armenian trading network was beset by many vicissitudes. In the second half of the sixteenth century, Armenians from the town of Djulfa on the Aras seem to have prospered in spite of recurrent Ottoman–Iranian wars, to witness the elaborate gravestones in the Djulfa cemetery, some of which survive until the present day. This was due to the fact that the local merchants, with access to Iranian raw silk, were able to plug themselves into the international silk trade, in which European purchasers were gaining in importance. In the early seventeenth century, when Shah 'Abbās succeeded in regaining the town of Nakhčhewān from the Ottomans, he had it destroyed because in his perspective, the resident elite had traitorously supported his major enemy. Furthermore, in order to prevent the rapid reconstruction of Nakhčhewān, he also deported the local traders' commercial partners, namely the Armenians of Djulfa, to a far-away site in the vicinity of Iṣfahān.[14] There the latter constructed the famous merchant diaspora which handled Iranian silk exports throughout the seventeenth century, as well as English and Indian goods.[15]

Armenian merchants formed part of a major commercial diaspora, which on the one hand linked the residents of New Djulfa near Iṣfahān to India and even Tibet, and on the other hand, to Izmir, Aleppo, Amsterdam and, at least temporarily, Marseilles. Another group of Armenians did business with Lvov (Lwiw), today a city in the Ukraine but which in the early modern period formed part of the commonwealth of Poland-Lithuania. All this activity must have resulted in more or less extended residences of Armenians based in New Djulfa in the major Ottoman centres of commerce.[16] Moreover, some of their counterparts domiciled in Amsterdam also traded with the Empire and thus visited Ottoman ports, especially Izmir.[17]

Most of the principal merchants of the Armenian diaspora lived permanently in Iran, and merely sent their junior partners, often younger relatives, on commercial trips. But there existed colonies of resident Armenian merchants in Ottoman cities as well. Thus from the eighteenth century onwards Roman Catholic Armenian immigrants from Iran were established in Izmir, where some of the wealthier members of the group soon came to intermarry with French merchants.[18] However, in the absence of the relevant records, it is not easy to determine when these immigrants from Armenia came to be regarded as subjects of the Ottoman sultan.

Although the Armenians are relatively well documented and currently constitute a focus of scholarly interest, Muslim Iranians should not be ignored either.

At least in Baghdad, Basra and Aleppo, Muslim traders occasionally found their way into Ottoman documents. Thus in 1610/1018–19, a caravan arrived in Aleppo with several very rich traders from Hamadān, who carried mainly indigo, perfume bottles, drugs and fabrics from Lahore.[19] By 'fabrics' the Aleppine scribe possibly meant not cottons, the most widespread Indian textile, but the famed shawls produced in the latter city.[20] Presumably commercial links to the north-western section of the Indo-Pakistani subcontinent were forged by traders from Multān, who regularly traversed the Hindukush to trade in Iran. Unfortunately our knowledge of the trade links between Indian merchants domiciled in Iran and their Iranian counterparts is as yet very limited.[21]

Even more enigmatic is the trade with Russia; the Ottoman side largely imported luxuries such as furs.[22] But the concept of luxury is relative, and the Ottoman administration passed out so many robes of honour, lined with exotic furs if intended for high-ranking personages, that the total demand for Russian furs must have been significant. If the examples still existing in the Kremlin collections are any indication, on the Russian side there was a substantial demand for rich horse-furnishings. Ottoman sultans occasionally sent out court merchants to purchase different types of fur.[23] But whether these people also carried all the luxury goods demanded in Moscow remains an open question.[24] It is quite possible that Tatars from Kazan or Astrakhan were also active in this commerce, to say nothing of the Armenian merchants who by the second half of the seventeenth century were exploring the possibilities of the Russian transit routes for Iranian silk.[25]

~ Merchants from a (not so) remote Christian country: the Venetians

Among merchants from Christian countries, in the late sixteenth and even in the early seventeenth century, the Venetians still retained a prominent position. The Venetian presence had originated in the division of the Byzantine Empire during the fourth crusade of 1204/600–1, which had netted Venice a number of islands and territories on the Aegean coasts. However, since these were mostly conquered by the sultans well before 1540/946–7, they will not concern us here. More importantly Cyprus, with its rich production of cotton and sugar, in 1489/894–5 had become a possession of Venice.[26] This island, the site of Shakespeare's Othello, remained under the Signoria's control until the Ottoman conquest of 1570–3/977–81. Moreover, until the mid-seventeenth century the island of Crete was still a Venetian possession; it too was finally conquered, by the Grand Vizier Köprülü-zade Fazıl Ahmed Paşa, on behalf of Sultan Mehmed IV (r. 1644–69/1053–80).[27] But even after the final loss of all Venetian possessions in the Aegean region (1718/1130–1) certain Ionian islands and sections of the Dalmatian coast remained in the Signoria's hands, so that Venice remained a neighbour of the Ottoman Empire until the very end of the ancient republic in 1797/1211–12.

In spite of rather numerous wars, Ottoman relations with this city were closer than with any other state of Christendom. Wealthy subjects of the sultans continued to purchase Venetian fabrics and glassware well into the seventeenth century, to say nothing of the cheeses that were highly esteemed by certain sixteenth-century Ottoman dignitaries.[28] Ottoman non-Muslims acquired books printed in Greek, in which Venice had already come to specialize by the sixteenth century.[29] In return, cotton was bought by the Signoria's subjects in Syria or Cyprus for sale in central Europe, where it was used for the manufacture of the fustian skirts worn by local peasant women. Venetian entrepreneurs of the seventeenth century also contributed, albeit indirectly, to the growth of the silk trade in Ottoman marts. In this period silk-reeling by water power spread in central Italy with towns on Venetian territory becoming a centre of the industry. While the mechanically reeled silk thread thus manufactured was made from Italian and not from imported raw material, due to its solidity it was considered desirable for the warp of silks woven in other European countries. Entrepreneurs in these latter localities employed the less durable Iranian silk for the weft, thus increasing demand for raw silk from the Middle East.[30] However, English and French merchants profited from this trade much more than their Venetian rivals.[31]

For a brief period before and after 1600/1008–9, certain Venetian traders also entered the none too broad and highly competitive market supplying woollen cloth to Ottoman customers. After about 1550/956–7 the severe, though temporary, crisis of the Venetian spice trade that occurred after Portuguese ships had gained access to India in the early 1500s encouraged local investors to put their money into craft production. For a short century Venice developed a significant woollen industry.[32] Venetian manufacturers concentrated on better-quality fabrics, which found favour among well-to-do Ottoman purchasers. But prosperity in this sector was of short duration. With high costs of living and numerous imposts resulting in relatively high prices, the industry was vulnerable to competition from Italian towns with easy access to Spanish wool, but also from English and Dutch importers. A further source of trouble was a decreasing demand on the part of Ottoman customers, whose purchasing power was seriously diminished by the provincial rebellions and financial crisis of the calamitous years around 1600/1008–9. But in spite of this crisis and the dangers often encountered en route, Ottoman–Venetian trade still gave rise to a considerable amount of travel between the two states, even during those years when Ottomans and Habsburgs were at war, and both Venetian and Ottoman markets in turmoil.[33]

During periods of war Venetian merchants were hampered in their business activities, having to use the certainly not disinterested services of trading partners from France, England, or even the Habsburg Empire.[34] This war-related disadvantage explains why the 'Doge and Lords of Venice', as they were called in Ottoman diplomatic parlance, attempted to end wars with the sultans within a few years, as long as the city's merchants still played an important role in the commerce of the eastern Mediterranean.[35] Only after the middle of the seventeenth century, when Venice's international trade was in full decline, do we encounter wars that dragged on over decades.

In peacetime, Venetian traders benefited from a widespread network of consuls, who often passed on complaints from individual traders to the *bailo* in Istanbul, who in turn applied, often successfully, to the Ottoman authorities. Thus a merchant who claimed to have been overcharged by the officials overseeing the unloading of his bales in Izmir could obtain redress from the Ottoman centre.[36] Something similar applied when merchants in Aleppo, who had spent considerable sums of money on the storerooms they rented in the khans of the city, were threatened with eviction by local foundation administrators hoping to derive higher rentals from a now much improved building.[37] Diplomatic channels might be of help in even more serious troubles: in the early seventeenth century, the previous prohibition to export cotton and raw wool had been rescinded, but certain provincial officials claimed to know nothing about this change of policy and forbade the Venetian traders to take out their wares. Once again a sultanic command was issued upon diplomatic mediation, expressly permitting the new trade.[38] Nor was it only in commercial matters that Venetians who got into trouble on Ottoman territory could count on the support of their *bailo*: when, sometime before 1028/1618–19, two men visiting the island of Bozcaada (Tenedos) had been accused of spying, the *bailo* was able to secure a sultanic command that the two men should be turned over to the Venetian consul in Gelibolu who in turn was assured of a hearing by the highest authorities.[39] Thus the quality of their diplomatic and consular representatives gave the Venetian traders advantages 'on the ground' even at a time when Venice's role in international trade had definitely passed its peak.[40]

~ Polish traders and gentlemanly visitors

In the sixteenth century, after Hungary had become an Ottoman province, competition between the Habsburgs and the sultans focused, among other things, on the Polish crown. After the extinction of the Jagiello dynasty in 1572/979–80, Poland became an elective monarchy. Immediately Sultan Selim II (r. 1566–74/ 973–82) made it clear that he would not tolerate a prince from any of the neighbouring territories on the Polish throne, and his threats of war applied particularly to any Habsburg candidate. As a result the crown was offered to a French prince, whom the sultan was willing to accept if no member of the local nobility could obtain sufficient support.[41] This episode demonstrates that the Ottoman sultans of the late sixteenth and early seventeenth centuries played a significant role in the formulation of the policies of the Polish-Lithuanian commonwealth. This fact is relevant here because commercial relations cannot be treated without reference to the political setting, especially when luxury items were of major significance, as is true in the present case.

Ottoman arms, as well as silk, velvet and mohair fabrics were very popular at the Polish court, and also among the male members of the Polish gentry.[42] After all, the so-called Sarmatian costume, by which this group during the seventeenth century defined its identity, was, certainly, an 'invented tradition'. But the inspiration came from Ottoman artefacts, quite abundant in Polish collections down to the present day.[43] Certain high-level commanders of the Polish-Lithuanian commonwealth carried the glorified version of an Ottoman war mace (*bozdoğan*) as a sign of their dignity and office. The seventeenth-century portraits of Polish gentlemen, often painted for use at funeral ceremonies, show them wearing garments in a style reminiscent of Ottoman kaftans.[44] The fabric designs favoured also are often visibly Ottoman in inspiration, sometimes originals imported from Istanbul or Anatolia. Others were local imitations, for the popularity of these textiles encouraged certain noblemen to sponsor workshops producing similar designs. Apart from silks, Ankara mohair fabrics were well liked; at the end of the sixteenth century, the kadi registers of this town mention traders exporting these items to Poland.[45] Possibly there was also some export of raw mohair and mohair yarn; a sultanic command of 1055/1645–6 mentions the delivery of such items to the ports of Sinop and Samsun, from where they were surely often carried to Poland.[46]

Some of the originals doubtless were not brought to Cracow and other places by professional merchants, but constituted the product of 'shopping trips' by the numerous young gentlemen for whom a visit to Istanbul formed part of their introduction to the world at large. The Polish embassies visiting Istanbul were numerous, and 'magnificence', as understood at the time, involved a numerous retinue. Moreover, for gentry families of moderate means, it was probably cheaper to send their sons travelling in the suite of an ambassador, than to pay for the conventional 'cavaliers' tour'. A grand vizier once joked that the retinue of a certain Polish ambassador was too small for the conquest of Istanbul, but too large for any other purpose.[47] Sometimes the king of Poland himself placed orders for textiles with gentlemen visiting the Empire: thus in 1553/960–1 Sigismund August asked the castellan Wawrzyniec Spytek Jordan to bring back no less than 132 textile items.[48] In fact quite a few gentlemanly visitors, in spite of a proclaimed aversion to commerce, made hefty profits from the goods they brought back: in 1742/1154–5 the envoy Paweł Benoe carried with him fifty carts full of goods. Those with no capital to invest at least sold the kaftans they had received at the Ottoman court, which, given the fashion for 'Sarmatian' attire, fetched good prices in Poland.[49]

But in addition, 'regular' merchants supplied their Polish customers. In the sixteenth century, Ottoman Muslims, Jews and others were involved in this trade, while after 1600/1008–9 Armenians gained the upper hand. A whole branch of the Armenian trade diaspora was, as we have seen, established in the then Polish city of Lvov. These traders could manage up to two return trips to Istanbul in one year, either travelling all the way by cart, traversing Moldavia and Walachia, or by entrusting themselves and their goods to boats that they hoped would weather the notorious storms of the Black Sea.[50] Those who planned to visit Anatolia or Aleppo might avoid the costs of a stay in Istanbul by transiting through the Black Sea ports of Trabzon, Samsun or Sinop. But the considerable funds that such merchants carried might make them vulnerable targets: thus in 984/1576–7, the Ottoman authorities struggled to clear up a case of robbery and murder whose victims were two Polish merchants carrying gold coins and woollens to Aleppo. Apparently the richness of these goods had struck the brother of the customs offi-cial in the port of Sinop, who seems to have found himself partners in crime among some merchants and truant *medrese* students. It would be good to know where the stolen woollens, which were retrieved at least in part, had been manu-factured, but our texts are of no help in this matter.[51] A certain number of the merchants importing textiles into Poland were domiciled in the Ottoman Black Sea port of Kefe/Kaffa/Feodosia. Judging from the names, some of them were Slavs, while others seem to have been German-speaking; we do not know whether these men had started out as subjects of the king of Poland, but it is possible.[52]

~ Merchants from the lands of a (doubtful) ally: France

Ottoman sultans of the sixteenth and seventeenth centuries were interested in friendly relations with rulers perceived as actual or potential allies in the struggle against the Habsburgs.[53] Capitulations granting privileges to foreign merchants were typically issued in this context. In a sense, this was applicable even to Ven-ice, whose government in this period felt particularly threatened by the Spanish presence in Naples and Milan, and thus was interested in a *modus vivendi* with the Ottoman Empire.[54] But the first Christian partner of the Ottomans in western Europe was King François I of France, whose alliance with Süleyman the Mag-nificent included provisions for the safety of French merchants on Ottoman territory.[55] Several times in the seventeenth century, the 'understanding' between the French and Ottoman rulers showed signs of considerable strain.[56] Yet conflict was contained, and in the period under discussion here, there never was any war between the Ottoman Empire and France.

However, in the sixteenth century, and even during the first half of the seven-teenth, there were not many French merchants who actually availed themselves of the opportunities provided by the Franco-Ottoman 'special relationship'. At first the so-called wars of religion and the civil war following the extinction of the royal house of Valois ruined the trade of Lyons, at that time the commercial centre of France. As a result the Italian bankers who had financed Lyons' eco-nomic activities either returned home or else sought assimilation into the French aristocracy.[57] Once Henri IV of the Bourbon dynasty had gained recognition as king of France, there was a brief period of commercial revival, reflected in a renewal of the capitulations (1604/1012–13). But the murder of this ruler in

1610/1018–19 inaugurated another period of civil wars, which only came to an end with the defeat of the provincial anti-tax rebellions and uprisings of the court nobility, known as the Fronde, in 1652/1062–3.

Yet even during this period, the 'special relationship' with the Ottoman sultans, established through the capitulations, was of considerable value to the budding French diplomacy of the time. For, while the Venetian capitulations were much older, they had lapsed during the period of tension and war which preceded and followed the Ottoman conquest of Cyprus. In consequence, for a while all European merchants wishing to trade in the Empire had to do so under the French flag. This explains why Valois and Bourbon diplomacy did not at all appreciate English and Dutch attempts to secure capitulations of their own.[58]

Domestic political troubles apart, there were also economic reasons for the relative lack of activity on the part of French traders. The seventeenth century was a period of economic difficulties in France, as it was in many other parts of Europe. Thus even after 1662/1072–3, when Louis XIV's chief minister Colbert reorganized French international trade so as to prepare future successful competition with the Dutch, the results were not immediately visible.[59] Only in the eighteenth century, with economic conjunctures once again favourable to expansion, did French traders reach the most prominent position among European businessmen active in the Ottoman Empire – and this was largely due to the voluntary withdrawal of their English competitors.[60]

In a more positive vein, Colbert's protectionist measures had made possible the emergence of a manufacture of woollen textiles in and around the Languedoc town of Carcassonne, whose products in the eighteenth century captured those Ottoman customers who could afford medium or good quality imported woollens.[61] Languedoc producers used the services of merchants established in Marseilles for the distribution of their goods. Traders of this Provençal port city in turn were protected from competition within France by a 20 per cent surtax payable on all goods imported into the kingdom from the Levant, and which had not passed through Marseilles.[62] Quality standards in woollen textiles were strictly enforced by numerous inspections. However, detailed regulation by privileges, controls and monopolies may well have left the industry vulnerable when, at the end of the eighteenth century, war in the Mediterranean and internal crisis in the Ottoman Empire left the producers of Carcassonne 'high and dry' without a market. In the absence of commercial links to any place but Marseilles, local entrepreneurs were not able to find alternative markets for their product, and Carcassonne was obliged to 'de-industrialize'.[63]

Merchandise apart, a source of 'invisible' earnings to southern French shipowners came from the use of their boats by Ottoman merchants, the so-called *caravane*. Due to the robberies of Maltese freebooters, which the sultan's navy was not able to eliminate, many Muslim merchants preferred to freight their goods on ships owned by non-Ottoman Christian shippers.[64] In the seventeenth-century provinces of Algiers, Tunis and Tripolis, moreover, a delicate balance was maintained between the interests of the local janissary garrisons and those of the privateers, who formed the Ottoman equivalent of the Maltese. Owners of merchant shipping, with their interests often diverging from those of the corsairs, would have been very difficult to accommodate in the local councils that possessed a major say in the politics of Algiers, Tunis and Tripolis. This was another reason why the traders of these provinces did not establish their own merchant marines, but relied on the services of foreign shippers, many of them French. A similar choice was made by those pilgrims to Mecca who did not traverse North Africa, but used the sea route as far as Egypt.[65] The Provençals who specialized in this business were usually small-time operators, who relied on the speed of their craft. Furthermore, the – for the most part – reasonably good relations of the French king with the governments of Tunis, Algiers and Tripolis were also helpful. However, by the eighteenth century, French *caravaniers* were to encounter serious competitors in the shape of Greek ship-owners, as yet still subjects of the Ottoman sultan.[66]

Compared to the Venetians or the Dutch, French merchants were hampered by the fact that representatives of commerce, on whatever level, had no immediate access to the holders of political power. Ambassadors were noblemen with no direct links to trade, although as we will see, this situation did not prevent some of them from holding strong opinions on commercial matters.[67] Consuls normally purchased their offices, and similarly to other tax farmers were concerned first and foremost with an adequate return on their investments. Nevertheless, the consuls had authority over the merchants, and could even forcibly repatriate those whom they considered recalcitrant.

Traders, if supplied with the necessary capital and official French residence permits, together formed the *nation*. This body held regular assemblies, and in the absence of consul or vice-consul, selected one of its members to act as a representative vis-à-vis both French and Ottoman authorities. Divergent political and economic interests of ambassador, consuls and merchants resulted in numerous conflicts, fought out acrimoniously and sometimes by involving the Ottoman authorities. A famous example was the story of the debts run up by the French ambassador the comte de Césy in the early seventeenth century, who supposedly had spent the money borrowed in order to procure advantages to French traders.[68] However, the latter refused to regard the issue in this light, and the dispute dragged on through the years.

In the 1720s/1132–42 and 1730s/1142–52 the Marseilles traders had to cope with the *dirigiste* ambitions of de Villeneuve, at this time the French ambassador in Istanbul. The latter believed that the price of French woollens, which had been on the decline for a while, could be sustained by having the importing merchants act in concert in order to limit the amount of textiles offered at any one time. Members of the relevant *nation* were to be bound to such a policy by a decision on the part of the entire group. Similar 'obligatory agreements' were to drive down the prices of those goods exported from the Ottoman Empire by traders subject to the king of France. De Villeneuve even conceived the plan of instituting binding agreements between the French merchants of different ports (*échelles*). But, even though Marseilles merchants by the eighteenth century enjoyed a strong position on the Ottoman market, they by no means possessed a monopoly. In consequence, both the principals in France and their agents on Ottoman soil were worried about the opportunities which de Villeneuve's decisions would provide to their European competitors. Enforcement was therefore erratic at best.[69]

In the second half of the eighteenth century, the *dirigisme* that de Villeneuve still had pursued without any doubts concerning its economic wisdom, came under increasing attack in French government circles.[70] One of the disputed issues was the monopoly of the Marseilles trading houses in French Levant commerce. Political expediency came to the aid of ideology. For, during the numerous wars fought out in this period, France and England were usually on opposite sides and – apart from the struggle over the independence of England's North American colonies – France was not spectacularly successful. As a result, French ships, under constant attack by privateers in the service of the English king, were quite unable to circulate normally in the Mediterranean.[71]

In order to salvage the business of French merchants established in the Levant under these adverse circumstances, Louis XV temporarily suspended the surtax of 20 per cent that secured the Marseilles monopoly. This involved a significant advantage for customers of imported raw materials such as the mohair manufacturers of Amiens. Even in peacetime, these people could purchase angora wool far more cheaply from Dutch importers, for the latter did not pay for expensive overland transportation through France in addition to internal customs duties. Amiens entrepreneurs thus attempted to prolong their wartime exemptions for as long as possible, claiming that the angora wool purchased from the Dutch was of higher quality. When the Marseillais attempted to refute this claim, a veritable war of pamphlets was the result. But it seems that both sides discussed the issue mainly as a kind of test case. In itself the importation of angora wool was not a major branch of trade, but if the Marseilles monopoly fell in this instance, there was no reason why it should continue in other trades.[72] However, in the end, the monopoly survived until the French Revolution, when it was abolished along with most other privileges of the Ancien Régime.

More than other European merchant colonies in foreign countries, Frenchmen were subjected to the interference of the government in the most minute details of their daily lives. Moreover, at least in some *échelles*, this interference was accepted as a fact of life and often actively solicited. Thus the submissive letters to the embassy in Istanbul, written by French merchants installed in Ankara during the second half of the eighteenth century, at times make it hard to believe that revolution was only a few decades away.[73] A recent study has demonstrated that once again, the gap between an extremely *dirigiste* policy and real life could be enormous.[74] Officially it was assumed that Frenchmen would come to the Levant without their families, refrain from marrying local Christian women and return to France within the span of a few years. Yet in reality, from the eighteenth century onwards certain families were installed in the Levant over generations, marriages to Catholic women of Greek or Armenian background were common and some people registered as Frenchmen had in fact ceased to speak French. Ambassadors and consuls were quite aware of this situation, yet it was normally tolerated; the French authorities were not alone in assuming that a numerous circle of more or less influential protégés was useful for the prestige of embassy and consulates, and by extension, for that of the king of France.[75]

~ Subjects of His/Her Majesty, the king/queen of England

English traders occasionally had appeared in the fifteenth-century Mediterranean, selling the woollen cloth that had begun to form the country's major export item. A hundred years later, after a brief interruption during the Veneto-Ottoman tensions of 1566–73/973–81, English merchants re-entered the Mediterranean in force, now with the intention of displacing the Venetian carrying trade by any means at their disposal, not excluding piratical attacks.[76] During the last decades of the sixteenth century, when the conflict with the Spanish crown had reached its height, Queen Elizabeth I consented to dispatch her first ambassadors to Istanbul; their salaries, however, were defrayed by the newly formed Levant Company.[77]

The latter's major source of profit was the trade in Iranian silk, brought to Aleppo and later Izmir by the Armenian merchants of New Djulfa.[78] English traders distributed this valuable raw material throughout northern Europe, although the nascent silk manufactures of London's Spitalfields district also absorbed a certain quantity. 'Public opinion' in contemporary England regarded the exportation of gold and silver as one of the more serious faults of the Levant trade. After all, these metals were considered the 'sinews of war' and thus the bases of state power. As we shall see later on, this was the one point that contemporary Ottoman and European concepts of trade had in common. In its defence, the Levant Company explained that much more bullion entered the country in consequence of silk re-sales in Europe than had ever left it in order to finance the original purchases. Yet, to use a latter-day expression, English merchants trading with the Levant were under considerable pressure to earn foreign currency demonstrably.[79]

One way of limiting currency exports was to sell English woollens in the Ottoman Empire; as the profits from the silk trade were high, woollens could be sold at relatively low prices without jeopardizing the profitability of the whole enterprise. This influx of English woollens gravely impaired the manufacture of woollen cloth in Salonica, practised by Ottoman Jews.[80] English woollens and those manufactured in the Macedonian port town, to say nothing of those imported from Venice, were directed at the same rather narrow market: the fabrics in question generally were purchased by the better-off inhabitants of Aleppo, Izmir or Istanbul. Villagers and even the inhabitants of towns at a distance from the major importing centres continued to rely on local products.

Several different factors caused the Salonica manufacturers to be particularly vulnerable to English competition. Firstly, the Balkan raw wool to which they had access was not of the highest quality, while English wool was. This affected the finished product, and meant that discriminating customers with money to spend would be attracted by the imported item. Secondly, there was Venetian and later French competition for raw wool, which drove up prices even though the Jews of Salonica possessed the privilege of purchasing Balkan wool before any other traders.[81] Thirdly, the manufacturers of Salonica owed their protection on the part of the Ottoman authorities to their deliveries of woollen cloth to the janissary corps. These woollens were either paid for at relatively low prices or, especially in the seventeenth century, were demanded in lieu of taxes and thus not paid for at all. For a livelihood, manufacturers relied on sales in the open market, which became increasingly difficult to achieve as the century progressed. A fourth source of problems was the financial crisis of the Ottoman state in the years around 1600/1008–9. For, as the Venetians also found out to their cost, many servitors of the sultans were left with a reduced disposable income. Under these circumstances, the low prices offered by English merchants contributed to their success even more than they would otherwise have done.

Throughout the seventeenth century, English traders constituted the most visible European presence in the Ottoman Empire; in an outlying province such as Morea (Peloponnese), we even occasionally find Englishmen as farmers of Ottoman dues.[82] However, English firms withdrew from the Ottoman market after about 1700/1111–12. On the one hand, the supply of Iranian raw silk became increasingly aleatory and in the end, almost dwindled to nothingness, as the wars which preceded and then followed the end of the Safavid dynasty discouraged producers from engaging in this delicate and labour-intensive enterprise.[83] Moreover, in both Bengal and China, English merchants found silk that was both cheaper and more appropriate to the expanding industries of Europe. As a result, European demand for Iranian silk practically collapsed. This phenomenon has been described as a loosening of the ties that bound Ottoman producers of textile fibres to their European customers, and Ottoman manufacturers were accorded a 'period of grace' before the full onslaught of European manufactures began in the early nineteenth century.[84] For the time being, English traders found themselves without goods to import from the Levant; and the Aleppo houses whose principals populated the vicinity of London's Devonshire Square closed down one by one.[85] This fact in itself demonstrates that in the eighteenth century we should not as yet speak of the Ottoman lands as a major outlet for English manufactured goods.

~ Links to the capital of the seventeenth-century world economy: the Dutch case

Dutch merchants and shippers were latecomers to the eastern Mediterranean, putting in a first appearance during the closing years of the sixteenth century. For a long time, the lifeline of northern Netherlanders had been the Baltic trade, which permitted large-scale imports of grain and, as a result, a level of urbanization unusually high for the early modern period. Where Dutch commerce outside Europe was concerned, involvement with the spice trade of the Moluccas and Ceylon – or even, in the seventeenth century, the abortive attempt to gain a position in the Americas – maintained priority over exports to or imports from the Ottoman domains.[86]

On the Ottoman side, it seems that the Dutch were welcomed because of the long and successful struggle they waged against Spanish–Habsburg hegemony. It has been suggested that the pattern of the war in the Netherlands between 1568/975–6 and 1609/1017–18 was at least partly due to Ottoman initiatives: the timing of sultanic naval actions in the Mediterranean may well have taken the vicissitudes of the war in the Netherlands into account.[87] After all, the prospect of the Spanish fleet free to act against Ottoman North Africa can scarcely have appealed to policy makers in Istanbul. We may therefore assume that the ultimate survival of the Dutch Republic was due to the fact that the Spanish 'defence of Catholicism' had to be conducted on two fronts, not only in the rebellious northern provinces, but also in the Mediterranean theatre of war.

When, though, at the beginning of the seventeenth century, the Dutch did apply for separate capitulations, they were not especially concerned with Ottoman political support. As happened so often in early modern history, the needs of a developing textile industry seem to have been decisive. For 'woollens' were being manufactured with considerable success in the city of Leiden, and some of these found buyers in the Levant. However, a very considerable share of this production, known in Dutch as *greinen*, was not made out of wool at all but out of the hair of angora goats.[88] Raw mohair came exclusively from Ottoman territories, for the most part from the Ankara area and, to a much lesser extent, possibly from the region of Aleppo.[89] This Leiden manufacture of *greinen* continued to flourish throughout the seventeenth century, but declined after 1700/1111–12, and ceased to be economically significant by about 1730/1151–2.[90]

In all likelihood the needs of the Leiden industry, and not the rather more limited demand from French manufacturing centres such as Amiens, constituted the reason why, in the seventeenth century, Ankara mohair weavers found it difficult to obtain the raw material they required. In the mid-seventeenth century, a tax farmer in charge of collecting the dues payable from the presses that gave the finished mohair fabric its characteristic sheen, was persuaded to intervene on behalf of the manufacturers. As a result in 1645/1054–5 the exportation of mohair yarn and raw mohair outside the province of Ankara was prohibited by sultanic command.[91] This prohibition was not fully enforced, or the manufacture of *greinen* would have died an early death. But from eighteenth-century French sources we know that at least the higher qualities of mohair were in fact set aside for local weavers, and early nineteenth-century Ottoman documents show that local artisans at that time were not having any trouble supplying themselves.[92] Occasional sales of mohair occurred in Holland even in the second half of the eighteenth century, after the demise of the Leiden *greinen*. Probably re-export to France allowed a few Dutch merchants to continue their activities in Ankara even at this late date.

~ How Ottoman merchants coped with foreigners and foreign trade

As our next step, we will discuss the activities of Ottoman merchants, both Muslim and non-Muslim, in foreign trade. For a long time, historians had assumed that Ottoman Muslims avoided commerce, apart from the heavily state-controlled trades supplying Istanbul, which at times seemed almost a branch of the Ottoman central administration.[93] But during the last decades, several studies have proved these assumptions to be quite erroneous for any period before the nineteenth century. To mention but one example, the establishment of the Fondaco dei Turchi in Venice around 1600/1008–9 can only be explained by the presence of numerous Anatolians, inhabitants of Istanbul and Muslim Bosnians. Figures are hard to come by; but in times of peace, the Ottoman presence in Venice may well have amounted to several hundred people.[94]

Moreover, a recent monograph on a late sixteenth- and early seventeenth-century Muslim merchant of Cairo has demonstrated the far-flung network that such a man could establish: Ismā'īl Abū Taqiyyah traded in Indian spices, drugs and fabrics, while dealing with colleagues in Venice through his partners.[95] Cairo continued to be a favourite venue for merchants, perhaps because its status as a large provincial centre with its own special customs house made it possible for merchants to operate more independently of the central administration than was possible in Istanbul. Among the commercial links to foreign lands, particular attention should be paid to the Yemen, after 1632/1041–2 no longer part of the Empire. Trade with Yemen assumed a novel importance because of the growing Ottoman demand for coffee, occasional sultanic prohibitions of the 'pernicious novelty' notwithstanding.[96]

Of course, engaging in foreign trade did not necessarily mean that a wealthy merchant visited the world beyond the Ottoman borders in person. Just as his counterparts in early modern or even late medieval Europe, a major businessman normally sat in his office in Cairo or Damascus, and relied on his correspondents to procure the goods required. Cairene merchants of Ismā'īl Abū Taqiyyah's times still dealt directly with western India. After 1700/1111–12, however, they merely sent their agents to Jiddah to accompany the goods along the very last leg of the journey.[97] In this later period transportation to a Red Sea port normally was assured by merchants from the producing regions, that is Indians or Yemenis.

Furthermore, the slave trade was not an insignificant source of profit. By definition, this involved commercial activities traversing the Ottoman borders, since
no subject of the sultan could be legally enslaved. Slave merchants were officially supposed to be Muslims, although 'unofficial' Jewish traders were also
active. In the steppe regions north of the Black Sea, slave dealers might be
Tatars, while at least in the mid-eighteenth century, people from north-eastern
Anatolia seem to have handled the trade in Caucasian slaves. However, the latter
sustained the competition of Abaza and Circassian traders from beyond the Ottoman borders.[98] To pay for the slaves, it was not unknown for Ottoman traders to
sell arms to the Caucasian tribesmen.[99]

Muslim traders were active in the Black Sea even at the time our study ends,
in the late eighteenth century, and this activity continued well into the nineteenth.
This can be determined from the kadi records of Istanbul's commercial suburb of
Galata, where quite a few of these men lived and conducted their businesses.
Some of them were active in the Istanbul supply trade, bringing in sheep, cattle,
grain and oil; the capital invested was often considerable. But possibly due to the
strict official controls prevailing in this branch of business, merchants often did
not continue in it for long and quite a few traders turned their hand to investments promising higher profits, particularly the slave trade.[100]

As to Ottoman Jewish merchants, these seem to have been most successful in
the sixteenth and early seventeenth centuries, when most of them were still fairly
recent immigrants from Spain or Italy. Since these traders were far less prosperous once they had been fully acclimatized in the Ottoman environment, their
case conforms to a pattern observed throughout the world; often so-called commercial diasporas do best as long as there remains a significant difference
between their members and the host society.[101] At the same time, we have seen
that sixteenth-century Jewish traders were well established, not only on Ottoman
territories, but also in Venice and in other Italian towns such as Ancona. Or at
least, this was true until 1556/963–4, when the papal inquisition in this city
seized and executed a sizeable number of Marranos: Jews who had been forced
to accept baptism in Spain and who later had reverted to their previous religion.
This relative success of Jewish merchants in Mediterranean trade, after a long
eclipse due to the growing prosperity of the medieval Italian communes, was due
to the protection of the Ottoman sultan, whose subjects many of them had
become.[102]

Among the successful competitors of Ottoman Jews, we have already encountered the Armenians who predominated during the seventeenth century, while in
the eighteenth, Greeks, Albanians and Serbs gained prominence. In the Balkan
peninsula, a positive economic conjuncture came into being after the end of the
long series of Ottoman–Habsburg wars in 1718/1130–1, the war of 1737–9/
1149–52, which netted the Ottomans the return of Belgrade, being too short to
seriously disrupt trade. Carriers and muleteers, who marketed the products of
their mountain villages, now were able to found independent commercial firms.
Their representatives visited Vienna, where, as Orthodox subjects of a foreign

ruler and also because of their ties to the Habsburgs' own Serbian subjects, they were closely watched by a mistrustful government. Some of these Balkan merchants even frequented the fairs of Leipzig.[103]

Greek maritime carriers prospered especially during times of war, when their competitors, the Provençals, were unable to carry on their business. Some of them even obtained *lettres de marque* as corsairs in the service of the king of England, which enabled them to use force against their commercial competitors without incurring the opprobrium connected with downright piracy.[104] Older research has focused on those traders who based their activities on certain of the smaller Aegean islands, a convenient choice for nationalist historians because these localities were settled almost exclusively by Greeks. But through more recent research we know that shipping also flourished in more 'multinational' contexts, such as Crete during the later seventeenth and early eighteenth centuries.[105]

Political factors allowed Greek entrepreneurs to expand the radius of their trading: after the peace of Küçük Kaynarca in 1774/1187–8, the Russian Empire gained access to the Black Sea, and, as there were no local ship-owners with the requisite capital, Greek entrepreneurs were offered advantageous conditions.[106] Secondly, the wars accompanying the French Revolution and the Napoleonic campaigns greatly increased the demand for grain, while the French navy soon was unable to operate in the Mediterranean and ensure the safety of the Provençal *caravaniers*.[107] Admittedly these events only occurred after the fatidic year of 1774/1187–8, when our account ends. But if Greek ship-owners had not been important entrepreneurs even before that date, they would not have been in a position to take advantage of the new commercial opportunities offered by the presence of Russian, English and French navies in the years before and after 1800/1214–15.

Thus Greek ship-owners struggled against their French competitors, attempting to gain a foothold in fairly remote lands, at times even including Spain. This shows that it is too simple to assume that non-Muslim Ottomans prospered merely because they serviced the trade of better capitalized and politically privileged traders from western Europe. There is no denying that some merchants from the Ottoman religious minorities did specialize in the provision of such services. We only need to evoke the numerous agents for western merchants, the dragomans of consulates both real and fictitious and a host of others. But at the same time, many of these Ottoman merchants, of whatever religious denomination, were competitors as much as they were associates of French or English traders. Even when they worked in concert with foreigners, they often attempted to use their superior knowledge of local conditions to protect their markets from the interference of the newcomers.[108] Moreover, in the generally expansive atmosphere of the years between about 1720/1132–3 and 1760/1173–4, carriers could become independent traders, and did so. Thus we should view the relationship of non-Muslim Ottoman merchants to foreign traders as a complicated one, in which a single individual might play the role of both associate and competitor

according to circumstances. Even the tendency of some Syrian and later Armenian Christians to accept Roman Catholicism should not be viewed merely as a
readiness to give up their own identities in favour of that of 'stronger' foreigners.
For, at the same time, such cultural assimilation might permit access to educational and other networks, which often permitted such converts a competitive
edge over their rivals.[109]

~ Revisiting an old debate: 'established' and 'new' commercial actors

Ever since the first appearance of Fernand Braudel's book on the sixteenth-
century Mediterranean, now over fifty years ago, scholars have been debating the
decline of Venice and the advent of the 'new-style' trading nations, such as the
Dutch, English and French.[110] In the 1970s things looked nice and simple: small-
scale traders of the Middle East were assumed unable to withstand the competition of the chartered companies with their greater supplies of capital, storage
space and market information.[111] In the seventeenth century, ocean travel supposedly eclipsed land routes, and Ottoman traders were marginalized. Admittedly
Braudel himself, in his later years, was inclined to modify this view; thus he
regarded Ottoman control of the overland routes as an important factor in the
Empire's capacity to hold off integration into the European world economy until
about 1800/1214–15.[112] But for most scholars, this was a minor aspect. Only specialists in Ottoman history were intrigued by the fact that studies of local
economies kept turning up examples of active merchants able to compete with
the Levant and Oostindische companies long after they 'should have' disappeared from the scene.[113]

Things only began to change in the second half of the 1980s, partly because of
the new emphasis on local agency vis-à-vis empire-building European diplomats
and merchants, a tendency which has characterized historiography from that time
onwards. In consequence, historians have attempted to 'fit in' the emerging
information about Ottoman commercial successes around 1600/1008–9 with
what we know about the retreat of Venice from international trade at approximately the same time. In the process, researchers have stressed that the inter-
continental importation of spices, while certainly one of the major revenue
sources of the Mamluk sultans in the fifteenth century, in the late 1500s was less
essential to Cairene merchants than to their Venetian counterparts. This was
especially due to the trade in coffee and Indian fabrics, which formed a ready
substitute for the Egyptians but in which the Venetians had no share.[114]

Moreover, we have come to appreciate the fact that merchants firmly established in a given branch of trade may use to good advantage the fact that they are,
so to speak, on home ground. As a result such traders may long resist the
attempts of outsiders to dislodge them. In this struggle rather unexpected alliances and even symbioses may occur. A recent study has shown how much both

the Ottomans and the Venetians of the seventeenth century formed part of an *ancien régime* world, which only came to an end when 'outsiders', in this case largely Frenchmen, established themselves in the ports of Crete.[115] All this happened for the most part well after the Ottoman conquest of the island. The reader may come away with the impression that, as far as Crete was concerned, 'incorporation into the European world economy' occurred at some time during the early 1700s, that is, somewhat later than in Izmir but earlier than, for instance, in the coastlands of the Black Sea.

Such judgements are often connected to the assumption that the government of France was able to establish firm control over trade in the Mediterranean region, by directing the activities of French merchants almost as if they had been government officials.[116] Yet other studies have demonstrated that Frenchmen resident in the Levant, Louis XIV's, Colbert's and de Villeneuve's ambitions notwithstanding, were quite adept at ignoring the regulations sent to them from Paris or Marseilles. To assume that all these people were perfectly docile can lead to misjudgements, even though such docility did in fact occur. French consuls stationed in one or another of the *échelles du Levant* often had their own reasons for tolerating disobedience against official rules. After all, the traders in question also were members of the French *nation*, with whom the consul needed to establish a modus vivendi.

Certainly, even traders who did not always follow the wishes of their home governments, and were firmly ensconced in Izmir or Hanya, could very well incorporate the Aegean region or Crete into the European world economy. Yet it would be naive to assume that such a thing could be done from one day to the next, at a speed which became possible only in the twentieth century. In the 1600s or 1700s foreign merchants often had far less power than they liked to imagine and, in order to continue trading, they had to adapt to Ottoman rules and customs. On the other hand, their activities were facilitated by the fact that the prices they offered were often better than what producers and traders subject to the sultans could hope to make if they sold their goods to Istanbul, where prices were rigidly controlled. In addition to competition between locals and foreigners, there also was a degree of cooperation.

~ The Ottoman ruling group and its attitudes to foreign trade

As the commercial policy of the Ottoman sultans has so often been discussed, only a few general features will be recapitulated here.[117] As in other polities of the pre-industrial age, trade was not regarded as a field of endeavour with its own laws, with which rulers could interfere only at the price of provoking unintended consequences, such as the disappearance of goods from the 'official' market. When the phenomenon of black marketing, probably widespread and known as *ihtikâr*, was discussed in Ottoman official documents, it was described as a moral failing, due to the desire for unlimited gain (*tama'-ı ham*). By contrast, it was never regarded as the reprehensible but unavoidable response to scarcity that we tend to see it as today. But then, phenomena which we denizens of the twenty-first century consider part of more or less autonomous 'economic' or political realms, to an Ottoman thinker formed part of an overarching realm of morality. As a literary genre, the 'mirrors of princes', of which numerous examples were composed, reflected this outlook in a particularly vivid fashion. Moreover, in contemporary western Europe, a similar way of thinking reigned unchallenged until the time of Machiavelli, and certainly had not disappeared even in the seventeenth century.[118]

Widespread in pre-industrial settings, both within the Middle East and elsewhere, was a tendency to see trade as an activity to be regulated by government, at least where the goods needed for day-to-day survival were concerned.[119] Regulation was legitimized by practical considerations, as given the low productivity of agriculture, large cities or armies could not be fed by market operations alone. But the dominance of morality over 'the economy' and politics provided additional justification, as the ruler could be seen, and in Islamic state theory was seen, as the guardian of moral order. In this perspective, regulation was both to the advantage of the ruler's treasury and to the benefit of his subjects. Government operated in a framework determined by religiously sanctioned laws and also by morality. If properly followed, these precepts would result in the prosperity of the population. And as 'ancient wisdom', known in an Islamic context as the circle of equity, would have it, the prosperity of the ruler's subjects permitted them to pay the taxes without which no state could hope to survive.[120]

It has long been known that the Ottoman sultans distinguished between the trade in foodstuffs and raw materials demanded by court, army and capital, and the business of long-distance and inter-state traders, who were often exempt from the detailed regulation to which other dealers needed to submit. These people were allowed to buy and sell without the government's interfering with their profit margins, while artisans and ordinary shopkeepers were permitted no more than a 10 to 20 per cent gain.[121] In all probability, this special treatment was due to the unspoken assumption that, for the most part, items carried by long-distance traders were few in number and were often luxuries rather than necessities. Such an interpretation incidentally fits in well with the concept of the Braudelian 'world economy', where usually little profit was to be expected from a crossing of the frontiers between different economic realms.[122]

However, the claim that the Ottoman government was not interested in regulating the trade in luxuries immediately demands qualification. For at least by the second half of the sixteenth century, the authorities seem to have assumed that members of the governing apparatus, to say nothing of the ruler himself, were entitled to certain goods that were not readily accessible to ordinary subjects. On the relatively modest level represented by the ordinary janissary, this meant, for instance, a regular publicly subsidized consumption of meat.[123] Or else 'robes of honour' were regularly distributed at festive occasions; thereby the recipients, who had not necessarily achieved a really elevated status, received quantities of silk fabric through the ruler's bounty. Here again we may think in terms of the entitlement of dignitaries to valuable goods.

When the sultan's palace was to be supplied, even long-distance trade was regulated more closely than was true in other contexts. It has been suggested that administratively decreed prices, of which detailed lists were published particularly in sixteenth- and seventeenth-century Istanbul, were enforced with special strictness when state authorities were the purchasers. Apparently more latitude was allowed to the merchant when dealing with ordinary customers.[124] The owners of goods required by the ruler might be asked to offer them at special prices as a sign of their devotion, and in certain sixteenth-century cases, special court traders visited Russia or even England in order to make their purchases directly 'at source'. Unfortunately we know nothing about their manner of doing business.[125]

Differently from the courtly and state elites, the Ottoman administration saw no particular need to protect the demand of well-to-do but 'ordinary' urbanites with respect to good-quality woollen cloaks, watches or painted Indian fabrics. Quite to the contrary, attempts on the part of such wealthy members of the subject population to use consumption as a means of asserting status were the targets of numerous anti-luxury rescripts. A tendency toward marking social status through elaborate consumption was especially noticeable during the first half of the eighteenth century, and was tolerated or even promoted as long as it occurred in a courtly context. But when contemporary merchants enriched through a burgeoning trade attempted to show their wealth through conspicuous consumption, a 'crackdown' in the shape of renewed anti-luxury laws was the result.[126] As is true of such regulations the world over, sultanic rescripts limiting consumption were not usually easy to enforce, and we may assume that Ottoman officials were as much aware of this fact as we are today. Quite possibly, by allowing long-distance merchants to charge what the market would bear, the Ottoman government quite effectively enforced sumptuary legislation among the less wealthy potential claimants to elevated social status.

But there were other reasons that might impel the Ottoman state to curtail foreign trade. These were linked to the problem of conserving bullion, regarded as an essential possession of any ruler preparing for war. Although the Ottoman state, at least in the eighteenth century, may have been a bad paymaster, silver and gold were needed to pay for soldiers and supplies. Without silver coin, no mercenaries could be hired, and from the seventeenth century onwards, these men were seen as absolutely essential. Moreover, in the course of the seventeenth century, most silver mines on Ottoman territory, already limited in number, were given up, as high costs of production made them uneconomic compared to their Peruvian and Mexican competitors.[127] But at the same time, from the late sixteenth century onwards a dramatic shortage of silver induced the Ottoman government to embark upon a long series of currency devaluations, which caused a good deal of socio-political upheaval and may have contributed towards a feeling of 'political decline' on the part of the people most seriously affected.[128] Obviously the 'secular drift' of money was eastwards, as it had been as far back as the Roman period. Thus even in the inflationary years around 1600/1008–9, much of the American bullion with which European merchants paid for their purchases did not stay within the Empire's borders for very long. As we have seen, Indian merchants had built up a major trade diaspora in Iran with extensions into Ottoman territory. They marketed indigo, Indian textiles, spices and drugs, and perhaps some Iranian silks as well. However, there were not many goods on the Ottoman market to interest purchasers back home. Thus Indian traders found themselves exporting silver in large quantities, and this influx of precious metal into the subcontinent accounted for the heaviness and high silver content of Mughul coins. This state of affairs began to worry members of the Ottoman elite in the early eighteenth century, when the official historian Naima suggested that merchants be required to purchase goods in exchange for the wares they brought into the Empire, singling out the Indians as major exporters of bullion.[129] But it was only at the end of the eighteenth century, when the Ottoman Empire once more found itself in the middle of war and crisis, that Selim III seriously attempted to forbid the importation of foreign fabrics.

European traders were not affected in any major way by this concern to prevent the outflow of silver. While in late Safavid Iran, when the silk trade had ceased to be profitable, European merchants did engage in a massive exportation of bullion, in the Ottoman lands this was not the case before the French financial speculations of the later eighteenth century.[130] Quite to the contrary, the Ottoman trade balance with European countries long continued to be positive, so that French and English merchants needed rather to import silver. By contrast, even during the sixteenth century, the Ottoman authorities had been extremely concerned about the outflow not only of silver, but even of copper to Iran. For here the question of bullion preservation was linked to the intention of denying metals to a potential opponent.[131] However, the purchase of raw silk from Iran by Bursa manufacturers, to say nothing of the importation of luxury goods, could most easily be balanced by the export of iron, copper and silver coin, so that smuggling must have been widespread.

When the Ottoman administration regulated trade, a concern to preserve the existing social order and discourage competition with the courtly, military and administrative elites thus combined with the desire to keep bullion in the country. Foodstuffs and raw materials that might benefit a potential enemy were not be exported, in any event, these goods might be needed by Ottoman soldiers, sailors or craftsmen.[132] We have encountered such policies with respect to copper and angora wool, but they were of even greater significance in the case of basic necessities such as wheat, cotton or leather. Taken together, all these considerations should have made the Ottoman elite extremely wary, if not outright hostile, with respect to foreign trade, at least in so far as it was not conducted in the service of the sultan himself.

This, however, was clearly not the case; quite to the contrary, foreign merchants were allowed considerable leeway. Where the 'Franks' were involved, this applied particularly to places such as Izmir, where they were allowed high visibility and even space in which to enjoy their leisure. For the most part Indian merchants also conducted their trade without let or hindrance. In a different vein, the continued existence of the minuscule trading city of Dubrovnik, which the Ottomans could have occupied any day but did not choose to take over, demonstrates the central government's interest in foreign trade (compare Chapter 3). Where imports were involved, a major motive was the 'consumerist' bias of the Ottoman administration; anything that increased the quantity of goods available on the domestic market was viewed in a positive light. Moreover, if importers were not to make themselves undesirable by exporting bullion, they had to be permitted to take out certain goods. In the perspective of the Ottoman administration, it was the prerogative of its servitors to determine which items were suitable for export and which ones were not. We do not know whether Ottoman officials were aware of the fact that, down into the eighteenth century, the trade with European countries resulted in a net inflow of silver, but it is highly probable. And while twentieth-century historians have viewed the entry of bullion in large quantities as a major destabilizing force in the late sixteenth-century Ottoman Empire, it is not very likely that treasury officials of the 1500s would have agreed with them.

At least as important in the eyes of the sultan's servitors, if not more so, was the gain in state revenues due to foreign trade. Ottoman customs duties were not high by modern standards; usually Muslim foreigners were to pay 3 per cent and non-Muslims 5 per cent, these payments were, however, augmented by various supplementary duties and 'gifts'.[133] When enforced, the capitulations granted to certain European rulers allowed the subjects of the beneficiaries to pay the 3 per cent rate as well. As the total quantities of goods involved were often large, even at the prevailing low rates, customs duties collected in any given port added up to major sums of money. If proof were needed, we might mention the fact that towards the end of our period, in the second half of the eighteenth century, local power magnates, such as the Kara Osmanoğulları in Izmir or Cezzar Ahmed Paşa in Acre, made special efforts to increase their control over foreign trade.[134] In addition, imports and exports produced revenues apart from customs duties: thus Iranian silk was weighed in special public scales, whose revenues, farmed out, constituted a not insignificant item in the Ottoman state budget.[135]

In the eighteenth century, foreign merchants, above all the French, might refuse to pay local imposts claiming exemption on the basis of the capitulations. But Ottoman tax collectors often found ways of getting around the foreigners' privileges, which included levying the dues in question on the brokers employed by foreign merchants. As Ottoman subjects, who did not usually 'enjoy foreign protection', these middlemen often could not claim exemption. On the other hand, their obvious lack of capital, and the impossibility of conducting trade without them, might oblige their French employers to contribute to the impost.[136]

Thus the local notables who so often made fortunes from tax farming developed vested interests in the continuance of foreign trade. Moreover, pious foundations profited from the khans they rented out, and in which foreign traders, especially the unmarried ones, were supposed to reside. In some places, both local dignitaries and the pious foundations they established built special housing to be rented out to foreign merchants. Last but not least, trade with the outside world provided work to numerous commercial agents, guides, owners of boats and camels, workmen in the ports and even state officials. All this employment was of some importance to the Ottoman administration as well, for any sultan could expect to gain legitimacy if a means of livelihood was made available to his 'poor subjects'. For most of the time, Ottoman rulers may not have made any special efforts to open up new routes of world trade. But they certainly were much concerned with the benefits to be derived from those already in existence.

This said, the Ottoman authorities do not seem to have worried over-much about the problems that might be generated by resident foreigners, at least as long as they were not at war with the relevant sovereigns, and/or the people in question were not sixteenth-century subjects of the shah of Iran. And even in times of war, there was no great official correspondence about the necessity of having the resident subjects of the adversary of the moment leave the realm as quickly as possible, even though these men were well advised to depart. In the period under discussion, the sultans were never at war with the rulers of England, France or the Netherlands, and this was doubtless a crucial factor in determining Ottoman attitudes; on the other hand, Austrian traders were not as yet of any special importance. We are entitled to think that the silence of Ottoman officials on this issue also indicates their conviction that they had the situation well in hand. Had matters been different, they probably would not have failed to write about the problem.

On the other hand, merchants were by no means the only foreigners who travelled the highways and byways of the Empire: after all, pilgrimage functioned as a third channel through which a denizen of the early modern age typically came into contact with the outside world. More specifically, how were foreign Muslim, Christian and Jewish pilgrims received on Ottoman territory? What kinds of relationships did missionaries and other non-trading strangers establish with Ottoman Muslims and non-Muslims? These matters will be discussed in the following chapter.

7 ~ Relating to pilgrims and offering mediation

When entering the Ottoman Empire, it was certainly necessary for the subjects of foreign rulers to apply to the nearest border post, pay customs duties and other taxes, and perhaps secure a *laissez-passer* for the journey to Istanbul or Aleppo.[1] However, obtaining the necessary permissions was, with some exceptions we will presently discuss, a relatively routine procedure, not to be compared with the difficulties encountered by would-be travellers to early modern Russia or China. That the accounts of seventeenth- or eighteenth-century private travellers say relatively little about the manner in which their authors obtained access to Ottoman territory indicates that these people encountered no insuperable difficulties. On the other hand, at least from the seventeenth century onwards, visitors from the Ottoman Empire when entering European states were often inconvenienced quite seriously by quarantine regulations.

Along the major routes of the Empire, quite a few strangers were thus engaged in their various errands: we have already encountered the merchants, British subjects, Frenchmen or else Iranian Armenians, travelling to Aleppo, Bursa or Izmir. In addition, there were non-commercial travellers of varying types, particularly pilgrims: Muslims from Morocco or India on their way to Mecca, Iranian Shi'ites visiting the sanctuaries of Ottoman Iraq, and also Christian and Jewish visitors to the Holy Land. But there were also European gentlemen in search of pleasure, instruction, and topics on which to write books, to say nothing of Dalmatian subjects of Venice seeking whatever employment they could get in the Ottoman capital.

Some of these people passed through the Ottoman lands entering into minimal contact with the local inhabitants. But others spent months or even years in the Empire, and must have had dealings with numerous Ottoman subjects. Moreover, even the most self-contained group of travellers was bound to put up in a khan, pay tolls, and perhaps use the services of guides. Thus there were always Ottoman subjects who, whether they wanted to or not, came into contact with foreign visitors. In addition, there were others for whom such encounters formed part of the everyday business of making a living. In this chapter we will try to trace the impressions that various foreigners left on their Ottoman interlocutors, both Muslim and non-Muslim.

Our major problem, however, is connected to the fact that such contacts between inhabitants of the Ottoman Empire and foreign travellers are but poorly documented. To highlight unofficial contacts, we are often obliged to use non-Ottoman sources in which this or that stranger has commented on the way in which he (or very rarely she) was received by various subjects of the sultan.[2] A commentator of this kind was Lady Mary Wortley Montagu who, as the wife of an English envoy and a cultured *femme de lettres*, visited Istanbul and Edirne in 1716–17/1128–30. Lady Mary discussed her relationships with Ottoman ladies and gentlemen quite extensively; other travel authors of less distinction also can be mined for this kind of information. But even so: throughout this study, both author and readers must contend with the unsystematic coverage of those issues that most interest us by the available primary sources. In the present chapter the difficulty is exacerbated. For we possess but few relevant texts written by Ottomans either Muslim or non-Muslim, to balance a multitude of European travelogues.[3] As a result our understanding of what the Empire's denizens thought about their foreign interlocutors is only known 'through a glass darkly'. We can only hope that more sources will come to light in the future and, for the present, make do with what we have got. A certain lack of systematic thinking on my part may have contributed to the difficulties as well.

A study of the reception of sixteenth-century Shi'ite Iranian pilgrims, for which Ottoman sources happen to be available, will thus be followed by the impressions of Christian and (albeit very briefly) Jewish visitors to the Holy Land, who wrote more or less extensively about the manner in which certain members of the local population interacted with them. As Christian pilgrimage accounts are so numerous, we will limit ourselves to a few exemplary texts. The reception of foreign Catholic missionaries by Ottoman Christians, which merits a more detailed discussion than is feasible here, will be followed by an equally brief analysis of the roles of Ottoman non-Muslims as mediators between different worlds, be it as translators or as medical men. These roles entailed close relationships between all the parties involved; these could be cordial or exactly the reverse, as the testimony of an eighteenth-century Istanbul writer will show with all the clarity we could possibly wish for. Discussing intermediaries will shade over into a final examination of an elusive and yet fundamentally important human relationship, namely making friends, and the degree to which it was possible for Ottoman subjects and foreigners to form ties of this kind.

~ The problems of Iranian pilgrims in Iraq and the Hijaz

Throughout the sixteenth century, and the early 1600s as well, there was much political rivalry between the Ottoman sultans and the shahs of Iran, exacerbated by the fact that the sultans defined themselves as protectors of Sunni Islam while the shahs had instituted Twelver Shi'ism as the dominant religion of their realm. On the other hand, the principal places of Shi'ite pilgrimage lay on Ottoman territory, and this included not only the two Holy Cities of the Hijaz, but also the mausoleums of Imām 'Alī, the Prophet Muhammad's son-in-law, and of the latter's grandson Ḥusayn in the Iraqi towns of al-Naḏjaf and Karbalā. In addition, the tombs of other descendants of the Prophet Muhammad too were visited by pious Shi'ites, and many of these were located in the Ottoman provinces making up modern Iraq. We also find that Iranian Shi'ites whose families could support the expense often had themselves buried close to the mausoleums of these holy personages.[4]

Ottoman attempts to cope with this situation have been studied in considerable detail for the middle and later nineteenth century.[5] However, even though the control of epidemic diseases – of considerable importance during this period – did not as yet worry the authorities of the sixteenth and seventeenth centuries, the authorities did feel that the need to guard against spies was a sufficient reason to control tightly the movements of pilgrims subject to the shah of Iran.[6] In wartime, Iranian pilgrims had no access to Ottoman territory at all. But even after the peace of Amasya in 1555/962–3 had regularized relations, officials in Istanbul were worried about emissaries of the shah establishing contact with disaffected Ottoman subjects, especially those who were themselves Shi'ites. Therefore visitors to the Hijaz were not allowed to cross the border until the pilgrimage season had actually begun, and their caravans were to be conducted as far as possible through sparsely inhabited territory.[7]

Official charities instituted by the shahs or their relatives in the pilgrimage cities of Al-Nadjaf and Karbalā were also unwelcome to the authorities in Istanbul. When turning down the Iranian request for permission to institute a soup kitchen for poor pilgrims from the shah's domains, the argument ran that any pilgrim should be able to fend for him/herself for the span of a few days, and a longer stay was undesirable anyway.[8] Presumably the reason for this attitude was that the sultan's officials wished to avoid what would have been a 'permanent representation' of the shah on Ottoman territory, particularly in a region where many of the inhabitants were themselves Shi'ites. But less formal alms distribution by emissaries of the shahs was difficult to prevent, and sometimes explicitly permitted. Moreover, wealthy Iranians settled in the region and even bought houses there; but in the sixteenth and early seventeenth centuries, a period of frequent warfare, the owners were liable to have their properties confiscated whenever the two empires were once again in conflict.

Iranian subjects traversing the desert route to Mecca through the Arabian peninsula were also regarded in Istanbul with considerable nervousness. This was presumably due to the presence of Shi'ites in the newly acquired province of al-Ḥasā (Laḥsa) and the doubtful loyalties of some of the local emirs, who even had established good relations with the Portuguese.[9] Furthermore, we can surmise that officials in Istanbul feared that Iranian pilgrims travelling in the interior of the Arabian peninsula, where the sultan's writ ran intermittently if at all, might establish links to the local Bedouins, who in turn might cause difficulties for the Ottoman state in the Hijaz. In any case, the pilgrimage route through the Arabian peninsula was periodically closed. Prospective pilgrims from Basra and Iraq – Ottoman subjects as well as pious travellers in transit from Iran – were enjoined to travel with the Damascene or Egyptian caravans. This was an enormous detour that for many candidate hajjis must have rendered the projected pilgrimage altogether unfeasible. A realistic official once commented that spies would get through even if the route to Mecca was closed, and that restrictive measures only made life difficult for legitimate travellers.[10] But he seems to have represented only a minority of sixteenth-century Ottoman bureaucrats.

In addition to periodic spy scares, cultural factors might be a further reason why Iranian visitors to Mecca at times were not welcome to the Ottoman authorities. In the second half of the sixteenth century, the sultans were much concerned about maintaining proper decorum in the Great Mosque of Mecca. Among other matters, this also meant that the use of the courtyard for 'profane' activities, such as sleeping or relaxation, was to be prevented. Thus a sultanic command complained that it was unacceptable to enjoy the evening cool in the mosque courtyard with 'cradles and pillows' (beşik ve döşek); but certain Iranian pilgrims obviously had quite a different view of what constituted pious behaviour.[11] It would appear that the formality of official Ottoman customs was unknown in Iran, and the relevant behaviour generated a degree of mutual incomprehension.[12]

~ Jewish visitors to Jerusalem

Jerusalem is, and was, a place of pilgrimage for Jews, Christians and Muslims alike; and the pious of all three monotheistic religions could scarcely have avoided seeing one another in the town's narrow streets. While in the sixteenth and seventeenth centuries the resident Jewish community was relatively small, pilgrimages by Jews both Ottoman and non-Ottoman were by no means rare. But very few of the ensuing reports seem to be available in translation. According to a memoir dated 1625–6/1034–6, Jewish pilgrims made charitable donations to the poor of their own religion settled in Jerusalem, as indeed they had done more than a century earlier, in the beginning years of Ottoman rule. Albeit on a smaller scale, this custom resembles the alms that pious Muslims used to give to the poor of Mecca and Medina. In the slightly over one hundred years that had elapsed between the Ottoman conquest and 1625–6/1034–6, many Jewish academies had been opened in the town, once again with outside support. The accumulated wealth was enough to tempt a rebellious commander of mercenaries, who probably around 1600/1008–9 robbed the local Jews but did not spare Muslims or Christians either. In the mid-seventeenth century there were fully-fledged guide books that told pious Jews planning to visit Jerusalem what they should take or avoid taking on their journey.[13]

~ Christian visitors writing about Palestine and the Sinai peninsula

While we do possess numerous records of sixteenth- and seventeenth-century Christian pilgrims – Orthodox, Gregorian Armenians, Catholics and even Protestants – who visited the places traditionally associated with the life of Jesus Christ and his mother Mary, the early modern period was a time of crisis as far as this practice was concerned. After about 1500/905–6 pilgrimages to the Holy Land possessed much less importance, at least in the eyes of western Christians, than had been true in earlier centuries. Persons concerned with the reform of the fifteenth-century Church, including Catholics, such as the highly respected spiritual leader Thomas à Kempis, were critical of the very notion of pilgrimage, and thought that people who often went on such journeys rarely became saints.[14] Even more radically, Lutherans and Calvinists alike rejected the notion that men and women, as sinful beings unable to obtain release from hell-fire except for the grace of an inscrutable deity, could do anything at all to further their salvation. This was a tenet which discredited the entire notion of 'good works' including pilgrimages. Even the Catholic Church, which continued to hold on to these concepts, attempted to control pilgrims more stringently. In principle it became necessary to obtain permission for every single pilgrimage to Jerusalem from papal officials in Rome. However, in practice, pious visitors at times obtained this permit from the Franciscans settled in Jerusalem.[15] With the diminished religious status of the pilgrimage, those people that did go tended to concentrate more on their worldly experiences, or at least on education and pious contemplation, as opposed to the gaining of religious merit.[16] Contemporaries were quite aware of this fact; and a Lutheran clergyman who showed up in late sixteenth-century Jerusalem was pointedly asked whether he had come for religious purposes or else to see foreign lands.[17]

Many western pilgrims visited Jerusalem and its environment on a guided tour, in a manner rather reminiscent of quite a few present-day travellers, and enumerated the sites they had seen in a fairly standard fashion. At times Protestants and Catholics seem to have used the same models, so that the sixteenth-century account by the Catholic Jean Palerne has features in common with the descriptions of Protestants such as Leonhart Rauwolff or Samuel Schweigger.[18] However, in connection with the sea-change described above, modifications of this standard pattern were not unknown. While biblical stories, as well the pious reflections inspired by the relevant texts, continued to form the main guideline for the organization of pilgrimage accounts, in the second half of the sixteenth century more broadly understood cultural concerns became typical for the better educated authors.[19] Learned Protestants especially liked to visit the sites mentioned in the gospels as a visual supplement to their Bible-reading. Thus the Augsburg physician and botanist Rauwolff, after a lengthy trip through Mesopotamia, took time off to visit the Holy Land in 1575/982–3, deploying the historical, architectural and geographical interests not uncommon, in a secular context, among contemporary European gentlemen with a humanist education.

Moreover, given this author's particular interest in accurate description, he included fairly detailed 'word pictures' of the Jerusalem monuments, including Ottoman structures such as the newly restored city walls.[20] Some of these pious travellers, with 'proto-archaeological' interests in mind, also ventured to places outside the Holy Land proper, particularly the Sinai, but also to sites where early Christian churches had been established according to the New Testament. Here pilgrimage easily shaded off into 'scholarly tourism'.

Pilgrimage accounts, especially those written by members of the Orthodox clergy, were meant as guides for future pilgrims and gave fairly standardized descriptions of the sites to be visited, particularly in the Holy City itself.[21] By comparison, the travel accounts in which the author gave his name and recounted some of his own adventures were comparatively rare.[22] A special case was that of Theodosios Zygomalas, proto-notary of the ecumenical patriarch Jeremias II and thus an Ottoman subject, who travelled from Istanbul to Jerusalem by way of Antalya and Acre, but mentioned the pilgrimage sites of the Holy Land only in a few brief phrases.[23] Yet from our viewpoint his work is most interesting, as he was friendly with the Protestant theologian Stephan Gerlach, who himself had written a diary covering his visit to Istanbul. Zygomalas' account was in fact addressed to Gerlach: as the Lutheran divine had not seen the monastery of St Catherine in the Sinai, this sanctuary was given pride of place. Since Zygomalas was addressing himself to a non-Orthodox friend, he especially mentioned the chapels used by pilgrims belonging to the western Church, a feature otherwise not customary in Orthodox pilgrimage literature. A contemporary (1577–92/ 984–1001) but more rhetorical and much longer description of the same site was composed by Paisios Hagiapostolites, metropolitan of Rhodes and thus an Ottoman subject. This text contained fairly detailed descriptions of the church of St Catherine and its auxiliary buildings, interspersed with miracle tales and pious exhortations.[24] Although Paisios wrote about a trip he had himself undertaken, and moreover at a time when his impressions were still fresh, his instructions concerning the state of mind desirable in a pilgrim were so detailed as to make his text resemble a formal pilgrimage guide. In such a work, there clearly was not much reason to discuss the relationships between Ottoman Orthodox subjects and non-Ottoman Christian visitors.

A much more personal account of a seventeenth-century pilgrimage to Jerusalem, this time by an Armenian from outside the Empire, was written by Simeon of Zamosc, a scribe and pious layman of the Gregorian persuasion (1584–after 1639/991–after 1049).[25] Although in later life Simeon was known for his opposition to any project of union between the Armenian and Catholic churches, during his visit to Jerusalem in 1617/1025–7 he stressed the close relations that many 'Franks' entertained with the Gregorian patriarchs, themselves subjects of the sultan and, further, closely supervised by the authorities in Istanbul. In Simeon's perspective, the solemn visits of 'Frankish' Christians to the Armenian Church of St James formed an important part of the ritual calendar of Jerusalem. When visiting the Church of the Nativity in Bethlehem, he conversely emphasized the welcome accorded to Armenian pilgrims by the 'Frankish' priests in charge of the sanctuary. At the same time, Simeon visibly took pride in the power and wealth of the Gregorian Armenian Church, and thus indirectly in its successful integration into the Ottoman state apparatus. Accordingly he tells us that, while most European pilgrims had to stay in the local khans, the monastery of St James belonging to his own church was large enough to accommodate 'ten thousand' pilgrims. But even more important to him was the Holy City of Jerusalem itself, to which Simeon came to form a strong emotional attachment, and that he greatly regretted having to leave.

~ Ottoman people and places in western accounts of Jerusalem

A comprehensive discussion of the pilgrimage reports written by western Christians between the mid-sixteenth and the late eighteenth century would take a separate book. Given the narrow limits of my competence, we will concentrate upon the reactions of Muslim and non-Muslim locals to pious foreign visitors, as pictured in a few of these texts. But in order to make sense of the often brief remarks that are all we possess, it is necessary to discuss them in a somewhat wider historical context.

Throughout the period under discussion there were acrimonious political disputes among Christian denominations for control of the main pilgrimage sites, especially the Church of the Holy Sepulchre (in Ottoman: Kamame/Kumame). Though foreign pilgrims rarely took note of this aspect of the question, it should be stressed that the disputes themselves were largely an internal Ottoman concern. After all, adherents of the Orthodox, Gregorian Armenian and Catholic churches all figured among the subjects of the sultan, and the relevant communities were recognized by the authorities. However, differently from all others, the Catholics received aid from outside potentates, namely the Habsburg emperors and the French kings. But a recent study has demonstrated that, on the whole, these activities of foreign rulers were of no major political importance on the Jerusalem scene before the late seventeenth century. It was only during the disastrous Ottoman–Habsburg war of 1683–99/1094–1111 that the Ottoman court attempted to secure the support of Louis XIV of France by making concessions to the Catholics with respect to possession of the Church of the Holy Sepulchre.[26]

In principle, the Protestant churches disparaged pilgrimages; but as we have seen, educated Anglicans and Lutherans still might visit Palestine for the purpose of pious edification. Though a convinced Lutheran, Leonhart Rauwolff spent time in contemplation of the place where Jesus supposedly was born, and of other presumed biblical sites.[27] A Lutheran clergyman, such as Samuel Schweigger in 1581/988–9, approached the Christian holy sites of Jerusalem and surroundings in much the same spirit. Moreover, a full century later (1696/1107–8) the same thing can be said of Henry Maundrell, chaplain to the English merchants residing in Aleppo, even though in more ways than one he was very much a man of the early enlightenment.[28]

Rauwolff seems to have talked extensively to local Christians, particularly Maronites. He also apparently had contacts with Druzes, and recorded that at the time of his stay, the two groups were allies; however, he had the astonishing notion that the Druzes were descended from crusaders once established in the Syrian territories.[29] Rauwolff's account also reflects the theological polemics between the different Christian denominations that had been going on for many centuries.[30] When discussing Orthodox and Nestorian Christians, his comments were quite hostile, while Ethiopians, Armenians and Maronites were described in positive or at least neutral terms. Writing about the various Christian denominations in the Holy Land was popular in the pilgrimage reports of the period: Rauwolff's contemporary Samuel Schweigger showed a similar concern, in his case informed by the interest of contemporary Protestant theologians in the Orthodox creed.[31]

Rauwolff had the typical prejudices of his milieu and time against Muslims, and also disliked Jews. In his pilgrimage account, local Muslims scarcely figured, except as collectors of dues and as a dominant group whose sensitivities were to be taken into account when moving around in Jerusalem. Something similar applied to Palerne, Schweigger and even Maundrell. At times one wonders whether perhaps copying was involved. Schweigger was peculiar in so far as he recorded minor physical confrontations with servants or cameleers, of a kind that happen during many trips but usually remain unrecorded in travel books; that this divine did think such incidents worth recounting may have had something to do with a particular sense of insecurity. Maundrell told a story of how his group asked for hospitality in a Shi'ite village but was refused; the reader does get the impression that Sunni travellers would not have been welcomed either. The point of his story was that the villagers, in a sense, were finally duped. For after some negotiation, the pilgrims were permitted to store their belongings but not to enter the settlement themselves; yet in the dead of night, they managed to creep into shelter none the less.[32] Thus contact with Muslims, at least in so far as it was recorded by these three authors, seems to have been minimal and mostly unfriendly. It is particularly striking that none of our authors recorded exchanges with locals in which the interlocutors said something like 'well, in the end, we all believe in one and the same God'. Did this really never happen?

However, a story recounted by Henry Timberlake (visit in 1601/1009–10) can be viewed as one of the few exceptions proving this rule. When the author insisted on entering Jerusalem while proclaiming himself both a subject of the queen of England and a Protestant he got himself arrested. From this unfortunate position he was extricated by the mediation of a Muslim shipmate who had become a friend.[33] This man went to see the governor and swore to Timberlake's good character, finally managing to get him released.

But, unfortunately, accounts of this kind must be regarded as voices crying in the wilderness. By contrast, amicable relations between individual members of the various Christian denominations, both Ottoman and foreign, are documented with somewhat greater frequency. Thus in a diffuse way, the pilgrimage to Jerusalem may have fostered the interest of Europeans in Ottoman Christians and vice versa.

~ The Christian pilgrimage to Jerusalem in Muslim eyes

While many Muslims must have commented orally on the oddities of Christian visitors to their city, they have not normally written about their observations and, as so often, we need to fall back upon Evliya Çelebi. While Evliya was certainly not a typical upper-class Ottoman, his tale does provide certain clues to the manner in which an educated Muslim saw this place of Christian pilgrimage. The author claimed to have been given a special 'guided tour' of the Church of the Holy Sepulchre, outside the pilgrimage season. As many details in his report resemble those given by Christian visitors like Rauwolff, it does seem probable

5. The Damascus gate in the walls of Jerusalem, these fortifications date from the Ottoman period.
Source: Bahattin Öztuncay, *James Robertson, Pioneer of Photography in the Ottoman Empire* (Istanbul: Eren, 1992): no. 29, p. 97. By kind permission from the publisher.

that Evliya reproduced certain stories told to him by his tour guide.[34] Thus, like the Augsburg physician and many other Christian visitors, the Ottoman traveller reported that the priests serving the sanctuary were locked up inside the church for a significant portion of the year, and that the building was only opened to pilgrims after the latter had paid a substantial entrance fee.[35] This remark thus may be regarded as 'standard', no matter whether Christians or Muslims authored the description. Whenever the building was closed, the priests were supplied through a window opened for this purpose in the wall of the compound. Evliya was much impressed by the ascetic life lived by the clergy serving in the church, and also by the pictorial qualities of the mosaics of the Pantocrator and the Virgin Mary. He also made a laudatory reference to the canopy set over what was considered to be the grave of Christ.[36] This was indeed 'a place worthy of being seen' (*temaşagâh*) and upon leaving, the author prayed that the church, whose porch and overall architecture he highly acclaimed, would one day be transformed into a mosque.[37]

Some ambiguity is apparent from this account. Evliya evidently found things to admire in the architecture and interior decoration of the church, and even in the lifestyle of the priests. At the same time, he was quite aware of the 'pious fraud' of the supposedly heaven-descended fire, which the Orthodox and Armenian clergies repeated every Easter, or as he called it, the *kızıl yumurta günleri* ('days of the red eggs') 'of evil reputation'.[38] Evliya was also cognisant of the material interests involved, observing that the wax of the Easter candles produced considerable revenue for the clergy; this was because the latter sold candles to the pilgrims whom they put up in their establishments. In addition, the numerous Orthodox and Armenians who, at the time of Maundrell's visit, lit their tapers at the Easter fire probably also bought them from priests and monks.[39] Evliya also claimed that his guide had himself admitted that the reason for having images in the church at all was not their intrinsic virtue, but rather the impression that 'our Orthodox (Rum) are a bunch of thick-headed and credulous men', who could not be moved by preaching alone but whose generosity could be stimulated by a judicious use of images.[40] Thus Evliya tells us that the priest who guided him was a 'an unbeliever, a heretic and a dissolute person' and thought nothing of addressing the man as 'you damned one'. But at the same time, Helena the mother of Constantine and herself a pious Christian – as Evliya was well aware – in this author's tale was made responsible for the restoration of the Muslim sanctuary known as the Mescid-i aksa. Apparently for Evliya Çelebi the pilgrimage church of the Kumame was an interesting site well worth visiting, where one could encounter strange people, assert the superiority of one's own faith and, last but not least, enjoy a piece of handsome architecture.

Other Muslims also entered the Church of the Holy Sepulchre on what we may call 'touristic' visits, of which we have at least indirect evidence. The Nuremberg soldier Hans Wild (1585–after 1613/992–after 1022), a prisoner of war in Ottoman lands between 1604/1012–13 and 1611/1019–20, was the slave of a merchant who, when passing through Jerusalem, decided to pay a visit to this church, and so did other members of the same caravan. Wild had in all likelihood converted to Islam and was taken along on the outing; he recorded that his fellow visitors scoffed at the explanations, probably given by a Christian guide, that Jesus had been mocked or crowned with thorns in this or that place now comprised within the church.[41]

When Maundrell visited the Church of the Holy Sepulchre, he also noted the presence of Muslim visitors. Some of them may once again have come 'as tourists', but there were others whose role it apparently was to testify that prior to the so-called miracle of the Holy Fire, celebrated by Orthodox and Armenians at Easter-time, all candles and lamps in the church had really been extinguished, so that the flame could not have originated within the building.[42] This Easter fire formed the culminating point of a ritual that already had been practised in the eleventh century, and that western and particularly Protestant observers treated with considerable scorn.[43] Maybe an investigation of the kadi registers of Jerusalem will one day tell us what at least a few of the Muslim witnesses present at the 'miracle' thought about all this.

Official Ottoman attitudes towards Christian pilgrims were reflected in these same record books and, at least occasionally, also in the central administration's main chancery registers (Mühimme Defterleri).[44] Some of the texts involved granted permission to the administrators of various Christian pilgrimage sites to effect repairs to the building fabric in their care, while others ordered investigations of various Muslim dues collectors who had demanded more than they were legally permitted to take. In other instances disputes between various Christian denominations concerning the control of this or that Palestinian sanctuary were decided by the highest authorities in Istanbul, with the idea in mind that all Christians should be allowed access to the main pilgrimage sites. Certainly the Ottoman government hoped in this fashion to increase pilgrim traffic. Recent research has shown, however, that pilgrims' dues were not typically a source of direct financial gain to the treasury. Rather, it was normal practice to spend the money thus received in order to enhance the Islamic character of Jerusalem, for instance by making such dues into foundations serving some Islamic pious purpose.[45] Thus religious, political and financial considerations encouraged the Ottoman administration to ensure the safety of Christian pilgrims to the Holy City.

~ Catholic missionaries in Ottoman lands

Western pilgrims in the area, as we have seen, were housed, fed, and guided by a mission consisting of non-Ottoman (often Italian) Franciscan friars, and it is to these missionaries and their reception by local Christians that we will now turn. At the Council of Trent (1542–64/948–72), the post-Reformation Roman Catholic Church had determined its organizational structures for the next few centuries.[46] Measures to compensate for the loss of a large part of Europe to Protestantism included increased missionary activity on other continents. While in a global context, India, China and for a while Japan were given pride of place, attempts to bring the Christian communities of western Asia to convert to Catholicism also intensified. At the very least, Middle Eastern Christians were to be persuaded to recognize the primacy of the pope while retaining their own customs and liturgies, the adherents of these newly formed churches being called Uniates.

Missionaries, who as part of their education studied the languages of the peoples among whom they were expected to serve, were trained for their tasks in special Roman colleges. For the most part these were instituted by Pope Gregory XIII (r. 1572–85/979–94), and instruction was entrusted to the Jesuits. Founded in 1577/984–5, the Collegium Graecum trained priests able to function in Greek, but also accepted lay students. A Collegium Maronitarum, established in 1584/ 991–2, was to bind the Maronites of Mount Lebanon, who had accepted union with Rome rather earlier, closer to the Catholic Church. These links were quite apparent to Rauwolff: at the time of his visit (1575/982–3) the Maronites were accustomed to elect their patriarch, who was then confirmed by the pope; and, as this author put it, a few years earlier the current incumbent had won his position by racing to Rome and putting forward his candidacy before his rival had had a chance to do so.[47]

From 1622/1030–1 onwards, all missions were supervised by the Roman congregation known as De Propaganda Fide. This bureaucratic entity in the papal service had an impact on the curricula of the various missionary colleges, stressing the importance of language training in addition to education in theology. The Propaganda committee also set out the rules by which missionaries 'in the field' were expected to operate, even though it was never able to completely eliminate rivalries between the various orders of monks and friars engaged in this activity. To the historian of the Ottoman realm, the Propaganda has made itself useful by demanding that all missionaries submit annual reports about their activities; for otherwise little documented areas such as Bosnia or Albania, these files contain much evidence on local social history. In the eighteenth century the Jesuits even made available several series of printed reports to a wider public, in order to introduce their missionary activities in the Levant and elsewhere to possible sponsors. Therefore these letters were meant to be both edifying and curious/ interesting.[48] Giving their names or else anonymously, Jesuit authors often wrote in the first person, and edited the writings of their deceased confreres. Some of the texts published seem to have originated as travel diaries; descriptions of places visited and of the varying conditions of the Christians residing therein alternated with 'edifying' accounts of the missionaries' lives and, above all, deaths. In spite of their brevity, the stories about people and places, in other words the 'curious' part of these travelogues, are valuable because they sometimes allow us to glimpse interactions of the missionaries with ordinary Ottoman subjects about which we would otherwise know nothing at all.

Among the different missionary orders, Franciscans and Jesuits were especially active on Ottoman territory, generally working under the protection of European ambassadors. While the Habsburgs were zealous in their patronage of post-Tridentine Catholicism, their frequent wars with the Ottomans caused the sponsoring of missionary activities to fall into the province of their arch-rival, the French king. In the reports of the French ambassadors, the affairs of the missionaries had a special place, quite comparable to political relations and matters of trade. However, the degree of support the clergy could expect varied with the political convictions of the various diplomats; particularly in the late seventeenth and early eighteenth centuries, the 'misplaced zeal' of certain missionaries formed a frequent complaint in French ambassadorial correspondence.[49]

Concerning the expectations that Christian subjects of the sultans might have concerning these missionaries, recent research has emphasized that, in a city like Aleppo, local eighteenth-century Orthodox merchants desired to increase their control over the local churches, which was easier to achieve if they shook off the patriarch in Istanbul. In addition, their adoption of Uniate status or even fully-fledged Catholicism permitted them to fit better into a wider Mediterranean world, in which French trade was dominant.[50] In outlying places, this desire to use Catholic mediation when trying to cope with the outside world might take on rather remarkable forms. Thus a report by an anonymous Jesuit father, printed in 1745/1157–8, described how Christian pirates commanded by an Italian free-booter had plundered villages on the Orthodox island of Samos (Sisam), in one case even kidnapping all the girls and women. Thereupon the locals hoped that the Jesuit father, who happened to be passing through, would remonstrate with the pirates and thus obtain the liberation of the kidnapped people. The author of the letter reported that he did not refuse, but did point out to the islanders that he and the captain came from different states, and that godless pirates were unlikely to be much impressed by the appearance of a clergyman. In the end, this particular piece of mediation proved to be unnecessary, as the pirates of their own accord returned the captives.[51]

In a sense, mediation, if unremunerated, can be considered a form of charity; and the anonymous Jesuit was willing to negotiate with the pirates for that very reason. In another instance he described himself as sharing a salve for healing surface wounds with a local family. As he refused payment, he thought that he had made an impression because of his désintéressement. But at the same time the author, as a person travelling alone, also depended on receiving charity from the locals; for in some cases that was apparently the only way in which he could find something to eat. In fact, the preparation of food seems to have to have been a matter in which our anonymous Jesuit was quite interested and which allowed him to communicate with various inhabitants of western Anatolia.[52] As he did not mention the religion of his interlocutors, we may assume that there were Muslims among them; in any event from these Anatolians the author learned to prepare pitta bread, pilav, which he was taught to distinguish from rice gruel, and what appears to have been a form of yoghurt soup (yayla çorbası). The author evidently enjoyed these novel dishes and also the relaxation of social constraints that travel brought with it – and his Ottoman interlocutors did not hesitate to make it all possible.

~ Mediations, ambiguities and shifts of identity

That mediation between members of the Ottoman elites and visiting or resident foreigners often fell to the lot of Ottoman non-Muslims has long been known. In this endeavour, the latter were all too often 'caught in the middle', that is, they attracted the reprobation of both sides. The dragomans attached to foreign embassies were mistrusted by their employers, on account of real or supposed venality but also because their status as subjects of the sultan made them liable to pressure by the Ottoman authorities. Venetians and Frenchmen especially made considerable efforts to teach young subjects of their own states the Ottoman language in order to avoid hiring locals.[53] Yet Christian dragomans subject to the sultan continued to work for many embassies, the family of the scholarly Armenian Catholic and luckless Swedish ambassador Mouradgea d'Ohsson (Muradcan Tosunyan) forming a case in point.[54] On the Ottoman side, there was the consideration that the dragoman might or actually did usurp the privileges of foreigners to which, as a subject of the sultan, he had no right. Moreover it was probably assumed that a denizen of the Empire owed his ruler undivided loyalty, and somebody who instead presumed to play a role 'between the fronts' must therefore have been viewed as faithless and unreliable.

However, mediators were necessary for many diplomatic negotiations, and while the motivations of these men for the most part remain obscure, their visible activities often have been well studied, especially where the sixteenth century is concerned. As a colourful example, we may refer to the doctor Solomon Ashkenazi from Udine, who studied in Padua and later settled in Istanbul.[55] There from the 1560s/967–77 onwards, he built up an important practice, which included the Grand Vizier Sokollu Mehmed Paşa and the chief translator to the sultan's council as well as the different Venetian ambassadors (*baili*) present in Istanbul during those years. In addition Ashkenazi did well in trade, and is known to have owned several ships.

The reason for the Jewish-Italian doctor's being the subject of several studies – the most recent dating from 1995 – is his share in bringing the war over Cyprus to an end.[56] The Signoria had entrusted this responsibility to the current *bailo* Marcantonio Barbaro, who was under house arrest in Pera and thus could only negotiate through a middleman. As such, Ashkenazi was a good choice because of his ongoing relationship with the grand vizier who, for his own reasons, wanted to end the war. But even so the undertaking was highly dangerous for the doctor and diplomat, as the grand vizier's political opponents tried to torpedo the negotiations by threatening the middleman. However Sokollu was successful in the end, and the peace was signed in 1573/980–1, with Solomon Ashkenazi one of the persons to draft the treaty. It has been suggested that this was a genuine case of 'double loyalty'; the doctor was willing to risk financial losses and personal danger in order to reestablish peace between the state where he had been born and that where he had made his home.[57]

On more modest levels of society as well, the borderline between Christians and Jews who owed allegiance to the sultan and those who were subject to foreign powers was often less clear in practice than in theory. In Islamic legal treatises, it was stipulated that the subject of a non-Muslim ruler who stayed in the Muslim world for over a year lost his status as a privileged foreigner and became a subject of the ruler on whose territory he lived. But at least in the early seventeenth century, this was not current practice in the Ottoman Empire.[58] To the contrary, as long as a foreigner did not acquire real estate and did not marry a subject of the sultan, he could retain his allegiance to the ruler of his own country of origin for an indefinite period of time – these stipulations also explain why English and French residents in the Levant were forbidden by their home authorities to do either of these two things. However, in practice, even these two conditions were often violated, and we know of eighteenth-century Frenchmen marrying Greek Catholic women, and yet remaining subjects of the kings of France. Eighteenth-century consuls in Izmir reported that some people claimed to be Frenchmen who had ceased to speak French, but who were accepted as such because, as we have seen, a large foreign community was a factor of prestige for the consul involved.[59] Practising the Catholic faith, though, does seem to have been a significant indicator of 'Frenchness', more perhaps than a command of the language. Perhaps for this reason a Catholic Greek from the island of Chios in the second half of the eighteenth century might manage to join the French merchant community in Ankara; and even though the man in question was denounced by a rival to the ambassador in Istanbul, this act did not apparently lead to his exclusion, at least not in the short run.

All this means that on a day-to-day level the association of Ottoman non-Muslims, and also for that matter recently converted Muslims, with various kinds of foreigners was often quite close. But this fact was rarely described in writing by the Ottoman subjects involved. Doubtless our ignorance is partly due to the fact that so little private correspondence survives. But, in addition, we must take into account that in narrating such relationships, the people in question admitted that they had violated the societal norms of their respective communities. After all, socializing across religious divides was highly problematic in the sixteenth and seventeenth centuries, not only within the Ottoman borders but also outside them.

~ An eighteenth-century Istanbul xenophobe

For information on the criticisms that such especially sociable persons might incur, we may consult an anonymous text from the eighteenth century, that recently has been published under the title *Risale-i garibe*.[60] The extant manuscript dates from the year 1720/1132–3. In this short text, the anonymous author has listed instances of what he saw as the rude and impolite behaviour of his fellow townsmen. While most of the cases mentioned seem to have taken place in the capital, dialectal forms indicate that the author may originally have come from western Anatolia. Present-day scholars have become interested in this text because of its 'ethnographic' aspect, that is, the numerous references to customs and expressions then current in non-elite Ottoman circles but now obsolete. However, in the present context, we are only concerned with what the anonymous author has to say about relationships with strangers.

Visibly the author had no love for any kind of outsiders to his own urban society. For quite a few of his curses were directed against Anatolian peasants (Türk) from the townlet of Gerede, who supposedly tried to hide their wretched poverty, Bosnian provincials unable to conceal their ignorance of 'civilization' or Tatars who, instead of killing the Cossacks they had captured, brought them to Istanbul, presumably for sale as slaves. Other vicious invective was reserved for people who had somehow entered the Islamic community, but whom the author suspected of less than total allegiance: 'Greeks who become Muslims for fear of the poll tax but who will continue to speak their native language whenever they see a fellow Greek'.[61] All these were of course Sunni Muslims of one kind or another, and subjects of the sultan to boot; yet if these people were unable to win approval in the author's eyes, it is not surprising that real outsiders were treated to at least equal invective. Thus Kalmuks – we are left to wonder where the writer had encountered them – were cursed as 'sons of dogs', the Shi'ites who swore at the first three caliphs were 'damned', the Moldavians 'traitors' and the Germans/ Austrians 'robbers'.[62]

It was not just the various outsiders themselves who were targeted by the anonymous writer, but also insiders who seemed to be friendly with unbelievers. Thus the author reserves various swearwords not only for the 'irreligious persons' who drank alcohol together with unbelievers, but also for those who merely observed the social niceties when encountering such people. Among other things, the author mentioned those who would speak 'the language of the unbelievers' even though the addressee knew Turkish, used friendly words when making purchases from an 'infidel', visited the homes of non-Muslims and made polite responses to the greetings of same.[63] All these strictures could broadly be based on sayings attributed to the Prophet or, more recently, on the legal opinions of sixteenth-century jurisconsults such as the Şeyhülislam Ebusu'ud, for whom it had been a major concern to keep Muslims and non-Muslims separate at all times.[64] But if there had not been any people who did all the things our anonymous writer considered so reprehensible, he would have had no occasion to write in the first place ...

~ Was friendship between an Ottoman Muslim and a foreigner an impossible proposition?

At first glance, the answer to this question would seem to be 'yes' in most contexts; or phrased differently, only somewhat unconventional personages should have been able to surmount the formidable social barriers preventing such friendships in the normal run. Maybe things were somewhat different for women, at least if the foreign partner was willing to learn Ottoman and was as gifted and energetic as the eighteenth-century travel author Lady Mary Wortley Montagu.[65] For it appears that, among highly placed Istanbul ladies, the requirements of social position and polite behaviour did not limit contacts with female strangers quite as stringently as was true among males. At least if Lady Mary's letters are at all realistic, her relationship with Fatma Hanım, the wife of the grand vizier's aide, the powerful *kâhya*, was what one would call a friendship. The two young women apparently went visiting together, and Fatma Hanım seems to have introduced Lady Mary to the wife of the grand vizier and even to female members of the ruling house. Thus the English travel writer much admired the social skills of this Istanbul lady, who she felt would easily have held her own at any European court.[66] However, as no testimony of Fatma Hanım's feelings has survived, these conclusions must remain hypothetical.

Certain relationships between former foreign slaves, Islamized or not, and their erstwhile masters also were described by the returnees in such a fashion that we may well wonder whether the master–servant relationship had not evolved in the direction of human fellow feeling. We will return once more to the Nuremberg ex-soldier Hans Wild, who was not in the normal run of things a considerate person. His book is full of the quarrels he got into with Muslims and non-Muslims, that often ended in fisticuffs; and that Wild was often punished for these affrays does not seem to have limited the zest with which he threw himself into anything that looked like a good fight.[67] Yet when he speaks of the last of his many masters, a janissary officer of Cairo, his tone changes. After the series of disasters that ended with his close brush with death in Antalya, Wild decided to return to the Egyptian capital and seek the aid of this personage, explaining that he had no better friend than him. The janissary commander took Wild back into his service and treated him well. As for the ex-soldier and ex-slave, he remained for a year, working hard to earn his welcome, until he had saved enough to re-embark. Once in Istanbul, he entered the service of the Habsburg ambassador, and this official gave him a testimonial that probably was meant to help him find employment once he had returned home. In this text and also in a similar document issued by the author's former commander in the Habsburg army, the aid of

Wild's 'good master' is strongly emphasized: the ex-slave visibly felt that the unnamed janissary commander had been the cause of his survival.[68]

But once again, one would like to know what the Ottoman officer thought of all this. Did he understand that Wild's conversion to Islam was shaky at best, and that above all, his former slave wanted to return home? We are unlikely to ever find out, nor will we know what the janissary officer may have learned about life in central Europe from his servitor. After all, while Wild's Arabic and Ottoman were certainly not perfect, the former slave was able to tell a story if required. These unanswered – and unanswerable – questions open up a series of others, concerning the sources of information on the outside world accessible to educated Ottomans. These we will treat in the following chapter.

8 ~ Sources of information on the outside world

Devising policies and campaigns, establishing business contacts, purchasing or freeing slaves, escorting pilgrims ... all these activities were predicated on the availability of at least a modicum of data concerning the world outside the sultan's realm. Compared to the information more or less accessible to an Ottoman of the nineteenth and early twentieth centuries, the sources that a person living between 1540/946–7 and 1770/1183–4 might turn to were doubtless limited, and the information obtained often out of date and not necessarily reliable.[1]

But then recent studies of the supposedly empirical travel accounts written by Europeans of the sixteenth century have shown that in these works as well, misinformation, to say nothing of occasional disinformation, was rife. Renaissance travellers from France, England or the Germanies had the greatest trouble imaginable distancing themselves from the authority of the geographers and philosophers of the Greco-Roman world. Eyewitnesses of people and places often found it hard to overcome their veneration for 'ancient wisdom', even when the authorities so much revered had not visited the places about which they wrote, and made claims that were manifestly false.[2] In consequence, forming world views and making decisions on the basis of poor information was by no means an Ottoman peculiarity.

In the present chapter, we will discuss the sources of knowledge about Asia, Europe and, intermittently, the Americas that were available to three different categories of people; for it would be naive to assume that what was known to one particular group would automatically be diffused within Ottoman society at large. To begin with, there were the high-ranking members of the sultan's court and administration who had access to whatever transpired in discussions between foreign ambassadors on the one hand, and on the other, the grand vizier and other officials including the chief scribe (re'isülküttab, re'is efendi) and the senior translator (baş tercüman).[3] From the early eighteenth century onwards, Ottoman ambassadors who visited the courts of Iran, Vienna, St Petersburg, Paris and, at the very end of our period, also Madrid and Berlin were officially encouraged to write about their experiences. Quite a few of these accounts (sefaretnames) have been located, even though only a minority is accessible in print.[4] The information brought back by these ambassadors will form a special category, that of the arcana imperii accessible only to a few high officials; at least for the first few years after writing, they were out of bounds to anyone less.

The second category will consist of scholars or educated men with an interest in travel and geography. This group includes famous personages such as Kâtib

Çelebi and his circle of collaborators, or else the Ottoman geographers to whom the translations of the Dutch *Atlas Minor* and *Atlas Maior* were entrusted, after these volumes had been submitted to the sultan and gained the interest of his court.[5] People such as Kâtib Çelebi and his associate Ebubekir Dimaşki were familiar with the Arab geographers of the medieval period, but also with the itineraries of sultanic campaigns that, already in the sixteenth century, were being composed either as independent texts or else inserted into Ottoman chronicles. In addition, some of these Istanbul-based scholars were interested in European cartography. Thus the famous sixteenth-century admiral Piri Re'is compiled a nautical handbook of the entire Mediterranean, including Barcelona and Marseilles as well as Cyprus and Crete; at his time of writing these two islands, after all, were still Venetian possessions.[6] There even was a handbook from which information on the West Indies could be culled, the *Tarih-i Hind-i garbi,* whose author remains unknown.[7] A further prominent aficionado of geography was Evliya Çelebi (1611–after 1683/1019–after 1095), the indefatigable traveller who visited, and wrote about, both Iran and Austria. Evliya read geographical works before composing his own account, characterized by a varying – and to us, disconcerting – mixture of imaginative literature and factual report.[8] However, his travels did not take him very far beyond the Ottoman borders and, apart from Vienna, Evliya's interest in factual information concerning the territories beyond the Hungarian or eastern Anatolian borderlands remained quite limited.

Our third category will consist of 'ordinary' subjects of the sultan, meaning here that they were not members of the governing class or relations of such men. Even the individuals in this third category were still highly privileged, for the most part inhabiting towns in a world populated by a vast majority of peasants and nomads. These men were often literate in Ottoman Turkish, at least if it was written in not too elevated a style, although they might not know Arabic or Persian. But even if unlettered themselves, they had easy access to people who could read to them. This latter group should thus have included janissaries and cavalry of the Porte, normally stationed in Istanbul, who were likely to acquire a modicum of information about the lands where they had been on campaign. But some military men of more provincial origins, for the most part private soldiers and low-ranking officers, also might fall into this category; those higher up in the hierarchy evidently would have belonged to the ruling group.

Other candidates for membership in this third group of Ottomans informed about the outside world were the merchants who, in the sixteenth and seventeenth centuries, routinely visited Venice and, albeit much less frequently, Ancona or even Marseilles.[9] Some Ottoman traders had contacts with Indian businessmen, the latter being numerous in the ports of Yemen and the Hijaz. But some of these Indians also visited Cairo, Aleppo and even Istanbul. Other Ottoman merchants, in Bursa, Izmir and elsewhere, had the opportunity to talk to their trading partners from Iran. In coastal areas, fishermen, sailors and returned captives must have relayed notions concerning the world outside the Ottoman borders. But to the frustration of today's historians, these people did not normally record their information in writing.

Quite a few Ottomans who travelled in Europe were non-Muslims; given my linguistic limitations, the present discussion is confined to authors either available in translation, or made accessible to me by friendly colleagues. While most Greek, Jewish or Armenian travellers must have been merchants, like their Muslim counterparts, they were not much given to the writing of memoirs. One of the most extensive accounts used here was written by an eighteenth-century rabbi who toured the Jewish communities of England, France and Holland in search of charitable donations.

Once their business had reached a certain level, merchants were literate. Yet some knowledge about foreign lands was also diffused among people with very slender access to written culture. Even totally unlearned mercenaries and seamen were likely to come back with stories of battle with or captivity among 'the infidel'. In addition, in Istanbul there were foreign labour migrants; as we have seen, in the eighteenth century, such men arrived from Venetian Dalmatia with some regularity.[10] For the most part, these people had no access to written culture even in their native southern Slavic language, and their Ottoman Turkish must have been limited indeed. But they were not totally without social contacts in the capital, and particularly those who came and went several times must have told stories about their difficult lives to their neighbours and employers.[11] While we have no way of reconstructing what was learned by ordinary inhabitants of Istanbul from casual contacts of this type, it would be a mistake to assume that such sources of information were of no importance whatsoever.

~ The knowledge of the ambassadors: some general considerations

As we have seen, ambassadorial reports were read by a small group of high-level bureaucrats and in most cases probably the sultan himself, that is, to return to our categorization, members of the first group. Only if, as sometimes happened, these texts were later incorporated into chronicles did a wider audience gain access to them. Presumably the readers of such chronicles belonged to the second and third groups, that is, they might be scholars or else simply literate townsmen. Thus these texts played a certain, albeit limited role in introducing upper-class and urban Ottomans to a variety of problems connected with inter-state relations.

When an Ottoman ambassador took pen in hand, his first responsibility was to describe his reception at the court to which he had been sent. After all, the ceremonies linked to this event indicated the esteem that the foreign ruler in question was willing to show the Ottoman sultan. Thus describing an honourable reception in many cases was equivalent to proclaiming the success of the ambassador's mission. Now the nuances of courtly ceremonial are certainly not without interest to the present-day historian, but they do tend to take second place vis-á-vis other concerns.[12] After all, we look mainly for what Ottoman diplomats had to say on the states and societies they encountered. Yet, a few exceptions apart, at least before the early to mid-eighteenth century such observations were mostly a matter of secondary importance to the authors whose writings have come down to us. About this time Ottoman sultans certainly did begin to ask their ambassadors to write about matters going beyond courtly receptions, as evident for the first time in connection with Yirmisekiz Mehmed Efendi's mission to Paris in 1720/1132–3. The quality of the socio-political information relayed depended on the training and personality of the ambassador in question. A systematic coverage of the world beyond the borders of the 'well-guarded domains' was not the concern of diplomats.

Why then do we bother to discuss such texts in detail? The main reason for our interest is the wide variety of solutions that Ottoman ambassadors might adopt in their reports for, in spite of all their limitations, these accounts were certainly not standardized. While some authors might indeed confine themselves to a simple description of the honours with which they were received, others did discuss broader patterns of behaviour typical of the Russian or Habsburg courts, at least where Ottoman affairs were concerned. And towards the end of our period, the character of a given ruler and even the socio-political information that we are so interested in might enter the picture in force.[13] We can thus follow a gradually increasing trend towards imparting information in writing, which in earlier periods must have been conveyed orally.

Moreover, in the sixteenth century and even later, Ottoman information on European courts was quite often gathered by non-Muslims, who were sent to negotiate with Christian courts and ambassadors; in some cases the intermediaries' position was semi-official rather than official.[14] But from the 1720s/1132–42 onwards more and more the tendency was to have that kind of information collected by Muslims, who often held official positions of some distinction. We can thus speak of an eighteenth-century antecedent of the nineteenth-century Tercüme Odası (Translation Office) that was founded in order to take over the functions of the (usually non-Muslim) chief translators (dragomans), no longer regarded as sufficiently reliable after the Greek uprising of 1821/1236–7. Or even more broadly speaking, we can compare the new obligations imposed upon Muslim envoys with the attempts on the part of the French and Venetian diplomatic services to ensure that translation work was not 'farmed out' to the sultan's non-Muslim subjects, but undertaken by people owing full allegiance to the state they served. Thus in this perspective the Ottoman ambassadorial reports allow us to follow how individual office-holders, usually of upper-middle rank, adapted to a set of demands that were now being made of them, and that their predecessors in the 1500s or 1600s had not frequently been called upon to fulfil.

~ Fleeting encounters: a sea captain and diplomat in sixteenth-century India

For the very beginning of our period, we possess the unique account of the Ottoman naval commander Seyyidî 'Ali Re'îs who, even though he had not been sent as an ambassador, wrote a report of his travels that already shows quite a few characteristics of the later *sefaretname*s.[15] Seyyidî 'Ali Re'îs is unique among sixteenth-century Ottomans in having visited India and written about his experiences. In late 1553/960–1, he had been sent out to rescue some Ottoman ships bottled up in Basra by the Portuguese holding the island of Hormuz. But driven into the Indian Ocean by violent storms, he lost his fleet, and thus had no option but to return overland to the Ottoman Empire, traversing the Mughul territories, Central Asia and Iran on highly difficult and dangerous routes.

This aspect of Seyyidî 'Ali Re'îs' story is perfectly credible. Yet at the same time, an emphasis on extraordinary hardships cleverly overcome evidently served the author's purposes: after all, he never tired of telling his readers that it was pure misery to live outside one's home region or, at the very least, outside the Ottoman sultan's well-guarded domains. Certainly this was not quite the whole story; and Seyyidî 'Ali Re'îs did on occasion treat his public to brief descriptions of monkeys, parrots and trees unknown on the Mediterranean coast, and even furnished some 'proto-ethnographic' data on the people encountered. Presumably the topos of the 'wonders of India', so well established in Ottoman literature, made it seem appropriate for a man who had actually visited the subcontinent to say something about these matters. But nowhere did Seyyidî 'Ali Re'îs express a more personal reaction to the wonders of nature and human activity that he had witnessed in Indian cities and royal courts. For instance, he never said that he would have liked to contemplate this fascinating place full of marvels at his leisure if his obligations had not forced him to return as quickly as possible.

Presumably the stranded sea captain composed his account as part of the strategy that he applied, not without success, after his return to Sultan Süleyman's court in Istanbul and Edirne. For, even though he made no intimation of his fears, the author must have been much worried about saving his own neck. Only a few years earlier (1553/960–1) Piri Re'is, arguably the Ottomans' most distinguished cartographer, had been executed because he too had lost ships to the Portuguese in the Persian Gulf.[16] If we understand Seyyidî 'Ali Re'îs' account as an exercise in self-defence, it becomes easy to explain why the author told us so much about his honourable receptions at a variety of Indian and Central Asian courts, not to mention the Safavid palace, and placed so much stress on his loyalty and faithful service to the Ottoman sultan. If he had failed in his assignment as a naval commander, at least his journey had not been totally in vain. This protestation of special loyalty to the Ottoman sultan, along with the first-hand diplomatic information furnished, seems to have gained the author some appreciation in high places; on his return, he was appointed to other offices and enabled to live out his life in Istanbul, as he claimed to have so ardently desired at the time of writing his book.

Although the author tells us repeatedly that he was in a great hurry to return to the Ottoman capital, in actual fact, Seyyidî 'Ali Re'îs was held up on the Indian subcontinent for a considerable length of time. When discussing the main reason for this situation, namely an enforced stay at the court of Bābur's son the Emperor Humāyūn, the account most resembles the *sefaretname*s of a later age: we learn that the author's poetry and witticisms were well received by Humāyūn, and we are even treated to copies of the flattering letters received from minor princes gravitating around the Mughul court. Of course Seyyidî 'Ali Re'îs did not neglect to mention that all these potentates performed some kind of obei-sance to the 'sultan of Rum', the implication being that his own skills as a courtier had been instrumental in furthering the prestige of the Ottoman Empire. This 'propagandistic' effort for the benefit of Süleyman the Magnificent reached its culmination point when in front of the Mughul ruler, the author claimed to have insisted that the landmass governed by the Ottomans was far larger than that ruled by Humāyūn himself. That Seyyidî 'Ali Re'îs wished to present him-self as a potential ambassador also became apparent from the manner in which he supposedly rejected a pressing offer on Humāyūn's part to stay for a longer period of time: he certainly would be happy to return, so Seyyidî 'Ali Re'îs replied, if only he could get himself appointed to an embassy.

Humāyūn finally accorded the author and his company permission to leave. But, just as the travellers were about to depart, the emperor suffered an accident and died a few days later (26 January 1556/13. Rabî I 963). This was an occasion for Seyyidî 'Ali Re'îs to present himself as an 'elder statesman'. To courtiers thrown into disarray by the death of their sovereign, the author, or so he told us, proposed a type of conduct well known at the Ottoman court, namely to keep the death secret for a while. As a model, he proposed the measures taken at the death of Selim I, and which, incidentally, were to be repeated in 1566/973–4, when Sultan Süleyman himself passed away.[17] Accordingly, messengers proclaimed *urbi et orbi* that the emperor was in good health and spirits, so as to give his suc-cessor Djalāl al-dīn Akbar time to reach the capital. In the meantime, Seyyidî 'Ali Re'îs attempted to use this period of confusion to absent himself from the Mughul domains, but was prevented from so doing. For, according to a rule also followed in the Ottoman context, all documents issued by the dead sovereign were no longer valid, and Akbar needed to confirm the *laissez-passer* issued by his deceased father.

Seyyidî 'Ali Re'îs thus seems to have fulfilled many of the functions of an ambassador even though he lacked the title: he even claimed to have persuaded Humāyūn – who was unable to contradict, being safely dead at the time of writ-ing – to admit the superior status of the sultan in Istanbul.[18] In addition, Seyyidî 'Ali Re'îs brought back valuable diplomatic information. Presumably, the Mughul ex-emperor's exile at the Safavid court was well known to Ottoman offi-cials, but it is quite likely that reliable news on his political comeback, his conquest of Agra and finally his fatal accident were first conveyed to Istanbul by Seyyidî 'Ali Re'îs. In our present perspective, this account is all the more interesting as later Ottoman embassy reports on India seem to have been very rare. Yet a few envoys continued to visit this country occasionally, and it is possible that some such report is still hidden away, un-catalogued, in one of the many collections of diverse texts (*mecmua*) so numerous in libraries both within and outside Turkey.[19]

~ The knowledge of the envoys: representing Ottoman dignity in Iran

Seyyidî 'Ali Re'îs had not originally planned to pass through Iran, but found himself obliged to do so because of the Russo-Ottoman conflict over Astrakhan. Passing through Mashhad, the author was received by the viziers who assisted the Safavid princes to whom this region had been assigned as apanages, and immediately, the thorny problem of Sunni–Shi'ite relations presented itself. The recently concluded peace of Amasya (1555/962–3) contained a clause that the Safavids were to desist from the ritual cursing of the first three caliphs of Islam, and also from reviling the Prophet Muhammad's spouse 'Ā'isha. But because of the opposition of these four personages to the Caliph 'Alī, whom the variety of Shi'ism espoused at the Safavid court considered the only legitimate successor to the Prophet, the caliphs Abū Bakir, 'Omar, 'Othmān as well as Sitt 'Ā'isha still were considered as highly controversial by Safavid dignitaries. Apparently the latter did their best to involve Seyyidî 'Ali Re'îs in discussions of these contentious issues, but our author refused to take the bait. Yet he was perfectly willing to write poetry in honour of the Prophet's descendants and thereby satisfy the Safavid court and Iranian religious scholars, without doing anything incorrect from the Sunni Ottoman point of view. He thus managed to conclude some rather thorny affairs in an elegant and conciliatory fashion.

If 'Ali Re'îs can be believed, it was his major concern to uphold the dignity of the Ottoman sultan no matter what risks he might incur. Thus he assured his readers that Shah Ṭahmāsp was completely submissive towards Süleyman the Magnificent; given the author's several close escapes at the hands of Safavid officials, at the Ottoman court this claim was probably taken with a grain of salt. In addition, we find Seyyidî 'Ali Re'îs upholding the warlike qualities of the Ottoman rulers as a model worthy of emulation. When shown the highly worked carpets, silk fabrics, decorated felts and ornamented tents in the Safavid treasury, he proclaimed that the storehouses of a great ruler should contain gold and silver capable of being rapidly transformed into weaponry, rather than textiles. Apart from praising his own ruler and embarrassing his host by an oblique reference to past Iranian defeats, Seyyidî 'Ali Re'îs probably adopted this stance because carpets and other precious textiles in the eyes of Safavid courtiers formed symbols of power.[20] Thus the author evidently saw his work as a testimony to his loyalty to the Ottoman sultan under whatever circumstances, while information about the Safavid court certainly was provided, but did not form the major topic of his description.

~ Lying abroad for the good of one's sovereign: obscuring Ottoman intentions in early eighteenth-century Iran

As the account of a later envoy to Iran – a 'real' one this time – we may cite Ahmed Dürri Efendi, who in 1721/1133–4 was accredited to the last Safavid shah of Iran. Due to the loss of his capital Işfahān to the Afghan invaders of his territory, Shah Ḥusayn, who died the following year, had been obliged to transfer his seat to Tehran.[21] At this time, Ahmed III's grand vizier Damad Ibrahim Paşa was planning to use the opportunity to occupy the western provinces of Iran, and this involved coming to an agreement with the equally expansionist Russian tsar Peter the Great. But at the same time, Ibrahim Paşa thought that it would be useful to both impress the shah with the sultan's power, and present the Ottoman Empire to the embattled Safavid dignitaries as a friendly state. Only in 1724/1136–7, after Shah Ḥusayn's death, were Ottoman expansionist intentions, which had long been suspected, to become completely obvious to the Iranian court.[22]

Ahmed Dürri Efendi, the ambassador chosen for this mission, had filled a variety of distinguished but not top-level scribal positions. For the occasion, he was given the status of an *orta elçi* (middle-level ambassador) and the ceremonial rank of a *şıkk-ı sani defterdarı* (finance director). He originated from the frontier town of Van and was fluent in Persian; probably this skill was one of the reasons why he had been selected in the first place. In order to emphasize the prestige of the Ottoman sultan at the Safavid court, Dürri Efendi told his readers that he was received with great pomp, the Vizier Rustam Khan meeting him at a distance from Tehran with a cortège of 3,000 men.[23] To further stress the respect that he had been shown, Dürri Efendi reported that the shah sent food from his own kitchen; but the ambassador availed himself of this courtesy for only a short period. Presumably it would have been a gesture of grave disrespect if Dürri Efendi had refused to accept any food at all. But at the same time it would not have done to create the impression that the envoy was dependent on the bounty of the court to which he had been dispatched. To maintain reciprocity, Dürri Efendi further distributed money and silk cloth among the court officials who had been sent to serve him.

At the Ottoman ambassador's first reception, the dignitary whom Ahmed Dürri describes as the 'Grand Vizier of the Persians', immediately entered *in medias res*, and attempted to find out which provinces the Ottomans planned to annex. By contrast the ambassador, in a long speech which appears as a verbatim citation, claimed that the frontier khan who had warned the Safavid court of Ottoman aggressive intentions had been completely misinformed.[24]

Presumably the negotiations of Dürri Efendi were 'top secret' at the time of writing; but this confidentiality did not last very long, as Mehmed Raşid soon was able to include the ambassador's account in his chronicle. Moreover, as early as 1735/1147–8 Dürri Efendi's text, of which there was apparently both a Turkish and a Persian version, was published in a Latin translation by P. Juda Krusinski SJ.[25] Of course, by the mid-eighteenth century, the Safavid dynasty no longer existed, so that Dürri Efendi's report now only possessed historical interest.[26] But other ambassadorial reports to Iran were to follow, and one of them, written in the early nineteenth century, even illustrated the principal stopping points by means of thirty-one miniatures, a tradition which had been instituted in the sixteenth century by Matrakçı Nasuh, but almost forgotten in later times.[27]

~ Reporting on European embassies

More numerous were the Ottoman embassies to European courts. But, as we have seen before 1700/1111–12, the ambassadors were not routinely required to file written reports about the foreign courts to which they had been accredited. In consequence, although in the sixteenth century Venice was probably the European capital most often visited by Ottoman envoys, we do not seem to possess any first-person accounts of these travels; nor did accompanying scribes record the successes of their masters as negotiators on behalf of the Ottoman sultans.[28] Only from official documents do we learn what the envoys to Venice usually dealt with, namely the problems of Ottoman subjects robbed while trading in the Adriatic region (compare Chapter 5). This deficiency is all the more regrettable as there survives ample documentation on the manner in which the Venetian authorities regarded these visitors from Istanbul, and it would be of great interest to know by what criteria the Ottoman envoys themselves evaluated the successes and failures of their missions.[29]

However, the number of studies undertaken on the basis of even the available embassy accounts is still remarkably limited. At least in part, this must be due to the fact that so many of them date from the eighteenth century, which as a whole, remains a much neglected period of Ottoman history. Of course there are some exceptions: thus after the battle of St Gotthard on the Raab (1664/1074–5), Mehmed Paşa was sent to Vienna in order to conclude a peace of twenty years' duration, and was accompanied by the famous traveller and creative writer Evliya Çelebi. The latter's account of this embassy is not only full of fascinating detail, both real and imaginary, but has received more scholarly attention than almost any other text of this type.[30] Particularly the amalgam of Ottoman stories about the 'Red Apple', the yet to-be-conquered capital of the 'German infidel' on the one hand, and the folklore of the Viennese celebrating their own city on the other, has been studied in considerable detail.[31] By comparison, the report of the ambassador himself is short and sober, and has aroused much less interest.[32]

From the 1720s/1132–42 dates another 'star' among Ottoman embassy reports, namely the book in which Yirmisekiz Mehmed Efendi reported on his visit to Paris and Versailles, where he was accredited to the boy-king Louis XV and the latter's regent Philip of Orleans. Translated into French upon the initiative of the Ottoman court shortly after the completion of the embassy, and republished several times since, this text has even become the subject of a separate monograph.[33] Furthermore, quite a few French sources on this embassy, including a large painting, have been made available in the context of a recent exhibition catalogue.[34] As to the late eighteenth-century report of Ahmed Resmi, covering his missions to Vienna and Berlin, it has been analysed as an important contribution to Ottoman intellectual and political life during those troubled years.[35] In the tradition initiated by Yirmisekiz Mehmed Efendi, Ahmed Resmi's account goes far beyond a simple description of his receptions at the two courts visited, an issue that, as we have seen, had formed the unavoidable centrepiece of older embassy accounts. On the other hand, Ahmed Resmi included quite a few observations of a socio-economic nature: thus he described the fascination of Prussian noblemen with the decorative possibilities of porcelain, and the attempts of King Frederick II to promote the manufacture of this precious material on Prussian territory in order to minimize the outflow of specie.[36]

Later reports by Ottoman envoys contain even more of such 'socio-economic' information. A good example is the work of Ebubekir Râtib Efendi, who visited the Habsburg capital almost twenty years after our story is supposed to end, namely in 1792/1206–7. But his account contains so many fascinating observations that we will for once ignore this constraint, and instead, Ebubekir Râtib's report will form the final point of our analysis of 'ambassadorial knowledge'.[37] In a sense, this text resulted from the order of Sultan Selim III, then recently enthroned, to collect information on European institutions which might be adapted to Ottoman conditions and thus help to ensure the Empire's survival.[38] However, the ambassador's interests were not limited to matters of immediate applicability. Thus an institution that he described in most detail was the Viennese Academy of Oriental Studies, where future translators and occasionally also other embassy personnel received instruction in Arabic, Persian and Ottoman Turkish. A library in the Transylvanian town of Sibiu was also described in considerable detail.

Ebubekir Râtib Efendi also noted that Ottoman music was of interest to educated Habsburg noblemen, and as he himself was competent in this field, he arranged for performances on the *saz* to be given, which were greatly appreciated; some of the people so honoured sent their own musicians in return.[39] Thus in line with Selim III's well-known interest in music and poetry, the ambassador understood his report also as a discussion of Viennese 'polite culture', and not as a mere description of institutions that might enhance military effectiveness. Moreover his presentation of the Ottoman court as a place where sophisticated music was highly esteemed shows a changing attitude vis-à-vis Habsburg courtly society. In the sixteenth century, 'cultural competition' had occurred mainly

6. The parade by which Ahmed Resmi entered Berlin in 1763, etching owned by the Staatsbibliothek-Preussischer Kulturbesitz Berlin, YB 9012m. Reproduced by permission.

Türcke: Legations secret: mit den Friden Contract

7. Secretary of the Ottoman embassy to Berlin, carrying the sultan's letter (after 1763). This image is part of a costume book documenting the embassy as a whole.

Source: The image has been reproduced in the exhibition catalogue *Im Lichte des Halbmonds, Das Abendland und der türkische Orient* (Dresden and Bonn: Staatliche Kunstsammlungen and Kunst- und Ausstellungshalle der Bundesrepublik Deutschland, 1995): 277 and 306, exhibit no. 352. The original volume is owned by the Staatsbibliothek-Preussischer Kulturbesitz Berlin, Sign. Libr.pictur. A151. Reproduced by permission.

when embassies were exchanged between the Ottoman and Iranian courts, and played but a minor role when an envoy visited the 'unbelievers'. On the other hand, Ebubekir Râtib Efendi evidently believed not only that music could be appreciated regardless of the Muslim–non-Muslim cultural divide, but also that displaying a rich musical culture could enhance the 'reputation' of the Ottoman court.[40]

~ Old opponents, new allies

We will continue the discussion of the reports of Ottoman ambassadors with a text by Vasıf Efendi, the author of an Ottoman chronicle known for its elaborate literary style.[41] As in 1787/1201–2, the Ottoman Empire found itself once again at war with both Russia and Austria, the government considered it necessary to secure the kingdom of Spain's absolute neutrality. A treaty of friendship and commerce had been concluded already in 1782/1196–7. It was also considered desirable to find out something about the effects of Spain's recent treaty with the autonomous Ottoman province of Algiers. For, in spite of the British fortress of Gibraltar, the Iberian kingdom remained one of the powers controlling access from the Atlantic to the Mediterranean. In the Ottoman perspective, the king of Spain thus occupied a strategic position; after all in 1770/1183–4 the unexpected appearance of a Russian fleet in the eastern Mediterranean had contributed to some degree to the Ottoman debacle. Good relations with Spain might forestall a repetition of these events.

A formal Hispano-Ottoman understanding was something of a novelty. Certainly the two states had not been at war for a long time. But well into the eighteenth century many members of the Spanish administration considered that their kingdom had throughout the centuries defined itself as the heir of the late medieval Reconquista, the 'reconquest' of the Iberian peninsula from the Muslims. This self-image implied an all-out defence of the Catholic faith and, as a corollary, the elimination of Muslims, Jews and Protestants from the Iberian peninsula. Following this political tradition, a strong faction within the governing elite took the position that Spain could not, without losing much of its credit within the community of Christian states, establish formal relations with an empire of 'unbelievers'.

However, by the late eighteenth century another group within the Spanish ruling circle increasingly considered the *respublica christiana* an outmoded concept that outside Spain had long been replaced by the notion of the sovereign ruler pursuing only the interests of his/her own dynasty and state. Thus by insisting on the aggrandizement of the Catholic Church as a major concern of public policy, Spain was merely allowing the benefits of commerce 'with the infidel' to go to other states. Thus the 1782/1196–7 treaty on the Spanish side can be regarded as an attempt to 'secularize' politics and, because of this implication, official relations with the Ottomans became a matter of domestic debate ranging far beyond the immediate content of the treaty.[42]

Vasıf Efendi, however, was only marginally concerned with the motives and political problems of his opposite numbers in Spain. Beyond his encounters with polite society, the ambassador's special interests were those of a literary figure. Similarly to his contemporary Ebubekir Râtib, who described in some detail the book collections he visited, Vasıf had something to say about the library of the Escorial. Here he found a large selection of Arabic manuscripts, collected in the royal library originally to facilitate censorship, but which had recently been catalogued.[43] Even though a large number of volumes had been lost in a fire, Vasıf Efendi was still quite impressed by the richness of this collection, which he was sorry to see in the hands of 'unbelievers'.[44]

~ In the empire of the tsars

As we have seen, the Russian Empire in the course of the eighteenth century emerged as arguably the most dangerous among the opponents of the Ottoman sultans. In consequence, examining the documentation produced by envoys who had visited the court of St Petersburg should have possessed high priority in the eyes of twentieth-century scholars. But that has not been the case, and neither has the new century begun with a great upsurge of interest in this issue.[45] Among Ottoman ambassadors who visited Russia, only the reports of Mehmed Emni Beyefendi, a bureaucrat promoted to the rank of *paşa* for the duration of his embassy (travelled 1739–42/1151–5) and of Abdülkerim Paşa (travelled 1775–6/ 1188–90) have been made available in full to the modern reader.[46]

According to the stipulations of the peace of Belgrade (1739/1151–2), which ended a war with the Russians and Austrians from which the Ottomans had emerged as highly successful, an exchange of ambassadors was to take place. As the sultan's envoy, it was Mehmed Emni's function to ensure the exchange of prisoners; in addition, he was to obtain the Tsarina Anna Ivanovna's signature to a document regulating this affair. On the other hand, the Ottoman side consented to accord the Russian rulers the title of emperor and also to destroy the long disputed fortress of Azak. Complications arose from the death of the tsarina before the Ottoman embassy had even reached Moscow, and the subsequent enthronement of a very young boy as tsar. 'On the ground' these tensions were expressed by long drawn-out disputes over matters of detail. For similar reasons, Mehmed Emni was later made to wait for a lengthy period of time before being admitted to St Petersburg.

All these delays resulted in a good deal of bad feeling, palpable even through the measured prose in which Mehmed Emni recounted his experiences. The Ottoman ambassador was particularly annoyed by the martial demonstrations of the Russian soldiers; these included a parade at which arms were presented ready for battle. Even though these events were supposedly organized in his honour, Mehmed Emni Beyefendi felt that such 'militaristic' behaviour was inappropriate to a peaceful mission, and did not hesitate to say so.[47]

In addition, the ambassador informed his superiors about the habits of his Russian interlocutors in a manner much more sophisticated and detailed than that of Seyyidî 'Ali Re'îs or Ahmed Dürri Efendi. At the time of the envoy's visit, the Russian armies had just fought out a small battle with the Swedes, whose great power status by the early eighteenth century was definitely on the wane. Mehmed Emni took the trouble to check the information concerning this encounter given to him by Russian ministerial personnel with the interpretation of these same events provided by an Ottoman-speaking nobleman attached to the French embassy. As a result, the ambassador informed his superiors that, like other European state officials, the Russian authorities were very anxious to keep secrets, and were inclined to spring information on him that he was unable to verify. Thus the envoy would be told about a 'victory' actually but of minor importance, after the very existence of the relevant conflict had been kept secret from him.[48]

Among the 'sights' with which the Russian court attempted to impress the ambassador, the gardens of Peterhof, with their canals, ponds and fountains, often adorned with statuary, rated a lengthy description by Mehmed Emni. We do not know whether the ambassador himself was interested in garden culture. Sultan Mahmud I (r. 1730–54/1142–68) may have shared the taste of his predecessor Ahmed III for decorative elements in the 'Frankish' style, and Mehmed Emni may thus have been instructed to pay particular attention to this aspect of Russian court life.[49] Also of some interest are the comparisons through which the author tried to give members of the Ottoman political establishment an idea of the appearance of Peterhof: thus he compared the hilly countryside adjacent to the river Neva to an Albanian village.[50] But in the end, Mehmed Emni judged that 'Frankish arts and crafts' lacked a sense of measure and harmony, the gardens were deficient in flowers, and the 'animal-like' labour expended on their construction was altogether in vain.[51]

~ Difficult beginnings: a new type of information-gathering

General observations about political tactics and diplomatic usage had doubtless been made by envoys from whatever period; but it was only in the eighteenth century that, as we have noted, recording them in writing became part of Ottoman diplomatic practice. We may surmise that this was also because, in an age in which embassies were more numerous, future envoys did well to read the reports of their predecessors, but this at present is just a hypothesis. Yet, as an argument in favour of this view, we may point out that in the course of the eighteenth century embassy reports tended to become more sophisticated, in other words, they were more frequently written up with an eye towards conveying information about the political practices of foreign courts. It is obvious that these data might be usable in future negotiations.

Certainly the Ottoman envoys, who as yet were not permanently stationed in the capitals to which they were accredited, often found it difficult to locate sources of information: Mehmed Emni's relief at finding an Ottoman-Turkish-speaking interlocutor in Russia is almost palpable. Yet it is also worth noting that he found it necessary to inform his superiors that he had in fact located such a person; presumably this documented his information-gathering skills.

At the same time it would seem that such new-style data-collecting was considered more important with respect to European states than when Iran was at issue. We may therefore hypothesize that Ottoman officials, especially those in the service of the *reisülküttab*, who were on their way towards becoming professional diplomats, realized that changing power relations made more and higher-quality information imperative. Wherever this constraint did not operate, Ottoman officials seem to have assumed that the old procedures would suffice.

They may also have concluded that it was people like themselves, and not the non-Muslim intermediaries of old, who could and should procure this type of knowledge. Yet one of the more remarkable aspects of these embassy accounts is the fact that religious concerns certainly were not absent, but did not exactly play a major role either. Our authors seem to have viewed themselves as part of the Islamic world mainly in a cultural sense. Thus Vasıf showed a close interest in the Arabic books of the Escorial, as did Ebubekir Râtib in the Viennese Academy for Oriental Studies. This matter-of-fact manner of reporting, without too many formulas glorifying the role of the sultan in spreading the dominion of Islam, may serve to remind us that the 'new style' Tanzimat officials of the mid-nineteenth century did not spring fully formed out of the Empire's recently established schools; quite to the contrary, they followed a tradition established by Ottoman envoys that went back several decades already.

~ Framing the world according to Ottoman geographers

When, from about 1500/905–6 onwards, some Ottomans began to write about geography, they were cognizant of the work that had been done by their medieval Arab predecessors, who had aimed at the description of the entire inhabited world – even though in practice, some regions were rather better known than others. But, as so often happens when making use of an ongoing scholarly tradition, in quite a few instances Ottoman authors were inclined to take over the findings of their mentors verbatim, without too much concern for the time elapsed since the collection of the data in question. In the case of Kâtib Çelebi, the reasons for this approach have been well elucidated.[52] Apparently this scholar considered that what was worthy of discussion were only those customs, political structures and distributions of varying ethnicities that supposedly had existed from the time of Noah's Flood. Transient phenomena, the entire realm of the contingent, thus did not seem worthy of the geographer's attention. Obviously, such *longue durée* phenomena might very well have been discovered by authors who had flourished in centuries long since past and whose works thus had achieved lasting validity. This attitude also explains why, for instance, Ottoman scholars were willing to use medieval sources, long out of date, when discussing a major empire such as China.[53]

In taking this view, they somewhat resembled their opposite numbers in Renaissance and sometimes even post-Renaissance Europe, who put a similar – and often misplaced – trust in the authors of Greco-Roman antiquity, to say nothing of more or less dubious travel accounts from their own times.[54] A recent study of late seventeenth- and early eighteenth-century Dutch geography has emphasized the tendency of authors working in Holland around 1700/1111–12 to eliminate from their works all matter that might have been regarded as 'contentious', and thus, to use a modern phrase, 'decontextualize' the information provided.[55] This proceeding resulted in an ahistorical picture not so dissimilar from that provided by medieval Islamic cosmographic literature, or for that matter, Christian *mirabilia*, that in their turn had often been derived from Islamic sources.

Even the lack of connectedness between the enormous variety of phenomena discussed, which makes Dutch geographic works published around 1700/1111–12 resemble cornucopias whose contents are emptied in front of a stupefied reader, is reminiscent of the *mirabilia* model. Certainly the accuracy of Dutch descriptions is novel, and so is the commercial motivation that has been suggested for this 'blandness' of content: if the historical contexts, potential generators of controversy, were left out of the picture, the books became more readily saleable.[56] After all, the atlases printed in Holland were of interest not just to European purchasers from a variety of countries often embroiled in war, but to the Ottoman court as well.

Yet at the same time, sixteenth-century geography, Ottoman or European, was not merely a scholarly and commercial endeavour. This was also the period when the sultan's navy was embarked on its triumphant career in the Mediterranean, and its admirals soon branched out into the Red Sea and the Indian Ocean. Naval expansion spurred interest in more modern discoveries, including regions of the world where the Ottomans were present only in a very limited sense, such as the Atlantic Ocean. Both Piri Re'is' and Seyyidî 'Ali Re'îs' interest in oceanic geography must be seen in this context. Thus there was not only a tension between the work of those authors who continued the traditions of medieval geographic literature and those who favoured contemporary sources, but also between those people whom we might describe as the 'schoolmen' and those who were interested in geographical knowledge for practical reasons.

To complicate matters yet further, geography might constitute an appropriate interest for a well-to-do gentleman able to afford lavishly produced books. For since the later 'Middle Period', to use Marshall Hodgson's terminology, geography had been considered as part of *adab*, the general knowledge expected from a cultivated man of letters. To satisfy this demand, there existed accounts of the Islamic world that contained occasional excursions into 'infidel' territories such as Byzantium.[57] In these works, the emphasis was often religious, that is, the ultimate aim was to teach veneration for the Creator and inculcate correct Islamic behaviour, by describing both the 'recurring features' and the 'extraordinary marvels' of the creation. These works showed humankind acting in the sublunar world between Noah's Flood and the Last Judgement. 'Monsters and wonders' readily found their places in this world view.[58]

Well into the eighteenth century, the principal texts of this literature in Arabic, often denoted by the term 'cosmography', were translated into Ottoman Turkish with relative frequency. They provided a framework within which authors could discuss places they had themselves visited, and others they could only describe at second hand. When, for instance, Mehmed Aşık (around 1555/962–after 1598/ 1007), a native of the Black Sea town of Trabzon, attempted to supplement the rather scanty medieval accounts of Rumelia and Anatolia by what he knew largely from first-hand observation, he adopted the cosmographer's framework. A similar proceeding was followed by the anonymous author of the late sixteenth-century work known as the *Tarih-i Hind-i garbi*, who framed a carefully researched secondary description of the Americas with topoi from cosmographic literature.[59] Throughout, this latter model must be taken into account when summarizing the contributions of Ottoman geographers to the knowledge that the sultan's subjects might acquire about the outside world.

We may thus distinguish between publications intended for naval men, of which almost nothing survives, books written by and for scholars and other volumes produced with the wealthy amateur in mind.[60] In terms of the categories set out at the beginning of this chapter, some readers might belong to the second category of specialist scholars, or else to the third category of literate townsmen. But of course a degree of overlap between the different categories must always have occurred. To see how this worked itself out, we will take a brief look at a rather early work, written just before the time covered in the present study, namely the lavishly illustrated travel account of the courtier, sportsman and artist Matrakçı Nasuh. Describing the itinerary of the Ottoman armies that conquered Iraq from the Safavids in 1533–6/939–43, he produced a book evidently not intended for a wide distribution. To the contrary, the readership envisaged must have belonged to a small highly privileged group, gravitating around the Ottoman palace, if only because the many miniatures contained in this volume must have raised its cost to prohibitive levels. But even so Matrakçı Nasuh did not write a mere 'coffee table book' *avant la lettre*. It makes more sense to consider him a pioneer who explored the uncertain boundary separating geography from the fine arts.

This is perhaps most obvious when we take a closer look at his map-like miniature of mid-sixteenth-century Istanbul.[61] The hills behind Galata, where today Beyoğlu is located, are covered with cypresses and spring flowers in the style of a miniature illustrating a literary text. As to the peninsula on which Istanbul is located, it is shown as a square rather than as a triangle, in order to better accommodate the sultan's palace, the Aya Sofya and the open space of the At Meydanı/ Hippodrome, which still possessed a range of columns that has since disappeared. In contrast with these stylized images, quite a few monuments are shown in such a fashion that with some imagination they are recognizable even today. At the same time the stylized depiction of buildings was accompanied by considerable care in showing the spatial relationships of the buildings to one another; here the miniature artist became the map-maker.

That Matrakçı Nasuh worked for courtiers is clearly apparent from his emphasis on public buildings: mosques, fortresses and palaces were given pride of place, while private dwellings are little in evidence. This aspect of Matrakçı's work is consonant with what the manufacturers of sixteenth-century town models for Central European princes also tended to do, showing public buildings larger than they were in relation to the houses surrounding them. However, there is one major difference: while in Central Europe streets and squares also were often overstressed, the opposite is true in Matrakçı's paintings. Istanbul's only open space is the At Meydanı, and even the ancient thoroughfare of the Divan-yolu remains invisible. Such a mode of depiction presumably reflected the priorities of sixteenth-century Ottoman urbanism: the erection of monumental structures as cores for town quarters yet to be established, and a limited interest in traffic flow.

With only slight exaggeration, we can say that what really counted for Matrakçı were the towns and cities, while the open countryside was paid much less attention. Different from what can be observed in his depiction of Istanbul's buildings, the watercourses, mountains, swamps and defiles of Anatolia were drawn without a great deal of attention to their spatial relationships. As rivers and streams so often follow a more or less horizontal course, dividing the miniatures into bands, it is likely that they were arranged according to compositional rather than according to geographical criteria; perhaps the idea was to depict the inexorable progress of Sultan Süleyman's ever victorious army.

~ Taking notice of the Americas

However, among sixteenth-century Ottoman geographers, the work of Piri Re'is is probably more famous today than that of Matrakçı Nasuh, due to the former's early knowledge of a Columbus map surviving only in this Ottoman rendition of 1513/918–19.[62] But Piri Re'is' geographical studies were for the most part undertaken long before 1540/946–7 and are thus outside the purview of our study; the author apparently was over eighty years old when he was executed in 1552–3/ 959–61.[63] Piri Re'is had been an admiral himself, and thus must have collected his information with some practical purpose in mind.[64] Yet scholarly discussion concerning his book on the Mediterranean coastline, written between 1521/ 927–8 and 1526/932–3, has stressed that, in spite of the numerous portulan maps that constitute one of the more fascinating aspects of this volume, most surviving manuscripts were not made to be used on board ship. Quite to the contrary, they seem to have been intended for library perusal, and in some cases, even as elegant appurtenances of a gentleman's study.

Among sixteenth-century Ottoman geographers, an interest in the Americas was not widespread, but neither was it uniquely limited to Piri Re'is. Of special interest is the anonymous author of the *Tarih-i Hind-i garbi*, or 'history of the western Indies', who hoped to encourage the sultan of his time, presumably Selim II (1566–74/973–82) and/or Murad III (1574–95/982–1004) to conquer at least a part of this remote continent.[65] How exactly these political suggestions should be understood remains a matter of dispute: the seventeenth-century author Kâtib Çelebi was quite contemptuous of such proposals, which he considered completely unrealistic. It has therefore been suggested that the author of the *Tarih-i Hind-i garbi* did not really intend them to be taken seriously either, but was simply engaged in a piece of courtly flattery.[66] Yet the earlier anonymous author was writing at a time when the memory of Ottoman exploits in the Indian Ocean was still vivid, and he also may have been more optimistic than the rather sceptical Kâtib Çelebi. Given Ottoman–Portuguese rivalries in the Indian Ocean and wars with the Spaniards in the Mediterranean, it is not, after all, so surprising that the author felt the sultans should not allow the Habsburg Empire to further increase its power. In addition to this political concern, the anonymous writer also expressed the more abstract hope of improving the geographic knowledge of his readers.[67]

Certainly the author of the *Tarih-i Hind-i garbi* was not the first Ottoman after Piri Re'is to show an interest in the New World; Seyyidî 'Ali Re'îs, the intrepid traveller across the Asian landmass, also had written a book about the oceans in which he included some information on America, apparently acquired from a Portuguese sea captain.[68] But the anonymous author of the *Tarih-i Hind-i garbi* probably had not seen the works of his Ottoman predecessors, but rather chose to translate very competently selections from books available in Italian. These texts originally had been written in Spanish, and in the last quarter of the sixteenth century they were considered authoritative on this subject.[69] Why the Italian versions were preferred to the Spanish originals remains unclear, as we know almost nothing about the person of the author. But evidently he was a Muslim, and with the exception of the Sephardic Jewish community, a knowledge of Italian was far more widespread in the eastern Mediterranean than that of Spanish.

One of the major attractions of the *Tarih-i Hind-i garbi* is the visual material that many of its copies contain. Some of the manuscripts are illustrated with maps including the American continent. For the historian who tries to determine how knowledge of the newly discovered lands was incorporated into the world view of people not necessarily ready to make room for this recently acquired information, these pictures constitute sources of the first order. Matters are complicated by the fact that relaying Americana of various kinds also involved conveying information about Spaniards, Portuguese or Genoese, and at least the first two figured among the major political opponents of the Ottoman sultans. Interest in realistic depiction thus may have been low. Some events difficult to imagine or interpret in an Ottoman context were simply left out: thus in some of the miniatures, Spaniards wear clothes typical of the eastern and not the western Mediterranean, and only their hats show that they are really foreigners.[70]

~ Kâtib Çelebi and his circle

To historians of Ottoman geography, Kâtib Çelebi (1609–57/1017–68) has long been a central figure. This is due to his interest in the work of his European colleagues that he incorporated into his synthesis known as the *Cihannüma*, a title that might be translated as 'the view of the world'. Twentieth-century scholarly attention was drawn to this work also because it was one of the earliest volumes put out by the first Ottoman printing press, founded by the Transylvanian convert Ibrahim Müteferrika.[71] The *Cihannüma*, along with the *Tarih-i Hind-i garbi* published two years earlier, was thus more readily accessible than other geographical works, which remained in manuscript well into the twentieth century.

With his impressive scholarly credentials Kâtib Çelebi must have primarily attracted a public of other scholars, that is members of what we have called the second category; but given the interest of the Grand Vizier Damad Ibrahim Paşa in the publication project, chances are that some high officials also figured among his readers. Non-scholarly educated townsmen, often with religious sympathies that favoured strict adherence to Islamic religious law, that is members of our third category, also appear to have bought *Cihannüma* manuscripts in sizeable numbers. How 'positive information' of the kind unearthed by Kâtib Çelebi and his collaborators fitted into the world view of these people is a question that I hope will be answered some day.[72]

To Kâtib Çelebi himself, geography formed part of a broad-ranging cultural project, which included a vast work of bibliography, a chronicle of the Empire, a discussion of contemporary political vicissitudes, an account of Ottoman naval matters, a treatise on coffee and tobacco and many other writings.[73] Moreover, Kâtib Çelebi was able to form a circle of collaborators, who brought to the project linguistic and cartographical skills that the principal author himself did not possess, and who were even willing to continue their activities after the latter's early death. The *Cihannüma* could not have been continued, and much less published, without this scholarly cooperation, which involved recent converts to Islam and at least one Armenian.

Several drafts of Kâtib Çelebi's geographical synthesis survive; but none of them is complete. This is due to a concern of the author that may appear rather modern, namely the wish to reflect the current 'state of the art'. After having written a first draft which encompassed Ottoman Rumelia, Bosnia and Hungary, according to his own statement Kâtib Çelebi gave up the project 'when he realized he would not find sufficient material in oriental geographic literature to describe the lands of the infidel'.[74] However, he continued adding to this draft as information became available to him. When, in 1653/1063–4, Kâtib Çelebi obtained access to the *Atlas Minor* of Gerhard Mercator, he first produced a translation into Ottoman with the help of a former Christian priest now converted to Islam. Furthermore, as a result of this encounter, he decided that his own work needed a complete rewriting, which he began in 1654/1064–5, but Kâtib Çelebi died rather suddenly before he could complete the project. In accordance with the outline of the *Atlas Minor,* the description of the world as given in the second version of the *Cihannüma* begins in eastern Asia and proceeds westwards. As the second draft ended at the eastern borders of the Ottoman Empire, Anatolia was never covered by Kâtib Çelebi himself, but his collaborators produced a description organized according to the administrative structure prevailing in the seventeenth century.[75] Thus the Ottoman translation of the *Atlas Minor* and the second version of the *Cihannüma* provided those readers who could gain access to them with a notion of the Asian landmass, including hitherto scarcely known countries such as Japan and China.

In this particular context, Kâtib Çelebi was closely concerned with locating and assimilating novel geographic sources. Thus his assumption that the important features of human life were those which had existed 'since Noah's Flood', did not mean that geographical knowledge was fixed once and for all. Possibly the Ottoman geographer felt that where his medieval Islamic colleagues had had ample opportunity for observation, their accounts were acceptable; but his work on the Dutch atlases had demonstrated that there were vast swathes of territory on which these scholars had nothing to say. Put differently, while the really important things in life may have all been of ancient vintage, by no means had all such 'ancient things' yet been discovered. Therefore obtaining access to the 'old' meant tireless hunting for the 'new'. But this reconstruction of Kâtib Çelebi's mindset is hypothetical, to be proven or disproved by future scholarship.

~ Non-Muslim Ottoman subjects and their travel writing

Doubtless the texts written in the various languages of Ottoman non-Muslims did not normally become accessible to Muslim Ottomans, and thus did not have any direct influence on the manner in which the latter viewed the world. But, first of all, Christians and Jews formed a substantial section of the Ottoman population, so what they could learn about the outside world is of interest in its own right. In addition, as we have seen, in the intellectual world of Istanbul as inhabited by the geographers, the cultural walls separating Muslims and non-Muslims were not as high as in other sectors of society. We thus should ask ourselves whether some of the knowledge of Ottoman non-Muslims was not passed on in one way or another, at least to people like Evliya or Kâtib Çelebi. Last but not least, the discussion of world views attempted here is predicated on the assumption that what was known to one social circle was not necessarily relayed to outsiders, and that certain kinds of information circulated only within small groups of people. Thus even texts that remained more or less confidential in their own times are to us still worth a closer look.

Among Jewish world-travellers of Ottoman background, one of the most exciting tales of adventure was certainly told by Sason Hai le-Veit Qastiel (from the House of Qastiel, probably meaning Castilia). A merchant of pearls and gems born in Istanbul, who visited Italy, Amsterdam and London among other places, he mostly travelled to the regions where jewels were produced. For pearls he went to Basra, which he seems to have used as a temporary trading base, while the gemstones in which he was interested were found in Ethopia, the Indian sub-continent and present-day Burma. In 1703/1114–15 Sason returned to Istanbul a very rich man, and in his memoirs he proudly recorded the grand seaside villa (*yalı*) he was able to buy for his mother. But on later voyages disaster struck: Sason lost a fortune while in Hormuz, and another major sum in the port of Pigum (Pegu), today in Burma. Ultimately he made his way to Balkh in present-day Afghanistan, where he remained for the rest of his life; for, as he put it in his memoirs, he was ashamed to return to Istanbul so wretchedly poor. It would be of interest to know who read and preserved his story for posterity, but to answer that question, we will need an edition (and translation) with numerous explanatory notes, to be published in the near future, ideally.

Another Jewish traveller was Ha'im Yosef David Azulai, born in Jerusalem, who, in the second half of the eighteenth century visited Holland, France and England in order to collect donations from local Jews for the poor scholars of Hebron (Ottoman: Halilürrahman).[76] In all likelihood his diary was not originally intended for publication. Many entries simply concern the frustrations familiar to anyone who travels in a strange country. Cultural features of the places visited thus inevitably took second place. However, there were some exceptions, including the elaborate Amsterdam city hall, today a royal palace and, above all, botanical gardens and collections of natural and man-made curiosities.[77] It would seem that Azulai generally appreciated places that were ornate and orderly, for these are the qualities that he stressed and praised in his diary.

Moreover, the account of Azulai's travels in Holland also contains quite a few indicators of the high degree of integration of at least the wealthier Amsterdam Jews into Dutch society. Not only does the traveller refer to the splendid furniture that some of these people had acquired, he also quite often mentions the custom of leaving calling cards in the houses of people whom the visitor failed to find at home. Or, as the author sometimes appears to have suspected, the men and women in question had their servants claim that they were out in order to avoid the vexed question of the donations that Azulai had come to demand. The diarist also notes that the originally Protestant custom of observing a special day of penance and prayer had been taken over by the local synagogues.[78]

Another image of life in Holland in the eighteenth century, once again seen through the eyes of an Ottoman non-Muslim, is found in the letters of the Greek merchant Stamatis Petru, a long-term resident of Amsterdam.[79] In spite of their rather mundane contents, these missives are of considerable interest, as they discuss the life of one of Stamatis Petru's associates, a young Greek named Adiamantos Korais, who in later life was to become a noted enlightenment scholar (1748–1833/1161–1249). Similar to Azulai, whose acquaintances included few gentiles, Stamatis Petru socialized mainly within the local Greek community. But, to the great scandal of our correspondent, Korais, who had learned some French already while in Izmir, made a pronounced effort to become fully at home in Amsterdam.

First of all, the transformation was sartorial, as it involved exchanging the long cloak worn by Greek merchants for the wigs, knee breeches and close-fitting coats demanded by French-style fashion. More seriously, Korais improved his French, the language of polite society in Holland as elsewhere in Europe. Just as Azulai had, Korais became interested in collections of natural curiosities, and Petru could only lament the money that the future scholar spent in trying to form a collection of his own. Korais also lost interest in Orthodox church ceremonies, visited Calvinist services 'on account of the music', and to top off Stamatis Petru's disgust, he got engaged to a Dutch girl, who, however, died before the marriage could take place. Unfortunately for us, Stamatis Petru was not able to leave much further evidence about the acculturation of the young Korais into Dutch society: for at one point, this future pillar of the enlightenment discovered that Stamatis Petru was spying on him, and unceremoniously chased the informer out of the house.

The letters concerning Korais' failed preparation for a merchant career, his largely successful acculturation in Holland and his later spectacular educational achievements must have caused much shaking of heads and clicking of tongues among the young man's relatives and friends back home. Yet Petru's missives are important for us, not because they were widely known among contemporaries, which evidently they were not, but because they describe the adaptation of Korais to Dutch life and customs, thus demonstrating that some few Ottoman non-Muslims might make such a choice and succeed. Azulai, by contrast, appears as a person to whom the idea of assimilation in Holland was as foreign as it could possibly be. But he too remarked that many well-to-do Jews residing in this state had in fact become Dutch in many aspects of their lives, in spite of their often Sephardic antecedents. Once again Azulai's tales upon his return may have caused a certain amount of head-shaking among the people of his Jerusalem or Hebron circles, but the diary itself was probably inaccessible.

While the published travel writings of Ottoman non-Muslims thus do not seem to have contributed spectacularly to the knowledge of the outside world among the Empire's denizens, it is quite conceivable that oral reports and private letters did have a certain impact. Moreover, towards the end of 'our' period, some time in the late eighteenth century, literate Armenians could find a considerable amount of information on the outside world in the geographical works of P. Ğugas (or Ğugios) İnciciyan (1758–1833/1171–1249), a scholarly Catholic Armenian of the Mechitarist order, who divided his time between Istanbul and Venice.[80] But that is part of another story.

~ Tracking down the knowledge of the educated Muslim townsman

Just as reading the ambassadorial reports in many cases remained the privilege of a few high officials, the works of Seyyidî 'Ali Re'îs or the author of the *Tarih-i Hind-i garbi*, if the number of extant copies is at all indicative, achieved a small or at most a moderate circulation. This makes it difficult to judge the kind of geographic information accessible to people who were educated at some level but not adepts of geography. Once again, it is worth stressing that much information must have been relayed orally. We thus have to use indirect ways to at least catch a glimpse of the stories that may have circulated in the Ottoman capital.

For this purpose, I contend that it is possible to use certain sections of Evliya Çelebi's travel account. Admittedly, there are some serious problems with this approach. For, while in present-day Turkey Evliya is probably the best-known representative of pre-nineteenth-century Ottoman-Turkish literature, his popularity only began about 150 years ago. In the eighteenth century, his work was known only to a few people, some of whom probably lived in Cairo, where the author appears to have spent the last decade of his life. Others must have belonged to the rarified milieu of the Ottoman palace. Thus we cannot claim that Evliya's accounts had a direct impact on shaping the geographic notions of his contemporaries, and it is not in this sense that we will study a sample of his writing about the non-Ottoman world. But on the other hand, Evliya told stories about the lands of the western 'infidels' that probably corresponded to what people knew or believed in seventeenth-century Istanbul – for nothing is ever invented 'out of thin air'.

Other objections can be linked to the fact that Evliya was anything but an 'average townsman', but, to the contrary, a highly original person. He had travelled at least as much as any other known Ottoman author, if not more, and read the writings of many Muslim geographers. But the use he made of his sources was not that of the scholar, geographer or historian, but rather that of the creative writer who employed factual accounts as an inspiration for a rather novel genre of writing, namely the romanced travelogue.[81] This proceeding has long been misunderstood and has resulted in Evliya's name becoming, until the revisions of recent years, almost a byword for unreliable 'travellers' tales'. Certainly, specialists who have studied his accounts during the last forty years or so have come to appreciate not only his artistic intentions, but also the numerous instances in which he was well informed indeed. Yet there is no denying that he sometimes told tales about places where he had obviously never been; but once again, even a person as original as Evliya was in the end a product of his milieu. We can therefore assume, although proof is impossible, that when he wrote about exotic localities, Evliya told stories reasonably consonant with the world view of his contemporaries, particularly since he himself liked to stress his knowledge of oral literature.[82] Moreover, we must keep in mind that, in seventeenth-century Istanbul or Bursa, story-telling was esteemed as a form of art, and by no means merely an amusement for the illiterate.

~ Evliya Çelebi's stories about Europe

Holland and the way thither

A good example of Evliya's reporting about exotic places concerns Holland, along with the city of Amsterdam; in the author's lifetime, this was the recognized centre of the European 'world economy'.[83] Given the presence of a Dutch embassy and traders from Holland in Istanbul, it should have been easy enough to acquire information about this city without ever leaving the capital of the sultans.[84] Men with bookish interests were likely to have heard about, or even perused, Dutch atlases; as we have noted, these publications were an important source of information for well-to-do Ottomans interested in seventeenth-century world geography. In addition, quite a few Armenian traders permanently established themselves in Amsterdam, and their relatives and friends in the sultan's territories must have heard from them what life was like in the Netherlands.[85] Thus, unlike more exotic European towns, there must have been some notions about Amsterdam and its surroundings circulating among educated Ottomans. It is unfortunate that we do not possess any written reactions of such people to the extraordinary tales told by Evliya, and probably by professional storytellers as well.

References to Holland and Amsterdam occur within the sixth volume of Evliya Çelebi's travel account.[86] The author's journey began in Uyvar and supposedly took him to a variety of countries and peoples. It was apparent to the author himself that he did not possess much information on Bohemia, the Germanies or even the Netherlands. To explain this deficiency, he pointed out that he had accompanied an army of raiding Tatars, who, as every Ottoman of his time was well aware, normally limited themselves to booty-taking in the open countryside, but were as a rule unable to take on fortified sites.[87] On the other hand, recounting the successes of this raid provided Evliya with an edifying adventure story, which probably interested both himself and his potential readers much more than the countries in which these events supposedly took place.

It is all but impossible to situate on a map the peoples, kingdoms and countries mentioned by Evliya, even though the terms Filimenk/Fiyaman (Dutch, Flemings), Nemse/Alaman (Germans), Leh (Poles), Çeh (Czechs) and İsfaç (Swedes, compare modern Turkish İsveç) are well known Ottoman-Turkish terms. All we can gather from Evliya's account was that these peoples should have been situated in central and western Europe. Some of the towns, among which we find the name of Daniska possibly derived from Gdansk/Danzig, the author described as being on the shores of the Bahr-i Muhit, the ocean sea surrounding the territories of the Ancient World. Particularly enigmatic is the great fortified city of Kallevine, whose name was perhaps derived from that of Calvin. Evliya placed it near the mouth of the river Vo, a huge body of water originating in the mountains of Daniska and flowing through the realm of the king of Sweden before entering the Bahr-i Muhit. In the port 'Indian ships' (perhaps 'Indiamen' belonging to the East India Company) in addition to Danish and Donkarkız vessels were to be found. As Donkarkız must be an Ottomanized version of Dunkerque/Dunkirk, I would suggest that, in a garbled fashion, Evliya referred to a port on the Baltic, that maintained trade relations with the Atlantic coast. As, in the seventeenth century, the Swedish kings had extensive possessions on the eastern and southern shores of the Baltic, I would further propose, but very tentatively, that the name of the river Vo is somehow linked to that of the Vistula. For it is obvious that when he discussed this river, Evliya once again returned to the shores of the Baltic. In this context our author dwells at some length upon amber, a famed product of this region and obtainable almost nowhere else, and also on pine tree sap treasured for its pleasant smell. Be that as it may; as Kâtib Çelebi would say, the responsibility for the story's truth lies with the narrator.[88]

From and to Kallevine, most routes should have been maritime, but Evliya's Tatars, of course, travelled by land. In his travelogue, the author did express the intention of setting out an itinerary, but in the end, the relevant heading promises more than the actual chapter provides. Evliya evidently assumed – shades of Shakespeare – that Bohemia, the territory of the Czechs, was adjacent to the sea, and that to the north, it bordered on the country of the Filimenk.

The Netherlands held an important place in the vision Evliya created of western Europe, at least this is what I would conclude from the frequency with which various terms referring to this region recurred in his tale. To begin with, there was 'Holandiye', which the author took to be the name of both a city and a province. But we also find 'Amıstırdam', which appeared as a stout fortress, and in addition, 'Filimenk Firengi'. Apart from Amsterdam, there was the major city of Karış, which I have not been able to identify; Evliya apparently considered this place the principal port of the Netherlands, as it was in the paragraph describing Karış that he mentioned the 'three thousand' ships of the Dutch, which travelled to the New World, India and China.[89]

Our author also thought that the Dutch had a king, and that in fact the latter was the owner of the ships putting in at the port of Karış. While the Netherlands of his time were an oligarchic republic, non-monarchical regimes were quite anomalous in mid-seventeenth-century Europe. Thus it is likely that the author's informants described the Stadhouders of the Oranje dynasty – military commanders whose relationship with the representative bodies of the Dutch republic was often rather strained – as the 'kings' of the country they were supposed to be serving. Evliya provided a description of the 'royal' palace with its domes, although he did have the good grace to admit that he never saw it but from a distance. For, as we have heard, the Tatars normally turned away from strongly fortified places, and 'Amıstırdam' was described as one such. Evidently the peculiar protection afforded by the country's numerous rivers, ponds and canals was not known to the person or persons who provided Evliya with his information on the Netherlands.

In addition, the Ottoman traveller had trouble finding his way through the different Christian denominations; even though once again the tensions between Catholics and – usually Calvinist – Protestants were quite often the cause of diplomatic incidents in Istanbul itself. Evliya knew that there were differences of *mezheb* between Christians. But this term is used in rather a remarkable fashion: in an Islamic context, it denotes schools of law whose opinions vary in matters of detail, but that are all recognized as equally acceptable to all believers. However, Evliya employed the term *mezheb* in order to denote Christian churches, whose members often enough considered one another as damnable heretics. In Evliya's perspective, the Christian variety of *mezheb* was closely linked to states and ethnic groups, not an unreasonable assumption in a period of *cuius regio eius religio* ('the ruler determines the religion of his subjects').

For the İsfaç (Swedes) the Ottoman traveller used the term 'Luturyan' (Lutheran). By contrast, in religious terms, the Dutch were likened to the English, which makes sense if one remembers that Calvinists dominated the principal Dutch towns, while Puritans had held power for two decades in mid-seventeenth-century England. Evliya knew that the Dutch and English did not fast before Easter, for which latter practice he used the picturesque name of 'German red-egg-fast' (*Nemse Kızılyumurtanın oruçları*).[90] However, it remains unclear what the author meant when he claimed that the English and Dutch were 'fire-worshippers in the pre-Islamic Iranian fashion' (*ateşperest mecûsîlerdir*), but that their holy book was the gospel. Equally astonishing is the claim that Amsterdam possessed a large number of monasteries with high domes; presumably the knowledge that such institutions existed in Orthodox towns made Evliya assume that they could be found in all Christian countries.

European frontiers: a *quantité négligeable*?

As to the ethnic and political frontiers that circumscribed Dutch territory, this also was apparently not a matter that interested the author very much; evidently the Tatar raiders of his story crossed European frontiers without let or hindrance. The one issue on which he had intended to provide information was the diversity of languages; in many of the territories he visited, he collected word lists that in some cases have become the subject of specialist studies.[91] But while the author included a chapter heading '*lisan-ı Filimenk-i pür-ceng*' (the language of the warlike Dutchmen), no such list follows in his text. As speakers of Dutch were not hard to find in Istanbul, one wonders whether this section of Evliya's travelogue was perhaps written during the author's later years, when he lived in Cairo, where speakers of this language would have been much less common.

Nor had Evliya been able to collect much information on the distribution of European peoples. When discussing the city of Holandiye and its environs, he claimed that they were inhabited by Poles and Czechs; whenever the Czech king was victorious, he controlled the region, and when the Swedish king won a war, the latter would take over. As the king of Bohemia of this period was identical to the Habsburg ruler, a circumstance of which Evliya seems to have been unaware, it is likely that here we have a rather vague allusion to the Habsburg–Swedish confrontation of the Thirty Years War, which had ended only in 1648/1057–8.[92] It is also possible that Evliya did not realize that the terms 'Holandiye' and 'Filimenk' often referred to one and the same political entity, even though to be exact, 'Holland' was but one of the 'Seven Provinces' that made up the Netherlands of this period. I am inclined to suspect that in his geography, the city of Holandiye was not located in Holland at all, but somewhere in the Baltic region.

And what about Evliya's intentions in writing?

It is obvious that in discussing Europe beyond the Ottoman borders, Evliya has mixed much more fancy and story-telling into his account than when covering places such as Bursa or Diyarbekir. Even when writing about Vienna, he had much more information to transmit, but then he had spent several weeks in the imperial capital. As I read it, the main point of his stories about the raid to Holland is that here are vast and prosperous lands and cities, with lively trade and stored-up riches, whose strongly fortified cities are difficult to conquer but whose countryside lies open to the raider, who can carry off slaves almost at will. That, beyond the borderlands of royal Hungary or the southern steppes bordering the realm of the tsars, this was not a realistic assessment of the seventeenth-century situation is immaterial in the present context. Our real problem lies in figuring out the reasons for such a narration. Quite possibly, Evliya thought that accurate information was not his priority, sometimes even in places he knew extremely well, but more particularly where non-Ottoman territories were involved.[93] Thus he relied on garbled accounts he could well have heard in Istanbul from recently Islamized Europeans whose notions of geography were shaky at best. It is also possible, although we cannot be sure, that by telling such stories he hoped to build up sentiment in favour of further wars of conquest in Central Europe – we must keep in mind that he wrote during the decades immediately preceding the second siege of Vienna in 1683/1094–5.

Viewed from another angle, Evliya may have written the way he did because he conformed to tales current in oral literature; but this is a question that only literary specialists will be able to answer. And did his listeners approve? Important though these questions are, at least to the second one there is no answer, for the simple reason that we do not possess any comments by people who heard Evliya tell his stories orally; and as to the manuscript, it became known outside a small circle of connoisseurs only in the nineteenth century. In consequence we do not have any reactions of contemporary readers to guide us. There is nothing comparable to the marginal notes in scholarly geographic works that were carefully read by the authors' colleagues and successors, and that provide such precious indicators concerning the acceptance or rejection of the claims made, for instance, by the anonymous writer of the *Tarih-i Hind-i garbi*.[94]

~ In conclusion

This chapter can make no claim to exhaust the possibilities provided by existing primary sources; it is no more than an outsider's summary of the research available today. Doubtless one of the most obvious gaps involves eighteenth-century writing on the non-Ottoman world by Ottoman subjects not ambassadors to foreign courts. It is hard to imagine that Ebubekir Dımeşkî did not train any successors in his chosen field of geography, or that there was absolutely no interest in the eighteenth-century expansion of Russia among Ottoman *literati*.[95] But the relevant works may not have been brought to light, or at least they have been largely neglected by twentieth-century historians. As a reason for this state of affairs, we must mention the disdain for the Ottoman eighteenth century, unfortunately still rather widespread outside a limited circle of aficionados. In addition, authors working in Istanbul during the 1700s presumably used European sources more extensively than their predecessors had done. In consequence, it appears that modern historians have often considered the geographers of a later age derivative and therefore unworthy of serious study.[96] But as we are here concerned not with the question of scientific originality, but with the notions of educated Ottomans concerning the outside world, this lack of interest on the part of twentieth-century scholars is a major drawback.

A further complication has made itself felt. In addition to Muslim scholars writing in Arabic or Ottoman Turkish, Jews, Greeks, Armenians and others have composed some works about the non-Ottoman world, but here the language barrier has proven formidable indeed. Thus, for instance, it is only in exceptional cases that geographical works by Armenian authors have been translated into a language normally mastered by Ottomanist historians.[97] Presumably given the great expansion of Greek maritime activity in the second half of the eighteenth century, there were Greek writers with something pertinent to say about the relationships Ottoman Christians formed in foreign lands, and *mutatis mutandis* something similar applies to Jews. But to sum it all up, the work of these authors has not been studied with reference to the information about the non-Ottoman world available to educated eighteenth-century Ottomans of whatever religion, and the present discussion has tried to make the most of an unfortunate situation.

When attempting an overview of the kind given here, it hard to escape the impression of a considerable discontinuity in the study of geography by Ottoman subjects. Information about the outside world was acquired by many writers more or less as a personal initiative, and only in the case of Kâtib Çelebi and his colleagues can we follow a transfer of knowledge across generations.[98] More-over, if the stories of Ottoman derring-do in a fictionalized environment were at all acceptable to those whom Evliya Çelebi targeted as his presumptive readers, we might conclude that the concrete information obtained, at considerable effort, by the author of the *Tarih-i Hind-i garbi* or else by Kâtib Çelebi, did not readily 'filter down' to the educated Ottoman public. Experiences of this type are unfortunately very familiar down to the present day, especially to scholars who try to disseminate information on the Ottoman world among an 'educated public' in Europe or North America.

But of course this is only one possible interpretation among several: after all, down to the 1970s, even though factual information on North America was readily available, audiences all over the world enjoyed the fictional 'Wild West' in comics and movies. Who knows whether an analogous state of mind was not widespread among Ottoman readers? Furthermore, we do not really know how valid is our impression that there yawned an abyss of discontinuity between the 'solid information' generated by authors such as Kâtib Çelebi and the romancing probably preferred by 'the average reader or rather listener'. There may well have been intermediate stages between the two extremes, resulting from transfers of knowledge that we have not as yet been able to discern.

When it comes to the reports of the ambassadors and also the accounts of quasi-ambassadors such as Seyyidî 'Ali Re'îs, they were one of the surest sources of knowledge about foreign lands available to those privileged Muslim Ottomans who were able to access them. Therefore it is an urgent desideratum to research what might be called the 'publishing history' of these texts. Even in those writings whose authors concentrated on highlighting the successes of their respective missions to the exclusion of other matters, we find itineraries and recorded impressions of the attitudes foreign court dignitaries adopted towards the Ottoman sultans, and all this information must have served as input when images of the outside world were created. To some readers, this approach may appear overly positivistic; and certainly, concrete information is only one of several 'ingredients' needed by a person or group embarking upon the formation of political attitudes towards the outside world. But on the other hand, such attitudes can only be operational if they have some kind of connection to events in the 'real world' – whatever 'real' may signify.

Sophisticated observers such as Seyyidî 'Ali Re'îs, Mehmed Emni Beyefendi or Ebubekir Râtib Efendi, moreover, provided a great deal more. Here we find evaluations of the political attitudes of the Russian or Habsburg courts, discussions of cultural institutions such as gardens, libraries and even the theatre, or else indications of how the Ottomans might culturally 'put themselves on the map' in an international context. As Seyyidî 'Ali Re'îs knew well, at Iranian or

Indian courts this might best be achieved by demonstrating a mastery of Iranian poetry. Or as Ebubekir Râtib tells us, when dealing with the Habsburg court of Joseph II or Leopold II, comparable ends might be served by highlighting the sophistication of Ottoman musical culture.

Such considerations have often been belittled by scholars of previous generations, for whom nothing counted but demonstrations of military prowess and diplomatic 'muscle'. However in our case, priorities are quite different. For we are concerned with the manner in which certain subjects of the Ottoman sultans, usually close to the political elite if not actually part of it, interacted with their 'opposite numbers' outside the Ottoman realm. For such a communication to work, the necessary pre-conditions had to be developed: in their very different ways, Kâtib Çelebi, Ahmed Resmi, Adiamantos Korais and Ebubekir Râtib all shared in this endeavour.

9 ~ Conclusion

~ A common world

Arguably, the first and most important point made by the present study is that, before the last quarter of the eighteenth century, or perhaps 1750/1163–4 if stricter criteria are preferred, the Ottomans and their European neighbours still inhabited a common world. Certainly this was not the way in which people of the period would have seen themselves: in the thinking of Muslim Ottomans, non-Muslim Ottoman subjects, and also the inhabitants of Christian states or empires, religious denomination was a central criterion by which people defined themselves, and were defined by others.

But viewed from a distance of two or three centuries, the shared social consequences of living in societies in which trade and petty commodity production largely depended on locally available agricultural resources, forcefully strike the eye. It is rather ironic that these commonalities, which existed in many walks of life, will have become especially apparent to the readers of this study in the treatment of prisoners of war. Enslaving such people and making them row on the galleys was an all-Mediterranean phenomenon, due to the capricious winds that well into the seventeenth century made it seem dangerous to rely exclusively on sailing ships. Forced labour in arsenals under dismal conditions was equally common, and so was the practice of making the captives partially fend for themselves whenever their labour was not urgently needed.

However, this commonality did not exclude significant nuances of difference. Thus Muslim prisoners in early modern Italy suffered particularly from the fact that there were so few free travellers from the sultans' lands that could have aided them through alms-giving and mediation; moreover, throughout Europe standards of charity towards people not of one's own religious denomination were not particularly high either, given a society where life was determined by such divisions. Last but not least, the arrangements by which Ottoman and Habsburg prisoners of war of some prominence could be ransomed or exchanged were, albeit informal, not too different from the agreements by which eighteenth-century European rulers among themselves 'determined the value of a prisoner'.[1]

~ The integration of foreigners

Throughout our study we have been concerned with the manner in which diplomats, foreign merchants and, on the lowest level, prisoners and slaves were integrated into the Ottoman world. Where free men were concerned, this normally was achieved by assigning the newcomers 'separate spheres', which allowed them to interact with the locals and yet kept them at a distance. This was handled in a flexible manner: thus merchants in Istanbul were not assigned any particular place of residence, but tended to gravitate towards Galata and Pera. In Aleppo by contrast, they were expected to reside in certain khans, while in Izmir, the 'street of the Franks' provided comfortable accommodation, at least to the wealthier traders. Organization in highly structured communities, that is in *nations* governed by consuls appointed by the relevant rulers, or else in chartered companies, gave these merchants a chance to operate within the Ottoman system.[2] Other traders, especially the Iranian Armenians, might prefer to operate as privately organized and highly cohesive commercial diasporas. As a result of these varying arrangements, the Ottoman authorities had officially sanctioned interlocutors available whenever problems arose. As the central government seems to have considered the situation well in hand, a closing of the borders, as we have seen, in peacetime was apparently not regarded as necessary.

Quite different was the situation of prisoners of war or victims of corsairs and pirates. By the period under investigation, it was no longer customary to settle such people in compact groups, as seems to have happened in the Istanbul region after 1453/857. If these men and women were not ransomed or exchanged, they were mostly incorporated as slaves into the households of the better off, unless they had the mischance to be assigned to the arsenal and the galleys. Manumission being reasonably frequent, and often preceded by conversion to Islam and accompanied by marriage to an Ottoman subject, these freedmen and freedwomen and their descendants normally joined the ranks of the sultan's Muslim subjects.

Perhaps we should conclude, as a second point, that those strangers who arrived as free men – and could therefore elect to leave – were expected to form organized social groups. These could be ambassadorial and consular households, *nations*, chartered companies or trade diasporas. Those to whom no such choice was offered, such as prisoners and slaves, might informally associate on the basis of a shared language denomination or land of origin. But from the Ottoman point of view, all these solidarities had no status at all, and the men and women involved were expected to fully assimilate, becoming part of the Empire's population in every respect. And unless they managed to flee, most of them must have done so.

~ Imperial cohesion, 'corruption' and the liberties of foreigners

Our third major point is concerned with the fact that throughout our period the Ottoman elites showed a significant degree of cohesion, thus enabling the Empire to play an active political role in spite of two serious military defeats. This statement contradicts the customary claim that a very short period of 'Ottoman greatness' was followed by a lengthy 'decline', in which it was largely the divisions of Christian princes that allowed the Empire to survive. At least for the time period treated here, down to 1774/1187–8, this no longer appears as a valid conclusion.

It has also been popular to link this notion of 'decline' with corruption on the part of office holders, of a kind somehow specific to the Ottoman realm.[3] However, it must be stressed that the sale of offices was no more an Ottoman peculiarity than the institution of tax farming, all of which flourished, for instance, in pre-revolutionary France. Certainly after the Empire had reached what may be called a 'stable state', members of the elite whose official functions had nothing to do with matters of 'foreign policy' did find opportunities for making their 'influence' felt in these matters. Whenever the interests of foreign powers were involved, these people often expected remuneration for their interventions. As so many official positions were obtained for money, office holders needed to recoup their fortunes by accepting more or less direct payment in exchange for their mediation; this custom was widespread in other early modern polities as well, including England or France.

But as we have seen, this state of affairs did not mean that outsiders to the Empire could readily get their way if only they paid the appropriate sums of money.[4] For in the end, the sultans' officials were bound to each other and to the ruler by strong ties of loyalty, especially if they were tax farmers, by the fact that they could only recoup their investments if the Empire remained a going concern.[5] Religious and moral reasons for adhesion to the *padişah* of Islam apart, these considerations acted powerfully in favour of cohesion. When all is said and done, the Ottoman polity held together reasonably well throughout our period, and only at the very end, the disasters of the 1768–74/1181–8 war caused major fissures to become visible, particularly where non-Muslims were concerned. Perhaps in the Ottoman context, the equivalent to the eighteenth-century American slogan of 'no taxation without representation' was 'no taxation without justice and protection'.

All this is especially remarkable as, throughout its existence – and this is a fourth point of some importance – the Ottoman lands were of relatively easy access to outsiders. Traders were allowed not only to come and go, but also to reside in the sultan's territories for many years without becoming the subjects of this potentate. Even the rule that such foreigners should not marry local women or acquire real estate was often ignored in practice. Catholic missionaries frequently complained about difficulties encountered. But the truly noteworthy aspect of missionary activity was surely the fact that they were allowed entry at all, especially if we keep in mind that in the late seventeenth and early eighteenth centuries quite a few Europeans were still required to leave their respective homelands on account of belonging to the 'wrong' denomination. Moreover, to my knowledge, the Ottoman elite never seriously considered instituting more stringent controls at entry points, of the kind that were customary in early modern Russia. As long as war had not officially been declared, the 'well-guarded domains' were traversed by many foreigners 'coming and going'.

~ Coping with the European world economy

Many of these foreigners being traders, who by the end of our period often concentrated on transactions involving bills of exchange, their activities produced what may be called a piecemeal integration of Ottoman territories into a world economy dominated by Europe. From this point of view, the period studied here is crucial: for at the end of the sixteenth century, there was an 'Ottoman world economy' in its own right, while this was no longer true in the years around 1800/1214–15. It would seem that selected commercial centres such as Izmir or Aleppo were the places where this integration into and appropriation by the European world economy first made itself felt.[6] In Izmir the second half of the seventeenth century was apparently decisive; in other places, different and later dates often will make more sense. However, in this period 'incorporation' throughout the Ottoman world economy was as yet in its beginning stages; thus the areas where it was under way operated as sources of foodstuffs and raw materials, but were not as yet ready markets for European industrial goods. This fragmented and piecemeal process makes it impossible to give an overall, definite date for the Ottoman world economy's dissolution.[7]

Another interesting issue is linked to the Braudelian version of world economies in general, and his statement that it is not normally profitable for trade goods to cross the boundaries of these major units.[8] We have, though, seen that even in the mid-sixteenth century, when the Ottoman world economy was going strong, it was profitable to export grain to Venice. In fact, there were years when ordinary Venetians would have starved without Ottoman wheat, which continued to arrive because traders both from Venice and the Empire made profits on these deals. Thus, to make this point once again, we can conclude that it is not very realistic to assume that trade across world economy limits is not profitable. Or else we may posit that the Ottoman world economy from its very inception in the fifteenth century maintained such close ties to Mamluk Egypt, Venice or Genoa that it is problematic to assume an independent world economy at any time. But in my view, this latter assumption creates more difficulties than it solves, and should be rejected.

~ Ottoman rule: between the centre and the margins

Whatever we may think of the boundaries of the Ottoman world economy, it is certain that the Empire as a political entity had more or less clearly demarcated borders. However, subjects of the sultan down to the late seventeenth century probably conceived of the latter not as hard and fast lines drawn on a map, but in form of a *serhad* that as a matter of principle was supposed to advance, and therefore could only be provisionally determined. In this context, raids by border warriors in enemy territory were considered 'normal' and, conversely, the Ottomans' Habsburg opponents operated in an analogous manner.[9] Moreover, given the peculiarities of early modern warfare, holding fortresses was considered more important than occupying tracts of swampy or extremely rugged territory.

Yet this did not mean that all principalities linked to the Empire by the tribute nexus ended up as provinces directly governed from the centre. While this transition may have constituted the 'royal road' of Ottoman conquest in the early years, by the sixteenth century we encounter Muslim provinces rapidly reverting to the state of dependent principalities. On the other hand, there were centrally located provinces important for reasons of strategy and revenue collection, in which direct central control was yet intermittent at best. On the other hand, in certain territories, especially in those previously in Christian hands, direct Ottoman rule was instituted without any dependent prince intervening to smooth the transition.

At one level, we may assume that more or less unique factors, due to a particular political conjuncture, conditioned the road that the Ottoman authorities allowed this or that province to take. However a few general rules were in operation, and this can be viewed as another major conclusion to be drawn from our study, the fifth to be exact: dependent principalities that retained their status over the centuries were normally located in border territory, and sometimes also provided the Ottoman centre with ready money, goods, services and information that an 'ordinary' provincial administration could not have easily procured. By contrast, the vicinity of a powerful opponent of the sultan's, such as the Habsburgs, did not necessarily mean that a dependent principality would soon be transformed into a province governed directly from Istanbul. Walachia, Moldavia and Transylvania can be cited as examples, further, the proximity of Safavid Iran also did not mean that the principalities of eastern Anatolia were rapidly transmitted into the charge of Ottoman governors-general.

Borderlands were areas in which Ottomans met outsiders to the sultan's realm; but at least as important for these purposes was Istanbul itself, seat of the sultanate and centre of the Ottoman world economy. This was the place where embassies were put up, first in a special khan and later in villas 'in the vineyards of Pera' (today: Beyoğlu).[10] Istanbul was also a centre of consumption and therefore frequented by traders, while its buildings and festivals attracted visitors from outside and inside the Empire. Ottoman geographers often worked in the capital, even if they might travel widely as well. In short, this city, rather than the often impoverished *serhad*, was the place where consumer goods from the world out-side the Ottoman borders and information about foreign lands could be procured with the greatest facility.

~ Providing information: what 'respectable people' might or might not write about

The Ottoman lands were of enormous extent. Border territories or urban centres such as Istanbul, Izmir or Aleppo apart, the need for information concerning the outside world must have been less apparent than in more exposed polities. More-over, apparently there were rules of polite behaviour in operation that prevented an Ottoman gentleman, or even a returned captive, from reporting what he had experienced in foreign parts at length and in writing. Thus Seyyidî 'Ali Re'îs did not think it appropriate to expand on the many remarkable buildings, landscapes and customs he must have encountered on the Indian subcontinent. Instead he chose to emphasize his permanent longing for Istanbul along with his role as a quasi-ambassador and upholder of Ottoman glory. A similar if less stringent rule seems to have applied even to a personage like Evliya Çelebi, who saw travelling and writing about travel as *the* major aim of his entire life; for at least one of this writer's interlocutors appears to have faulted him for being too friendly with infi-dels. This approach has often been linked to religious rulings, which advised Muslims to avoid close contact with those of other faiths.

However, Ottoman Jews or members of the various Christian denominations were no different in this respect, having been brought up to prefer the company of their coreligionists. Although a few travel diaries and correspondences do exist, writing about experiences made abroad was not a popular genre among Armenians, Greeks or Jews, at least not before the late eighteenth century. It would seem that even though many non-Muslim Ottoman merchants visited Amsterdam, Rotterdam, Leipzig, Vienna and Trieste, people such as Adiamantos Korais, who did develop a serious interest in the culture of their places of resi-dence, were but a small minority. How much more would we know if at least Mouradgea d'Ohsson had left an account of his late eighteenth- and early nineteenth-century travels in France, Sweden and the Ottoman Empire ...

Not only religious precepts, but also socio-economic factors played a role in accentuating the isolation of the members of every individual religion or denom-ination. After all, Armenians, Greeks and Jews active in western and central Europe all operated as trading diasporas. A high value therefore was placed on intra-community cohesion, for this was the precondition for credit-based busi-ness transacted over long distances. Staunch adherence to the prevailing religion or denomination thus was a *conditio sine qua non* for commercial creditworthi-ness. Therefore it was only a man like Korais, a complete failure as a merchant, who could afford to ignore the criticisms levied at him by colleagues or ex-colleagues in the Greek commercial environment. This link between trading diasporas and a lack of interest in foreign customs may be retained as a sixth conclusion to be drawn from the present book.

~ Embassy reports: much maligned but a sign of changing mentalities

Some historical information about the lands of Christian 'unbelievers' and Shi'ite 'miscreants' was collected by the Ottoman central authorities, probably to serve as an aid in policy-making. This must have applied to works such as the sixteenth-century collection of biographies of French rulers that has recently been edited and translated into French.[11] Other volumes of this kind survive, but do not seem to have been systematically studied.[12] Further historical information was found in the reports of returning ambassadors, who apart from the details of their honourable receptions, might discuss the changes of rulers or chief ministers witnessed in foreign capitals. We may assume, although we have no way of being sure, that an Ottoman ambassador before setting out from Istanbul typically immersed himself in the reports of his predecessors.

At an early stage, eighteenth-century embassy reports doubtless were akin to official documents, and thus of restricted circulation. But as we have seen, chroniclers appointed by the Ottoman government soon included some of these texts in their works, thus making them accessible to a broader spectrum of Ottoman literati. Presumably it was especially ambassadors of known literary distinction who attracted Ottoman readers. Perhaps it was not so much the fact that he wrote about the otherwise virtually unknown kingdom of Spain that made the report of Vasıf Efendi interesting to subsequent generations, but rather the author's fame as a notable stylist. At the present state of our knowledge, we can surmise that some ambassadorial reports elicited more interest than others, but we often are hard put to tell what exactly an eighteenth-century non-official Ottoman reader expected of a successful embassy report.

It is easy enough to point out the deficiencies of embassy reports as sources of information on foreign lands, and yet their growing frequency and sophistication in the course of the eighteenth century is of great significance. It would seem that demanding written reports of ambassadors was part of what we would today call a package deal. Sultans and viziers of the period seem to have considered that a knowledge of foreign courts and countries was now more important than it had been in the sixteenth or seventeenth centuries. Therefore it was no longer appropriate to rely largely on information obtained from foreign embassy personnel stationed in Pera, or from non-Muslim Ottomans active as the sultan's diplomats, including the medical doctor Solomon Ashkenazi from Udine, the prince Vasile Lupu or the scholarly Alexander Mavrocordato.

Rather, Muslims from within the scribal service were now recruited for these positions, in a manner that was to be repeated in the nineteenth century, when

8. A visit of the Ottoman ambassador Mehmed efendi, accompanied by his son Hüseyin, at the court of King Augustus of Poland in 1731; he announced the advent of Sultan Mahmud I. The ambassador was received twice, once at his arrival and once at his departure only a week later. The drawing was probably made before the reception took place, so that the master of ceremonies would know whom to place where.

Source: The image has been reproduced in the exhibition catalogue *Im Lichte des Halbmonds. Das Abendland und der türkische Orient* (Dresden and Bonn: Staatliche Kunstsammlungen and Kunst- und Ausstellungshalle der Bundesrepublik Deutschland, 1995): 190 and 225. The drawing belongs to the Sächsisches Hauptstaatsarchiv, Kartenabteilung, Rißschrank VII, No 90, fol. 1. Reproduced by permission.

elite Muslim officials trained in the 'Translation Chamber' took over from the now disgraced chief dragomans. A modernization of government, and that would be my seventh and final point, was thus accompanied by a takeover, on the part of Muslim officials, of duties earlier performed by non-Muslims. The reports produced by these new-style officials were usually quite sober and matter-of-fact, with few flourishes of religiously motivated rhetoric legitimizing the sultan; and this manner of writing may also be viewed as part of the growing 'secularization' of the Ottoman elites, a process that, I should think, began long before the age of Mahmud II.

~ Bibliography

The comments which follow certain publications are not intended to convey systematic information, but simply guide the beginner to some works that I have found especially stimulating. Apart from a very few exceptions, there are no comments on articles; they are usually short enough that the reader can see for him/herself.

In some cases, it is possible to dispute whether a certain item is mainly a publication of a primary source, with a more or less ample introduction, or else a monograph with a large appendix containing primary sources. When in doubt, I have tended to record such items as secondary material. The other ambiguity derives from the fact that in many publications the editor of a given primary source appears as the author, and the original author's name forms part of the title. In some instances only, I have added the original author in parentheses and relegated the editor to a secondary position; however as both names are always present, there should not be any problem in locating the books in question.

~ Reference works

Collective work (1992). *Başbakanlık Osmanlı Arşivi Rehberi* (Ankara: Başbakanlık, Devlet Arşivleri Genel Müdürlüğü).

Collective work (1993–5). *Dünden Bugüne İstanbul Ansiklopedisi*, 8 vols (Istanbul: Kültür Bakanlığı and Tarih Vakfı) (*DBİA*).

The Encyclopedia of Islam (1913–34). ed. by M. T. Houtsma, T. W. Arnold, R. Basset, R. Hartmann *et alii*, 4 vols (Leiden: E. J. Brill).

The Encyclopedia of Islam (2nd edition, 1960–2004). ed. by H. A. R. Gibb *et alii* (Leiden: E. J. Brill) (*EI*).

Ihsanoğlu, Ekmeleddin, *et alii* (2000). *Osmanlı Coğrafya Literatürü Tarihi, History of Geographical Literature during the Ottoman Period*, 2 vols (Istanbul: IRSICA). (Vol. 1 covers the years down to the end of the 19th century).

İslâm Ansiklopedisi, İslâm Âlemi Tarih, Coğrafya,Etnografya ve Biyografya Lugati (1st edition, completed 1988), ed. by Adnan Adıvar *et alii* (Istanbul: Milli Eğitim Bakanlığı) (*İA*).

Redhouse Yeni Türkçe–İngilizce Sözlük, New Redhouse Turkish–English Dictionary (1968), ed. by U. Bahadır Alkım, Sofi Huri, Andreas Tietze *et alii* (Istanbul: Redhouse Press).

Türkiye Diyanet Vakfı İslam Ansiklopedisi (1988–). (Istanbul: Türkiye Diyanet Vakfı).

Yurt Ansiklopedisi, Türkiye İl İl: Dünü, Bugünü, Yarını (1981–4). (Istanbul: Anadolu Yayıncılık AŞ).

~ Primary sources

Adler, Elkan ed. (reprint 1987). *Jewish Travellers in the Middle Ages, 19 First-hand Accounts* (New York: Dover Publications). (Wider than the title suggests; contains the travel account of Samuel Jemsel the Karaite, who visited Gelibolu and Rhodes in 1641, and also an extract of the travel diary of Azulai, *q.v.*).

Aigen, Wolffgang (1980). *Sieben Jahre in Aleppo (1656–1663), ein Abschnitt aus den 'Reiß-Beschreibungen' des Wolffgang Aigen*, ed. by Andreas Tietze (Vienna: Verlag des Verbandes der wissenschaftlichen Gesellschaften Österreichs). (A vivid experience of mid-17th-century northern Syria, with an excursion to the silk growers of Lebanon).

Andreasyan, Hrand (1976). 'Celâlilerden Kaçan Anadolu Halkının Geri Gönderilmesi', in *İsmail Hakkı Uzunçarşılı'ya Armağan* (Ankara: Türk Tarih Kurumu): 45–54. (Translation of a 17th-century Armenian source).

Anonymous (1998). *XVIII. Yüzyıl İstanbul Hayatına Dair Risâle-i Garîbe*, ed. and commented by Hayati Develi (Istanbul: Kitabevi). (On the notions of proper behaviour entertained by a rather misanthropic Istanbullu).

Anonymous Jesuit (1745). *Nouveaux mémoires des missions de la Compagnie de Jésus dans le Levant*, Vol. VIII (Paris: Frères Guérin). (Concerns a trip to Aleppo by way of the Izmir region and the Aegean islands).

Ayn-ı Ali (1979). *Kavânîn-i Âl-i Osman der Hülâsa-i Mezâmin-i Defter-i Dîvân*, intr. by Tayyib Gökbilgin (Istanbul: Enderun). (Reprint of the 19th-century edition, with a new introduction by a specialist on Ottoman tax registers).

['Azîz Efendi] (1985). *Kanûn-nâme-i sultânî li 'Azîz Efendi, Aziz Efendi's Book of Sultanic Laws and Regulations*, ed. by Rhoads Murphey (Cambridge, MA: Harvard University). (Advice by an Ottoman official to his presumed successors).

Azulai, Ha'im Y. (1997). *The Diaries of Rabbi Ha'im Yosef David Azulai, Ma'agal Tov', The Good Journey*, ed. by Benjamin Cymerman (Jerusalem: Bnei Issakhar Institute). (On an 18th-century Jerusalem rabbi who travelled in France, Holland and England).

Bacqué-Grammont, Jean-Louis (1981). 'Un plan inédit de Van au XVIIe siècle', *Osmanlı Araştırmaları*, II: 97–122. (On an Ottoman sketch map of both the fortress and the town).

Bacqué-Grammont, Jean-Louis (tr. and ed.) (1997). *La première histoire de France en turc ottoman, Chroniques des padichahs de France 1572* (Istanbul and Paris: Institut Français d'Études Anatoliennes and L'Harmattan). (Translation into French from the Ottoman original, that was in its turn based on French 16th-century chronicles; this proceeding permits us to envisage how the political institutions of France 'translated' into the Ottoman terminology of the time).

Berindei, Mihnea, and Veinstein, Gilles (1987). *L'Empire ottoman et les pays roumains 1544–1545* (Paris and Cambridge, MA: Éditions de l'ÉHÉESS and Harvard Ukrainian Research Institute). (Contains an important discussion of the information which the earliest Registers of Important Affairs provide on Walachia, Moldavia and Transylvania).

Beydilli, Kemal, and Erünsal, İsmail E. (2001–2). 'Prut Savaşı Öncesi Diplomatik Bir Teşebbüs Seyfullah Ağa'nın Viyana Elçiliği (1711) (142 sayfa belge ile birlikte)', *Belgeler*, XXII, 26: 1–182.

Binark, Ismet *et alii* (eds) (1993). *3 Numaralı Mühimme Defteri (966–68/1558–60)*, 2 vols (Ankara: Başbakanlık Devlet Arşivleri Genel Müdürlüğü).

Binark, Ismet *et alii* (eds) (1994). *5 Numaralı Mühimme Defteri (973/1565–66)*, 2 vols (Ankara: Başbakanlık Devlet Arşivleri Genel Müdürlüğü).

Binark, Ismet *et alii* (eds) (1995). *6 Numaralı Mühimme Defteri 972/1564–65*, 3 vols (Ankara: Başbakanlık Devlet Arşivleri Genel Müdürlüğü).

Binark, Ismet *et alii* (eds) (1996). *12 Numaralı Mühimme Defteri 978–979/1570–72*, 3 vols (Ankara: Başbakanlık Devlet Arşivleri Genel Müdürlüğü).

Bonnac, Jean-Louis Dusson, Marquis de (1894). *Mémoire historique sur l'Ambassade de France à Constantinople*, ed. and intr. by Charles Schefer (Paris: Ernest Leroux). (Valuable introduction by Schefer, and Bonnac's own accounts are fascinating; unfortunately, because of the poor quality of the paper used, the book has become rather difficult to find).

Busbecq, Ogier Ghiselin de (1968). *The Turkish Letters of Ogier Ghiselin de Busbecq, Imperial Ambassador at Constantinople 1554–1562*, tr. by Edward Seymour Forster (Oxford: Clarendon Press).

Busbequius, Augerius Gislenius (1994). *Legationis turcicae epistolae quatuor*, ed. by Zweder von Martels, tr. into Dutch by Michel Goldsteen (Hilversum: Verloren). (Excellent index makes this version the most 'user-friendly' of all that I have seen).

Cantemir, Demetrius (1734). *The History of the Growth and Decay of the Ottoman Empire*, tr. by N. Tindal, 2 vols (London: John James & Paul Knapton). (Still the most accessible edition although the Latin original, long lost, has now been retrieved).

Cantemir, Demetrius (1743). *Histoire de l'Empire Othoman où se voyent les causes de son agrandissement et de sa décadence*, tr. by M. de Joncquières, 4 vols (Paris: Huart).

Cantemir, Dimitrie (reprint 1973a). *Beschreibung der Moldau, Faksimiledruck der Originalausgabe von 1771*, postscriptum by Constantin Maciuca (Bucharest: Kriterion). (Information on political institutions, but also on the role of the Orthodox Church; interesting material on folklore).

Cantemir, Dimitrie (1973b). *Dimitrie Cantemir, Historian of South East European and Oriental Civilizations, Extracts from 'The History of the Ottoman Empire'*, ed. by Alexandru Dutu and Paul Cernovodeanu, preface by Halil Inalcik (Bucharest: Association Internationale d'Études du Sud-Est Européen). (Contains mainly the 'footnotes' to Cantemir's historical work, rich on Istanbul folklore).

Costin, Miron (1980). *Grausame Zeiten in der Moldau, Die Moldauische Chronik des Miron Costin 1593–1661*, tr. and comments by Adolf Armbruster (Graz, Vienna and, Cologne: Styria) (The author, a high official and aristocrat, participated in quite a few of the events described).

Dernschwam, Hans (1923). *Hans Dernschwams Tagebuch einer Reise nach Konstantinopel und Kleinasien (1553–1555)*, ed. by Franz Babinger (Munich and Leipzig: Duncker und Humblodt). (Xenophobic and bad-tempered account by a retired businessman of the 16th century, but with an informed interest in everyday technology).

Doughty, Charles M. (1936). *Travels in Arabia Deserta*, intr. by T. E. Lawrence, 2 vols (London: Jonathan Cape). (Late 19th-century British traveller who learned

Arabic and lived with the Bedouin as a 'participant observer' *avant la lettre*; synthetically 'Elizabethan' language).

Dourry Efendy (1810). *Relation de Dourry Efendy ambassadeur de la Porte ottomane auprès du roi de Perse* ... (Paris: Ferra). (Translation by De Fienne of following item, should be checked against the original).

Dürri Efendi, Ahmed, published in Raşid, Mehmed (1282/1865–6), *Tarih-i Raşid*, Vol. 5: 382–98. (Embassy report to Iran).

Düzdağ, Ertuğrul (1972). *Şeyhülislam Ebusuud Efendi Fetvaları Işığında 16. Asır Türk Hayatı* (Istanbul: Enderun). (The *fetva*s of Sultan Süleyman's *şeyhülislam*, at the interface of religion and politics).

Emnî, Mehmed (1974). *Mehmed Emnî Beyefendi (Paşa)'nın Rusya Sefâreti ve Sefâret-nâmesi*, ed. by Münir Aktepe (Ankara: Türk Tarih Kurumu). (Contains descriptions of the palaces and gardens near St Petersburg).

Evliya Çelebi (1314/1896–7 to 1938). *Seyahatnamesi*, 10 vols (Istanbul, Ankara: Ikdam and others). (Unsatisfactory, new edition to be used for the first eight vols).

[Evliya Çelebi] (2nd edition, 1987). *Im Reiche des Goldenen Apfels, des türkischen Weltenbummlers Evliya Çelebi denkwürdige Reise in das Giaurenland und in die Stadt und Festung Wien anno 1665*, tr. and annotated by Richard F. Kreutel, Erich Prokosch and Karl Teply (Vienna: Verlag Styria). (Evliya's trip to Vienna, commented on by three connoisseurs of Ottoman and Viennese folklore).

Evliya Çelebi (1988). *Evliya Çelebi in Diyarbekir*, ed. and tr. by. Van Bruinessen *et alii* (Leiden: E. J. Brill). (With an exhaustive commentary by a team of Dutch specialists).

Evliya Çelebi (1990). *Evliya Çelebi in Bitlis, the Relevant Sections of the Seyahatname, edited with translation, commentary and introduction by Robert Dankoff* (Leiden: E. J. Brill).

Evliya Çelebi b Derviş Mehemmed Zılli (1995). *Evliya Çelebi Seyahatnâmesi, Topkapı Sarayı Bağdat 304 Yazmasının Transkripsyonu –Dizini*, Vol. 1, ed. by Orhan Şaik Gökyay and Yücel Dağlı (Istanbul: Yapı Kredi Yayınları). (This is one of the last productions of Gökyay, a well-known connoisseur of Ottoman literature).

Evliya Çelebi b Derviş Mehemmed Zılli (1999a). *Evliya Çelebi Seyahatnâmesi, Topkapı Sarayı Bağdat 304 Yazmasının Transkripsyonu –Dizini*, Vol. 2, ed. by Zekerya Kurşun, Yücel Dağlı, and Seyit Ali Kahraman (Istanbul: Yapı Kredi Yayınları).

Evliya Çelebi b Derviş Mehemmed Zılli (1999b). *Evliya Çelebi Seyahatnâmesi, Topkapı Sarayı Bağdat 305 Yazmasının Transkripsyonu –Dizini*, Vol. 3, ed. by Yücel Dağlı and Seyit Ali Kahraman (Istanbul: Yapı Kredi Yayınları).

Evliya Tchélébi (2000). *La guerre des Turcs, Récits de batailles extraits du 'Livre de voyages'*, tr. and annotated by Faruk Bilici (Aix-en-Provence: Sindbad and Actes Sud).

[Evliya Çelebi] (2000). *Kairo in der zweiten Hälfte des 17. Jahrhunderts beschrieben von Evliya Celebi*, tr. by Erich Prokosch (Istanbul: Simurg).

Evliya Çelebi b Derviş Mehemmed Zılli (2001a). *Evliya Çelebi Seyahatnâmesi, Topkapı Sarayı Bağdat 305 Yazmasının Transkripsyonu –Dizini*, Vol. 4, ed. by Yücel Dağlı and Seyit Ali Kahraman (Istanbul: Yapı Kredi Yayınları).

Evliya Çelebi b Derviş Mehemmed Zılli (2001b). *Evliya Çelebi Seyahatnâmesi, Topkapı Sarayı Bağdat 307 Yazmasının Transkripsyonu –Dizini*, Vol. 5, ed. by Yücel Dağlı, Seyit Ali Kahraman and Ibrahim Sezgin (Istanbul: Yapı Kredi Yayınları).

Evliya Çelebi b Derviş Mehemmed Zılli (2002). *Evliya Çelebi Seyahatnâmesi, Topkapı Sarayı Bağdat 305 Yazmasının Transkripsyonu –Dizini*, Vol. 6, ed. by Yücel Dağlı and Seyit Ali Kahraman (Istanbul: Yapı Kredi Yayınları).

Galland, Antoine (reprint 2002). *Voyage à Constantinople (1672–1673)*, ed. by Charles Schefer, new preface by Frédéric Bauden (Paris: Maisonneuve and Larose). (In this diary Galland has recorded everyday encounters, probably in order to collect observations later to be used in more formal writings).

Gökbilgin, M. Tayyip (1964). 'Venedik Devlet Arşivlerindeki Vesika Külliyatında Kanunî Sultan Süleyman Devri Belgeleri', *Belgeler*, I, 1–2: 234.

Gölpınarlı, Abdülbaki (1963). *Alevî-Bektaşî Nefesleri* (Istanbul: Remzi). (Religious poetry with comments by a major connoisseur of Ottoman dervish life).

Haedo, Diego de (reprint 1998). *Histoire des rois d'Alger*, tr. by Henri-Delmas de Grammont, new introduction by Jocelyne Dakhlia (Paris: Editions Bouchene). (An Italo-Spanish Benedictine of the early 17th century on the Ottoman governors of Algiers).

Hattî Efendi, Mustafa (1999). *Viyana Sefâretnâmesi*, ed. by Ali Ibrahim Savaş (Ankara: Türk Tarih Kurumu). (An 18th-century embassy to Vienna).

Heberer von Bretten, Johann Michael (reprint 1967). *Aegyptiaca Servitus*, intr. by Karl Teply (Graz: Akademische Druck- und Verlagsanstalt). (The memoirs of an articulate Protestant who for several years in the 1580s served on Ottoman galleys; has a great deal to say on survival in a harsh environment).

Hibri, Abdürrahman (1975, 1976, 1978). 'Menasik-i Mesalik', ed. by Sevim İlgürel, *Tarih Enstitüsü Dergisi*, 6: 111–128, *Tarih Dergisi*, 30: 55–72, *Tarih Dergisi*, 31: 147–62 (17th-century account of the pilgrimage to Mecca, describes the perils of the desert journey in considerable detail).

Hiltebrand, Conrad Jacob (1937). *Conrad Jacob Hiltebrandts Dreifache Schwedische Gesandtschaftsreise nach Siebenbürgen, der Ukraine und Constantinopel (1656–1658)*, ed. with commentary by Franz Babinger (Leiden: E. J. Brill). (A young preacher accompanying Swedish embassies to Moldavia and Istanbul).

Ibn Jubayr (1952). *The Travels of Ibn Jubayr ...*, tr. by R. J. C. Broadhurst (London: Jonathan Cape). (12th-century Andalusian pilgrim).

İnciciyan, P. Ğ[ugas] (1956). *XVIII. Asırda İstanbul*, tr. and commentary by Hrand Andreasyan (Istanbul: İstanbul Fethi Derneği İstanbul Enstitüsü). (By a sophisticated Mechitarist priest from Istanbul, who spent much of his time in Venice).

İsmâ'îl 'Asım Küçük Çelebizade, published in Raşid, Mehmed (1282/1865–6), *Tarih-i Raşid*, Vol. 6. ('Standard' Ottoman chronicle).

Jahn, Karl (1963). *Türkische Freilassungserklärungen des 18. Jahrhunderts (1702–1776)* (Naples: Istituto Universitario Orientale di Napoli). (Document publication with interesting sidelights on Ottoman peace-making in the 18th century).

Kal'a, Ahmet, *et alii* (eds) (1997–). *İstanbul Külliyatı I, İstanbul Ahkâm Defterleri ...* (Istanbul: İstanbul Büyükşehir Belediyesi). (Rich collection of sultans' commands dealing with the affairs of the Ottoman capital, ten vols to date).

Kâtib Çelebi (1145/1732). *Cihân-numâ* (Istanbul: Ibrahim Müteferrika). (One of the major works of Ottoman geography).

Kömürcüyan, Eremya Çelebi (1952). *İstanbul Tarihi, XVII. Asırda İstanbul*, tr. and annotated by Hrand Andreasyan (Istanbul: İstanbul Üniversitesi Edebiyat Fakültesi). (Detailed description by a 17th-century Istanbul Armenian scholar).

Kütükoğlu, Mübahat (ed.) (1983). *Osmanlılarda Narh Müessesesi ve 1640 Tarihli Narh Defteri* (Istanbul: Enderun Kitabevi). (Most informative notes and a comprehensive introduction).

Lâtifî (2001). *Éloge d'Istanbul suivi du Traité de l'invective (anonyme)*, tr. and comments by Stéphane Yérasimos ([Aix-en-Provence]: Sindbad-Actes Sud). (The *Traité* is the text published by Develi).

[Lubenau, Reinhold] (1912 and 1915). *Beschreibung der Reisen des Reinhold Lubenau*, ed. by W. Sahm (Königsberg/ Kaliningrad: Ferdinand Beyers Buchhandlung).

Martelli, Claudio Angelo de (1689). *Relatio captivo-redempti, das ist warhafft: und eigentliche Beschreibung der Anno 1683 ... außgestandenen Gefaengnuß* (Vienna: Matthias Sischowitz). (The story of a Habsburg officer taken prisoner in the Vienna campaign, with an emphasis on conditions in the numerous jails in which he was kept).

Maundrell, Henry (reprint 1963), *A Journey from Aleppo to Jerusalem in 1697*, intr. by David Howell (Beirut: Khayats). (A scholarly writer whose work makes good reading).

Mehmed Efendi (1981). *Le paradis des infidèles, Un ambassadeur ottoman en France sous la Régence*, with an introduction by Gilles Veinstein (Paris: François Maspéro). (The account, by an educated Ottoman, of the French court in 1720, compare Göçek, 1987).

Mende, Rana von (ed.) (1989). *Mustafā 'Ālī's Fursat-nāme, Edition und Bearbeitung einer Quelle zur Geschichte des persischen Feldzugs unter Sinān Paša 1580–81* (Berlin: Klaus Schwarz Verlag).

Montagu, Lady Mary Wortley (1993). *Turkish Embassy Letters*, ed. by Anita Desai and Malcolm Jack (London: Pickering). (No comment needed: a classic).

[Nahifi Mehmed Efendi] (1970). *Mubadele – An Ottoman-Russian Exchange of Ambassadors*, tr. and annotated by Norman Itzkowitz and Max Mote (Chicago and London: University of Chicago Press).

Nasuhü's-silahî (Matrakçı) (1976). *Beyan-ı Menazil-i Sefer-i 'Irakeyn-i Sultan Süleyman Han*, ed. by Hüseyin G. Yurdaydın (Ankara: Türk Tarih Kurumu). (The 'official' illustrated account of the Ottoman conquest of Iraq).

Orhonlu, Cengiz (ed.) (1970). *Osmanlı Tarihine âid Belgeler, Telhîsler 1597–1607* (Istanbul: İ.Ü. Edebiyat Fakültesi). (On collections of reports submitted by grand viziers to their rulers).

Osman Ağa (1962). *Der Gefangene der Giauren, die abenteuerlichen Schicksale des Dolmetschers Osman Ağa aus Temeschwar, von ihm selbst erzählt*, tr. and commented by Richard Kreutel and Otto Spies (Cologne, Graz, Vienna: Styria). (Osman Ağa not only had a series of horrible adventures as a prisoner in the war of 1683–99, he was also a fine storyteller. A French translation by Frédéric Hitzel, published in 1998, is available: *Prisonnier des infidèles, un soldat ottoman dans l'empire des Habsbourg*, Aix-en-Provence: Sindbad-Actes Sud).

Osman Ağa (1980). *Die Autobiographie des Dolmetschers 'Osman Aga aus Temeschwar,* ed. by Richard Kreutel (Cambridge: Gibb Memorial Trust). (The Ottoman original).

Palerne, Jean (reprint 1991). *D'Alexandrie à Istanbul, Pérégrinations dans l'empire ottoman 1581–1583*, ed. by Yvelise Bernard (Paris: L'Harmattan). (How to combine pilgrimage and sightseeing).

[Papa Synadinos of Serres] (1996). *Conseils et mémoires de Synadinos prêtre de Serrès en Macédoine (XVIIe siècle)*, ed., tr. and commented by Paolo Odorico, with S. Asdrachas, T. Karanastassis, K. Kostis and S. Petmézas (Paris: Association 'Pierre Belon'). (The rich chronicle of a Balkan town, with superb commentaries).

Pedani Fabris, Maria Pia (1994a). *I 'Documenti turchi' dell'Archivio di Stato di Venezia* (Roma: Ministero per i beni culturali e ambientali, Ufficio centrale per i beni archivistici). (Archival catalogue, with long summaries of many of the relevant documents, often by Alessio Bombaci).

Piri Reis (1935). *Kitabı Bahriye*, ed. by Haydar Alpagut and Fevzi Kurtoğlu (Istanbul: Türk Tarih Kurumu).

Prohazka-Eisl, Gisela (ed.) (1995). *Das Surname-i Hümayun, Die Wiener Handschrift in Transkription, mit Kommentar und Indices versehen* (Istanbul: The Isis Press).

Raşid, Mehmed (1282/1865–66). *Tarih-i Raşid*, 6 vols (Istanbul: Matba'a-yı amire).

Ratib Efendi, Ebubekir (1999). *Ebubekir Ratib Efendi'nin Nemçe Sefaretnamesi* (Istanbul: Kitabevi). (Embassy to Vienna by a sophisticated member of Selim III's 'think tank').

Rauwolff, Leonhard (reprint 1971). *Aigentliche Beschreibung der Raiß inn die Morgenländer*, intr. by Dieter Henze (Graz: Akademische Druck- und Verlagsanstalt). (The author made his reputation by his detailed description of Mesopotamia).

Refik, Ahmed (1932). *On altıncı Asırda Râfizîlik ve Bektaşilik. On altıncı Asırda Türkiye'de Râfizîlik ve Bektaşîliğe dair Hazinei Evrak Vesikalarını Havidir* (Istanbul: Muallim Ahmed Halit Kütüphanesi). (A collection of documents from the Mühimme registers concerning the 16th-century persecution of heterodox Muslims).

Resmi, Ahmed (1303/1885–6). *Sefâretnâme-i Ahmed Resmî* (Istanbul: Kitâbhâne-i Ebuzziyâ). (A lively description of late 18th-century Berlin).

Sahillioğlu, Halil (ed. and analysis) (1985a). 'Yemen in 1599–1600 Yılı Bütçesi', in *Yusuf Hikmet Bayur Armağanı* (Ankara: Türk Tarih Kurumu): 287–319. (Both edition and interpretation).

Sahillioğlu, Halil (ed. and analysis) (2002). *Topkapı Sarayı Arşivi H. 951–952 Tarihli ve E–12321 Numaralı Mühimme Defteri* (Istanbul: IRSICA).

Schweigger, Samuel (reprint 1964). *Eine Newe Reyssbeschreibung auss Teutschland nach Constantinopel und Jerusalem*, intr. by Rudolf Neck (Graz: Akademische Druck- und Verlagsanstalt). (By a Lutheran divine with good contacts to the late 16th-century ecumenical patriarchate).

Şener, Murat, *et alii* (eds) (1997). *7 Numaralı Mühimme Defteri 975–976/1567–69*, 3 vols (Ankara: Başbakanlık Devlet Arşivleri Genel Müdürlüğü).

Sestini Domenico (1785). *Opuscoli del Signor Abate Domenico Sestini* (Florence). (There exists a contemporary translation into German by Christian Joseph Jagemann, *Beschreibung des Kanals von Konstantinopel*, Hamburg: Carl Ernst Bohn, 1786).

Seyyidî 'Ali Re'îs (1999a). *Le miroir des pays, Une anabase ottomane à travers l'Inde et l'Asie centrale*, tr. and comments by Jean-Louis Bacqué-Grammont ([Aix-en-Provence]: Sindbad-Actes Sud). (In spite of its factual tone, a great adventure story).

[Seyyidî 'Ali Re'îs] (1999b). *Seydi Ali Reis, Mir'âtü'l-Memâlik, İnceleme, Metin, Index*, ed. by Mehmet Kiremit (Ankara: Türk Dil Kurumu).

Shaw, Stanford J. (ed.) (1968). *The Budget of Ottoman Egypt 1005–1006/1596–1597* (The Hague and Paris: Mouton). (Publication of the original document, with translation and comments).

Simeon, Polonyalı (1964). *Polonyalı Simeon'un Seyahatnâmesi, 1608–1619* (Istanbul: İstanbul Üniversitesi Edebiyat Fakültesi).

Skilliter, Susan A. (1977). *William Harborne and the Trade with Turkey 1578–1582, A Documentary Study of the First Anglo-Ottoman Relations* (London: The British Academy and Oxford University Press). (An exhaustively commented edition of the surviving documents).

Sofroni von Vratsa (2nd edition 1979). *Leben und Leiden des sündigen Sofroni*, tr. and notes by Norbert Randow (Leipzig: Insel-Verlag). (A classic of Bulgarian literature, and very informative on provincial life, but unfortunately almost unknown to Ottomanists).

Vraca'lı Sofroni (2003). *Osmanlı'da Bir Papaz, Günahkâr Sofroni'nin Çileli Hayat Hikâyesi 1739–1813*, tr. by Aziz Nazmi Şakir-Taş (Istanbul: Kitap Yayınevi). (Now that this translation is on the market, the situation described above hopefully will change).

Stamates Petru (1976). *Grammata apo to Amsterntam*, with a postscriptum by Philippos Eliu (Athens: Nea Hellenike Bibliotheke). (Original not seen, tr. by Anna Vlachopoulos).

Teply, Karl (1983). 'Das österreichische Türkenkriegszeitalter', in Zygmunt Abrahamowicz *et alii*, *Die Türkenkriege in der historischen Forschung* (Vienna: Franz Deuticke): 5–51. (An anthology of primary sources on the Ottoman–Habsburg wars, in German translation).

Tulum, Mertol, *et alii* (eds) (1993). *Mühimme Defteri 90* (Istanbul: Türk Dünyası Araştırmaları Vakfı).

Ünal, Mehmet Ali (ed.) (1995). *Mühimme Defteri 44* (Izmir: Akademi Kitabevi).

Vasıf, Ahmed, 'Sefaretname-i Vasıf Efendi', published in Cevdet, Ahmed (1309/1893–4). *Tarih-i Cevdet, Tertib-i Cedid*, Vol. 4 (Istanbul: Matbaa-yı Osmaniye): 348–58.

Veselà, Zdenka (1961). 'Quelques chartes turques concernant la correspondance de la Porte Sublime avec Imre Thököly', *Archiv Orientální*, 29: 546–74.

Webbe, Edward (1895). *Edward Webbe Chief Master Gunner, his Travails 1590*, ed. by Edward Arber (Westminster: Constable & Co). (The story of a soldier of fortune who also spent time as a galley slave in the Istanbul Arsenal, to be taken with more than just two grains of salt).

Wild, Johann (reprint 1964). *Reysbeschreibung eines Gefangenen Christen Anno 1604* (Stuttgart: Steingrüben). (By a Nuremberg soldier in the 'Long War', who, as a probably Islamized slave, visited Cairo, Jerusalem, Mecca and the Yemen; returned in 1611 after manumission).

Wilkinson, William (reprint 1971). *An Account of the Principalities of Walachia and Moldavia with Various Political Observations Relating to them* (New York: Arno Press and The New York Times). (As a former British consul the author was well-infomed on many issues; but ethnocentrism and even racism are pervasive in this book).

Wüstenfeld, Ferdinand (reprint 1981). *Die Chroniken der Stadt Mekka, Teil III–IV*, in one vol.: III. *Cutb ed-Dins Geschichte der Stadt Mekka*, IV. *Geschichte der Stadt Mekka, nach den Arabischen Chroniken bearbeitet, Die Scherife von Mekka im 11.*

(17.) Jahrhundert (Hildesheim and New York: Georg Olms Verlag). (Translation of important Meccan chronicles into German).

Yıldırım, Hacı Osman, *et alii* (eds) (1997). *7 Numaralı Mühimme Defteri 975–976/ 1567–69*, 5 vols (Ankara: Başbakanlık Devlet Arşivleri Genel Müdürlüğü).

~ Monographs and articles

Abdel Nour, Antoine (1982). *Introduction à l'histoire urbaine de la Syrie ottomane (XVIe–XVIIIe siècle)* (Beyrouth: Université Libanaise and Librairie Orientale). (On the basis of kadi registers, fundamental on the problems of private housing).

Abdullah, Thabit A. J. (2000). *Merchants, Mamluks and Murder, The Political Economy of Trade in Eighteenth-Centuy Basra* (Albany, NY: SUNY Press).

Abou-El-Haj, Rifa'at A. (1974a). 'Ottoman Attitudes toward Peace-making: The Karlowitz Case', *Der Islam*, 51: 131–7.

Abou-El-Haj, Rifa'at A. (1974b). 'The Ottoman Vezir and Pasha Households 1683–1703: A Preliminary Survey', *Journal of the American Oriental Society*, XCIV: 438–47.

Abou-El-Haj, Rifa'at A. (1983). 'An Agenda for Research in History: The History of Libya between the Sixteenth and Nineteenth Centuries', *International Journal of Middle East Studies*, 15: 305–19.

Abou-El-Haj, Rifa'at A. (1984). *The 1703 Rebellion and the Structure of Ottoman Politics* (Istanbul and Leiden: Nederlands Historisch-Archeologisch Instituut).

Abou-El-Haj, Rifa'at A. (1991). *Formation of the Ottoman State, The Ottoman Empire Sixteenth to Eighteenth Centuries* (Albany, NY: SUNY Press). (The Ottoman Empire in a comparative perspective, most stimulating).

Abrahamowicz, Zygmunt (1983). 'Der politische und ökonomische Hintergrund des Wiener Feldzuges von Kara Mustafa', *Studia Austro-Polonica*, 3: 7–44.

Abu-Husayn, Abdul-Rahim (1985). *Provincial Leaderships in Syria 1575–1650* (Beirut: AUB).

Adanır, Fikret (1982). 'Haiduckentum und osmanische Herrschaft. Sozialgeschichtliche Aspekte der Diskussion um das frühneuzeitliche Räuberunwesen in Südosteuropa', *Südost-Forschungen*, 41: 43–116.

Adnan-Adıvar, Abdülhak (1943). *Osmanlı Türklerinde İlim* (Istanbul: Maarif Vekilliği).

Aghassian, Michel, and Kévonian, Kéram (1999). 'The Armenian Merchant Network: Overall Autonomy and Local Integration', in Sushil Chaudhuri and Michel Morineau (eds), *Merchants, Companies and Trade, Europe and Asia in the Early Modern Era* (Cambridge: Cambridge University Press): 74–94.

Ágoston, Gábor (1993). 'Gunpowder for the Sultan's Army: New Sources on the Supply of Gunpowder to the Ottoman Army in the Hungarian Campaigns of the Sixteenth and Seventeenth Centuries', *Turcica*, 25: 75–96.

Ágoston, Gábor, (1994). 'Ottoman Artillery and European Military Technology in the Fifteenth to Seventeenth Centuries', *Acta Orientalia Hungarica*, 47: 15–48.

Ágoston, Gábor (1999). 'Ottoman Warfare in Europe 1453–1826', in Jeremy Black (ed.), *European Warfare, 1453–1815* (Basingstoke: Macmillan): 118–44 and

262–3. (A brief and incisive treatment of the problems confronted by the Ottoman military establishment).

Ak, Mahmut (1991). 'Menâzırü'l-Avâlim ve Kaynağı Takvîmü'l-Buldân', in *Professor Dr. Bekir Kütükcğlu'na Armağan* (Istanbul: İstanbul Üniversitesi Edebiyat Fakültesi): 101–20.

Akarlı, Engin (1986). 'Gedik: Implements, Mastership, Shop Usufruct and Monopoly among Istanbul Artisans, 1750–1850', *Wissenschaftskolleg Berlin: Jahrbuch*: 223–31.

Akarlı, Engin (1988). 'Provincial Power Magnates in Ottoman Bilad al-Sham and Egypt, 1740–1840', in Abdeljelil Temimi (ed.), *La vie sociale dans les provinces arabes à l'époque ottomane* (Zaghouan: CEROMDI): 41–56. (A good discussion of an often misrepresented topic).

Akdağ, Mustafa (1963). *Celâlî İsyanları 1550–1603* (Ankara: A Ü Dil ve Tarih-Coğrafya Fakültesi). (Basic monograph on the military uprisings which shook late 16th-century Anatolia).

Aksan, Virginia (1986–8). 'Ottoman Sources on Europe in the Eighteenth Century', *Archivum Ottomanicum*, 11: 5–16.

Aksan, Virginia (1993). 'Ottoman Political Writing, 1768–1808', *International Journal of Middle East Studies*, 25: 53–69.

Aksan, Virginia (1995). *An Ottoman Statesman in War and Peace, Ahmed Resmi Efendi, 1700–1783* (Leiden: E. J. Brill). (The perspective of an author-*cum*-diplomat on the possibilities and limitations of the 18th-century Ottoman Empire, important).

Aksan, Virginia (1999a). 'Locating the Ottomans among Early Modern Empires', *Journal for Early Modern History*, 3, 2: 103–34.

Aksan, Virginia (1999b). 'An Ottoman Portrait of Frederick the Great', *Oriente Moderno*, 18: 203–15.

Aksan, Virginia (2002). 'Ottoman Military Matters', *Journal for Early Modern History*, 6, 1: 52–62.

Akşin, Sina (ed.) (1990–5). *Türkiye Tarihi*, Vol. 1: *Osmanlı Devletine kadar Türkler*, Vol. 2: *Osmanlı Devleti 1300–1600*, Vol. 3: *Osmanlı Devleti 1600–1908*, Vol. 4: *Çağdaş Türkiye 1908–1980*, Vol. 5: *Bügünkü Türkiye 1980–1995* (Istanbul: Cem Yayınevi). (With contributions by numerous authors).

Aktepe, Münir (1958). *Patrona İsyanı* (Istanbul: İstanbul Üniversitesi Edebiyat Fakültesi). (An important monograph which has aged well).

Aktuğ, İlknur (1992). *Nevşehir, Damat İbrahim Paşa Külliyesi* (Ankara: Kültür Bakanlığı).

Allmeyer-Beck, Christoph Johann, and Lessing, Erich (1978). *Die kaiserlichen Kriegsvölker, von Maximilian I bis Prinz Eugen 1479–1718* (Munich: Bertelsmann Verlag). (Lively and, above all, superbly illustrated).

Allouche, Adel (1983). *The Origins and Development of the Ottoman-Safavid Conflict (906–962/1500–1555)* (Berlin: Klaus Schwarz).

Anastassiadou, Meropi (1997). *Salonique, 1830–1912, Une ville ottomane à l'age des Réformes* (Leiden: E. J. Brill). (The emphasis is on the 'Ottomanness' of the city).

Anderson, Matthew S. (reprint 1998). *War and Society in Europe of the Old Regime 1618–1789* (Phoenix Mill: Sutton Publishing Ltd).

Anderson, Sonia (1989). *An English Consul in Turkey, Paul Rycaut at Smyrna, 1667–1678* (Oxford: Clarendon Press). (On the author of a widely read history of the Ottoman Empire).

Angelomate-Tsoungarake, Eleni (2000). 'Hellenika periegetika keimena (16os–19os ai.)', *Mesaionika kai Nea Hellenika*: 155–80. (Original not seen, tr. by Nicolas Pissis).

Anonymous (ed.) (1999). *Topkapı à Versailles, Trésors de la cour ottomane* (Paris: Réunion des Musées Nationaux and Association Française d'Action Artistique). (Magnificent illustrations, covering items very rarely shown before).

Arbel, Benjamin (1995). *Trading Nations, Jews and Venetians in the Early Modern Eastern Mediterranean* (Leiden: E. J. Brill). (Very instructive on the links between Venice and Istanbul as mediated by Jewish merchants).

Arens, Meinolf (2001). *Habsburg und Siebenbürgen 1600–1605, Gewaltsame Eingliederungsversuche eines ostmitteleuropäischen Fürstentums in einen frühabsolutistischen Reichsverband* (Cologne, Weimar, Vienna: Böhlau). (Careful monograph; highlights the reasons how 'Counter-Reformation politics' made it impossible for the Habsburgs to gain the hearts and minds of their Hungarian subjects).

Argenti, Philip (1954). *The Occupation of Chios by the Genoese and their Administration of the Island 1346–1566*, 3 vols (Cambridge: Cambridge University Press).

Arıkan, Zeki (1991). 'Osmanlı İmparatorluğunda İhracı Yasak Mallar (Memnu Meta)', in *Professor Dr. Bekir Kütükoğlu'na Armağan* (Istanbul: İstanbul Üniversitesi Edebiyat Fakültesi): 279–307.

Artan, Tülay (1993). 'From Charismatic Leadership to Collective Rule, Introducing Materials on the Wealth and Power of Ottoman Princesses in the Eighteenth Century', *Toplum ve Ekonomi*, 4: 53–94.

Atıl, Esin (1999). *Levni and the Surname, The Story of an Eighteenth-century Ottoman Festival* (Istanbul: Koçbank). (Superbly illustrated).

Aymard, Maurice (1966). *Venise, Raguse et le commerce du blé pendant la seconde moitié du XVIe siècle* (Paris: S.E.V.P.E.N.). (On grain supplies reaching Venice from Ottoman territories).

Aynural, Salih (2002). *İstanbul Değirmenleri ve Fırınları, Zahire Ticareti* (Istanbul: Tarih Vakfı Yurt Yayınları). (Very well documented study on Ottoman state control at its most intrusive).

Babinger, Franz (1982). *Osmanlı Tarih Yazarları ve Eserleri*, tr. with supplementary information by Coşkun Üçok (Ankara: Ministry of Culture and Tourism). (This is a reference work; the original dates from 1927, and many more manuscripts have since been discovered. A revision is long overdue, but even as it stands, the book is a mine of information).

Baghdiantz McCabe, Ina (1999). *The Shah's Silk for Europe's Silver, the Eurasian Trade of the Julfa Armenians in Safavid Iran and India (1530–1750)* (Atlanta: Scholars Press and University of Pennsylvania). (Uses Safavid sources and describes the functioning of the New Djulfan community 'from within').

Bağış, Ali Ihsan (1983). *Osmanlı Ticaretinde Gayri Müslimler, Kapitülasyonlar, Beratlı Tüccarlar ve Hayriye Tüccarları (1750–1839)* (Ankara: Turhan Kitabevi). (On privileged non-Muslim – and to some extent also Muslim – traders at a time of European economic expansion).

Balard, Michel (1978). *La Romanie génoise (XIIème–début du XVème siècle)* (Rome: École française de Rome).

Barbir, Karl K. (1980). *Ottoman Rule in Damascus, 1708–1758* (Princeton: Princeton University Press). (On the organization of the Damascus pilgrimage caravan).

Barkan, Ömer Lütfi (1939). 'Türk-İslam Hukuku Tatbikatının Osmanlı İmparatorluğunda Aldığı Şekiller I: Malikane Divani Sistemi', *Türk Hukuk ve İktisat Tarihi Mecmuası*, 1: 119–85.

Barkan, Ömer Lütfi (1951–3). 'Tarihi Demografi Araştırmaları ve Osmanlı Tarihi', *Türkiyat Mecmuası*, X: 1–26.

Barkan, Ömer Lütfi (1963). 'Şehirlerin Teşekkül ve Inkişafı Tarihi Bakımından: Osmanlı İmparatorluğunda İmaret Sitelerinin Kuruluş ve İşleyiş Tarzına ait Araştırmalar', *İstanbul Üniversitesi İktisat Fakültesi Mecmuası*, 23, 1–2: 239–96. (On pious foundations and their role in Ottoman urbanism: still fundamental).

Barkan, Ömer Lütfi (1972, 1979). *Süleymaniye Cami ve İmareti İnşaatı*, 2 vols (Ankara: Türk Tarih Kurumu). (*The* fundamental study of Ottoman monumental construction from an organizational and financial point of view; the second posthumous volume contains a publication of the relevant documents).

Barkan, Ömer Lütfi (1975). 'The Price Revolution of the Sixteenth Century: A Turning Point in the Economic History of the Near East', *International Journal of Middle East Studies*, VI: 3–28. (Has aroused considerable debate).

Barkey, Karen (1994). *Bandits and Bureaucrats, the Ottoman Route to State Centralization* (Ithaca, NY, and London: Cornell University Press). (Comparative perspective; emphasizes the 'inclusiveness' of the early modern Ottoman state apparatus).

Bartl, Peter (1974). *Der Westbalkan zwischen spanischer Monarchie und Osmanischem Reich, Zur Türkenkriegsproblematik an der Wende vom 16. zum 17. Jahrhundert* (Wiesbaden: Albanien-Institut and Otto Harrassowitz). (On diverse projects to disrupt Ottoman rule in the western Balkans, and their ultimate failures).

Bayly, Christopher A. (1983). *Rulers, Townsmen and Bazaars, North Indian Society in the Age of British Expansion, 1770–1870* (Cambridge: Cambridge University Press).

Bayly, Christopher A. (1989). *Imperial Meridian, the British Empire and the World 1780–1830* (Harlow: Longman). (The 'World' discussed here includes the Ottoman Empire).

Behar, Cem (1990). *Ali Ufkî ve Mezmurlar* (Istanbul: Pan Yayıncılık). (A stimulating biography of a very unusual personage, a 'wanderer between two worlds').

Behrens-Abouseif, Doris (1994). *Egypt's Adjustment to Ottoman Rule, Institutions, waqf and Architecture in Cairo* (Leiden: E. J. Brill). (By an art historian and connoisseur of Cairo, the chapter on Egyptian opinions of the Ottomans is particularly remarkable).

Bellan, Lucien-Louis (1932). *Chah 'Abbas I, sa vie, son histoire* (Paris: Librairie Orientaliste Paul Geuthner).

Béller-Hann, Ildikó (1987). 'Ottoman Perception of China', in *Comité International d'Études Pré-ottomanes et Ottomanes, VIth Symposium, Cambridge, 1st–4th July 1984*, ed. by Jean-Louis Bacqué-Grammont and Emeri van Donzel (Istanbul, Leiden and Paris: IFEA and Divit Press): 55–64.

Belting, Hans (1993). *Bild und Kult, eine Geschichte der Bilder vor dem Zeitalter der Kunst* (Munich: C. H. Beck). (A magnificent discussion on the way icons, often of Byzantine provenance, were treated in the medieval west).

Bennassar, Bartolomé, and Lucile (1989). *Les Chrétiens d'Allah, l'histoire extraordinaire des renégats, XVIe–XVIIe siècles* (Paris: Perrin). (Remarkable studies of people who spent time in the Ottoman Empire as captives or emigrants, and ultimately returned to the Christian world; based on Inquisition documents).

Bennigsen, Alexandre, and Lemercier-Quelquejay, Chantal (1970). 'Les marchands de la Cour ottomane et le commerce des fourrures moscovites dans la seconde moitié du XVIe siècle', *Cahiers du monde russe et soviétique*, XI, 3: 363–90.

Bennigsen, Alexandre, and Lemercier-Quelquejay, Chantal (1976). 'La Moscovie, la Horde Nogay et le problème des communications entre l'Empire ottoman et l'Asie centrale en 1552/1556', *Turcica*, VIII, 2: 203–36.

Bennigsen, Alexandre, *et alii* (1978). *Le Khanat de Crimée dans les archives du Musée du Palais de Topkapı* (Paris: ÉHÉSS and Mouton).

Bergasse, Louis, and Rambert, Gaston (1954). *Histoire du commerce de Marseille*, Vol. 4: *De 1599 à 1660, De 1660 à 1789* (Paris: Plon). (Lots of information on Marseilles' trade with Syria, Egypt and western Anatolia).

Berkes, Niyazi (1969, 1970). *100 Soruda Türkiye İktisat Tarihi*, 2 vols (Istanbul: Gerçek Yayınevi). (Now out of date, but interesting for the history of Ottomanist historiography).

Berktay, Halil (1990). 'The "Other" Feudalism, A Critique of 20th Century Turkish Historiography and its Particularisation of Ottoman Society' (unpublished PhD dissertation, Birmingham).

Berktay, Halil (1991). 'Der Aufstieg und die gegenwärtige Krise der nationalistischen Geschichtsschreibung in der Türkei', *Periplus*, 1: 102–25.

Beydilli, Kemal (1974). *Die polnischen Königswahlen und Interregnen von 1572 und 1576 im Lichte osmanischer Archivalien, Ein Beitrag zur Geschichte der osmanischen Machtpolitik* (Munich: Dr Dr Rudolf Trofenik). (On the basis of Mühimme Registers).

Beydilli, Kemal (1984). 'Ignatius Mouradgea D'Ohsson (Muradcan Tosunyan)', *Istanbul Üniversitesi Edebiyat Fakültesi Tarih Dergisi*, 34: 247–314.

Beydilli, Kemal (1985). *Büyük Friedrich ve Osmanlılar, XVIII. Yüzyılda Osmanlı-Prusya Münasebetleri* (Istanbul: İstanbul Üniversitesi). (First part of a two-volume study on 18th-century Ottoman–Prussian relations).

Beydilli, Kemal (1995). *Türk Bilim ve Matbaacılık Tarihinde Mühendishâne, Mühendishâne Matbaası ve Kütüphânesi (1776–1826)* (Istanbul: Eren). (Important in our context for the references to 18th-century book production in general).

Biddle, Martin (1999). *The Tomb of Christ* (Phoenix Mill: Sutton Publishing) (An archaelogical study, demonstrates that, contrary to what had been previously assumed, the present *edicula* in the Church of the Holy Sepulchre is not entirely a 19th-century creation; invaluable for the interpretation of pilgrimage accounts).

Biedrońska-Słota, Beata (1999). 'The History of Turkish Textile Collections in Poland', in *War and Peace, Ottoman–Polish Relations in the 15th–19th Centuries* (Istanbul: Turkish Ministry of Culture and Polish Ministry of Culture and Art): 62–9.

Biegman, N. H. (1963). 'Ragusan Spying for the Ottoman Empire', *Belleten*, XXVII: 237–55.

Biegman, N. H. (1967). *The Turco-Ragusan Relationship, According to the Firmans of Murad III (1575–1595) Extant in the State Archives of Dubrovnik* (The Hague and Paris: Mouton). (A pioneering study).

Bilici, Faruk (1992). *La politique française en Mer Noire, Vicissitudes d'une implantation* (Istanbul: The Isis Press). (Concerns the period after 1774, when the French established a consulate on the northern shore of the Black Sea).

Bode, Andreas (1979). *Die Flottenpolitik Katharinas II und die Konflikte mit Schweden und der Türkei (1768–1792)* (Wiesbaden: Otto Harrassowitz). (Uses the reports of Swedish diplomats in Istanbul written in Swedish; interesting).

Bono, Salvatore (1999). *Schiavi musulmani nell' Italia moderna, Galeotti, vu' cumprà, domestici* (Naples: Edizioni Scientifiche Italiane). (On the survival of slavery in Italy into the early 19th century and the fate of Muslim slaves and freedman, this book should be much better known).

Bostan, İdris (1992). *Osmanlı Bahriye Teşkilâtı: XVII. Yüzyılda Tersane-i amire* (Ankara: Türk Tarih Kurumu). (A careful archival study).

Boulanger, Patrick (1996). *Marseille marché international de l'huile d'olive, un produit et des hommes, 1725–1825* (Marseilles: Institut Historique de Provence). (Contains much information on trade with the Ottoman Empire).

Bracewell, Catherine Wendy (1992). *The Uskoks of Senj, Piracy, Banditry and Holy War in the Sixteenth-Century Adriatic* (Ithaca, NY, and London: Cornell University Press). (Attempts to reconstruct the world of the Uskoks 'from within').

Braude, Benjamin (1979). 'International Competition and Domestic Cloth in the Ottoman Empire: A Study in Undevelopment', *Review*, II, 3: 437–54.

Braudel, Fernand (1st edition in 1 vol., 1949, 2nd edition, 1966). *La Méditerranée et le monde méditerranéen à l'époque de Philippe II*, 2 vols (Paris: Librairie Armand Colin). (Has aged well; full of stimulating ideas).

Braudel, Fernand (1979). *Civilisation matérielle, économie et capitalisme*, 3 vols (Paris: Armand Colin). ('Required reading').

Brotton, Jerry (2002). *The Renaissance Bazaar, From the Silk Road to Michelangelo* (Oxford: Oxford University Press). (A thought-provoking essay).

Brummett, Palmira (1991). 'Competition and Coincidence: Venetian Trading Interests and Ottoman Expansion in the Early Sixteenth Century Levant', *New Perspectives on Turkey*, 5–6: 29–52.

Bulut, Mehmet (2001). *Ottoman–Dutch Economic Relations in the Early Modern Period, 1571–1699* (Hilversum: Verloren).

Bushkovitch, Paul (1980). *The Merchants of Moscow 1580–1650* (Cambridge: Cambridge University Press).

Çağatay, Neşet (1971). 'Osmanlı İmparatorluğunda Riba-Faiz Konusu, Para Vakıfları ve Bankacılık', *Vakıflar Dergisi*, IX: 39–56.

Camariano, Nestor (1970). *Alexandre Mavrocordato, le Grand Drogman, son activité diplomatique (1673–1709)* (Thessaloniki: Institute for Balkan Studies). (Important monograph on a man about whom, his prominence notwithstanding, surprisingly little is known).

Carter, Francis W. (1972). *Dubrovnik (Ragusa) A Classic City-state* (London and New York: Seminar Press). (Especially rich on Dubrovnik's economy, includes much information on the local archives).

Chagniot, Jean (2001). *Guerre et société à l'époque moderne* (Paris: PUF-Nouvelle Clio). (In the traditional format of Nouvelle Clio: bibliography, an account of the issues involved and a section on historiographical debates).

Chaudhuri, K. N. (1985). *Trade and Civilisation in the Indian Ocean, An Economic History from the Rise of Islam to 1750* (Cambridge: Cambridge University Press). (An attempt to write a 'companion volume' to Braudel's *Méditerranée*; short and stimulating).

Chaunu, Pierre (1977). 'L'état', in *Histoire économique et sociale de la France*, Vol. 1: *1450–1660, L'état et la ville*, by Pierre Chaunu and Richard Gascon (Paris: Presses Universitaires de France): 1–228.

Chérif, Mohamed-Hédi (1984, 1987). *Pouvoir et société dans la Tunisie de H'usayn bin 'Ali (1705–1740)*, 2 vols (Tunis: Université de Tunis). (Wide-ranging monograph).

Chew, Samuel C. (reprint 1965). *The Crescent and the Rose, Islam and England during the Renaissance* (New York: Octagon Books). (A mine of information on English travellers in the Ottoman Empire).

Çizakça, Murat (1985). 'Incorporation of the Middle East into the European World Economy', *Review*, VIII, 3: 353–78. (Based on tax-farming data, shows that the speed of 'incorporation' slowed down in the 17th century).

Çizakça, Murat (reprint 1987). 'Price History and the Bursa Silk Industry: A Study in Ottoman Industrial Decline, 1550–1650', in Huri Islamoğlu-Inan (ed.), *The Ottoman Empire and the World Economy*, (Cambridge and Paris: Cambridge University Press and Maison des Sciences de l'Homme): 247–61. (A comparison of raw material prices and the prices paid for finished fabrics, demonstrates the existence of 'price scissors' in the late 16th century).

Clayer, Nathalie (1994). *Mystiques, état et société, Les Halvetis dans l'aire balkanique de la fin du XVème siècle à nos jours* (Leiden, New York and Cologne: E. J. Brill). (On a dervish order upholding the Ottoman state in the Balkans).

Concina, Ennio (1997). *Fondaci, Architettura, arte e mercatura tra Levante, Venezia e Alemagna* (Venice: Marsilio Editori). (Includes the Fondaco dei Turchi in Venice).

Cook, Michael A. (1972). *Population Pressure in Rural Anatolia, 1450–1600* (London: Oxford University Press).

Costantini, Vera (2001). 'Chypre, Venise, les Ottomans au XVIe siècle' (unpublished manuscript).

Crane, Howard (1991). 'The Ottoman Sultan's Mosques: Icons of Imperial Legitimacy', in Irene Bierman, Rifa'at A. Abou-El-Haj and Donald Preziosi (eds), *The Ottoman City and its Parts* (New Rochelle, NY: Aristide Caratzas Publishers): 173–243.

Croce, Guiseppe (1998). 'Die orientalischen Kirchen', in *Die Geschichte des Christentums, Religion, Politik, Kultur*, Vol. 9, *Das Zeitalter der Vernunft 1620/30–1750*, ed. by Marc Venard *et alii* (Freiburg, Basle, Vienna: Herder).

Curtin, Philip D. (1984). *Cross-Cultural Trade in World History* (Cambridge: Cambridge University Press). (On the functioning of commercial diasporas).

Czapliski, W. (reprint 1978). 'The Reign of Władysław IV, 1632–48', in W. F. Reddaway *et alii* (eds), *The Cambridge History of Poland*, Vol. 1: *From the Origins to Sobieski (to 1696)*, (New York: Octagon Books): 488–501.

Dale, Stephen Frederic (1994). *Indian Merchants and Eurasian Trade, 1600–1750* (Cambridge: Cambridge University Press). (Concerns Astrakhan).

Dalsar, Fahri (1960). *Türk Sanayi ve Ticaret Tarihinde Bursa'da İpekçilik* (Istanbul: İstanbul Üniversitesi İktisat Fakültesi). (Includes many original documents, still fundamental).

Daniel, Norman (1993). *Islam and the West, the Making of an Image* (Oxford: Oneworld Publications).

Dankoff, Robert (1991). *The Intimate Life of an Ottoman Statesman, Melek Ahmed Pasha (1588–1662) As Portrayed in Evliya Çelebi's* Book of Travels, intr. by Rhoads Murphey (Albany, NY: SUNY Press). (contains one of the very few accounts of married life in the Istanbul upper class).

Dankoff, Robert (2004). *An Ottoman Mentality, The World of Evliya Çelibi* (Leiden: E. J. Brill). (The standard monograph on this important Ottoman writer).

Darling, Linda (Fall 2001). 'Review of Suraiya Faroqhi, Subjects of the Sultan: Culture and Daily Life in the Ottoman Empire', *History: Reviews of New Books*, 3: 1.

Dávid, Geza, and Fodor, Pál (eds) (1994). *Hungarian–Ottoman Military and Diplomatic Relations in the Age of Süleyman the Magnificent* (Budapest: Loránd Eötvös University).

Dávid, Geza, and Gerelyes, Ipolya (1999). 'Ottoman Social and Economic Life Unearthed. An Assessment of Ottoman Archaeological Finds in Hungary', in Raoul Motika, Christoph Herzog and Michael Ursinus (eds), *Studies in Ottoman Social and Economic Life* (Heidelberg: Heidelberger Orientverlag, 1999): 43–80. (Fascinating report on Hungarian rural archaeology in the Ottoman period; a real find).

Dávid, Géza and Fodor, Pál (2002). 'Hungarian Studies in Ottoman History', in Fikret Adanır and Suraiya Faroqhi (eds), *The Ottomans and the Balkans, A Discussion of Historiography*, (Leiden: E. J. Brill): 305–50.

Dávid, Géza (2002). 'The Mühimme Defteri as a Source for Ottoman–Habsburg Rivalry in the Sixteenth Century', *Archivum Ottomanicum*, 20:167–210.

Davies, Brian L. (1999). 'The Development of Russian Military Power', in Jeremy Black (ed.), *European Warfare 1453–1815*, (Houndmills: Macmillan): 145–79.

Davis, Ralph (1967). *Aleppo and Devonshire Square, English Traders in the Levant in the Eighteenth Century* (London: Macmillan). (By a non-Ottomanist, based on the traders' correspondence in English libraries and archives).

de Groot, Alexander H. (1978). *The Ottoman Empire and the Dutch Republic, A History of the Earliest Diplomatic Relations 1610–1630* (Leiden, Istanbul: Nederlands Historisch-Archaeologisch Instituut).

Delumeau, Jean (1967). *La civilisation de la Renaissance* (Paris: Arthaud). (Now dated, but still worth reading: by one of the major historians of the *Annales* school).

Desmet-Grégoire, Hélène, and Georgeon, François (eds) (1997). *Cafés d'Orient revisités* (Paris: CNRS).

Demetz, Peter (1997). *Prague in Black and Gold, Scenes from the Life of a European City* (New York: Hill and Wang).

Denny, Walter B. (1970). 'A Sixteenth-Century Architectural Plan of Istanbul', *Ars Orientalis*, 8: 49–63.

Deringil, Selim (1991). 'Legitimacy Structures in the Ottoman State: The Reign of Sultan Abdülhamid II (1876–1909)', *International Journal of Middle East Studies*, 23: 345–59.

Deringil, Selim (1998). *The Well-Protected Domains, Ideology and the Legitimation of Power in the Ottoman Empire 1876–1909* (London: I. B. Tauris).

Doğru, Halime (1990). *Osmanlı İmparatorluğunda Yaya-Müsellem-Taycı Teşkilatı (XV.ve XVI. Yüzyılda Sultanönü Sancağı* (Istanbul: Eren).

Duchhardt, Heinz (1997). *Balance of Power und Pentarchie, 1700–1785* (Paderborn: Ferdinand Schöningh). (Part of a series covering international relations in the European context from 1450 to the present; has the great merit of viewing the Ottoman Empire as an integral part of the European political game).

Dürr, Renate, Engel, Gisela, and Süßmann, Johannes (eds) (2003). *Eigene und fremde Neuzeiten, Genese und Geltung eines Epochenbegriffs, Beihefte* of the *Historische Zeitschrift*, 35 (Munich: Oldenbourg).

Dursteler, Eric (2002). 'Commerce and Coexistence: Veneto-Ottoman Trade in the Early Modern Era', *Turcica*, 34: 105–134.

Dziubinski, Andrzej (1999). 'Polish-Turkish Trade in the 16th to 18th Centuries', in *War and Peace, Ottoman–Polish Relations in the 15th–19th Centuries* (Istanbul: Turkish Ministry of Culture and Polish Ministry of Culture and Art): 38–45. (Based on the author's book which is only available in Polish).

Eberhard, Elke (1970). *Osmanische Polemik gegen die Safawiden im 16. Jahrhundert nach arabischen Handschriften* (Freiburg: Klaus Schwarz-Verlag).

Eickhoff, Ekkehard (2nd edn 1988). *Venedig, Wien und die Osmanen, Umbruch in Südosteuropa 1645–1700* (Stuttgart: Klett-Cotta). (Informative).

Eldem, Edhem (1999). *French Trade in Istanbul in the Eighteenth Century* (Leiden: E. J. Brill). (Much broader than the title might suggest; highly stimulating).

Eldem, Edhem, Goffman, Daniel, and Masters, Bruce (1999). *The Ottoman City between East and West, Aleppo, Izmir and Istanbul* (Cambridge: Cambridge University Press).

Eldem, Sedad Hakkı (1977). *Sa'dabad* (Ankara: Kültür Bakanlığı). (Uses imagery otherwise little known).

Elton, G. R. (ed.) (1958) *The New Cambridge Modern History*, Vol. 2: *The Reformation 1520–1559* (Cambridge: Cambridge University Press).

Eren, Meşkûre (1960). *Evliya Çelebi Seyahatnâmesi Birinci Cildinin Kaynakları Üzerinde bir Araştırma* (Istanbul: n.p.). (Fundamental on Evliya's use of sources).

Ergenç, Özer (1975). '1600–1615 Yılları Arasında Ankara Iktisadi Tarihine Ait Araştırmalar', in Osman Okyar and Ünal Nalbantoğlu (eds), *Türkiye İktisat Tarihi Semineri, Metinler-Tartışmalar ...*, (Ankara: Hacettepe Üniversitesi): 145–68.

Ergenç, Özer (1995). *Osmanlı Klasik Dönemi Kent Tarihçiliğine Katkı, XVI. Yüzyılda Ankara ve Konya* (Ankara: Ankara Enstitüsü Vakfı). (Worthwhile monograph on Ankara and Konya in the late 16th century).

Erim, Neşe (1991). 'Trade, Traders and the State in Eighteenth Century Erzurum', *New Perspectives on Turkey*, 5–6: 123–50.

Ersanlı, Büşra (2002). 'The Ottoman Empire in the Historiography of the Kemalist Era: A Theory of Fatal Decline', in Fikret Adanır and Suraiya Faroqhi (eds), *The Ottomans and the Balkans, A Discussion of Historiography*, (Leiden: E. J. Brill): 115–54.

Eyice, Semavi (1970). 'Elçi Hanı', *Tarih Dergisi*, XXIV: 93–130.

Fahmi, Khaled (1997). *All the Pashas Men, Mehmed Ali, his Army and the Making of Modern Egypt* (Princeton: Princeton University Press).

Farooqi, Naim R. (1988). 'Moguls, Ottomans and Pilgrims: Protecting the Routes to Mecca in the Sixteenth and Seventeenth Centuries', *The International History Review*, X, 2: 198–220.

Faroqhi, Suraiya (1969). 'Das telhīs, eine aktenkundliche Studie', *Der Islam*, 45, 1–2: 96–116.

Faroqhi, Suraiya (1971). 'Der Aufstand des Yaḥya ibn Yaḥya as-Suwaydī', *Der Islam*, 47: 67–92.

Faroqhi, Suraiya (1979). 'Sixteenth Century Periodic Markets in Various Anatolian *sancaks*: İçel, Hamid, Karahisar-i Sahib, Kütahya, Aydın and Menteşe', *Journal of the Economic and Social History of the Orient*, XXII, 1: 32–79.

Faroqhi, Suraiya (1981). 'Seyyid Gazi Revisited: The Foundation as Seen Through Sixteenth and Seventeenth-Century Documents', *Turcica*, XIII: 90–122.

Faroqhi, Suraiya (1983). 'Die osmanische Handelspolitik des frühen 17. Jahrhunderts zwischen Dubrovnik und Venedig', *Wiener Beiträge für die Geschichte der Neuzeit*, 10: 207–22.

Faroqhi, Suraiya (1984). *Towns and Townsmen in Ottoman Anatolia, Trade, Crafts and Food Production in an Urban Setting 1520–1650* (Cambridge: Cambridge University Press).

Faroqhi, Suraiya (1986). 'Town Officials, Timar-holders and Taxation: The Late Sixteenth-Century Crisis as seen from Çorum', *Turcica*, XVIII: 53–82.

Faroqhi, Suraiya (reprint 1987). 'The Venetian Presence in the Ottoman Empire', in Huri Islamoğlu Inan (ed.), *The Ottoman Empire and the World Economy* (Paris and Cambridge: Maison des Sciences de l'Homme and Cambridge University Press): 311–44.

Faroqhi, Suraiya (1991). 'Red Sea Trade and Communications as Observed by Evliya Çelebi (1671–72)', *New Perspectives on Turkey*, 5–6: 87–106.

Faroqhi, Suraiya (1993a). 'Sainthood as a Means of Self-Defense in Seventeenth-Century Ottoman Anatolia', in Grace Smith and Carl Ernst (eds), *Saints in Islam* (Istanbul: ISIS Press): 193–208.

Faroqhi, Suraiya (1993b). 'Trade Controls, Provisioning Policies and Donations: The Egypt–Hijaz Connection during the Second Half of the Sixteenth Century', in Halil Inalcik and Cemal Kafadar (eds), *Süleyman the Second (sic) and his Time* (Istanbul: The Isis Press): 131–44.

Faroqhi, Suraiya (1994). *Pilgrims and Sultans* (London: Tauris Press). (On the Ottoman way of organizing the pilgrimage to Mecca, concerns the 16th and 17th centuries).

Faroqhi, Suraiya (1996). 'Seeking Wisdom in China: An Attempt to Make Sense of the Celali Rebellions', in Rudolf Vesely and Eduard Gombar (eds), *Zafar nama, Memorial Volume to Felix Tauer* (Prague: Enigma): 101–24.

Faroqhi, Suraiya (1998). 'Migration into Eighteenth-Century "Greater Istanbul" as Reflected in the Kadi Registers of Eyüp', *Turcica*, 30: 163–83.

Faroqhi, Suraiya (2001). 'Research on the History of Ottoman Consumption: a Preliminary Exploration of Sources and Models', in Donald Quataert (ed.), *Consumption Studies and the History of the Ottoman Empire, 1550–1922, an Introduction*, (Albany, NY: SUNY Press, 2000): 15–44.

Faroqhi, Suraiya (2002). 'Ottoman Views on Corsairs and Piracy in the Adriatic', in Elizabeth Zachariadou (ed.), *The Kaptan Paşa's Province* (Rethymnon: University of Crete Press): 357–70.

Faroqhi, Suraiya (2003). 'Representing France in the Peloponnesus: A Wealthy French Dwelling in 1770', in Suraiya Faroqhi and Christoph Neumann (eds), *The Illuminated Table, the Prosperous House* (Istanbul and Würzburg: Orient-Institut and Ergon Verlag): 255–73.

Ferrier, R. W. (1973). 'The Armenians and the East India Company in Persia in the Seventeenth and early Eighteenth Centuries', *Economic History Review*, XXVI: 38–62.

Fennell, J. L. I. (1958). 'Russia 1462–1583', in G. R. Elton (ed.), *The New Cambridge Modern History*, Vol. 2: *The Reformation* (Cambridge: Cambridge University Press): 70–250.

Findley, Carter (1995). 'Ebu Bekir Ratib's Vienna Embassy Narrative: Discovering Austria or Propagandizing Reform in Istanbul?', *Wiener Zeitschrift für die Kunde des Morgenlandes*, LXXXV: 41–80.

Findley, Carter (1998). 'Mouradja d'Ohsson (1740–1807). Liminality and Cosmopolitanism in the Author of the *Tableau général de l'empire ottoman*', *The Turkish Studies Association Bulletin*, 22,1: 21–35.

Fink, Carole (1991). *Marc Bloch, A Life in History* (Cambridge: Cambridge University Press).

Finkel, Caroline (1988). *The Administration of Warfare: the Ottoman Military Campaigns in Hungary, 1593–1606*, 2 vols (Vienna: VWGÖ). (Shows the role of Bosnia as a staging ground for Ottoman campaigns).

Fischer, Fritz (reprint 1994). *Der Griff nach der Weltmacht, Die Kriegszielpolitik des kaiserlichen Deutschland 1914/18* (Düsseldorf: Droste).

Fisher, Alan W. (1978). *The Crimean Tatars* (Stanford, CA: Hoover Institution Press).

Fisher, Alan W. (1993). 'The Life and Family of Süleymân I', in Halil Inalcik and Cemal Kafadar (eds), *Süleyman the Second (sic) and his Time,* (Istanbul: The Isis Press): 1–19.

Fisher, H. J. (1977). 'The Eastern Maghrib and the Central Sudan', in Roland Olivier (ed.), *The Cambridge History of Africa*, Vol. 2: *c. 1050–c. 1600*, (Cambridge: Cambridge University Press): 241–59.

Fleet, Kate (1999). *European and Islamic Trade in the Early Ottoman State, the Merchants of Genoa and Turkey* (Cambridge: Cambridge University Press).

Fleischer, Cornell H. (1983). 'Royal Authority, Dynastic Cyclism and "ibn Khaldunism" in Sixteenth-century Ottoman Letters', *Journal of Asian and African Studies*, 18: 198–220.

Fleischer, Cornell H. (1986). *Bureaucrat and Intellectual in the Ottoman Empire, The Historian Mustafâ 'Âlî (1541–1600)* (Princeton: Princeton University Press). (Problems encountered by a high-level Ottoman official, who had no inkling of his posthumous fame).

Fleischer, Cornell H. (1992). 'The Lawgiver as Messiah: The Making of the Imperial Image in the Reign of Süleyman', in *Soliman le Magnifique et son temps, Actes du Colloque de Paris, Galeries Nationales du Grand Palais, 7–10 mars 1990* (Paris: La Documentation Française): 159–78. (On apocalyptic ideas at the mid-16th-century Ottoman court).

Fleming, Katherine E. (1999). *The Muslim Bonaparte, Diplomacy and Orientalism in Ali Pasha's Greece* (Princeton: Princeton University Press).

Flemming, Barbara (1987). 'Sahib-kıran und Mahdi: Türkische Endzeiterwartungen im ersten Jahrzehnt der Regierung Süleymans', in György Kara (ed.), *Between the Danube and the Caucasus* (Budapest: The Academy of Sciences): 43–62.

Fletcher, Joseph F. (reprint 1995). 'Turco-Mongolian Monarchic Tradition in the Ottoman Empire', in Beatrice Manz (ed.), *Studies on Chinese and Islamic Inner Asia* (Aldershot: Variorum Reprints).

Fodor, Pál (reprint 2000). 'The View of the Turk in Hungary: the Apocalyptic Tradition and the Red Apple in [the] Ottoman Hungarian Context', in Pál Fodor, *In Search of the Golden Apple, Imperial Ideology, Politics and Military Administration in the Ottoman Empire* (Istanbul: The Isis Press): 71–104.

Frangakis-Syrett, Elena (1992). *The Commerce of Smyrna in the Eighteenth Century (1700–1820)* (Athens: Centre for Asia Minor Studies). (Based on a careful analysis of French and British import and export figures).

Frank, André Gunder (1969). *Capitalism and Underdevelopment in Latin America, Historical Studies of Chile and Brazil* (New York: Monthly Review Press).

Fukasawa, Katsumi (1987). *Toilerie et commerce du Levant, d'Alep à Marseille* (Paris: Editions du CNRS). (Has information on Ottoman imitations of Indian printed fabrics that found their way to Marseilles).

Gascon, Richard (1971). *Grand commerce et vie urbaine au XVIe siècle, Lyon et ses marchands (environs de 1520–environs de 1580)* (Paris and The Hague: Mouton).

Gascon, Richard (1977). 'La France du mouvement: les commerces et les villes', in Fernand Braudel and Ernest Labrousse (eds), *Histoire économique et sociale de la France*, Vol. 1: 231–479.

Genç, Mehmet (1975). 'Osmanlı Maliyesinde Malikâne Sistemi', in Osman Okyar and Ünal Nabantoğlu (eds), *Türkiye İktisat Tarihi Semineri, Metinler-Tartışmalar* ... (Ankara: Hacettepe Üniversitesi): 231–96. (Fundamental article on lifetime tax farms).

Genç, Mehmet (1984). 'Osmanlı Ekonomisi ve Savaş', *Yapıt*, 49, 4: 52–61; 50, 5: 86–93; French version (1995): 'L'économie ottomane et la guerre au XVIIIème siècle', *Turcica*, XXVII: 177–196. (Economic-financial explanation for Ottoman military failures in the 18th century).

Genç, Mehmet (1987). '17–19. Yüzyıllarda Sanayi ve Ticaret Merkezi Olarak Tokat', in *Türk Tarihinde ve Kültüründe Tokat Sempozyumu, 2–6 Temmuz 1986* (Tokat: Tokat Valiliği Şeyhülislâm İbn Kemal Araştırma Merkezi): 145–69.

Genç, Mehmet (1994). 'Ottoman Industry in the Eighteenth Century: General Framework, Characteristics and Main Trends', in Donald Quataert (ed.), *Manufacturing in the Ottoman Empire and Turkey 1500–1950* (Albany, NY: SUNY Press): 59–86.

Gerelyes, Ipolya (1990–2). 'The Influence of Ottoman-Turkish Art in Hungary, 1: The Spread and Use of Turkish Ornamental Weapons on the Basis of the Sixteenth- and Seventeenth-Century Probate Inventories', *Acta Historiae Artium Academiae Scientiarum Hungaricae*, 35: 181–91.

Göçek, Fatma Müge (1987). *East Encounters West, France and the Ottoman Empire in the Eighteenth Century* (New York, Oxford and Washington: Oxford University Press and The Institute of Turkish Studies). (On the 1720 embassy of Yirmisekiz Mehmed Efendi to Paris and Versailles).

Goffman, Daniel (1990a). *Izmir and the Levantine World, 1550–1650* (Seattle: University of Washington Press). (On the Aegean regional economy as a basis for foreign trade).

Goffman, Daniel (1990b). 'Review of Sonia Anderson, An English Consul in Turkey, Paul Rycaut at Smyrna, 1667–1678, Oxford, 1989', *New Perspectives on Turkey*, 4: 105–10.

Goffman, Daniel (1998). *Britons in the Ottoman Empire 1642–1660* (Seattle and London: University of Washington Press). (How Royalists and Parliamentarians intrigued against one another on Ottoman soil).

Goffman, Daniel (2002). *The Ottoman Empire and Early Modern Europe* (Cambridge: Cambridge University Press).

Gökçe, Cemal (1979). *Kafkasya ve Osmanlı İmparatorluğunun Kafkasya Siyaseti* (Istanbul: Şamil Eğitim ve Kültür Vakfı).

Goldstone, Jack A. (1991). *Revolution and Rebellion in the Early Modern World* (Berkeley and Los Angeles: University of California Press). (On population growth as a destabilizing factor in the political realm).

Gomez-Géraud, Marie-Christine (1999). *Le crépuscule du Grand Voyage: les récits des pèlerins à Jérusalem, 1458–1612* (Paris: H. Champion).

Gondicas, Dimitri, and Issawi, Charles (eds) (1999). *Ottoman Greeks in the Age of Nationalism* (Princeton: The Darwin Press).

Gonzalez-Raymond, Anita (1992). *La croix et le croissant, Les inquisiteurs des îles face à l'Islam, 1550–1700* (Paris: CNRS). (On returnees from the Islamic world).

Goodrich, Thomas (1990). *The Ottoman Turks and the New World, A Study of Tarih-i Hind-i Garbi and Sixteenth-century Ottoman Americana* (Wiesbaden: Otto Harrassowitz). (Contains both a translation and a facsimile, in addition to an erudite introduction).

Goubert, Pierre (1977). 'Le "tragique" XVIIe siècle', in Fernand Braudel and Ernest Labrousse (eds), *Histoire économique et sociale de la France* (Paris: PUF), Vol. 2: 329–66.

Göyünç, Nejat (1969). *XVI. Yüzyılda Mardin Sancağı* (Istanbul: Istanbul Üniversitesi Edebiyat Fakültesi).

Göyünç, Nejat (1976). 'XVIII. Yüzyılda Türk İdaresinde Nauplia (Anabolu) ve Yapıları', in *Ord. Prof İsmail Hakkı Uzunçarşılı'ya Armağan* (Ankara: Türk Tarih Kurumu): 461–85.

Grabar, Oleg (1973). *The Formation of Islamic Art* (New Haven, CT, and London: Yale University Press).

Gradeva, Rositsa (1994). 'Ottoman Policy towards Christian Church Buildings', *Etudes Balkaniques*, 4: 14–36.

Gradeva, Rositsa (2001). 'War and Peace along the Danube: Vidin at the End of the Seventeenth Century', *Oriente Moderno*, XX, n. s., Kate Fleet (ed.), *The Ottomans and the Sea*: 149–75.

Grafton, Anthony, with Shelford, April, and Siraisi, Nancy (2000). *New Worlds, Ancient Texts, The Power of Tradition and the Shock of Discovery* (Cambridge, MA, and London: The Belknap Press of Harvard University Press) (On the difficulty of Renaissance scholars in accepting that the Americas were in fact a new world, about which the authors of antiquity had nothing to say).

Greene, Molly (2000). *A Shared World, Christians and Muslims in the Early Modern Mediterranean* (Princeton: Princeton University Press). (On the economic commonalities between Venice and the Ottoman Empire, when compared to the 'new economy' of 17th-century England and France).

Gregorovius, Ferdinand (reprint n.y.) 'Geschichte der Stadt Athen im Mittelalter', in Johann Pruss (ed.), *Athen und Athenais, Schicksale einer Stadt und einer Kaiserin im byzantinischen Mittelalter* (Essen: Emil Vollmer Verlag). (A 19th-century study, still worth reading).

Griswold, William (1983). *The Great Anatolian Rebellion 1000–1020/1591–1611* (Berlin: Klaus Schwarz). (Concerns both Anatolia and northern Syria, points to the role of climatic deterioration among the factors promoting the rebellions).

Gronke, Monika (1993). *Derwische im Vorhof der Macht, Sozial- und Wirtschaftsge-schichte Nordwestirans im 13. und 14. Jahrhundert* (Stuttgart: Franz Steiner). (On the early history of the Safavids).

Güçer, Lütfi (1949–50). 'XVIII. Yüzyıl Ortalarında İstanbul'un İaşesi için Lüzumlu Hububatın Temini Meselesi', *İstanbul Üniversitesi İktisat Fakültesi Mecmuası*, 11, 1–4: 397–416.

Güçer, Lütfi (1951–2). 'Osmanlı İmparatorluğu dahilinde Hububat Ticaretinin Tabi Olduğu Kayıtlar', *İstanbul Üniversitesi İktisat Fakültesi Mecmuası*, 13, 1–4: 79–98.

Güçer, Lütfi (1964). *XVI–XVII. Asırlarda Osmanlı İmparatorluğunda Hububat Meselesi ve Hububattan Alınan Vergiler* (Istanbul: İstanbul Üniversitesi İktisat Fakültesi). (Important also for the light it throws on war financing).

Guilmartin Jr, John Francis (1974). *Gunpowder and Galleys, Changing Technology and Mediterranean Warfare at Sea in the Sixteenth Century* (Cambridge: Cambridge University Press). (Includes the economic and social aspects of changes in military technology; discusses the Ottomans at considerable length, very important).

Gürbüz, Adnan (2001). *XV.–XVI. Yüzyıl Osmanlı Sancak Çalışmaları, Değerlendirme ve Bibliyografik bir Deneme* (Istanbul: Dergâh Yayınları).(A bibliography of studies based upon Ottoman tax registers, a useful research aid).

Haarmann, Ulrich (1976). 'Evliya Çelebi's Bericht über die Altertümer von Gize', *Turcica*, VIII, 1: 157–230.

Haase-Dubosc, Danielle (1999). *Ravie et enlevée, De l'enlèvement des femmes comme stratégie matrimoniale au XVIIe siècle* (Paris: Albin Michel).

Hadrovics, Ladislas (1947). *Le peuple serbe et son église sous la domination turque* (Paris: Presses Universitaires de France). (Discovered the 'tax-farm-like' aspects of the Orthodox Church on Ottoman territory).

Hagen, Gottfried (1982–98). 'Kâtib Çelebi and Târîh-i Hind-i Garbî', *Güney-Doğu Avrupa Araştırmaları Dergisi*, 12: 101–15.

Hagen, Gottfried (1995–6). 'Überzeitlichkeit und Geschichte in Kâtib Čelebis Ğihān-nümā', *Archivum Ottomanicum*, 14: 133–60.

Hagen, Gottfried (1998a). 'Kâtib Čelebis Darstellung der Eyālets und Sanğaks des Osmanischen Reiches', *Archivum Ottomanicum*, 16: 101–24.

Hagen, Gottfried (1998b). 'The Traveller Mehmed Aşık', in *Essays on Ottoman Civ-ilization, Proceedings of the XIIth Congress of the Comité International d'Études Pré-ottomanes et Ottomanes, Praha, 1996* (Prague: Academy of Sciences of the Czech Republic, Oriental Institute): 145–54.

Hagen, Gottfried (2000). 'Some Considerations on the Study of Ottoman Geographi-cal Writings', *Archivum Ottomanicum*, 18: 183–94.

Hagen, Gottfried (unpublished m.s.) 'Das Fremde im Eigenen, Mehmed 'Aşıq's Reisen über den osmanischen Balkan'.

Hagen, Gottfried (2003). *Ein osmanischer Geograph bei der Arbeit. Entstehung und Gedankenwelt von Katib Celebis Ğihānnümā* (Berlin: Klaus Schwarz Verlag).

Haldon, John (1992). 'The Ottoman State and the Question of State Autonomy', in Halil Berktay and Suraiya Faroqhi (eds), *New Approaches to State and Peasant in Ottoman History* (London: Frank Cass): 18–108.

Haldon, John (1993). *The State and the Tributary Mode of Production* (London and New York: Verso). (Broadly-based comparative study, with considerable emphasis on the Ottoman Empire).

Hale, John R. (1998). *War and Society in Renaissance Europe 1450–1620* (Phoenix Mill: Sutton Publishing). (By an expert on Italy; important from the metho-dological point of view).

Hammer[-Purgstall], Joseph von (1828). *Geschichte des osmanischen Reiches, großenteils aus bisher unbenutzten Handschriften und Archiven*, Vol. 3: *Vom Regierungsantritte Suleiman des Ersten bis zum Tode Selims II. 1520–1574* (Budapest: C. A. Hartleben). (Still useful in spite of its age, French translation available).

Hanna, Nelly (1998). *Making Big Money in 1600, the Life and Times of Isma'il Abu Taqiyya, Egyptian Merchant* (Syracuse: Syracuse University Press). (Sensational: demonstrates that a Cairene merchant could succeed in business without involving himself with the Ottoman state bureaucracy).

Harley, J. B., and Woodward, David (eds), *The History of Cartography*, Vol. 2: 1 *Cartography in the Traditional Islamic and South Asian Societies* (Chicago and London: University of Chicago Press). (A fundamental research tool; Ahmet Karamustafa, John Michael Rogers and Svat Soucek have contributed important articles on Ottoman map-making).

Hassiotis, Giovanni K. (1977). 'Venezia e i domini veneziani tramite di informazioni sui Turchi per gli Spagnoli nel sec. XVI', in Hans-Georg Beck, Manoussos Manoussacas and Agostino Pertusi (eds), *Venezia, Centro di mediazione tra Oriente e Occidente (secoli XV–XVI)* (Florence: Leo S. Olschki): 117–36. (Based on material in the Simancas archives).

Hathaway, Jane (1997). *The Politics of Households in Ottoman Egypt, The Rise of the Qazdağlıs* (Cambridge: Cambridge University Press). (Important new study).

Hauser, Henri (1930). *La modernité du XVIe siècle* (Paris: Librairie Félix Alcan). (Published lectures, still make interesting reading even though many issues are today seen differently).

Heers, Jacques (1961). *Gênes au XVe siècle, Activité économique et problèmes sociaux* (Paris: SEVPEN). (On the role of Chios).

Heilingsetzer, Georg (1988). 'Prinz Eugen und die Führungsschicht der österreich-ischen Grossmacht', in Erich Zöllner *et alii* (eds), *Österreich und die Osmanen, Prinz Eugen und seine Zeit* (Vienna: Österrreichischer Bundesverlag): 120–37.

Hellie, Richard (1971). *Enserfment and Military Change in Muscovy* (Chicago and London: University of Chicago Press).

Hering, Gunnar (1968). *Ökumenisches Patriarchat und europäische Politik 1620–1638.* (Wiesbaden: Franz Steiner) (Biography of the 'Protestant Patriarch' Kyrillos Lucaris; the analysis of the European power games impinging on Lucaris' career is masterly; translation into modern Greek available).

Herzig, Edmund (1996). 'The Rise of the Julfa Merchants in the Late Sixteenth Century', in Charles Melville (ed.), *Safavid Persia, The History and Politics of an Islamic Society* (London: I. B. Tauris): 305–22.

Herzog, Christoph (1996). *Geschichte und Ideologie: Mehmed Murad und Celal Nuri über die historischen Ursachen des osmanischen Niedergangs* (Berlin: Klaus Schwarz Verlag). (On the perception of Ottoman history by late Ottoman intellectuals).

Hess, Andrew (1972). 'The Battle of Lepanto and its Place in Mediterranean History', *Past and Present*, 57: 53–73.

Hess, Andrew (1978). *The Forgotten Frontier, A History of the Sixteenth-Century Ibero-African Frontier* (Chicago and London: University of Chicago Press). (On the division of the Mediterranean world between Christians and Muslims).

Heyd, Uriel (1960). *Ottoman Documents on Palestine 1552–1615, A Study of the Firman according to the Mühimme Defteri* (Oxford: Clarendon Press). (Contains translations of the relevant texts into English, apart from the diplomatic study promised by the title).

Heywood, Colin (1988). 'Between Historical Myth and "Mythohistory": the Limits of Ottoman History', *Byzantine and Modern Greek Studies*, 12: 315–45.

Hiestand, Rudolf (1996). 'Nova Francia – Nova Grecia. Morea zwischen Franken, Venezianern und Griechen', in Reinhard Lauer and Peter Schreiner (eds), *Die Kultur Griechenlands in Mittelalter und Neuzeit, Bericht über das Kolloquium der Südosteuropa-Kommission 28.–31. Oktober 1992* (Göttingen: Vandenhoeck and Rupprecht): 55–72.

Hinds, Martin and Victor Ménage (1991). *Qasr Ibrim in the Ottoman Period, Turkish and Further Arabic Documents* (London: Egypt Exploration Society).

Hitzel, Frédéric (2001). 'Osmân Ağa, captif ottoman dans l'empire des Habsbourg à la fin du XVIIe siècle', *Turcica*, 33: 191–216.

Hochedlinger, Michael (2003). *Austria's Wars of Emergence 1683–1797* (Harlow and London: Longman and Pearson Education). (Makes available the results of 'war and society studies, Austrian style' to the English-speaking reader).

Hochhut, Pia (1986). 'Zur Finanzierung des Baus einer Sultansmoschee: Die Nûruosmaniye', in Hans Georg Majer (ed.), *Osmanische Studien zur Wirtschafts- und Sozialgeschichte. In Memoriam Vanco Boskov* (Wiesbaden): 68–75.

Hodgson, Marshall G. S. (1973–4). *The Venture of Islam, Conscience and History in a World Civilization*, Vol. 1: *The Classical Age of Islam*, Vol. 3: *The Gunpowder Empires and Modern Times* (Chicago and London: Chicago University Press). (The third volume was put together, posthumously, from Hudgson's notes by his friends and students).

Hoensch, Jörg K. (1998). *Matthias Corvinus, Diplomat, Feldherr und Mäzen* (Graz, Vienna and Cologne: Styria). (Ottoman–Hungarian conflict is given full weight in this important biography).

Hoffmann, Peter (1974). 'Zur Editionsgeschichte von Cantemirs Descriptio Moldaviae', in Anonymous (ed.), *Ein bedeutender Gelehrter an der Schwelle zur Frühaufklärung: Dimitrie Cantemir (1673–1723)* (Berlin: Akademie Verlag).

Hohrath, Daniel (1999). '"In Cartellen wird der Werth eines Gefangenen bestimmet" Kriegsgefangenschaft als Teil der Kriegspraxis im Ancien Régime', in Rüdiger Overmans and die Arbeitskreis Militärgeschichte (ed.), *In der Hand des Feindes*.

Geschichtsschreibung zur Kriegsgefangenschaft von der Antike bis zum Zweiten Weltkrieg, (Cologne, Weimar and Vienna: Böhlau Verlag): 141–70.

Horden, Peregrine, and Purcell, Nicholas (2000). *The Corrupting Sea, A Study of Mediterranean History* (Oxford: Blackwell).

Howard, Deborah (2000). *Venice and the East* (London and New Haven: Yale University Press).

Huizinga, Johan (1954). *The Waning of the Middle Ages, A Study of the Forms of Life, Thought and Art in France and the Netherlands* (Garden City, NY: Doubleday and Anchor). (Fine background reading for those wishing to know more about the state of mind of 15th-century western pilgrims).

İlgürel, Mücteba (1979). 'Osmanlı İmparatorluğunda Ateşli Silahların Yayılışı', *Tarih Dergisi*, 32: 301–18.

Imber, Colin (1979). 'The Persecution of the Ottoman Shiites According to the Mühimme Defterleri 1565–1585', *Der Islam*, 56: 245–73.

Imber, Colin (1997). *Ebu's-su'ud, the Islamic Legal Tradition* (Edinburgh: Edinburgh University Press).

Inalcik, Halil (1948). 'Osmanlı-Rus Rekabetinin Menşei ve Don-Volga-Kanalı Teşebbüsü, 1569', *Belleten*, XII: 349–402.

Inalcik, Halil (1954). 'Ottoman Methods of Conquest', *Studia Islamica*, III: 103–29. (On the manner in which newly conquered provinces were made part of the Ottoman Empire: basic).

Inalcik, Halil (1960). 'Bursa and the Commerce of the Levant', *Journal of the Economic and Social History of the Orient*, 3: 131–47.

Inalcik, Halil (1969). 'Capital Formation in the Ottoman Empire', *Journal of Economic History*, XXIX, 1: 97–140. (Fundamental study of 16th- and 17th-century economic history).

Inalcik, Halil (1970a). 'The Ottoman Economic Mind and Aspects of the Ottoman Economy', in Michael Cook (ed.), *Studies of the Economic History of the Middle East* (London, Oxford: Oxford University Press): 207–18. (Important complement to Inalcik, 1969).

Inalcik, Halil (1970b). 'The Policy of Mehmed II toward the Greek Population of Istanbul and the Byzantine Buildings of the City', *Dumbarton Oaks Papers*, 24: 231–49.

Inalcik, Halil (1973). *The Ottoman Empire, The Classical Age 1300–1600*, tr. by Norman Itzkowitz and Colin Imber (London: Weidenfeld and Nicolson). (Has become a classic in its genre; introduces political and economic history 'in a nutshell').

Inalcik, Halil (1975). 'The Socio-Political Effects of the Diffusion of Firearms in the Middle East', in M. E. Yapp (ed.), *War, Technology and Society in the Middle East*, (London and Oxford: Oxford University Press): 195–297.

Inalcik, Halil (1977). 'An Outline of Ottoman-Venetian Relations', in Hans-Georg Beck, Manoussos Manoussacas and Agostino Pertusi (eds), *Venezia, Centro di mediazione tra Oriente e Occidente (secoli XV-XVI)*, (Florence: Leo S. Olschki): 83–90.

Inalcik, Halil (1979). 'The Question of the Closing of the Black Sea under the Ottomans', *Archeion Pontou*, 35: 74–110.

Inalcik, Halil (1979–80). 'Osmanlı Pamuklu Pazarı, Hindistan ve İngiltere: Pazar Rekabetinde Emek Maliyetinin Rolü', *Gelişme Dergisi*, special issue, *Türkiye*

İktisat Tarihi Üzerine Araştırmalar: 1–65. (Discusses the importation of Indian fabrics into the Ottoman Empire).

Inalcik, Halil (1980). 'Military and Fiscal Transformation in the Ottoman Empire, 1600–1700', *Archivum Ottomanicum*, VI: 283–337. (Important discussion of the rise of provincial notables).

Inalcik, Halil (reprint 1992). *Tanzimat ve Bulgar Meselesi, Doktora Tezi'nin 50. Yılı* (Istanbul: Eren). (On a mid-19th-century rural rebellion in the Vidin area).

Inalcik, Halil (1997). 'The Ottoman State: Economy and Society, 1300–1600', in Halil Inalcik with Donald Quataert (eds), *An Economic and Social History of the Ottoman Empire, 1300–1914* (Cambridge: Cambridge University Press). (Paperback version, Inalcik's work appears as Vol. 1).

Iserloh, Erwin, Glazik, Josef, and Jedin, Hubert (1985). *Handbuch der Kirchengeschichte*, Vol. IV: *Reformation, Katholische Reformation und Gegenreformation*, ed. by Hubert Jedin (Freiburg, Bâle, Vienna).

Islamoğlu-Inan, Huri, (ed.) (1987). *The Ottoman Empire and the World Economy*, (Cambridge and Paris: Cambridge University Press and Maison des Sciences de l'Homme).

Islamoğlu-Inan, Huri (1994). *State and Peasant in the Ottoman Empire, Agrarian Power Relations and Regional Economic Development in Ottoman Anatolia during the Sixteenth Century* (Leiden: E. J. Brill). (On the socio-political background of rural crafts and trade).

Isom-Verhaaren, Christine (1996). 'An Ottoman Report about Martin Luther and the Emperor: New Evidence of the Ottoman Interest in the Protestant Challenge to the Power of Charles V', *Turcica*, 28: 299–318.

Israel, Jonathan I. (1989). *Dutch Primacy in World Trade, 1585–1740* (Oxford: Clarendon Press).

Jahn, Karl (1961). 'Zum Loskauf christlicher und türkischer Gefangener und Sklaven im 18. Jahrhundert', *Zeitschrift der Deutschen Morgenländischen Gesellschaft*, 111, NF 36: 63–85.

Jardine, Lisa (1996). *Worldly Goods, A New History of the Renaissance* (London and Basingstoke: Macmillan).

Jardine, Lisa and Jerry Brotton (2000). *Global Interests, Renaissance Art Between East and West* (London: Reaktion Books).

Jelavich, Barbara (1983). *History of the Balkans*, Vol. 1: *Eighteenth and Nineteenth Centuries* (Cambridge: Cambridge University Press). (Informative and wide-ranging).

Jennings, Ronald (1980). 'Firearms, Bandits and Gun Control: Some Evidence on Ottoman Policy toward Firearms in the Possession of reaya, from Judicial Records of Kayseri, 1600–1627', *Archivum Ottomanicum*, VI: 339–58. (By one of the early connoisseurs of Ottoman kadi registers).

Kafadar, Cemal (1986a). 'When Coins Became Drops of Dew and Bankers became Robbers of Shadows: The Boundaries of Ottoman Economic Imagination in the Sixteenth Century' (unpublished PhD dissertation, McGill University, Montreal).

Kafadar, Cemal (1986b). 'A Death in Venice (1575): Anatolian Muslim Merchants Trading in the Serenissima', *Journal of Turkish Studies*, 10, *Raiyyet Rüsumu, Essays presented to Halil Inalcik* ...: 191–218. (An eye-opener).

Kafadar, Cemal (1989). 'Self and Others: The Diary of a Dervish in Seventeenth-century Istanbul and First-person Narratives in Ottoman Literature', *Studia Islamica*, LXIX: 121–50.

Kafadar, Cemal (1991). 'Les troubles monétaires de la fin du XVIe siècle et la conscience ottomane du déclin', *Annales ESC*, 43: 381–400.

Kafadar, Cemal (1994). 'Eyüp'te Kılıç Kuşanma Törenleri', in Tülay Artan (ed.), *Eyüp: Dün/ Bugün, 11–12 Aralık 1993* (Istanbul: Tarih Vakfı Yurt Yayınları, 1994): 50–61.

Kafadar, Cemal (1995). *Between Two Worlds, The Construction of the Ottoman State* (Berkeley and Los Angeles: University of California Press). (Intelligent discussion of both history and historiography).

Kasaba, Reşat (1988). *The Ottoman Empire and the World Economy, The Nineteenth Century* (Albany, NY: SUNY Press).

Kaufmann, Thomas DaCosta (1995). *Court, Cloister & City, The Art and Culture of Central Europe, 1450–1800* (London: Weidenfeld and Nicolson).

Kévonian, Kéram (1975). 'Marchands arméniens au XVIIe siècle, à propos d'un livre arménien publié à Amsterdam en 1699', *Cahiers du monde russe et soviétique*, 16, 2: 199–244. (On a trader's *vade mecum*).

Keyder, Çağlar (1987). *State and Class in Turkey, a Study in Capitalist Development* (London and New York: Verso). (The first chapter contains a bold comparison between the Byzantine and Ottoman social formations: stimulating).

Khachikian, Levon (1967). 'Le registre d'un marchand arménien en Perse, en Inde et au Tibet (1682–1693)', *Annales Économies Sociétés Civilisations*, 22, 2: 231–78. (Important; unfortunately this merchant's travels did not include the Ottoman Empire).

Khaddouri, Majid (1955). *War and Peace in the Law of Islam* (Baltimore: Johns Hopkins Press).

Khoury, Dina (1997). *State and Provincial Society in the Ottoman Empire Mosul 1540–1834* (Cambridge: Cambridge University Press). (Particularly interesting: the analysis of the socio-political attitudes taken by local intellectuals).

Kırzıoğlu, Fahreddin (1976). *Osmanlılar'ın Kafkas-Elleri'ni Fethi (1451–159)* (Ankara: Atatürk Üniversitesi-Erzurum).

Kissling, Hans Joachim (1977). 'Venezia come centro di informazioni sui Turchi', in Hans-Georg Beck, Manoussos Manoussacas and Agostino Pertusi (eds), *Venezia, Centro di mediazione tra Oriente e Occidente (secoli XV-XVI)*, (Florence: Leo S. Olschki): 99–109.

Köhbach, Markus (1983a). 'Die osmanische Gesandtschaft nach Spanien in den Jahren 1787–88. Begegnung zweier Kulturen im Spiegel eines Gesandtschafts-berichts', *Wiener Beiträge für die Geschichte der Neuzeit*, 10: 143–52.

Köhbach, Markus (1983b). 'Der Tarih-i Mehemmed Giray – eine osmanische Quelle zur Belagerung Wiens durch die Türken im Jahre 1683', *Studia Austro-Polonica*, 3: 137–64.

Köhbach, Markus (1994). *Die Eroberung von Fülek durch die Osmanen 1554, Eine historisch-quellenkritische Studie zur osmanischen Expansion im östlichen Mitteleuropa* (Vienna and Cologne: Weimar).

Kołodziejczyk, Dariusz (2000). *Ottoman-Polish Diplomatic Relations (15th–18th Century), An Annotated Edition of 'Ahdnames and Other Documents* (Leiden:

E. J. Brill). (Contains a monograph on the topic, in addition to the edition of materials in Ottoman, Polish and Latin).

Kołodziejczyk, Dariusz (2003). 'Polish Embassies in Istanbul or How to Sponge on your Host without Losing your Self-Esteem', in Suraiya Faroqhi and Christoph Neumann (eds), *The Illuminated Table, the Prosperous House* (Istanbul and Würzburg: Orient-Institut and Ergon Verlag): 51–8.

Konyalı, İbrahim Hakkı (1974). *Âbideleri ve Kitabeleri ile Niğde Aksaray Tarihi*, 3 vols (Istanbul: n.p.).

Köprülü, Mehmed Fuad (1935). *Türk Halkedebiyatı Ansiklopedisi, Ortaçağ ve Yeniçağ Türklerinin Halk Kültürü Üzerine Coğrafya, Etnografya, Etnoloji, Tarih ve Edebiyat Lugatı, fasc. 1* (Istanbul: n.p.). (The article 'Abdal' is insightful and still a mine of information).

Köprülü, Mehmed Fuad (1959). *Osmanlı Devletinin Kuruluşu* (Ankara: Türk Tarih Kurumu). (Based on the author's lectures held at the Sorbonne in the 1930s; still a classic).

Kortepeter, Carl Max (1972). *Ottoman Imperialism During the Reformation: Europe and the Caucasus* (London and New York: London University Press, New York University Press). (Deals, among other matters, with the 'Long War' of 1593–1607 and, woven into the richly textured narrative of political events, there is a biography of the Crimean khan Gazi Giray).

Kortepeter, Carl Max (1979). 'A Source for the History of Ottoman-Hijaz Relations: The Seyahatnâme of Awliya Chalaby and the Rebellion of *Sharif* b Zayd in the Years 1671–1672/1081–82', in Abdelgadir Mahmoud Abdalla *et alii* (eds), *Sources for the History of Arabia*, Vol. 1, parts 1 and 2, (Riyadh): 229–46.

Kreiser, Klaus (1975). *Edirne im 17. Jahrhundert nach Evliyā Çelebi, ein Beitrag zur Kenntnis der osmanischen Stadt* (Freiburg: Klaus Schwarz Verlag). (Important discussion of Evliya's way of working).

Kreiser, Klaus (1979). 'Über den Kernraum des Osmanischen Reiches', in Klaus-Detlev Grothusen (ed.), *Die Türkei in Europa ?*, (Göttingen: Vandenhoeck & Rupprecht): 53–63.

Kreiser, Klaus (reprint 1998). 'Germano-Turcica: 1. Gefangene, Pilger und Kaufleute: Die Transkriptionstexte des späten Mittelalters und der Neuzeit, 2. "Zwecke ohne die nöthigen Mittel ..." Vom letzten habsburgischen Türkenkrieg (1781–1791) bis zum Frieden von Paris (1856)', in Klaus Kreiser, *Türkische Studien in Europa* (Istanbul: The Isis Press): 65–74.

Kreiser, Klaus (2001). *Der osmanische Staat 1300–1922* (With a stupendous bibliography and insightful reviews of what these studies have brought us).

Kretschmayr, Heinrich (1896). 'Ludovico Gritti, eine Monographie', *Archiv für österreichische Geschichte*, 83: 3–85. (Written from an Austro-Hungarian viewpoint, very full documentation).

Külzer, Andreas (1994). *Peregrinatio graeca in Terram Sanctam, Studien zu Pilgerfahrten und Reisebeschreibungen über Syrien, Palästina und den Sinai aus byzantinischer und metabyzantinischer Zeit* (Frankfurt: Peter Lang).

Kunt, Metin (1974). 'Ethnic-Regional (*Cins*) Solidarity in the Seventeenth-Century Ottoman Establishment', *International Journal of Middle East Studies*, 5: 233–9.

Kunt, Metin (1977). 'Derviş Mehmed Paşa, Vezir and Entrepreneur: A Study in Ottoman Political-Economic Theory and Practice', *Turcica*, 9, 1: 197–214.

Kunt, Metin (1981). *Bir Osmanlı Valisininin Yıllık Gelir-Gideri Diyarbekir, 1670–71* (Istanbul: Boğaziçi Üniversitesi). (The budget of a 17th-century provincial governor, edition and analysis).

Kunt, Metin (1983). *The Sultan's Servants, the Transformation of Ottoman Provincial Government, 1550–1650* (New York: Columbia University Press).

Kuran, Aptullah (1987). *Sinan, the Grand Old Master of Ottoman Architecture* (Washington and Istanbul: Institute of Turkish Studies and Ada Press).

Kuran, Aptullah (1994). 'Eyüp Külliyesi', in Tülay Artan (ed.), *Eyüp: Dün/ Bugün, 11–12 Aralık 1993* (Istanbul: Tarih Vakfı Yurt Yayınları): 129–35.

Kurz Otto (1975). *European Clocks and Watches in the Near East* (London and Leiden: The Warburg Institute, University of London and E. J. Brill).

Kurz, Otto (reprint 1977). 'A Gold Helmet Made in Venice for Sulayman the Magnificent', in Otto Kurz, *The Decorative Arts of Europe and the MiddleEast* (London: Dorian Press): 249–58.

Kütükoğlu, Bekir (2nd edition 1993). *Osmanlı-İran Siyasi Münasebetleri (1578–1612)* (Istanbul: İstanbul Fetih Cemiyeti). (This edition, unfortunately posthumous, is much more comprehensive than its predecessor).

Kütükoğlu, Mübahat (1994). *Osmanlı Belgelerinin Dili (Diplomatik)* (Istanbul: Kubbealtı Akademisi Kültür ve Sanat Vakfı). (This is the standard discussion of Ottoman diplomatics; more or less supersedes previous work).

Kut, Turgut (1994). 'Terekelerde Çıkan Kitabların Matbu Satış Defterleri', *Müteferrika*, 2: 3–24.

Lane, Frederic C. (1973). *Venice, A Maritime Republic* (Baltimore, MD: Johns Hopkins University Press). (Fundamental).

Layton, Evro (1994). *The Sixteenth Century Greek Book in Italy, Printers and Publishers for the Greek World* (Venice: The Hellenic Institute of Byzantine and Post-Byzantine Studies). (A mine of information; I have especially relished the story of a scholarly Orthodox bishop – see p. 390 – who got into trouble with both the Inquisition and his own hierarchy when he suggested that 'the prejudice of centuries' had something to do with the split between the two churches).

Le Roy Ladurie, Emmanuel (1977). 'Révoltes paysannes et histoire sociale', in Fernand Braudel and Ernest Labrousse (eds), *Histoire économique et sociale de la France* (Paris: PUF), Vol. 1, 2: 819–59.

Lesure, Michel (1972). *Lepante, la crise de l'Empire ottoman* (Paris: Julliard). (With numerous Mühimme documents in translation, most informative).

Lesure, Michel (1986). 'Les relations franco-ottomanes à l'épreuve des guerres de religion (1560–1594)', in Hâmit Batu and Jean-Louis Bacqué-Grammont (eds), *L'Empire Ottoman, la République de Turquie et la France* (Paris and Istanbul: Association pour le Développement des Études Turques and The Isis Press): 38–57.

Lewis, Bernard (1982). *The Muslim Discovery of Europe* (New York and London: Norton).

Llewellyn Smith, Michael (reprint 1998). *Ionian Vision, Greece in Asia Minor 1919–1922* (London: Hurst & Company). (The war in Asia Minor with a focus on Greece).

Lory, Bernard (1985). *Le sort de l'héritage ottoman en Bulgarie, l'exemple des villes bulgares 1878–1900* (Istanbul: The Isis Press).

Mack, Rosamund (2002). *Bazaar to Piazza, Islamic Trade and Italian Art, 1300–1600* (Los Angeles: University of California Press). (On the commerce and imitation of artefacts from the Islamic world).

Majer, Hans Georg (1969). *Vorstudien zur Geschichte der Ilmiye im osmanischen Reich* (Munich: Dr Rudolf Trofenik).

Majoros, Ferenc and Bernd Rill (1994). *Das Osmanische Reich (1300–1922), Die Geschichte einer Grossmacht* (Ratisbon and Graz: Friedrich Pustet and Styria).

Mantran, Robert (1962). *Istanbul dans la seconde moitié du XVIIᵉ siècle, Essai d'histoire institutionelle, économique et sociale* (Paris and Istanbul: Institut Français d'Archéologie d'Istanbul and Adrien Maisonneuve). (Fundamental on food supply, guilds and activities of foreigners in 17th-century Istanbul).

Marquié, Claude (1993). *L'industrie textile carcassonnaise au XVIIIe siècle, Étude d'un groupe social: les marchands-fabricants* (Carcassonne: Société d'Etudes Scientifiques de l'Aude). (On an industry completely geared to the Ottoman market).

Masson, Paul (1911). *Histoire du commerce français dans le Levant au XVIIIe siècle* (Paris: Librairie Hachette). (Emphasis on the institutional framework, still important on this particular topic).

Masters, Bruce (1988). *The Origins of Western Economic Dominance in the Middle East, Mercantilism and the Islamic Economy in Aleppo, 1600–1750* (New York: New York University Press).

Masters, Bruce (1992). 'The Sultan's Entrepreneurs: The Avrupa tüccarı and the Hayriye tüccarıs in Syria', *International Journal of Middle East Studies*, 24: 579–97.

Masters, Bruce (1994a). 'The Evolution of an Imagined Community: Aleppo's Catholics in the 18th and 19th Centuries' (paper delivered at the 11th Symposium of CIEPO, Amsterdam, June 1994, unpublished).

Masters, Bruce (1994b). 'The View from the Province: Syrian Chronicles of the Eighteenth Century', *Journal of the American Oriental Society*, 114, 3: 353–62.

Masters, Bruce (2001). *Christians and Jews in the Arab World, The Roots of Sectarianism* (Cambridge: Cambridge University Press). (A fine explanation of the reasons that, in the 18th century, prompted a majority of Aleppo's Christians to become Catholics).

Matar, Nabil (1999). *Turks, Moors and Englishmen in the Age of Discovery* (New York: Colombia University Press).

Matthee, Rudolph P. (1999). *The Politics of Trade in Safavid Iran, Silk for Silver 1600–1730* (Cambridge: Cambridge University Press). (Important, with a strong emphasis on Dutch sources).

Matschke, Klaus Peter (2004). *Das Kreuz und der Halbmond, Die Geschichte der Türkenkriege* (Düsseldorf: Artemis & Winkler). (Events plus the views of contemporaries).

Matuz, Joseph (1992). 'A propos de la validité des capitulations de 1536 entre l'Empire ottoman et la France', *Turcica*, XXIV: 183–92. (A relatively recent contribution to an old discussion).

Maxim, Mihai (reprint 1999a) 'Recherches sur les circonstances de la majoration du kharaj de la Moldavie entre les années 1538 et 1574', in Mihai Maxim, *L'Empire ottoman au nord du Danube et l'autonomie des Principautés Roumaines au XVIe siècle, Études et documents* (Istanbul: The Isis Press): 185–214.

Maxim, Mihai (reprint 1999b) 'L'Autonomie de la Moldavie et de la Valachie dans les actes officiels de la Porte au cours de la seconde moitiè du XVIe siècle', in Mihai Maxim, *L'Empire ottoman au nord du Danube et l'autonomie des Principautés Roumaines au XVIe siècle, Études et documents* (Istanbul: The Isis Press): 11–82.

McCarthy, Justin (1995). *Death and Exile, The Ethnic Cleansing of Ottoman Muslims 1821–1922* (Princeton: The Darwin Press).

McGowan, Bruce (1981). *Economic Life in Ottoman Europe, Taxation, Trade and the Struggle for Land, 1600–1800* (Cambridge and Paris: Cambridge University Press and Maison des Sciences de l'Homme). (Has placed the study of the '*çiftlik*' on a new footing).

Mélikoff, Irène (1975). 'Le problème kızılbaş', *Turcica*, VI: 49–67.

Motika, Raoul (1993). 'Bezüglich des Buches von Lucile und Bartolomé Bennassar, *Les Chrétiens d'Allah: l'histoire extraordinaire des rénégats, XVIᵉ-XVIIᵉ siècles*', *Turcica*, XXV: 189–204.

Mousnier, Roland (1971a). *La vénalité des offices sous Henri IV et Louis XIII* (Paris: Presses Universitaires de France).

Mousnier, Roland (1971b). *Peasant Uprisings in Seventeenth Century France, Russia and China* (London: Allen & Unwin).

Mraz, Gottfried (1980). 'Die Rolle der Uhrwerke in der kaiserlichen Türkenverehrung im 16. Jahrhundert', in Klaus Maurice and Otto Mayr (eds), *Die Welt als Uhr, Deutsche Uhren und Automaten 1550–1650*, (Munich: Deutscher Kunstverlag): 39–54.

Müller, Wolfgang *et alii* (1985). *Handbuch der Kirchengeschichte*, Vol. IV: *Die Kirche im Zeitalter des Absolutismus und der Aufklärung*, ed. by Hubert Jedin (Freiburg, Bâle, Vienna: Herder).

Murphey, Rhoads (1999). *Ottoman Warfare, 1500–1700* (London: UCL Press). (Especially valuable on the motivations of Ottoman military men; shows them as human beings and not as automata).

Nagata, Yuzo (1982). *Muhsin-zâde Mehmed Paşa ve Ayânlık Müessesesi* (Tokyo: Institute for the Study of Languages and Cultures of Asia and Africa).

Nagata, Yuzo (1997). *Tarihte Ayânlar, Karaosmanoğulları üzerinde bir İnceleme* (Ankara: Türk Tarih Kurumu). (Has much information on the landholdings of these major notables of western Anatolia).

Necipoğlu-Kafadar, Gülru (1986a). 'Plans and Models in 15th and 16th Century Ottoman Architectural Practice', *Journal of the Society of Architectural Historians*, XLX, 3: 224–43.

Necipoğlu-Kafadar, Gülru (1986b). 'The Süleymaniye Complex in Istanbul: an Interpretation', *Muqarnas*, III: 92–117.

Necipoğlu, Gülru (1989). 'Süleyman the Magnificent and the Representation of Power in the Context of Ottoman-Habsburg-Papal Rivalry', *The Art Bulletin*, LXXI, 3: 401–27.

Necipoğlu, Gülru (1991). *Architecture, Ceremonial and Power, The Topkapı Palace in the Fifteenth and Sixteenth Centuries* (Cambridge, MA: The Architectural History Foundation and MIT Press). (Fascinating perspectives on political history as well).

Necipoğlu, Gülru (1992). 'The Life of an Imperial Monument: Hagia Sophia after Byzantium', in Robert Mark and Ahmet Ş. Çakmak (eds), *Hagia Sophia from the*

Age of Justinian to the Present (Cambridge: Cambridge University Press): 195–226.

Nehring, Karl (1983). *Adam Freiherr zu Herbersteins Gesandtschaftsreise nach Konstantinopel, Ein Beitrag zum Frieden von Zsitvatorok (1606)* (Munich: Oldenbourg). (Both an analysis and a publication of primary source material).

Neumann, Christoph K. (1993). 'Decision Making Without Decision Makers: Ottoman Foreign Policy circa 1780', in Caesar Farah (ed.), *Decision Making and Change in the Ottoman Empire*, (Kirksville MO: Thomas Jefferson University Press): 28–39.

Neumann, Christoph (1994). *Das indirekte Argument, Ein Plädoyer für die Tanzîmat vermittels der Historie, Die geschichtliche Bedeutung von Ahmed Cevdet Paşas Ta'rih* (Münster and Hamburg: Lit Verlag). (Spirited and scholarly).

Neumann, Christoph (unpublished manuscript) 'The Russian Experience: Necati Efendi in Captivity'.

Nolte, Hans-Heinrich (1998). *Kleine Geschichte Russlands* (Stuttgart: Reclam).

Nora, Pierre (1997). *Les lieux de la mémoire*, 3 vols (Paris: Gallimard).

Nouzille, Jean (1991). *Histoire des frontières, L'Autriche et l'Empire ottoman* (Paris: Berg International). (Based on Austrian archival materials; for specialist readers).

Nowak, F. (reprint 1978). 'Sigismund III 1587–1632', in W. F. Reddaway *et alii* (eds), *The Cambridge History of Poland*, Vol. 1: *From the Origins to Sobieski (to 1696)*, (Cambridge: Cambridge University Press): 451–75.

Ocak, Ahmet Yaşar (2002). *Sarı Saltık, Popüler İslâmın Balkanlar'daki Destanî Öncüsü* (Ankara: Türk Tarih Kurumu).

Ohanian Mechitarista, Vahan (2000). 'La Bibbia armena dell' Abbate Mechitar', in Simonetta Pelusi (ed.), *Le civiltà del Libro e la stampa a Venezia, Testi sacri ebraici, cristiani, islamici dal Quattrocento al Settecento* (Venice: Libreria Sansoviniana and Il Poligrafo): 95–104.

Orhonlu, Cengiz (1967). *Osmanlı İmparatorluğunda Derbend Teşkilatı* (Istanbul: Istanbul Üniversitesi Edebiyat Fakültesi). (On villagers responsible for security on Ottoman roads).

Orhonlu, Cengiz (1974). *Osmanlı İmparatorluğunun Güney Siyaseti, Habeş Eyaleti* (Istanbul: İ.Ü. Edebiyat Fakültesi). (On the forgotten 'Far South': The Ottomans on the African coast of the Red Sea).

Overmans, Rüdiger (1999a). '"In der Hand des Feindes". Geschichtsschreibung zur Kriegsgefangenschaft von der Antike bis zum Zweiten Weltkrieg', in Rüdiger Overmans and the Arbeitskreis Militärgeschichte (eds), *In der Hand des Feindes. Geschichtsschreibung zur Kriegsgefangenschaft von der Antike bis zum Zweiten Weltkrieg* (Cologne, Weimar and Vienna: Böhlau Verlag): 1–40.

Overmans, Rüdiger (1999b). 'Ein Silberstreifen am Forschungshorizont? Veröffentlichungen zur Geschichte der Kriegsgefangenschaft', in Rüdiger Overmans and the Arbeitskreis Militärgeschichte (eds), *In der Hand des Feindes. Geschichtsschreibung zur Kriegsgefangenschaft von der Antike bis zum Zweiten Weltkrieg* (Cologne, Weimar and Vienna: Böhlau Verlag): 483–506.

Özbaran, Salih (1986). 'The Ottomans' Role in the Diffusion of Fire-arms and Military Technology in Asia and Africa in the Sixteenth Century', *Revue internationale d'histoire militaire* (Ankara), 67: 77–83, reprinted in Salih Özbaran, *The Ottoman Response to European Expansion, Studies on*

Ottoman–Portuguese Relations in the Indian Ocean and Ottoman Administration in the Arab Lands during the Sixteenth Century (Istanbul: The Isis Press): 61–6.

Özbaran, Salih (1994a). 'The Ottoman Budgets of Yemen in the Sixteenth Century', in Salih Özbaran, *The Ottoman Response to European Expansion, Studies on Ottoman–Portuguese Relations in the Indian Ocean and Ottoman Administration in the Arab Lands during the Sixteenth Century* (Istanbul: The Isis Press): 49–60.

Özbaran, Salih (1994b). *The Ottoman Response to European Expansion, Studies on Ottoman–Portuguese Relations in the Indian Ocean and Ottoman Administration in the Arab Lands during the Sixteenth Century* (Istanbul: The Isis Press).

Palumbo Fossati Casa, Isabella (1997). 'L'École venitienne des "giovani di lingua"', in Frédéric Hitzel (ed), *Istanbul et les langues orientales* (Istanbul and Paris: IFÉA, INALCO, L'Harmattan): 109–22.

Pamuk, Şevket (1999). *Osmanlı İmparatorluğunda Paranın Tarihi* (Istanbul: Tarih Vakfı Yurt Yayınları).

Pamuk, Şevket (2000). *A Monetary History of the Ottoman Empire* (Cambridge: Cambridge University Press). (A fundamental text).

Panaite, Viorel (2000). *The Ottoman Law of War and Peace, The Ottoman Empire and Tribute Payers* (Boulder, CO, and New York: Columbia University Press). (This is an interesting piece of scholarship badly in need of an editor).

Panzac, Daniel (1996a). 'Négociants ottomans et capitaines français: la caravane maritime en Crète au XVIIIe siècle', reprinted in *Commerce et navigation dans l'Empire ottoman au XVIIIe siècle* (Istanbul: The Isis Press): 77–94.

Panzac, Daniel (1996b). 'Affréteurs ottomans et capitaines français à Alexandrie: la caravane maritime au milieu du XVIIIe siècle', reprinted in *Commerce et navigation dans l'Empire ottoman au XVIIIe siècle* (Istanbul: The Isis Press): 57–76.

Panzac, Daniel (1999). *Les corsaires barbaresques, la fin d'une épopée 1800–1820* (Paris: Editions du CNRS). (Much broader than the title suggests: the manner in which corsairs operated during the 18th century, and their last-ditch effort to change over to commerce, frustrated by European exclusiveness).

Pappas, Nicholas Charles (1991). *Greeks in Russian Military Service in the late 18th and early 19th centuries* (Thessaloniki: Institute for Balkan Studies).

Paris, Robert (1957). *Histoire du commerce de Marseille*, Vol. 5: *Le Levant, de 1660 à 1789* (Paris: Plon). (Discusses quantitative data on the 17th- and 18th-century commerce of Marseilles).

Parker, Geoffrey (revised edition 1990). *Spain and the Netherlands, 1559–1659, Ten Studies* (London: Fontana Press). (Did the Ottoman sultans decisively aid the northern Netherlands against Philip II?).

Parker, Geoffrey (1998). *The Grand Strategy of Philip II* (New Haven, London: Yale University Press).

Parmaksızoğlu, İsmet (1953). 'Bir Türk Kadısının Esaret Hatıraları', *Tarih Dergisi*, V: 77–84.

Parry, V. J. (1958). 'The Ottoman Empire, 1520–66', in G. R. Elton (ed.), *The New Cambridge Modern History*, Vol. 2: *The Reformation* (Cambridge: Cambridge University Press): 510–33.

Pastor, Ludwig Freiherr von (1923). *Geschichte der Päpste im Zeitalter der katholischen Reformation und Restauration*, Vol. 9 *Gregor XIII (1572–1585)* (Freiburg: Herder): 179–88, 734–46.

Pedani Fabris, Maria Pia (1994b). *In nome del Gran Signore, Inviati ottomani a Venezia dalla caduta di Costantinopoli alla guerra di Candia* (Venice: Deputacione Editrice). (Shows the intensity of 16th- and early 17th-century Ottoman–Venetian relations).

Pedani Fabris, Maria Pia (2000). 'Safiye's Household and Venetian Diplomacy', *Turcica*, 32: 9–32.

Pedani Fabris, Maria Pia (2002). *Dalla frontiera al confine* (Venice: Herder Editrice and Università Ca Foscari di Venezia).

Peirce, Leslie (1993). *The Imperial Harem, Women and Sovereignty in the Ottoman Empire* (New York and Oxford: Oxford University Press).

Peri, Oded (2001). *Christianity under Islam in Jerusalem, The Question of the Holy Sites in Early Ottoman Times* (Leiden, Cologne and Boston: E. J. Brill).

Peters, Francis E. (1985). Jerusalem, *The Holy City in the Eyes of Chroniclers, Visitors, Pilgrims, and Prophets from the Days of Abraham to the Beginnings of Modern Times* (Princeton: Princeton University Press). (A very full and instructive selection of primary sources translated into English, with a commentary by the author tying them together; modern times means here the mid-19th century).

Petritsch, Ernst (1983). 'Die tatarisch-osmanischen Begleitoperationen in Niederösterreich', *Studia Austro-Polonica*, 3: 207–40.

Pistor-Hatam, Anja (1991). 'Pilger, Pest und Cholera: Die Wallfahrt zu den Heiligen Stätten im Irak als gesundheitspolitisches Problem im 19. Jahrhundert', *Die Welt des Islam*, 31: 228–45.

Pitcher, Donald Edgar (1972). *An Historical Geography of the Ottoman Empire* (Leiden: E. J. Brill). (Published posthumously; dated and for general information only).

Piterberg, Gabriel (2003). *An Ottoman Tragedy, History and Historiography at Play* (Berkeley, Los Angeles and London: University of California Press).

Planhol, Xavier de (2000). *L'Islam et la mer, La mosquée et le matelot, VIIe–XXe siècle* (Paris: Perrin).

Po'Chia Hsia, Ronnie (1998). *Gegenreformation, Die Welt der katholischen Erneuerung 1540–1770*, tr. by Holger Fliessbach (Frankfur: Fischer Taschenbuch Verlag).

Pomian, Krzysztof (1987). *Collectionneurs, amateurs et curieux, Paris-Venise: XVIe–XVIIIe siècle* (Paris: Gallimard).

Poni, Carlo (1982). 'Maß gegen Maß: Wie der Seidenfaden rund und dünn wurde', in Berdahl, Lüdtke, Medick, Poni, Reddy, Sabean, Schindler, Sider (eds), *Klassen und Kultur, Sozialanthropologische Perspektiven in der Geschichtsschreibung* (n.p.: Syndicat): 21–53.

Porchnev, Boris (1972). *Les soulèvements populaires en France au XVIIe siècle* (Paris: Flammarion).

Poumarède, Géraud (1997). 'Justifier l'injustifiable: l'alliance turque au miroir de la chrétienté (XVIe–XVIIe siècles)', *Revue d'histoire diplomatique*, 3: 217–46.

Poumarède, Géraud (1998). 'Négocier près de la Sublime Porte, Jalons pour une nouvelle histoire des capitulations franco-ottomanes', in L. Bély (ed.), *L'invention de la diplomatie* (Paris: n.p.): 71–85.

Preto, Paolo (1975). *Venezia e i Turchi* (Florence: Sansoni Editore and Facoltá di Magistero dell'Universitá di Padova) (Especially precious the section on conversions to Islam; should be much better known).

Preto, Paolo (1999). *I servizi secreti di Venezia, Spionaggio e controspionaggio al tempo della Serenissima: cifrari, intercettazioni, delazioni, tra mito e realtà* (Milan: EST). (Fantastic information concerning Venetian 'secret service' activities on Ottoman territory. As gripping as a spy novel).

Quataert, Donald (1993). *Ottoman Manufacturing in the Age of the Industrial Revolution* (Cambridge: Cambridge University Press). (Has pointed out that many Ottoman artisans found ways and means of coping with the vicissitudes of 'integration into the European world economy').

Quataert, Donald (1997). 'Clothing Laws, State and Society in the Ottoman Empire, 1720–1829', *International Journal of Middle East Studies*, 29: 403–25.

Rafeq, Abdul-Karim (1970). *The Province of Damascus 1723–1783* (Beirut: Khayats).

Rafeq, Abdul-Karim (2000). 'Ottoman Jerusalem in the Writings of Arab Travellers', in Sylvia Auld and Robert Hillenbrand (eds), *Ottoman Jerusalem, The Living City 1517–1917* (London: Altajir World of Islam Trust): 63–72.

Raymond, André (1973–4). *Artisans et commerçants au Caire, au XVIIIᵉ siècle*, 2 vols (Damascus: Institut Français de Damas). (Fundamental; on the basis of inheritance inventories the author deals with Red Sea trade, artisanal activities and the penetration of paramilitary corps into artisan lives).

Raymond, André (1986). *Grandes villes arabes à l'époque ottomane* (Paris: Sindbad). (Masterly overview).

Raymond, André (1995). *Le Caire des janissaires, L'apogée de la ville ottomane sous 'Abd al-Rahmân Katkhuda* (Paris: CNRS Editions) (Shows what can be said in a short volume, if the person saying it is André Raymond).

Raymond, André (1998). *Égyptiens et Français au Caire 1798–1801* (Cairo: IFAO).

Redlich, Fritz (1956). *De Praeda Militari, Looting and Booty 1500–1815* (Wiesbaden: Vierteljahrschrift für Sozial- und Wirtschaftsgeschichte and Franz Steiner).

Redlich, Fritz (1964–5). *The German Military Enterpriser and his Work Force, A Study in European Economic and Social History* (Wiesbaden: Vierteljahrschrift für Sozial- und Wirtschaftsgeschichte and Franz Steiner).

Reinert, Stephen W. (1998). 'The Muslim Presence in Constantinople, 9th–15th Centuries: Some Preliminary Observations', in Hélène Ahrweiler and Angeliki E. Laiou (eds), *Studies on the Internal Diaspora of the Byzantine Empire*, (Washington: Dumbarton Oaks and Harvard University Press): 125–50.

Renda, Günsel (1989). 'Die traditionelle türkische Malerei und das Einsetzen der westlichen Einflüsse', in *Geschichte der türkischen Malerei* (Istanbul: Palasar SA): 15–86.

Restle, Marcell (1976), *Reclams Kunstführer, Istanbul, Edirne, Iznik* (Stuttgart: Philipp Reclam).

Revere, Robert B. (1957). 'No Man's Coast: Ports of Trade in the Eastern Mediterranean', in Karl Polanyi, Conrad M. Arensberg and Harry W. Pearson (eds), *Trade and Market in the Early Empires, Economies in History and Theory* (Glencoe, IL: Free Press, Falcon's Wing Press): 38–63.

Richards, John (1993). *The New Cambridge History of India, The Mughal Empire* (Cambridge: Cambridge University Press).

Roemer, Hans Robert (1986). 'The Safawid Period', in Peter Jackson and Lawrence Lockhart (eds), *The Cambridge History of Iran*, Vol. 6: *The Timurid and Safavid Periods* (Cambridge: Cambridge University Press): 189–350.

Rogers, John Michael (1982). 'The State and the Arts in Ottoman Turkey', *International Journal of Middle East Studies*, 14: 71–86; 283–313.

Roosen, William (1980). 'Early Modern Diplomatic Ceremonial: A Systems Approach', *The Journal of Modern History*, 52, 3: 452–76.

Rosenthal, Steven (1980). *The Politics of Dependency; Urban Reform in Istanbul* (Westport, CT: Greenwood Press).

Rothenberg, Gunther E. (1970). *Die österreichische Militärgrenze in Kroatien 1522 bis 1881*, tr. by Helga Zoglmann (Vienna: Herold Druck- und Verlagsgesellschaft) (Translation, in one volume, of Rosenberg's classical study).

Rozen, Minna (2002). *A History of the Jewish Community in Istanbul, the Formative Years, 1453–1566* (Leiden: E. J. Brill).

Runciman, Steven (1968). *The Great Church in Captivity, A Study of the Patriarchate of Constantinople from the Eve of the Turkish Conquest to the Greek War of Independence* (Cambridge: Cambridge University Press). (A standard work of reference).

Rüpke, Jörg (1999). 'Kriegsgefangene in der römischen Antike, Eine Problemskizze', in Rüdiger Overmans and the Arbeitskreis Militärgeschichte (eds), *In der Hand des Feindes. Geschichtsschreibung zur Kriegsgefangenschaft von der Antike bis zum Zweiten Weltkrieg* (Cologne, Weimar, Vienna: Böhlau Verlag): 83–98.

Sadok, Boubaker (1987). *La Régence de Tunis au XVIIᵉ siècle: ses relations commerciales avec les ports de l'Europe méditerranéenne, Marseille et Livourne* (Zaghouan: CEROMA). (A clever methodological approach: how French commercial data can be made to yield information about the Tunisian economy).

Sahillioğlu, Halil (1968). 'Bir Tüccar Kervanı', *Belgelerle Türk Tarih Dergisi* (Istanbul), 9: 63–9.

Sahillioğlu, Halil (1985b). 'Slaves in the Social and Economic Life of Bursa in the late 15th and early 16th Centuries', *Turcica*, XVII: 43–112.

Said, Edward (1978), *Orientalism* (New York: Random House).

Salzmann, Ariel (1993). 'An Ancien Régime Revisited: "Privatization" and Political Economy in the Eighteenth-century Ottoman Empire', *Politics and Society*, XXI, 4: 393–423.

Salzmann, Ariel (2004). *Toqueville in the Ottoman Empire, Rival Paths to the Modern State* (Leiden: E. J. Brill).

Sarıcaoğlu, Fikret (1991). 'Cihânnümâ ve Ebubekir b. Behrâm ed-Dımeşkî-İbrahim Müteferrika', in *Professor Dr. Bekir Kütükoğlu'na Armağan* (Istanbul: İstanbul Üniversitesi Edebiyat Fakültesi): 121–42.

Schaser, Angelika (1993). 'Die Fürstentümer Moldau und Walachei 1650–1850', in Wolfram Fischer *et alii* (eds), *Handbuch der europäischen Wirtschafts- und Sozialgeschichte*, Vol. 4: Ilya Mieck (ed.), *Von der Mitte des 17. Jahrhunderts bis zur Mitte des 19. Jahrhunderts* (Stuttgart: Klett-Cotta): 971–93. (Very informative).

Schmidt, Jan (n.d., probably 1992). *Pure Water for Thirsty Muslims, A Study of Mustafa 'Ali of Gallipoli's Künhü l-ahbar* (Leiden: n.p.).

Schmidt, Jan (2000). *The Joys of Philology*, 2 vols (Istanbul: The Isis Press).

Schulin, Ernst (1999). *Kaiser Karl V, Geschichte eines übergroßen Wirkungsbereiches* (Stuttgart: W. Kohlhammer). (Summary of recent research, for the general reader).

Schulze, Winfried (1978). *Reich und Türkengefahr im späten 16. Jahrhundert, Studien zu den politischen und gesellschaftlichen Auswirkungen einer äusseren Bedrohung* (Munich: C. H. Beck). (How the Habsburgs got money from the German princes for their wars against the Ottomans).

Sella, Domenico (1968a). 'The Rise and Fall of the Venetian Woollen Industry', in Brian Pullan (ed.), *Crisis and Change in the Venetian Economy in the Sixteenth and Seventeenth Centuries* (London: Methuen & Co): 106–26.

Sella, Domenico (1968b). 'Crisis and Transformation in Venetian Trade', in Brian Pullan (ed.), *Crisis and Change in the Venetian Economy in the Sixteenth and Seventeenth Centuries*, (London: Methuen & Co): 88–105.

Sevinçli, Efdal (1993). 'Theater in Izmir', in *The Three Ages of Izmir, Palimpsest of Cultures*, tr. by Virginia Taylor Saçlıoğlu (Istanbul: Yapı ve Kredi Yayınları): 369–86.

Shaw, Stanford J. (1962). *The Financial and Administrative Development of Ottoman Egypt 1517–1798* (Princeton: Princeton University Press). (A basic work of reference).

Shaw, Stanford J. (1971). *Between Old and New: The Ottoman Empire under Selim III, 1789–1807* (Cambridge, MA: Harvard University Press).

Shaw, Stanford J. (1977). *History of the Ottoman Empire and Modern Turkey*, 2 vols, Vol. II coauthored with Ezel Kural Shaw (Cambridge: Cambridge University Press).

Singer, Amy (1994). *Palestininan Peasants and Ottoman Officials, Rural Administration around Sixteenth-century Jerusalem* (Cambridge: Cambridge University Press).

Singer, Amy (2002). *Constructing Ottoman Beneficence: An Imperial Soup Kitchen in Jerusalem* (Albany, NY: SUNY Press). (Apart from the Jerusalem case, this important study covers Ottoman charity in general, and that of royal women in particular).

Skilliter, Susan (1975). 'Catherine de' Medici's Turkish Ladies in Waiting – A Dilemma in Franco-Ottoman Diplomatic Relations', *Turcica*, VII: 188–204.

Skilliter, Susan A. (1976). 'The Sultan's Messenger, Gabriel Defrens; An Ottoman Master-Spy of the Sixteenth Century', *Wiener Zeitschrift für die Kunde des Morgenlandes*, 68: 47–60.

Smyrnelis, Marie-Carmen (1995). 'Les Arméniens catholiques aux XVIIIème et XIXème siècles', *Revue du Monde Arménien moderne et contemporain*, 2: 25–44.

Smyrnelis, Marie-Carmen (1999). 'Les Européens et leur implantation dans l'espace urbain de Smyrne', in Jacques Bottin and Donatella Calabi (eds), *Les étrangers dans la ville* (Paris: Editions de la Maison des Sciences de l'Homme): 65–75.

Smyrnelis, Marie-Carmen (2000). 'Une société hors de soi: Identités et relations sociales à Smyrne aux XVIIIème et XIXème siècles' (unpublished PhD thesis, Ecole des Hautes Études, Paris).

Snouck Hungronje, Christiaan (1923). 'Een Mekkaansch gezantshap naar Atjeh in 1683', in Hungronje Snouk, *Verspreide Geschriften*, Vol. III *Geschriften betreffende Arabie en Turkije* (Bonn and Leipzig: Kurt Schroeder): 137–48.

Sohrweide, Hanna (1965). 'Der Sieg der Safawiden in Persien und seine Rückwirkungen auf die Schiiten Anatoliens im 16. Jahrhundert', *Der Islam*, 41: 95–223. (Anatolian heterodox Muslims and their relationship to Safavid Iran; an important study).

Soucek, Svat (1992). *Piri Reis and Turkish Mapmaking after Columbus* (London: The Nour Foundation).

Sourdel-Thomime, Janine (1971), *Clefs et serrures de la Ka'ba, notes d'épigraphie arabe* (Paris: Geuthner).

Spies, Otto (1968). 'Schicksale türkischer Kriegsgefangener in Deutschland nach den Türkenkriegen', in Erwin Graef (ed.), *Festschrift Werner Caskel*, (Leiden: E. J. Brill).

Springborn, Patricia (1992). *Western Republicanism and the Oriental Prince* (Cambridge and Oxford: Polity Press and Basil Blackwell).

Stchoukine, Ivan (1966). *La peinture turque d'après les manuscrits illustrés*, Vol. 1: *De Süleyman I à 'Osman II* (Paris: Paul Geuthner).

Steensgaard, Niels (1967). 'Consuls and Nations in the Levant from 1570 to 1650', *Scandinavian Economic History Review*, 1, 2: 13–54.

Steensgaard, Niels (1973). *The Asian Trade Revolution of the Seventeenth Century, The East India Companies and the Decline of the Caravan Trade* (Chicago and London: Chicago University Press). (While the main thesis of this book is difficult to accept today, it remains interesting reading).

Steensgaard, Niels (1978). 'The Seventeenth-Century Crisis', in Geoffrey Parker and Lesley Smith (eds), *The General Crisis of the Seventeenth Century*, (London: Routledge and Kegan Paul): 26–56.

Stepánek, Petr (2001). 'War and Peace in the West (1644/5): A Dilemma at the Threshold of Felicity?', *Archiv Orientální*, 69, 2: 327–40.

Stoianovich, Traian (1960). 'The Conquering Balkan Orthodox Merchant', *Journal of Economic History*, XX: 234–313.

Stoye, John (1994). *Marsigli's Europe* (New Haven and London: Yale University Press).

Stoye, John (reprint 2000). *The Siege of Vienna* (Edinburgh: Birlinn). (Originally published in 1964; uses those Ottoman sources which had been translated at that time; fine narrative).

Streit, Christian (1978). *Keine Kameraden. Die Wehrmacht und die sowjetischen Kriegsgefangenen 1941–1945* (Stuttgart: Deutsche Verlagsanstalt). (A fundamental study of the mistreatment of Soviet prisoners of war by the Wehrmacht, melancholy but essential reading for those who try to measure the risks undergone by war captives).

Strong, Roy (1991). *Feste der Renaissance*, tr. by Susanne Höbel and Maja Ueberle-Pfaff (Freiburg and Würzburg: Pfaff). (Political symbolism at the court of Charles V, Catherine de Medici, Grand Duke Ferdinand of Florence, Charles I of England and Scotland).

Strong, Roy (reprint 1995). 'Queen and City: The Elizabethan Lord Mayor's Pageant', in *The Tudor and Stuart Monarchy, Pageantry, Painting, Iconography*, 2 vols (Woodbridge: Boydell Press), Vol. 2: 17–32. (One of the author's early pieces, when he was still a student of Frances Yates).

Subrahmanyam, Sanjay (1988). 'Persians, Pilgrims and Portuguese: the Travails of Masulipatnam Shipping in the Western Indian Ocean, 1590–1665', *Modern Asian Studies*, 22, 3: 503–30.

Subtelny, Orest (1991). 'The Contractual Principle and Right of Resistance in the Ukraine and Moldavia', in R. J. W. Evans and T. V. Thomas (eds), *Crown, Church and Estates, Central European Politics in the Sixteenth and Seventeenth Centuries*

(London and New York: School of Slavonic and East European Studies and St Martin's Press): 287–99.

Sumner, Benedict (1949). *Peter the Great and the Ottoman Empire* (Oxford: Basil Blackwell).

Szakály, Ferenc (1986). *Hungaria eliberata, Die Rückeroberung von Buda im Jahr 1686 und Ungarns Befreiung von der Osmanenherrschaft (1683–1718)* (Budapest: Corvina). (Focuses on military history).

Szakály, Ferenc (1995). *Ludovico Gritti in Hungary, 1529–1534, A Historical Insight (sic) into the Beginnings of Turco-Habsburgian Rivalry* (Budapest: Akadémiai Kiadó). (On a uniquely colourful character: the natural son of a famous Venetian doge who made a career for himself in the service of Süleyman the Magnificent).

Tabakoğlu, Ahmet (1985). *Gerileme Dönemine Girerken Osmanlı Maliyesi* (Istanbul: Dergâh Yayınları).

Taeschner, Franz (1923). 'Die geographische Literatur der Osmanen', *Zeitschrift der Deutschen Morgenländischen Gesellschaft*, 2, 1: 31–80.

Tchentsova, Vera (1998). 'Le fonds des documents grecs (f.52. "Relations de la Russie avec la Grèce") de la collection des Archives Nationales des Actes anciens de la Russie et leur valeur pour l'histoire de l'Empire ottoman', *Turcica*, 30: 383–96. (Contains much more than the title promises, in fact the beginnings of a study of the 17th-century relationship of the Orthodox patriarchs with the tsars).

Temimi, Abdeljelil (1989). *Le gouvernement ottoman et le problème morisque* (Zaghouan: CEROMDI). (Based on documentation in the Mühimme Defterleri).

Teply, Karl (1973). 'Vom Los osmanischer Gefangener aus dem grossen Türkenkrieg 1683–1699', *Südost-Forschungen*, XXXII: 33–72. (Important article, should be much better known).

Terzioğlu, Derin (1995). 'The Imperial Circumcision Festival of 1582: An Interpretation', *Muqarnas*, 12: 84–100.

Theolin, Sture; and Findley, Carter V.; Renda, Günsel; Mansel, Philip; Ciobanu, Veniamin; Beydilli, Kemal; Temimi, Abdeljelil; Tlili Sellaouti, Rachida; Ludwigs, Folke (2002). *The Torch of the Empire, Ignatius Mouradgea d'Ohsson and the Tableau général of the Ottoman Empire in Eighteenth Century / İmparatorluğun Meşalesi, XVIII. Yüzyılda Osmanlı İmparatorluğunun Genel Görünümü ve Ignatius Mouradgea d'Ohsson* (Istanbul: Yapı Kredi Yayınları).

Theunissen, Hans (1991). 'Ottoman-Venetian Diplomatics: The *ahidname*s. The Historical Background and the Development of a Category of Political-Diplomatic Instruments together with an Annotated Edition of a Corpus of Relevant Documents' (PhD dissertation, Utrecht). (Only available on the Internet).

Thomas, Lewis V. (1972). *A Study of Naima*, ed Norman Itzkowitz (New York: New York University Press). (Rather descriptive; but then the work is much older than the date of publication indicates).

Tietze, Andreas (1942). 'Die Geschichte vom Kerkermeister-Kapitän, Ein türkischer Seeräuberroman aus dem 17. Jahrhundert', *Acta Orientalia*, 19: 152–210.

Tilly, Charles (1981). *As Sociology Meets History* (New York and London: Academic Press).

Tilly, Charles (1985). 'War Making and State Making as Organized Crime', in Peter B. Evans, Dietrich Rueschemeyer and Theda Skocpol (eds), *Bringing the State back in* (Cambridge: Cambridge University Press): 169–91. (Beautiful demystification of the activities of early modern monarchs).

Tinguely, Frédéric (2000). *L'écriture du Levant à la Renaissance* (Geneva: Droz). (Important work on the difficulties of Renaissance scholars when confronted with the contradiction between antique texts and their own observations).

Todorova, Maria (1996). 'The Ottoman Legacy and the Balkans', in L. Carl Brown (ed.), *Imperial Legacy, The Ottoman Imprint on the Balkans and the Middle East*, (New York: Columbia University Press): 45–77.

Togan, Isenbike (1992). 'Ottoman History by Inner Asian Norms', in Halil Berktay and Suraiya Faroqhi (eds), *New Approaches to State and Peasant in Ottoman History*, (London: Frank Cass): 185–210. (Stimulating article, by a historian of Central Asia).

Toledano, Ehud (1990). *State and Society in Nineteenth-Century Egypt* (Cambridge: Cambridge University Press).

Topping, Peter (1972). 'The Post-Classical Documents', in *The Minnesota Messenia Expedition, Reconstructing a Bronze Age Environment* (St Paul, MN): 64–80.

Toumarkine, Alexandre (2000). 'L'Abkhazie et la Circassie dans le *Cihân-nümâ* de Kâtib Çelebi: un regard ottoman sur le Caucase du Nord-Ouest', in Raoul Motika and Michael Ursinus (eds), *Caucasia between the Ottoman Empire and Iran, 1555–1914* (Wiesbaden: Reichert): 31–40.

Tuchscherer, Michel (ed.) (2001). *Le commerce du café avant l'ère des plantations coloniales* (Cairo: IFAO).

Tunçer, Hadiye and Hüner (2nd printing 1998). *Osmanlı Diplomasisi ve Sefaretnameler* (Ankara: Ümit Yayıncılık).

Turan, Şerafettin (1961). *Kanuni'nin Oğlu Şehzâde Bayezid Vak'ası* (Ankara: Ankara Üniversitesi Dil ve Tarih-Coğrafya Fakültesi).

Turan, Şerafettin (1968). 'Venedik'te Türk Ticaret Merkezi', *Belleten*, 32, 126: 247–83.

Uebersberger, Hans (1913). *Russlands Orientpolitik in den letzten zwei Jahrhunderten ...*, Vol. 1: *Bis zum Frieden von Jassy* (Stuttgart: Deutsche Verlagsanstalt). (Uses the ample Russian literature on the 'Eastern question'; very informative).

Ülgener, Sabri F. (reprint 1981). *İktisadi Çözülmenin Ahlak ve Zihniyet Dünyası* (Istanbul: DER). (An original attempt to apply Weberian categories to Ottoman artisan history).

Ülker, Necmi (1987). 'The Emergence of Izmir as a Mediterranean Commercial Center for French and English Interests, 1698–1740', *International Journal of Turkish Studies*, 4, 1: 1–38.

Unat, Faik Reşat (1968). *Osmanlı Sefirleri ve Sefaretnâmeleri*, completed and ed. by Bekir Sıtkı Baykal (Ankara: Türk Tarih Kurumu). (A basic work of reference, even though some of the texts unpublished at the time of writing have since been made available).

Ursinus, Michael (1989). 'Klassisches Altertum und europäisches Mittelalter im Urteil spätosmanischer Geschichtsschreiber', *Zeitschrift für Türkeistudien*, 2, 2: 69–78.

Uzunçarşılı, İsmail Hakkı (1972). *Mekke-i mükerreme Emirleri* (Ankara: Türk Tarih Kurumu). (A reference work).

Uzunçarşılı, İsmail Hakkı (reprint 1977, 1982, 1983). *Osmanlı Tarihi*, 4 vols; Vol. 1: *Anadolu Selçukluları ve Anadolu Beylikleri hakkında bir Mukaddime ile Osmanlı Devleti'nin Kuruluşundan İstanbul'un Fethine kadar*; Vol. 2: *İstanbul'un Fethinden Kanunî Sultan Süleyman'ın Ölümüne kadar*; Vol. 3, part 1: *II Selim'in*

Tahta Çıkışından 1699 Karlofça Andlaşmasına kadar; Vol. 3, part 2: *XVI. Yüzyıl Ortalarından XVII. Yüzyıl Sonuna Kadar*; Vol. 4, part 1: *Karlofça Anlaşmasından XVIII. Yüzyılın Sonuna kadar*; Vol. 4, part 2: *XVIII. Yüzyıl* (Ankara: Türk Tarih Kurumu). (A reference work, now rather old-fashioned, but still useful on occasion).

Valensi, Lucette (1969). 'Islam et capitalisme: production et commerce des chéchias en Tunisie et en France aux XVIIIe et XIXe siècles', *Revue d'histoire moderne et contemporaine*, XVII: 376–400.

Valensi, Lucette (1987). *Venise et la Sublime Porte, la naissance du despote* (Paris: Hachette). (On European intellectual history: how the Ottoman sultan became a despot in the eyes of the Venetian *baili*).

Van Luttervelt, R. (1958). *De 'Turkse' Schilderijen van J. B. Vanmour en zijn school, De verzameling van Cornelis Calkoen, ambassadeur bij de Hoge Porte 1725–1743* (Istanbul, Leiden: Nederlands Historisch-Archaeologisch Instituut in het Nabije Oosten). (On a painter who, while not himself a great artist or even documentarist, was instrumental in starting the fashion for *orientalia* in 18th-century Europe).

Várkonyi, Agnes (1987). 'Gábor Bethlen and Transylvania under the Rákóczis at the European Peace Negotiations 1648–1714', in Kálmán Bénda *et alii* (eds), *Forschungen über Siebenbürgen und seine Nachbarn, Festschrift für Atilla T. Szabó und Zsigmund Jakó* (Munich: Dr Dr Rudolf Trofenik): 151–62.

Vatin, Nicolas (1995). 'Aux origines du pèlerinage à Eyüp des sultans ottomans', *Turcica*, XXVII: 91–100. (Ably sums up what is known about a rather confused issue).

Vatin, Nicolas, and Veinstein, Gilles (1996). 'Les obsèques des sultans ottomans de Mehmed II à Ahmed Ier', in Gilles Veinstein (ed.), *Les ottomans et la mort, permanences et mutations* (Leiden: E. J. Brill): 208–44. (Discusses the religious and political considerations behind the funerary ceremonies of Ottoman sultans).

Vatin, Nicolas (2001). 'Une affaire interne: le sort et la libération de personnes de condition libre illégalement retenues en esclavage', *Turcica*, 33: 149–90. (Based on broad Ottoman evidence, very instructive).

Vatin, Nicolas, and Veinstein, Gilles (2003). *Le sérail ébranlé* (Paris: Fayard). (Fascinating stories of what happened when the Ottoman throne fell vacant).

Veinstein, Gilles (1975). 'Ayân de la région d'Izmir et le commerce du Levant (deuxième moitié du XVIIIe siècle)', *Revue de l'Occident musulman et de la Méditerranée*, XX: 131–46.

Veinstein, Gilles (1988). 'Du marché urbain au marché du camp: l'institution ottomane des *orducu*', in Abdelgelil Temimi (ed.), *Mélanges Professeur Robert Mantran,* (Zaghouan, CEROMDI): 299–327.

Veinstein, Gilles (1996). 'L'oralité dans les documents d'archives ottomans: paroles rapportés ou imaginées?', *Oral et écrit dans le monde turco-ottoman,* special issue of *Revue du monde musulman et de la Méditerranée* (Aix-en-Provence: Edisud), 75–6: 133–42.

Veinstein, Gilles (1999). 'Commercial Relations between India and the Ottoman Empire (late Fifteenth to late Eighteenth Centuries): a few Notes and Hypotheses', in Sushil Chaudhuri and Michel Morineau (eds), *Merchants, Companies and Trade, Europe and Asia in the Early Modern Era* (Cambridge: Cambridge University Press): 95–115.

Veinstein, Gilles (2003). 'Les Ottomans: Fonctionnarisation des clercs, cléricalisation de l'état?', in Dominique Iogna-Prat and Gilles Veinstein (eds), *Histoires des hommes de Dieu dans l'Islam et le christianisme* (Paris: Flammarion): 179–204.

Versteeg, Annemieke (1997). '"Zich te bedienen van den arbeid van anderen". Bronnen voor de beschrijving van Turkije', in *'Ik hadde de nieusgierigheid', De reizen door het Nabije Oosten van Cornelis de Bruijn (ca. 1652–1727)* (Leiden and Leeuwen: Ex Oriente Lux and Peeters): 71–82.

Viallon, Marie (1995). *Venise et la Porte ottomane (1453–1566), Un siècle de relations vénéto-ottomanes de la prise de Constantinople à la mort de Soliman* (Paris: Economica).

Vigié, Marc, with van Wilder-Vigié, Muriel (1985). *Les galériens du roi, 1661–1715* (Paris: Fayard, 1985).

Wacquet, Jean Claude (1984). *De la corruption. Morale et pouvoir à Florence aux XVIIe et XVIIIe siècles* (Paris: Fayard).

Wallerstein, Immanuel (1974, 1980, 1989). *The Modern World-System*, 3 vols (New York: Academic Press).

Wallerstein, Immanuel, Decdeli, Hale, and Kasaba, Reşat (reprint 1987). 'The Incorporation of the Ottoman Empire into the World Economy', in Huri Islamoğlu-Inan (ed.), *The Ottoman Empire and the World Economy*, (Cambridge and Paris: Cambridge University Press and Maison des Sciences de l'Homme): 88–100.

Windler, Christian (2001). 'Diplomatic History as a Field for Cultural Analysis: Muslim–Christian Relations in Tunis, 1700–1840', *Historical Journal*, 44, 1: 79–106.

Wirth, Eugen (1986). 'Aleppo im 19. Jahrhundert – ein Beispiel für Stabilität und Dynamik spätosmanischer Wirtschaft', in Hans Georg Majer (ed.), *Osmanische Studien zur Wirtschafts- und Sozialgeschichte. In Memoriam Vančo Boškov* (Wiesbaden: Harrassowitz): 186–206.

Wittram, Reinhard (1964). *Peter I, Czar und Kaiser, Die Geschichte Peters des Grossen in seiner Zeit*, 2 vols (Göttingen: Vandenhoeck and Rupprecht).

Wood, Alfred C. (1964). *A History of the Levant Company* (London: Frank Cass).

Woodhead, Christine (1983). *Ta'lîkî-zâde's Şehnâme-i hümâyun, A History of the Ottoman Campaign into Hungary 1593–94* (Berlin: Klaus Schwarz).

Woods, John E. (1976). *The Aqquyunlu, Clan, Confederation, Empire, A Study in 15th/19th Century Turko-Iranian Politics* (Minneapolis and Chicago: Bibliotheca Islamica).

Wurm, Heidrun (1971). *Der osmanische Historiker Hüseyn b. Ğafer, genannt Hezârfenn und die Istanbuler Gesellschaft in der zweiten Hälfte des 17. Jahrhunderts* (Freiburg: Klaus Schwarz Verlag). (Still the standard work on an interesting figure).

Yates, Frances (1975). *Astraea: The Imperial Theme in the Sixteenth Century* (London: Ark Paperbacks). (By a scholar working in the tradition of Aby Warburg, on French and English parades of the 16th century; inspiring).

Yavuz, Hulûsi (1984). *Kâbe ve Haremeyn için Yemen'de Osmanlı Hâkimiyeti (1517–1571)* (Istanbul: n.p.). (On the basis of documents in the Mühimme registers).

Yérasimos, Stephane (1990). *La Fondation de Constantinople et de Sainte-Sophie dans les traditions turques* (Istanbul and Paris: Institut Français d'Études Anatoliennes und Librairie d'Amérique et d'Orient). (A stimulating interpretation of late 15th-century intra-Ottoman political conflict concerning the fate of Istanbul).

Yérasimos, Stephane (1991). *Les voyageurs dans l'Empire ottoman (XIVe–XVIe siècles), Bibliographie, itinéraires et inventaire des lieux habités* (Ankara: Türk Tarih Kurumu). (Much more than the title indicates: introduces travel accounts as source material for cultural history).

Yérasimos, Stephane (1995). 'La communauté juive d' Istanbul à la fin du XVIe siècle', *Turcica*, 27: 101–30.

Yılmaz, Serap (1992). 'Osmanlı İmparatorluğunun Doğu ile Ekonomik İlişkileri: XVIII. Yüzyılın İkinci Yarısında Osmanlı-Hind Ticareti ile İlgili bir Araştırma', *Belleten*, LVI, 215: 31–68. (On 18th-century trade between the Ottoman Empire and India).

Yinanç, Refet (1989). *Dulkadir Beyliği* (Ankara: Atatürk Kültür, Dil ve Tarih Yüksek Kurumu).

Young, I. (1965). 'Russia', in A. Goodwin (ed.), *The New Cambridge Modern History*, Vol. VIII: *The American and French Revolutions 1763–93*, (Cambridge: Cambridge University Press): 306–32.

Zach, Cornelius (1987). 'Über Klosterleben und Klosterreformen in der Moldau und in der Walachei im 17. Jahrhundert', in Kálmán Bénda *et alii* (eds), *Forschungen über Siebenbürgen und seine Nachbarn, Festschrift für Atilla T. Szabó und Zsigmund Jakó* (Munich: Dr Dr Rudolf Trofenik): 111–22

Zarinebaf-Shahr, Fariba (1991). 'Tabriz under Ottoman Rule (1725–1730)' (unpublished doctoral dissertation, University of Chicago).

Zeller, Gaston (1955). 'Une légende qui a la vie dure: Les capitulations de 1535', *Revue d'Histoire Moderne et Contemporaine*, 2: 127–32.

Zhelyazkova, Antonina (2002). 'Islamization in the Balkans as a Historiographical Problem: the Southeast European Perspective', in Fikret Adanır and Suraiya Faroqhi (eds), *Ottoman Historiography: Turkey and Southeastern Europe*, (Leiden: E. J. Brill): 223–66.

Zilfi, Madeline (1988). *The Politics of Piety, The Ottoman Ulema in the Classical Age* (Minneapolis: Bibliotheca Islamica).

Zilfi, Madeline (1993). 'A *Medrese* for the Palace: Ottoman Dynastic Legitimation in the Eighteenth Century', *Journal of the American Oriental Society*, CXIII.

Zilfi, Madeline (1995). 'Ibrahim Paşa and the Women', in Daniel Panzac (ed.), *Histoire économique et sociale de l'Empire ottoman et de la Turquie (1326–1960)*, (Louvain and Paris: Peeters): 555–9.

Zilfi, Madeline (1996). 'Women and Society in the Tulip Era, 1718–1730', in Amira Al-Azhary Sonbol (ed.), *Women, the Family and Divorce Laws in Islamic History*, (Syracuse: Syracuse University Press): 290–306.

Zilfi, Madeline (2000). 'Goods in the *Mahalle*: Distributional Encounters in Eighteenth Century Istanbul', in Donald Quataert (ed.), *Consumption Studies and the History of the Ottoman Empire, 1550–1922, an Introduction,* (Albany, NY SUNY Press): 289–312.

Zygulski, Zdzisław (1999). 'The Impact of the Orient on the Culture of Old Poland', in Jan Ostrowski *et alii*, *Land of the Winged Horseman, Art in Poland 1572–1764* (Alexandria, VA: Art Service International with Yale University Press): 69–80.

~ Notes

The notes only contain references to publications. Some of these have been mined for factual information, while others are sources and secondary works discussed for their intellectual content. Given the format of the notes it is not possible to distinguish between the two categories without consulting the works in question.

The following abbreviations have been used in the notes:

EI: *Encyclopedia of Islam*

İA: *İslam Ansiklopedisi*

MD: Mühimme Defterleri (Chancery registers, in the Başbakanlık Arşivi-Osmanlı Arşivi, Istanbul).

1 ~ Introduction

1 I use the term 'Ottomanist' for scholars of whatever nationality who have studied the Ottoman Empire according to the criteria current in twentieth-century historiography, in contradistinction to those who have done so within the parameters of Ottoman civilization itself. The latter will be called 'Ottoman.' When the word 'empire' is capitalized, the Ottoman Empire is always intended.

2 Fodor, reprint 2000.

3 Güçer, 1964 and Finkel, 1988.

4 Düzdağ, 1972: 109–12.

5 'Imtiyâzât', in *EI*, 2nd edn.

6 Inalcik, 1969.

7 Fischer, reprint 1994; Aktepe, 1958; Abou-El-Haj, 1984 and Piterberg, 2003.

8 Kunt, 1974.

9 See Abou-El-Haj, 1974a.

10 Eickhoff, 2nd edn 1988: 20.

11 Sella, 1968b.

12 Fleischer, 1986: 49–54.

13 Pedani Fabris, 1994b; Goffman, 2002.

14 Compare Göçek, 1987.

15 Goffman, 1998: 10–12.

16 De Bonnac, 1894: 50.

17 Pedani Fabris, 2000.

18 De Groot, 1978: 60–1.

19 Hering, 1968: 30–59.

20 Poumarède, 1997.

21 Murphey, 1999.

22 See also Finkel, 1988 and Ágoston, 1993 and 1994.

23 Goffman, 2002: 1–4.
24 Steensgaard, 1978.
25 Tilly, 1985.
26 Kołodziejczyk, 2000.
27 Fleischer, 1986 and Abou-El-Haj 1991.
28 Evliya, 1995: 85.
29 Dürr, Engel and Süßmann (eds), 2003.
30 Pedani Fabris, 2000.
31 Viallon, 1995: 217–26.
32 Kretschmayr, 1896; Szakály, 1995.
33 Compare Matuz, 1992 and Poumarède, 1998.
34 Kafadar, 1986b.
35 Curtin, 1984; Veinstein, 1975 and Nagata, 1997; see also Smyrnelis, unpublished.
36 Erim, 1991.
37 Goffman, 2002: 9–12.
38 See Haase-Dubosc, 1999.
39 Hochedlinger, 2003.
40 Farooqi, 1988.
41 Raymond, 1973–4, Vol. 1: 107–64.
42 Orhonlu, 1974.
43 Güçer, 1949–50; Faroqhi, 1998.
44 Seyyidî 'Alî Re'îs, 1999: 28–31.
45 See Veinstein, 2003.
46 Düzdağ, 1972; Imber, 1997; Majer, 1969; Zilfi, 1988.
47 Pamuk, 2000: 18.
48 Braudel, 1979, Vol. 3: 16.
49 Aymard, 1966: 125–40.
50 Braudel, 1979, Vol. 3: 402–16.
51 Valensi, 1969; Sadok, 1987: 134–5; Faroqhi, 1994: 164–6.
52 Braudel, 1979, Vol. 3: 16.
53 Ibid.: 14–63.
54 Ibid.: 17.
55 Ibid.: 16.
56 Finkel, 1988, Vol. 1: 42.
57 Compare Bayly, 1983: 62–3.
58 See Braudel, 1979, Vol. 3: 17–21.
59 Raymond, 1973–4; Hanna, 1998.
60 Braudel, 1979, Vol. 3: 20.
61 Goffman, 2002: 134–5.
62 Eldem, 1999: 148–226.
63 See Goffman, 1998: 10–11.
64 Darling, 2001.
65 Evliya, 1990; Dankoff, 1990 1991.
66 See Abu-Husayn, 1985; Chérif, 1984; 1987; Singer, 1994 and 2002; Hathaway, 1997; Khoury, 1997; Masters, 2001; Raymond, 1973–4, 1995 and 1998; Sadok, 1987; Frangakis-Syrett, 1992; Goffman, 1990a; Greene, 2000; Ülker, 1987; Dávid and Fodor (eds), 1994; Dávid and Gerelyes, 1999 and Dávid and Fodor, 2002.

67 Khoury, 1997; Abdullah, 2000.
68 Baghdiantz McCabe, 1999; Rozen, 2002; Hanna, 1998; Dale, 1994.
69 Hiltebrand, 1937: 82ff.
70 See Pedani Fabris, 2002.
71 Kołodziejczyk, 2000: 57–67.
72 Hochedlinger, 2003.
73 Inalcik, 1979.
74 Said, 1978: *passim.*
75 Tinguely, 2000 and Grafton, 2000.
76 Yérasimos, 1991: 17–20; Tinguely, 2000: 36.
77 Eren, 1960.
78 Evliya, 1987: 238–40, 131 and 64.
79 Busbequius, 1994: 103 and 179; Valensi, 1987: 33.
80 Jardine, 1996; Jardine and Brotton, 2000; Howard, 2000; Mack, 2002.
81 Valensi, 1987: 98.
82 Mack, 2002.
83 Brotton, 2002: 3.
84 Kuran, 1987: 245–6.
85 Fleischer, 1986; Schmidt, 1992; Stoye, 1994; Wurm, 1971 and Galland, reprint 2002.
86 Fink, 1991: 117–18.
87 Greene, 2000: 11–12.
88 See Stoye, 1994: 137–215.

2 ~ On sovereignty and subjects

1 Abou-El-Haj, 1991.
2 Aksan, 1993 and 1995.
3 ['Azîz Efendi], 1985.
4 Hadrovics, 1947: 127. Compare the article 'Imtiyâzât' in *EI*, 2nd edn.
5 Smyrnelis, 1999.
6 De Bonnac, 1894: 138.
7 Hering, 1968: 42–3.
8 Mehmed Efendi, 1981; Göçek, 1987.
9 Fleming, 1999; Fahmi, 1997: 4–7.
10 Veinstein, 2003.
11 Khoury, 1997: 76–7.
12 Inalcik, 1980.
13 Togan, 1992.
14 Neumann, 1993.
15 Binark, 1993, 1994, 1995, 1996; Yıldırım 1997; Collective work, 1992.
16 Nouzille, 1991: 228–9.
17 Young, 1965: 325–8.
18 Szakály, 1986; Dávid and Fodor, 2002; Shaw, 1962: 286–305; Hathaway, 1997.
19 Uebersberger, 1913: 317.

20 Hiestand, 1996; Hoensch, 1998: 77–96; Kołodziejczyk, 2000: 99–128; Lane, 1973: 234–37; Heers, 1961.
21 Dávid and Fodór, 2000.
22 Schulin, 1999; Parker, 1998.
23 Poumarède, 1997.
24 Lane, 1973: 245–8; Inalcik, 1977.
25 Woods, 1976.
26 Nasuhü's-silahî, 1976.
27 Delumeau, 1967: 144–70; Elton (ed.), 1958: 70–250.
28 Fennell, 1958: 543–61.
29 Hering, 1968: 273–81; Peri, 2001.
30 Gronke, 1993.
31 Refik, 1932.
32 Eberhard, 1970: 33; Necipoğlu, 1986b.
33 Mélikoff, 1975; Clayer, 1994: 63–112.
34 Hammer[-Purgstall], 1828, Vol. 3: 326.
35 Von Mende, 1989: 2; Sohrweide, 1965; Eberhard, 1970: 25–44; Imber, 1979; Allouche, 1983; B. Kütükoğlu, 2nd edn 1993: 236–41.
36 Lesure, 1986: 43ff.
37 Ibid.: 45.
38 Busbecq, 1968; Busbequius, 1994; Dernschwam, 1923.
39 Rothenberg, 1970: 35–6.
40 Fleischer, 1992; Evliya Çelebi, 1987.
41 Köhbach, 1994.
42 Fisher, 1977: 241–59.
43 Hess, 1972.
44 Temimi, 1989: 19–22; Costantini, 2001.
45 MD 26: 51–2, nos 132–3 (982/1574–5); see also Vatin, 2001.
46 Parry, 1958: 532.
47 Poumarède, 1997.
48 Hassiotis, 1977.
49 Sahillioğlu, 1985b.
50 Inalcik, 1948.
51 Ibid. and Bennigsen and Lemercier-Quelquejay, 1976.
52 Farooqi, 1988. See MD 28: 139, no. 331 (984/1576–7).
53 Richards, 1993: 15.
54 MD 14: 385, no. 542 (978/1570–1).
55 Faroqhi, 1994: 137–9.
56 Fleischer, 1986: 154–9.
57 Dávid and Fodor, 2002: 314–18.
58 Hering, 1968: 24.
59 Hering, 1968.
60 Lesure, 1972 and Bartl, 1974.
61 Hering, 1968: 6–7.
62 Ibid.: 2–4.
63 Ersanlı, 2002: 117; Berktay, 1991.
64 Herzog, 1996.
65 Köprülü, 1959: 67–83.

66 Mousnier, 1971a; Wacquet, 1984; Hathaway, 1997 and Khoury, 1997.
67 Hering, 1968; Goffman 1990b; Bracewell, 1992; Goffman, 1998; Peri, 2001.
68 Bode, 1979: 69 and 154, n. 294.
69 Duchhardt, 1997: 172–87.
70 Abou-el-Haj, 1974b; Kunt, 1983.
71 Peri, 2001.
72 Tapu ve Kadastro Arşivi, Ankara, Kuyudu kadime no. 110, fols 143b–146a (991/1583–4).
73 Sohrweide, 1965: 171–83.
74 Köprülü, 1935: 36; Gölpnarlı, 1963: 86–7.
75 Faroqhi, 1993a; see also MD 78: 81, no. 212 (1018/1609–10).
76 Inalcik, 1975; Ilgürel, 1979; Jennings, 1980.
77 MD 78: 882, no. 4007 (1018/1609–10).
78 MD 48: 121, no. 323 (990/1582).
79 Hadrovics, 1947: 124–7; Tchentsova, 1998 (important).
80 Ibid.; Preto, 1999.
81 Bartl, 1974; MD 30: 161, no. 380 (985/1577–8).
82 Lesure, 1972: 67–9.
83 MD 27: 20, no. 60 (983/1575–6). Uzunçarşılı, 1972: 23; Faroqhi, 1994: 156–63; Kortepeter, 1979.
84 Yavuz, 1984.
85 Özbaran, 1994b: 52–4.
86 Ibid.: 65.
87 Fleischer, 1986: 47–53.
88 Yavuz, 1984.
89 Papa Synadinos, 1996: 93–5.
90 Andreasyan, 1976.
91 B. Kütükoğlu, 2nd edn 1993; Kırzıoğlu, 1976.
92 'Azîz Efendi, 1985: 12–18.
93 Kołodziejczyk, 2000; MD 5: 35, no. 83 (973/1565–6); MD 22: 110, no. 225 (981/1573–4).
94 Nowak, reprint 1978 and Czapliński, reprint 1978.
95 Uebersberger, 1913: 21–3.
96 Stepánek, 2001; Faroqhi, 1969 and Orhonlu, 1970.
97 Sella, 1968b.
98 Lane, 1973: 297–304, 334, 384ff.; Sella, 1968a and 1968b.
99 Steensgaard, 1967.
100 Kissling, 1977 and Hassiotis, 1977.
101 Aigen, 1980: 7; Greene, 2000: 74–5, 172ff.
102 Bartl, 1974: 179–89.
103 Compare Tapu ve Kadastro Arşivi, Ankara, Kuyudu kadime no. 167, fol. 3bff.
104 Faroqhi, 1984: 75–103; Goffman, 1990a: 9–24.
105 Faroqhi, 1984: 102–3.
106 Ibid.: 120.
107 Braudel, 2nd edn 1966, Vol. 2: 451ff.
108 Matthee, 1999: 42, 224–5; Baghdiantz McCabe, 1999: 115–40.
109 Matthee, 1999: 144.
110 Goffman, 1990: 52–3; Çizakça, reprint 1987.

111   Abdel Nour, 1982: 278–9.
112   Wallerstein, Decdeli and Kasaba, 1987.
113   For variant interpretations: Islamoğlu-Inan, 1987; Quataert, 1993. See Chapter 9, below.
114   Braudel, 1979, Vol. 3: 16; Aymard, 1966: 125–40.
115   Roemer, 1986; see also the article 'Tabrīz', in *EI*, 2nd edn.
116   Wittram, 1964, Vol. 2: 488.
117   Sumner, 1949: 79.
118   Cantemir, 1734, 1743 and 1973b; Pappas, 1991.
119   Rothenberg, 1970: 71.
120   Skilliter, 1976; Tchentsova, 1998: 393.
121   Veselà, 1961; Szakály, 1986: 23–4.
122   Szakály, 1986: 126–8; Abou-El-Haj, 1984: 22 and 54.
123   Nouzille, 1991: 91.
124   Ibid.: 93; Zhelyalzkova, 2002.
125   Nouzille, 1991: 92ff.
126   Abou-El-Haj, 1974a and 1984: 22.
127   Szakály, 1986: 93 and 102.
128   Eickhoff, 2nd edn 1988: 428; Gregorovius, reprint n.d.: 572.
129   Topping, 1972.
130   Compare the article 'Mora', in *İA*.
131   Gradeva, 2001: 153–62.
132   Genç, 1975.
133   Orhonlu, 1967: 53, 73, 103 and 108.
134   Başbakanlık Arşivi-Osmanlı Arşivi, section Anadolu Ahkâm Defterleri 35: 250, no. 753 (1174/1760–1).
135   Dalsar, 1960: 131–4.
136   Bağış, 1983: 18–32.
137   Frangakis-Syrett, 1992: 59.
138   Pedani Fabris, 1994b: 53–4.
139   Bağış, 1983: 29.
140   Valensi, 1987: 123–5 and 91–111.
141   Cantemir, 1734.
142   Veinstein, 1975.
143   Stoianovich, 1960: 269ff.
144   Paris, 1957: 574–8.
145   Göyünç, 1976.
146   Inalcik, 1980; McGowan, 1981: 60–1.
147   Inalcik, 1997: 144.
148   Nagata, 1997: 114.
149   Veinstein, 1975.
150   Nouzille, 1991: 203–54.
151   Ibid.: 246.
152   Uebersberger, 1913: 248–9.
153   Compare the article 'Belgrad', in *EI*, 2nd edn.
154   Aksan, 1995: 195–6.
155   Bilici, 1992: 104–37.
156   Uebersberger, 1913: 346–9.

157 Beydilli, 1985.
158 Beydilli, 1985: 97–107; Hochedlinger, 2003.
159 Duchhardt, 1997: 7–18; Uebersberger, 1913: 302–38.
160 Duchhardt, 1997: 121; Uebersberger, 1913: 318.
161 Ibid.: 318 and 362–8.
162 Sofroni von Vratsa, 2nd edn 1979.
163 Ibid.: 62–5.
164 Griswold, 1983: 78-85 and 110–56; see also the article 'Fakhr al-Dīn Ma'n', in *EI*, 2nd edn.
165 Masson, 1911: 142 and *passim*.
166 Veinstein, 1975.
167 Akarlı, 1988.
168 Mantran, 1962: 179; Eldem, 1999: 131–40.
169 Ibid.: 129.
170 Ibid.: 284–8.
171 Raymond, 1973–4, Vol. 1: 98–100, 240; Fukasawa, 1987; Genç, 1987.
172 Genç, 1984.
173 Ülgener, reprint 1981: 65–94 and *passim*.
174 Inalcik, 1969: 135–9.
175 Genç, 1984.
176 Rafeq, 1970: 198–9, 214–15.
177 Ibid.: 214–19; Barbir, 1980.
178 See the articles 'Ibn 'Abd al-Wahhāb' and 'Al-Su'ūd', in *EI*, 2nd edn.
179 Imber, 1997: 67–9.
180 Uebersberger, 1913: 309.
181 Szákaly, 1986: 28; Aksan, 1995: 198–200.
182 Duchhardt, 1997: 132.
183 Abou-El-Haj, 1983.

3 ~ At the margins of empire: clients and dependants

1 Inalcik, 1954.
2 Kafadar, 1995: 122–8.
3 Barkan, 1939.
4 Arens, 2001: 151.
5 Yinanç, 1989: 104–5.
6 'Ramazan-oğulları', in *İA*.
7 Arens, 2001: 22.
8 Dávid and Fódor, 2002.
9 Arens, 2001: 10.
10 M. Kütükoğlu, 1994: 100–8; Pedani Fabris, 1994a: 307.
11 Maxim, reprint 1999a: 188.
12 Arens, 2001; Várkonyi, 1987.
13 Pitcher, 1972: map XXIV; Abdullah, 2000: 10.
14 Greene, 2000: 175–9.
15 Dávid and Fodor, 2002: 324.

16 Yavuz, 1984: 92ff.
17 Braudel, 2nd edn 1966, Vol. 1: 165–6.
18 Akarlı, 1988.
19 Faroqhi, reprint 1987.
20 Abu-Husayn, 1985.
21 Ibid.: 167–8.
22 Dávid and Fodor, 2002.
23 Costin, 1980: 20–32; Cantemir, reprint 1973a; Hoffmann, 1974; Hiltebrandt, 1937: 82ff. and Wilkinson, reprint 1971.
24 Compare the article 'Khayr el-Dīn Pasha', in *EI*, 2nd edn.
25 Compare the article 'Algeria, Turkish period', in *EI*, 2nd edn.
26 Faroqhi, 1971.
27 Chérif, 1984, 1987, Vol. 1: 124–5.
28 Panzac, 1999: 26–7.
29 Ibid.: 14.
30 Haedo, reprint 1998: 7–16.
31 Abou-El-Haj, 1974b and Kunt, 1981.
32 On the situation in Egypt: Hathaway, 1997 and Raymond, 1995.
33 Wüstenfeld, reprint 1981, Vol. IV; Uzunçarşılı, 1972; Shaw (ed.), 1968; Farooqi, 1988.
34 Fleischer, 1986: 276.
35 Hinds and Ménage, 1991.
36 Ibn Jubayr, 1952: 71–2.
37 Wüstenfeld, reprint 1981, Vol. IV: 304–5.
38 Uzunçarşılı, 1972: 23; Faroqhi, 1994: 66.
39 MD 58: 201, no. 527 (993/1585).
40 Kortepeter, 1979.
41 Evliya Çelebi, 1314/1896–7 to 1938, Vol. 9: 679.
42 Raymond, 1973–4, Vol. 1: 132–3; Evliya Çelebi, 1314/1896–7 to 1938, Vol. 9: 796.
43 Faroqhi, 1993b.
44 Faroqhi, 1994, p. 43.
45 Wüstenfeld, reprint 1981, Vol. IV: 304–5.
46 Faroqhi, 1994: 48–52.
47 Evliya Çelebi, 1314/1896–7 to 1938, Vol. 9: 584–5.
48 Hibri, 1975, 1976, 1978.
49 Barbir, 1980: 175–6.
50 Compare the article 'Ḥadd', in *EI*, 2nd edn.
51 Uzunçarşılı, 1972: 86f.
52 Evliya Çelebi, 1314/1896–7 to 1938, Vol. 9: 702.
53 Kortepeter, 1972: 236.
54 Farooqi, 1988.
55 MD 39: 238, no. 471 (988/1580–1); Farooqi, 1988.
56 Farooqi, 1988; Evliya Çelebi, 1314/1896–7 to 1938, Vol. 9: 772.
57 Subrahmanyam, 1988.
58 Fleischer, 1986: 180–87; Evliya Çelebi, 1314/1896–7 to 1938, Vol. 9: 796 calls the governor a *paşa*.
59 Biegman, 1967; Faroqhi, 1984: 105–21.

60 Revere, 1957.
61 Gascon, 1971, Vol. 1: 49, 50 and 339–40; Curtin, 1984.
62 Argenti, 1954, Vol. 3.
63 Biegman, 1967: 27; Carter, 1972: 355.
64 Ibid.: 349–404.
65 Ibid.: 354.
66 Biegman, 1967: 35.
67 Carter, 1972: 379.
68 Biegman, 1967: 129.
69 Carter, 1972: 346–7.
70 Pedani Fabris, 1994a: 322; Faroqhi, 2002.
71 Biegman, 1967: 130–1.
72 The title of Costin, 1980 is the source for this heading.
73 Ibid.: 178.
74 Berindei and Veinstein, 1987: 47; Maxim, reprint 1999a suggests the reign of
    Süleyman the Magnificent. But a booklet put out by Dariusz Kołodziejczyk,
    'Exhibition of Ottoman and Crimean Documents' for the CIÉPO 16 (Warsaw:
    n.p., 2004), no. 9 refers to a document dated 1455 in which the sultan demands a
    tribute (Polish State Archives, A6AD, AKW Dz. tur. k. 66, t. 1, nr.1).
75 Ibid.: 192.
76 Ibid.: 195.
77 Maxim, reprint 1999a: 192.
78 Ibid.: 194–7; Costin, 1980: 20–7, 295.
79 Cantemir, reprint 1973a: 260.
80 Subtelny, 1991: 293–7.
81 Cantemir, reprint 1973a: 262–5.
82 Ibid.: 260.
83 Compare the article 'Mamlūk', in EI, 2nd edn and Toledano, 1990: 56–9.
    Thanks to Christoph Neumann for this reference.
84 Dankoff, 1991: 8–9.
85 Costin, 1980: 160; Kortepeter, 1972.
86 Maxim, reprint 1999a: 161, 195.
87 Cantemir, reprint 1973a: 245.
88 Ibid.: 239.
89 Ibid.: 186–208 and 260–70.
90 Ibid.: 242.
91 Kortepeter, 1972: 232.
92 Zach, 1987.
93 Cantemir, reprint 1973a: 320–9.
94 Wilkinson, reprint 1971: 60.
95 Ibid.: 75–7.
96 Schaser, 1993: 984–5.
97 Wilkinson, reprint 1971: 171.
98 Costin, 1980: 198 and elsewhere.
99 Ibid.: 167.
100 Schaser, 1993: 990.
101 Evliya Çelebi, 1995: 246.
102 Kortepeter, 1972: 144–5 and 218–19.
103 Salzmann, 1993.

4 ~ The strengths and weaknesses of Ottoman warfare

1 Majoros and Rill, 1994: 28–30; Ágoston, 1999: 127.
2 Murphey, 1999.
3 Ibid.: 141–6.
4 Eickhoff, 2nd edn 1988: 50ff.
5 Kortepeter, 1972, Murphey, 1980 and B. Kütükoğlu, 2nd edn 1993.
6 Berkes, 1969, 1970, Vol. 1: 28–9; Abrahamowicz, 1983.
7 Inalcik, 1969: 135–40.
8 Quataert, 1993, *passim.*
9 Murphey, 1999: 147.
10 Redlich, 1956: 74 and elsewhere.
11 Redlich, 1956.
12 Dankoff, 2004.
13 Redlich, 1956: 56 and 67.
14 Köhbach, 1983 and Petritsch, 1983.
15 Barkan, 1951–3: 11.
16 Inalcik, 1960, 1969, 1997; Raymond, 1973–4; Hanna, 1998 and Dursteler, 2002: against Stoianovich, 1960.
17 Braudel, 1979, Vol. 3: 402–16.
18 Dale, 1994.
19 Busbecquius, 1994: 165, 177.
20 Vatin and Veinstein 2003: 99–109.
21 Busbecquius, 1994: 267.
22 Kretschmayr, 1896.
23 Duchhardt, 1997: 396, on the end of Venetian rule in 1715.
24 Arens, 2001.
25 Redlich, 1964–5.
26 Ibid., Vol. 2: 14–19 and Allmeyer-Beck and Lessing, 1978: 237–8.
27 Ibid.: 176; Redlich, 1964–5, Vol. 2: 154; Abrahamowicz, 1983: 33.
28 Lane, 1973: 386–7, 391–2.
29 Schulze, 1978, *passim.*
30 Duchhardt, 1997: 80–1.
31 Kortepeter, 1972, *passim.*
32 Kołodziejczyk, 2000: 137.
33 Hauser, 1930: 62.
34 Stoye, 1994: 247–50.
35 Heilingsetzer, 1988: 131–2; Allmeyer-Beck and Lessing, 1978: 213.
36 Stoye, 1994: 238–52.
37 Barkan, 1975; Barkey, 1994.
38 Genç, 1975.
39 Genç, 1987.
40 Inalcik, 1980.
41 Inalcik, 1973: 107–18.
42 Kunt, 1981.
43 Inalcik, 1980.
44 Doğru, 1990: 114, 140–1.
45 Barkan, 1972, 1979, Vol. 1: 130–1; Sahillioğlu (ed.), 2002: 309 (No. 426).

46 Fleischer, 1986: 5–7.
47 See Finkel, 1988, Vol. 1: 36–7, 173–8, on cost-cutting in the Ottoman army.
48 Faroqhi, 1984: 129–30.
49 Akarlı, 1986.
50 Çağatay, 1971; Faroqhi, 1984: 233–9.
51 Tabakoğlu, 1985: no loans mentioned.
52 M. Kütükoğlu, 1983.
53 Güçer, 1964.
54 Aynural 2002: 5–84.
55 Braude, 1979.
56 Faroqhi, 1984: 127.
57 Veinstein, 1988.
58 Bostan, 1992: 199ff.
59 Aktepe, 1958: 94–5.
60 Genç, 1984.
61 Murphey, 1999: 179–84.
62 Ágoston, 1994.
63 Allmayer-Beck and Lessing, 1978: 235;.
64 Duchhardt, 1997: 52.
65 Güçer, 1964; Finkel, 1988; Ágoston, 1993 and 1994.
66 Konyalı, 1974, Vol. 1: 851.
67 Ágoston, 1993: 87.
68 Hale, reprint 1998: 217–18.
69 Stoye, reprint 2000: 156.
70 Ágoston, 1999.
71 Dávid and Gerelyes, 1999.
72 Dávid and Gerelyes, 1999; Dávid and Fódor, 2002.
73 Gerelyes, 1990–2.
74 See Chapter 3, section on Moldavia.
75 Binark et alii (eds), 1993, Özet ve Transkripsyon: 640; Vatin, 2001.
76 Kortepeter, 1972, passim.
77 Imber, 1997: 84–6; Düzdağ, 1972.
78 Kołodziejczyk, 2000; 129.
79 Bennigsen et alii, 1978.
80 Compare the article 'Idris Bitlisi', in İA.
81 Evliya Çelebi, 1990, passim.
82 Faroqhi, 1984: 52.
83 Gürbüz, 2001.
84 Göyünç, 1969; Bacqué-Grammont, 1981.
85 Fleischer, 1986: 66.
86 Kunt, 1974, Fleischer, 1986: 165.
87 Fleischer, 1986: 65.
88 Salzmann, 1993.
89 Braudel, 1979, Vol. 3: 47.
90 Adanır, 1982.
91 Goffman, 1998: 52.
92 Eickhoff, 2nd edn 1988: 426–34.
93 Jelavich, 1983: 77.

94 Ibid.: 73–8.
95 For a conspectus of the – enormous – secondary literature: Teply, 1983.
96 Hale, 1998: 46; Guilmartin, 1974: 229ff.
97 Evliya Çelebi, 1314/1896–7 to 1938, Vol. 9: 821.
98 Guilmartin, 1974: 98–109.
99 Davies, 1999.
100 Chagniot, 2001.
101 Abou-El-Haj, 1974a.
102 Faroqhi, 1986.
103 Kal'a *et alii* (eds), 1997–.

5 ~ Of prisoners, slaves and the charity of strangers

1 Overmans, 1999b: 486.
2 Overmans, 1999a, *passim*.
3 Rüpke, 1999.
4 Overmans, 1999b: 506; Spies, 1968; Teply, 1973; Jahn, 1963.
5 Streit, 1978.
6 Anderson, reprint 1998.
7 Hohrath, 1999.
8 Heberer von Bretten, reprint 1963: X.
9 McCarthy, 1995.
10 Panzac, 1999: 81.
11 Panaite, 2000: 283–301.
12 Pedani Fabris, 1994b: 179–85; Faroqhi, 2002; Gökbilgin, 1964: 211–12.
13 Tietze, 1942.
14 Bracewell, 1992.
15 Ibid.: 187–9.
16 Berktay, 1990.
17 Faroqhi, 1984: 108.
18 Ibid.: 100–1.
19 Stoye, 1994: 20–1.
20 De Martelli, 1689: *passim*.
21 Panzac, 1999 and Bono, 1999.
22 Parmaksızoğlu, 1953 and Neumann, unpublished manuscript.
23 Jahn, 1961; Spies, 1968 and Teply, 1973.
24 Bono, 1999: 21–36.
25 Pedani Fabris, 1994b: 168–9; Preto, 1999: 348–60.
26 Panzac, 1999: 97–103; Bono, 1999: *passim*.
27 Osman Ağa, trans. by Kreutel and Spies, 1962; and trans. by Hitzel, 2001.
28 De Martelli, 1689.
29 Heberer von Bretten, reprint 1963: 164; Vatin, 2002.
30 Guilmartin, 1974: 111–18.
31 Heberer von Bretten, reprint 1963: 164–5.
32 For an exception: Matar, 1999: 20.
33 Bono, 1999: 482–6.

34 Ibid.: 497–9.
35 Guilmartin, 1974: 223 and 268.
36 Heberer von Bretten, reprint 1963: 179–80.
37 Ibid.: XXXV–XXXVI.
38 Rauwolff, reprint 1971: 358.
39 Singer, 2002.
40 Kreiser, reprint 1998.
41 Heberer von Bretten, reprint 1963: 158–9.
42 Ibid.: XXVII–XXIX, 296–7, 323–4.
43 Ibid.: 191ff.
44 Ibid.: 219.
45 Ibid.: 249.
46 Wild, reprint 1964: 240–6.
47 De Martelli, 1689: 86.
48 Ibid.: 97.
49 Ibid.: 86.
50 Bennassar and Bennassar, 1989: 362.
51 Webbe, 1895.
52 Sahillioğlu, 1985b.
53 Heberer von Bretten, reprint 1963: *passim*.
54 Ibid.: 245.
55 Ibid.: 243 and elsewhere.
56 Vigié, 1985: 225.
57 Teply, 1973: 60.
58 Spies, 1968.
59 Skilliter, 1975.
60 Osman Ağa, 1962: 147ff.
61 Bono, 1999: 252–304. Teply, 1973: 63.
62 Bennassar and Bennassar, 1989: 125–44.
63 De Martelli, 1689: 109 and 133.
64 Ibid.: 110.
65 Teply, 1973.

6 ~ Trade and foreigners

1 Inalcik, 1969; Başbakanlık Arşivi-Osmanlı Arşivi Maliyeden müdevver 6004: 49 (1033/1623–4).
2 Kunt, 1977.
3 Kafadar, 1986b; Arbel, 1995.
4 Faroqhi, 2002.
5 Sahillioğlu, 1968.
6 Evliya Çelebi, 1314/1896–7 to 1938, Vol. 9: 804–5; Faroqhi, 1991.
7 Inalcik, 1981; Veinstein, 1999.
8 Raymond, 1973–74, Vol. 1: 117.
9 Binark *et alii* (eds), 1995: MD 6: 166, no. 355 (972/1564–5).
10 Binark *et alii* (eds), 1994: MD 5: 629, no. 1755 (973/1565–6).

11 Dale, 1994.
12 Dalsar, 1960: 132–6.
13 Herzig, 1996.
14 Herzig, 1996.
15 Aghassian and Kévonian, 1999.
16 Bergasse and Rambert, 1954: 64–70; Khachikian, 1967; Aghassian and Kévonian, 1999; Kévonian, 1975; Braudel, 1979, Vol. 2: 133; Dziubinski, 1999.
17 Kévonian, 1975: 210.
18 Smyrnelis, 1995.
19 Sahillioğlu, 1968.
20 Ibid.: 68.
21 Dale, 1994: 46–54; Subrahmanyam, 1988.
22 Bennigsen and Lemercier-Quelquejay, 1970.
23 Yıldırım *et alii* (eds), 1997: MD 7: 62, no. 169 (975–6/1567–9).
24 Ibid.
25 Kévonian, 1975.
26 Lane, 1973: 298.
27 Greene, 2000.
28 Arbel, 1995: 15; Pedani Fabris, 1994b.
29 Layton, 1994.
30 Çizakça, reprint 1987: 253; Poni, 1982.
31 Aigen, 1980: 12ff.
32 Sella, 1968.
33 Turan, 1968; Kafadar, 1986b and Concina, 1997; Arbel, 1995: 66; Kafadar, 1986b: 212.
34 Aigen, 1980.
35 Lane, 1973: 248.
36 Başbakanlık Arşivi-Osmanlı Arşivi, section Maliyeden müdevver, no. 6004: 10 (1029/1619–20).
37 Maliyeden müdevver 6004: 140 (undated).
38 Maliyeden müdevver 6004: 49 (1033/1623–4).
39 Maliyeden müdevver 9829: 8.
40 Steensgaard, 1967.
41 Beydilli, 1976: 19–48.
42 Binark *et alii* (eds), 1995: MD 6: 93, no. 194 (972/1564–5).
43 Biedrońska-Słota, 1999.
44 Zygulski, 1999.
45 Ergenç, 1975.
46 Istanbul, Başbakanlık Arşivi/ Osmanlı Arşivi, Maliyeden müdevver, no. 7527: 69.
47 Kołodziejczyk, 2003.
48 Biedrońska-Słota, 1999.
49 Kołodziejczyk, 2003.
50 Dziubinski, 1999.
51 MD 27: 361, no. 861; MD 28: 214, no. 502; 215, no. 504; 373, no. 966; 374, no. 967; 375, no. 970; 377, no. 975; 386, no. 1003; 393, no. 1024 (all from 984/1576–7). Akdağ, 1963: 89 and Faroqhi, 1984: 67–8.
52 Biedrońska-Słota, 1999.

53 De Groot, 1978: 94ff.
54 Lane, 1973: 399–400.
55 Poumarède, 1997 and 1998.
56 Eickhoff, 2nd edn, 1988: 212–13, 250–9.
57 Gascon, 1977, Vol. 1: 326–8.
58 Poumarède, 1997: 244.
59 Goubert, 1977, Vol. 2: 329–66.
60 Davis, 1967: 242ff.
61 Marquié, 1993.
62 Paris, 1957: 9–35.
63 Marquié, 1993: 76–81.
64 Greene, 2000: 75–7.
65 Panzac, 1999: 124–7.
66 Stoianovich, 1960.
67 Steensgaard, 1967; Paris, 1957: 44ff.
68 Goffman, 1990a: 120.
69 Masson, 1911: 1–32; Paris, 1957: 328–34.
70 Masson, 1911: 32–42.
71 Ibid.: 317–62.
72 Archives of the Chambre de Commerce de Marseille, file H201, *Défenses de la Chambre du Commerce de Marseille contre les fabricans de camelots d'Amiens et de Lille* (Marseilles: Jos Ant Brebion, 1764).
73 Ministère des Affaires Etrangères, Nantes archives, file 2mi1958, Correspondance entre l'échelle d'Angora et l'ambassadeur à Constantinople.
74 Smyrnelis, 2001.
75 Bağış, 1983.
76 Braudel, 2nd edn 1966, Vol. 1: 557–81.
77 Skilliter, 1977; Goffman, 1998: 1–44.
78 Ferrier, 1973; Frangakis-Syrett, 1992: 107.
79 Wood, 1964; Matthee, 1999: 91–118.
80 Braude, 1979.
81 MD 43: 15, no. 27 (988/1580–1).
82 Goffman, 1998: 60–5.
83 Erim, 1991.
84 Çizakça, 1985.
85 Davis, 1967: 240–2.
86 Israel, 1989; see index.
87 Parker, revised edn 1990.
88 Israel, 1989: 262–3.
89 Bulut, 2001, *passim*.
90 Israel, 1989: 397–8.
91 Istanbul, Başbakanlık Arşivi/Osmanlı Arşivi, Maliyeden müdevver, no. 7527: 69 (1055/1645–6).
92 Istanbul, Başbakanlık Arşivi/ Osmanlı Arşivi, Cevdet İktisat, no. 971.
93 Kafadar, 1986b: 191–2.
94 Arbel, 1995: 67–8.
95 Hanna, 1998.
96 Desmet-Grégoire and Georgeon (eds), 1997 and Tuchscherer (ed.), 2001.

97 Hanna, 1998: 34–5, 58, 77; Raymond, 1973–4, Vol. 1: 117–19.
98 Istanbul, Başbakanlık Arşivi/ Osmanlı Arşivi, Maliyeden müdevver, no. 10349: 14–17.
99 MD 19: 130, no. 276; 67, no 146; 65, no. 142 (all 980/1572–3).
100 Çizakça, 1996: 92–122.
101 Curtin, 1984.
102 Arbel, 1995: 3–4, 44–54; Faroqhi, 1994: 165–6.
103 Stoianovich, 1960.
104 Panzac, 1996a: 79–80.
105 Greene, 2000: 153–4.
106 Bilici, 1992: 119.
107 Frangakis-Syrett, 1992: 94.
108 Ibid.: 105ff.
109 Masters, 1994b.
110 Braudel, 1949 and 2nd revised edn 1966.
111 Steensgaard, 1973, *passim.*
112 Braudel, 1979, Vol. 3: 409ff.
113 Panzac, 1996b.
114 Hanna, 1998.
115 Greene, 2000: 205.
116 Masson, 1911: 1–32.
117 Inalcik, 1969.
118 Springborn, 1992: 230.
119 Güçer, 1951–2 and Aymard, 1966.
120 Fleischer, 1986: 262.
121 Inalcik, 1969: 106.
122 Braudel, 1979, Vol. 3: 16.
123 Faroqhi, 1984: 222; MD 71: 334, no. 636 (1001/1592–3).
124 Kafadar, 1986a; M. Kütükoğlu, 2nd edn 1983.
125 MD 5, nos 1311 and 1312 (973/1565–6); Binark *et alii* (eds), 1994: 212.
126 Quataert, 1997.
127 Pamuk, 2000: 139.
128 Kafadar, 1991.
129 Inalcik, 1970b: 215.
130 Eldem, 1999: 148–202.
131 Faroqhi, 1984: 54; MD 7: 705, no. 1939 (976/1568–9) and MD 47: 199, no. 1466 (990/1582–3).
132 Barkan, 1975; Faroqhi, 1983.
133 Compare the article 'Imtiyāzāt', in *EI*, 2nd edn.
134 Veinstein, 1975 and the article 'Al-Djazzār Pasha', in *EI*, 2nd edn.
135 Dalsar, 1960: 244–77.
136 For an exception: Eldem, 1999: 223–5.

7 ~ Relating to pilgrims and offering mediation

1 See Chapter 8, for the special situation of ambassadors.
2 Montagu, 1993: XLI–XLII.

3 Goffman, 1998: 11.
4 MD 24: 43–4, no. 124 (981/1573–4).
5 Pistor-Hatam, 1991.
6 Faroqhi, 1994: 134–9.
7 MD 23: 203, no. 430 (981/1573–4).
8 MD 6: 17, no. 39 (972/1564–5). See also Binark *et alii* (eds), 1995.
9 Özbaran, 1994b: 127.
10 MD 14: 385, no. 542 (978/1570–1).
11 MD 26: 241, no. 693 (980/1572–3).
12 Necipoğlu, 1991: 255.
13 Peters, 1985: 484–9, 525–7.
14 Huizinga, 1954: 161–2.
15 Rauwolff, reprint 1971: 320–1.
16 Gomez-Géraud, 1999.
17 Schweigger, reprint 1964: 289 (visit in 1581/988–9).
18 Palerne, reprint 1991 (visit also in 1581/988–9).
19 Peters, 1985: 515–16.
20 Rauwolff, reprint 1971: 327 and elsewhere; Yérasimos, 1991: 300–1.
21 Rafeq, 2000.
22 Külzer, 1994; Yérasimos, 1991: 21.
23 Külzer, 1994: 351–5 (text dated to 1587/985–6).
24 Ibid.: 355–95.
25 Simeon, 1964.
26 Peri, 2001.
27 Rauwolff, reprint 1971: 448–58.
28 Schweigger, reprint 1964; Maundrell, reprint 1963.
29 For historical information: article 'Al-Durūz', in *EI*, 2nd edn.
30 Rauwolff, reprint 1971: 406–31.
31 Schweigger, reprint 1971: XXII–XXIII; Runciman, 1968: 244–58.
32 Maundrell, reprint 1963: 13.
33 Peters, 1985: 510–11.
34 Evliya Çelebi, 1314/1896–1938, Vol. 9: 488–95.
35 Rauwolff, reprint 1971: 376–7; Evliya Çelebi, 1314/1896–7 to 1938, Vol. 9: 490.
     See also Simeon, 1964: 126–9.
36 Biddle, 1999: 120.
37 Evliya Çelebi, 1314/1896–7 to 1938, Vol. 9: 493.
38 Ibid.: 491; Peri, 2001.
39 Peters, 1985: 520; Maundrell, reprint 1963: 129.
40 Evliya Çelebi, 1314/1896–7 to 1938, Vol. 9: 493; but compare also Evliya Çelebi,
     2nd edn 1987: 161; Belting, 1993.
41 Wild, reprint 1964: 200.
42 Maundrell, reprint 1963: 129.
43 Ibid.: 127–31.
44 Heyd, 1960: 180–4.
45 Peri, 2001: 198–200.
46 Pastor, 1923: 179–88; 734–46; Iserloh, Glazik and Jedin, 1985: 526–8; Müller
     et alii, 1985: 248–55; Croce, 1998: 602.
47 Rauwolff, reprint 1971: 427.

48 Anonymous Jesuit, 1745.
49 De Bonnac, 1896: 149.
50 Masters, 2001: 71–2.
51 Anonymous Jesuit, 1745: 55–7, 100.
52 Ibid.: 68, 118–21.
53 Hitzel (ed.), 1997; Palumbo Fossati Casa, 1997; Bacqué-Grammont, 1997.
54 Beydilli, 1984; Findley, 1998; Theolin *et alii*, 2002.
55 Arbel, 1995: 78–86.
56 Arbel, 1995.
57 Above, Chapter 5.
58 Khadduri, 1955; Faroqhi, reprint 1987.
59 Smyrnelis, 2000.
60 Anonymous, 1998; Latifi, 2001.
61 Anonymous, 1998: 41.
62 Ibid.
63 Ibid.: 33.
64 Ibid.; Masters, 2001: 16–40; Düzdağ, 1972: 87–109.
65 Montagu, 1993.
66 Ibid.: 89–91.
67 Wild, reprint 1964: 73.
68 Ibid.: 345–8.

8 ~ Sources of information on the outside world

1 Ihsanoğlu, 2000, Vol. 1.
2 Tinguely, 2000; Yérasimos, 1991: 17.
3 Camariano, 1970.
4 Unat, 1968; Tunçer and Tunçer, 1997; Hattî Efendi, 1999: 4–8 (Introduction).
5 Hagen, 1982–98.
6 Piri Reis, 1935; Soucek, 1992.
7 Goodrich, 1990.
8 Eren, 1960.
9 Bergasse and Rambert, 1954: 500–5.
10 Sestini, 1785.
11 Ibid.
12 Roosen, 1980; Windler, 2001.
13 Aksan, 1999b.
14 Camariano, 1970.
15 Seyyidî 'Ali Re'îs, 1999a with copious annotation; Kiremit (ed.), 1999, with linguistic study.
16 Soucek, 1992: 103.
17 'Süleyman I', in *İA*; Vatin and Veinstein, 2003, *passim*.
18 Deringil, 1991: 351; Seyyidî 'Ali Re'îs, 1999a: 88.
19 Unat, 1968: 82–4.
20 Faroqhi, 1994: 139.
21 Unat, 1968: 59–61.
22 Ibid.: 59; Zarinebaf-Shahr 1991.

23 Dourry Efendy, 1810: 4–5; Raşid, 1282/1865–6, Vol. 5: 373.
24 Dourry Efendy, 1810: 6–10. Raşid, 1282/1865–6, Vol. 5: 374; Veinstein, 1996.
25 Palumbo Fossati Casa, 1997.
26 Dourry Efendy, 1810: III–IV.
27 Nasuhü's-silahî, 1976; Unat, 1968: 206–10 (by Bekir Sıtkı Baykal).
28 Pedani Fabris, 1994b.
29 Ibid.: 196ff.
30 Evliya Çelebi, 2nd edn 1987.
31 Fodor, reprint 2000.
32 Beydilli and Erünsal, 2001–2.
33 Göçek, 1987; Mehmed Efendi, 1981.
34 Anonymous, 1999: 314–21.
35 Aksan, 1995; Unat, 1968: 116.
36 Resmi, 1303/1885–6: 35–6.
37 Findley, 1995.
38 Râtib Efendi, 1999.
39 See the entry on *saz* in *EI*, 2nd edn; Râtib Efendi 1999: 78–9.
40 Evliya Çelebi, 2nd edn 1987: 159–60.
41 Köhbach, 1983a; Vasıf in Ahmed Cevdet, *Tarih-i Cevdet*, 1309/1893–4, Vol. 4: 348–58 (abridged).
42 Windler, 2001.
43 Köhbach, 1983; Tunçer and Tunçer, 1998: 86–93.
44 Vasıf Efendi, 1309/1893–4: 354–5.
45 Unat, 1968: 116–28; Neumann, unpublished.
46 Emnî, 1974; Nahifi Mehmed Efendi, 1970.
47 Emnî, 1974: 47.
48 Ibid.: 69–70.
49 Nahifi Mehmed Efendi, 1970: 112–13.
50 Emnî, 1974: 66–8.
51 Nahifi Mehmed Efendi, 1970: 87.
52 Hagen, 1995–6.
53 Béller-Hann, 1987.
54 Versteeg, 1997.
55 Schmidt, 2000, *passim*.
56 Ibid.: 357–9.
57 Hodgson, 1973–4, Vol. 1: 96, 453–7.
58 Hagen, unpublished.
59 Hagen, 1998b; Ak, 1991.
60 Salzmann, 2004: 31ff.
61 Denny, 1970; Nasuhü's-silahî, 1976: 50–1, 8b and 9a.
62 Adnan-Adıvar, 1943; Ahmet Karamustafa, John Michael Rogers and Svat Soucek, in Harley and Woodward (eds), 1992; Ihsanoğlu, 2000, Vol. 1.
63 Piri Reis, 1935; compare the article 'Pīrī Re'īs', in *EI*, 2nd edn.
64 Soucek, 1992.
65 Goodrich, 1990; Bacqué-Grammont, 1997: XVII, LXIV, LXVI–LXVIII.
66 Hagen, 1982–98: 108.
67 Goodrich, 1990: 19–20.
68 Ibid.: 11–15.

69 Ibid.: 32–3.
70 Ibid.: 58; on 'recycling in a Dutch context': Schmidt, 2000: 360–1.
71 Kâtib Çelebi, 1145/1732.
72 Hagen, 2003
73 Compare the relevant article in *EI*, 2nd edn; Ihsanoğlu, 2000.
74 Hagen, 1982–98: 105.
75 Hagen, 1998a; Sarıcaoğlu, 1991.
76 Azulai, 1997.
77 Ibid.: 214–15, 248–9, 258–9.
78 Ibid.: 216.
79 Stamates Petru, 1976; Angelomate-Tsoungarake, 2000.
80 İnciciyan, 1956: 9, 39; article 'Inciciyan', in Collective work, 1993–5.
81 Eren, 1960, Kreiser, 1975, Haarmann, 1978 and Evliya Çelebi, 1988.
82 Evliya Çelebi, 1999a, Vol. 2: 18.
83 Braudel, 1979, Vol. 3: 145–234.
84 De Groot, 1978; Bulut, 2001.
85 Kévonian, 1975; Bulut, 2001.
86 Evliya Çelebi, 2002, Vol. 6: 219–25; Eren, 1960, Haarmann, 1978 and Evliya Çelebi, 1987.
87 Evliya Çelebi 2002, Vol. 6: 222.
88 Hagen, 1982–98: 105.
89 Evliya Çelebi, 2002, Vol. 6: 221 and 223.
90 Ibid.: 222; above, Chapter 7.
91 Evliya Çelebi, 1987: 243–4.
92 Evliya Çelebi, 2002, Vol. 6: 221.
93 Eren, 1960.
94 Hagen, 1982–98: 108.
95 Hagen, 2000.
96 Taeschner, 1923: 73–5.
97 İnciciyan, 1956.
98 Goodrich, 1990: 15.

9 ~ Conclusion

1 Hohrath, 1999.
2 Masson, 1911: 149–84.
3 Ersanlı, 2002; Fleischer, 1986: 85–6, 104.
4 Peri, 2000, *passim.*
5 Salzmann, 1993.
6 Masters, 1988; see, however, Wirth, 1986 on continuing connections to India.
7 Wallerstein, Decdeli and Kasaba, reprint 1987; Braudel, 1979, Vol. 3: 12–70.
8 Ibid.: 16.
9 Dávid, 2002: 194–5.
10 Eyice, 1970.
11 Bacqué-Grammont, 1997.
12 Osman Ağa, 1962: 13; Babinger, 1982.

Index

'Abbās I, shah of Iran, 49, 54, 139
Abdülkerim Paşa, 192
ahidname, 3, 60, 122, 144f, 150, 159
Ahmed I, sultan, 52
Ahmed III, sultan, 58f, 108, 186, 193
Ahmed Dürri Efendi, 186f, 193
Ahmed Paşa, Cezzar, 159
Ahmed Resmi, 28, 74, 188, 210
Akbar, Djalāl al-dīn, Mughul emperor, 41, 184
Albania(n), 12, 64, 114, 116, 152, 172, 193
Aleppo, 3, 10, 17, 29, 54f, 80, 138–40, 142, 144, 148f, 161, 168, 173, 180, 212, 214, 216,
Algiers, 79, 81–3, 121, 125, 131, 134, 145f, 191
Ali Paşa, Canbuladoğlu, 69
Ali Paşa, of Janina, 70
alms, 129f, 211
Amasya, 45
Amasya, treaty of, 36, 163, 185
ambassadors,
    Dutch, 42
    English, 42, 61, 134, 148
    French, 6, 28, 35, 37, 42, 61, 134, 146–8, 173, 175
    Ottoman, 6, 182, 217
    Russian, 51
    Venetian see *bailo*
America, 197f
Amsterdam ('Amıstırdam'), 10, 15, 139, 201, 204, 206, 216
Anatolia(n), 10, 34, 36, 44, 46, 53, 60, 62, 71, 76, 83, 101, 106, 108, 114, 123, 137, 143f, 173, 176, 180, 196, 200, 215
ancien régime, 52, 116, 147, 155
angora wool see mohair,
Ankara, 150f
Anna Ivanovna, Russian tsarina, 192

anti-luxury laws see luxury, 157
artisans, service to the Ottoman army, 108
Arab(ia), Arabian, Arabic, 18, 20, 72, 77, 101, 138, 163, 180, 192, 194, 208
Ardabīl, 35f
Armenia(n), 10, 18, 54, 60, 139f, 143, 148, 152, 154, 161, 165–8, 170f, 181, 199, 203f, 208, 212, 216
arsenal(s), 211f
    naval, Ottoman, 127, 131
    Istanbul, 132
    Marseilles, 132, 135
Arsenius Crnojevic III, Serbian patriarch, 58, 64
Ashkenazi, Solomon, 174f, 217
Astrakhan, 40, 50, 138, 140, 185
Austria(n) see Habsburg(s)
ayan (Muslim notables), 63
Azak, fortress of, 192
Aziz Efendi, 49
Azov, 50f
Azulai, Ha'im Yosef David, 201f

Bābur, Mughul emperor, 41, 184
Baghdad, 12, 31, 34, 49, 140
Bahçesaray, 112f
bailo, 28, 40, 51, 142, 174
'balance of power', 67f, 73f
Balkans, the, 12, 20, 101–3, 106, 115, 149, 152f
Bal**kh**, 20, 201
banditry see *eşkiya, eşkiyalık*
Basra, 11f, 34, 138, 140, 163, 183, 201
Bayezid II, sultan, 33, 36
Bedouin(s), 72, 82, 85–8, 163
Belgrade, 31, 58, 62, 64f, 127, 130f, 152
Belgrade, treaty of, 192
Belon, Pierre, 23
beylerbeyi, beylerbeylik, 76–8, 80–3, 89, 97

Bitlis, 113
Black Sea, 16, 22, 32, 50, 56, 63, 67, 82, 95, 98, 100, 112, 123, 144, 152f, 155, 196
Bloch, Marc, 25
Bohemia(n), 4, 29, 110, 204f, 207
Bonnac, marquis de, 29
boom, war-induced, 71, 109
booty, 99f, 113, 121, 204
Bosnia(n), 16, 114, 125, 137, 172, 176, 200
Braudel, Fernand, 15–7, 100, 154, 156, 214
Brotton, Jerry, 24
Bulgaria(n), 18, 62f, 69, 90
Bursa, 1, 10, 14, 40, 54, 113, 131, 138, 158, 161, 180, 204, 207
Busbecq, Ogier Ghiselin de, 24f, 38, 101

Cairo, 11, 15–8, 20, 85f, 101, 130, 151, 177, 180, 203, 207
Calvinist(s), Calvinism, 34, 42, 102, 165, 202, 206
Cantemir, Dimitrie (or Demetrius), 56, 82, 92–4, 96
capital formation, Ottoman, problems in, 71, 99, 109
capitulations see *ahidname*
captive(s), 18, 40, 119–21, 125f, 129, 135, 192, 211f, 216
captivity accounts, 121, 125f, 129f
Capuchins, 35
caravane, caravaniers, 145f, 153
Carcasonne, 145
cash payments, to soldiers, 105f
Caspian Sea, 56
Catherine II, Russian tsarina and empress, 22, 29, 67–9, 77, 115f
Catherine de Medici, 37
Catholic(s), 17, 32, 34f, 37, 42, 46, 61f, 73, 78, 80–2, 89, 130f, 133, 148, 150, 154, 162, 165, 167, 171–5, 191, 203, 206, 213
Caucasus, Caucasian, 12, 41, 56, 92, 99, 102f, 152
çavuş (messenger, envoy), 6, 123
Central Asia(n), 1

'centralism', Ottoman, 37, 48, 81, 96, 101
'centralism', Ottoman, limits of, 79
Çeşme, battle of, 61, 67
charity, to prisoners, 129f
Charles V, Habsburg emperor and king of Spain, 22, 32f, 38, 57
Chios, 89, 175
Church of the Holy Sepulchre, 35, 167, 169f
Church of the Nativity in Bethlehem, 166
çiftlik (piece of agricultural land), 63
Circassia(n), 12, 92, 152
coalition warfare, problems inherent in, 103
competition, between Ottoman and non-Ottoman traders, 62
consuls, 61
   French, 70, 146, 155
corsairs, 121f, 124f, 146, 153, 212
Cossacks, 50–2, 94, 112f, 123, 176
Costin, Miron, 82, 91, 94f
Counter-Reformation, 7, 47, 102
Crete, 5, 10, 22, 33, 58, 78, 115, 140, 155, 180
Crimea, 31, 67f, 78f, 103, 113
'cultural competition' between courts, 188, 191
customs duties, 137, 159, 161
Cyprus, Cypriot, 5, 21, 34, 38, 46–8, 78, 102, 130, 140f, 145, 174, 180

Damascus, 80, 87, 89, 151, 163
Darülharb, 2, 21, 73, 138
Darülislam, 2, 73
debts, of the Ottoman state, to tax-farmers, 106
'decline', Ottoman, 42f, 61, 97, 158, 213
defterdar, 13
Delhi, 41
deliveries, to the Ottoman state, in war-time, 107
'dependent principalities', 78–85, 95f, 215
   in international politics, 88
desert route, to Mecca, 163
deserts, as frontier regions, 72, 84

diaspora
  Armenian, 20, 54, 60, 139
  commercial, 152, 212, 216
  Jewish, 20
diplomatic and consular services, Venetian, 142
dirigiste policy, French, 146f
Diyarbekir, 207
Don Sebastian, king of Portugal, 138
dragomans, 7, 61, 153, 174, 182, 219
Druzes, 168
Dubrovnik, 2, 20, 52, 80–2, 89–91, 96f, 131, 159
Dutch see Netherlands, the

Ebubekir Dimaşkî (or Dımeşkî), 180, 208
Ebubekir Râtib Efendi, 188, 191f, 194, 209f
Ebusu'ud Efendi, *şeyhülislam*, 13, 176
economic rationality, absent from early modern warfare, 110
Edirne, 16, 162, 183
  treaty of, 38
Egypt(ian), 5, 10, 15f, 31, 45, 51, 71f, 77, 79, 85, 87, 138, 146, 163, 177, 214
embassy accounts, Ottoman, 179, 181, 183–5, 194, 203, 209, 217
England, English, 3, 11, 14, 28f, 34, 37, 52f, 111, 141, 145, 147, 153f, 157, 160, 175, 177, 179, 181, 201, 206, 213
enslavement, 125f
entitlement, to scarce goods, 156f
eşkiya, eşkiyalık (banditry, rebellion), 45, 59, 69, 87, 115
Eugene of Savoy, prince, 102, 104
Evliya Çelebi, 13, 20, 23, 25, 86f, 95, 100, 113, 169f, 180, 187, 201, 203–9, 216
export prohibitions, Ottoman, 53, 158
  exceptions from, 55, 142
exportation
  of cotton, by Venetian merchants, 141
  of Iranian silk, 54, 139
  of Iranian silk, to Europe, 141
  of Ottoman textiles, to Poland, 143

Fahreddin Ma'n, 69, 80
Fazıl Ahmed Paşa, Köprülüzade, 140
Ferdinand I, Habsburg emperor, 22, 33, 38, 40, 76
Feyzullah Efendi, *şeyhülislam*, 57f
Fondaco dei Turchi, 51
food supplies, for Istanbul, 69, 95, 98, 107, 151f, 156
'foreign policy', 4–7, 28, 83, 213
'foreign politics' see 'foreign policy'
France, French, 3, 6, 7, 9, 10f, 14, 17, 25, 29f, 33f, 42f, 52f, 73, 104, 117, 120, 132f, 142, 145, 148f, 154, 160, 173–5, 179, 181f, 188, 193, 201f, 213, 216f
Franciscans, 35
Franco-Ottoman alliance, 33, 73
François I, king of France, 8, 33, 37, 103, 144
Frederick II, king of Prussia, 68, 188

Galata, 28
Galland, Antoine, 25
galleys, 108, 127, 129, 130–3, 135, 211f
Gazi Giray, khan of the Crimean Tatars, 113
geography,
  Ottoman, 194, 203, 215
  Dutch, 195
Georgia(n), 2, 12, 55
Gerlach, Stephan, 166
governors,
  Christian, 97
  from pre-Ottoman elites, 75
  Ottoman, 13, 22, 27, 93, 96, 112, 121f
grain deliveries, Moldavian, to the 19th-century Ottoman Empire, 94f
grains delivered to the Ottoman state, 53
grand vizier, 7f, 21
Great Britain, British see England,
Greece, Greek, 10, 12, 18, 62f, 92, 141, 146, 148, 152, 172, 175f, 181f, 202, 208, 216f
Gregorian, 62, 165–7
Grenzer, 58, 64f

Gritti, Ludovico/Alvise, 10
gunpowder, 111
Gyllius, Petrus, 23

Habsburg(s), 2, 4f, 8f, 12, 21, 24f, 27f,
    31–3, 37f, 40, 52, 56, 58f, 61f, 73,
    76–9, 87, 95f, 98, 101–5, 110–5,
    117f, 120f, 123, 125, 141f, 144, 152f,
    167, 173, 177, 182, 188, 191f, 198,
    207, 209, 210f, 215
Habsburg lands, the, 11, 22, 64f, 122,
    132, 134
Hagiapostolites, Paisios, 166
Hai le-Veit Castiel, Sason, 201
Hayreddin Barbarossa, *kapudan paşa*,
    33, 38, 82
Heberer, Michael, 129–32
Henri IV, king of France, 9, 144
Hijaz, 11, 47, 72, 79, 82, 84–8, 96, 138,
    163, 180
Holland see Netherlands, the
'Holy League', 103, 115
'holy war', 98
'house of Islam' see Darülislam
'house of war' see Darülharb
households, political, Ottoman, 11, 30,
    44, 72, 82, 84, 97
Humāyūn, Mughul emperor, 41, 184
Hungary, Hungarian, 1, 9f, 21f, 27,
    31–4, 37f, 40, 52, 57–9, 64, 76–8, 80,
    96, 102–3, 106, 110, 115–7, 130, 142,
    180, 200, 207
Hurrem Sultan, 40
Hüseyin Hezarfenn, 25, 77

Ibrahim I, sultan, 5, 50
Ibrahim Müteferrika, 199
Ibrahim Paşa, Damad, 29, 186, 199
importation,
    of French woollens, 145
    of Indian textiles, 140, 158
    of Venetian woollens, 141
Inalcik, Halil, 75, 79f, 96
İnciciyan, P. Ğugas (or Ğugios), 203
'incorporation' into the European-
    dominated world economy, 54f, 65,
    154f, 214
'independence', of the Crimea, 67f

India(n), 2, 11f, 14f, 41, 47, 86, 88,
    138–40, 151, 154, 159, 161, 172,
    180, 183f, 201, 205, 209f, 216
Indian Ocean, 11, 48, 183, 195, 198
Innocent XI, pope, 57
integration, economic, 15
invincibility, Ottoman reputation for,
    98, 102
Iran(ian), 1, 2, 5, 10–2, 28, 31, 34, 41,
    45, 48f, 56, 60, 99, 108, 138–41,
    148f, 158–64, 179f, 183, 185–7, 191,
    194, 209, 212, 215
Iraq, 34, 41, 106, 161, 163, 196
Islamization, 81
Ismā'īl I, shah of Iran, 34, 36, 60, 138
Işfahān, 41, 54–6, 139, 186
Islamic religious law, 2, 21, 28, 30, 74,
    113, 199
Istanbul, 1, 3–6, 10f, 15–8, 20f, 25, 27,
    29, 35, 41f, 51–3, 60, 63, 69f, 72,
    79–81, 83, 85f, 90, 97, 100, 106f,
    113–5, 122f, 125, 133f, 143f, 146,
    151, 155, 162f, 166, 171, 173, 176f,
    180f, 183, 197, 200f, 203f, 206f, 212,
    215–7
Izmir, 3, 10, 14, 17, 29, 53–5, 61–3, 70,
    113, 139, 142, 148, 155, 159, 161,
    175, 180, 202, 212, 214, 216

janissaries, 5, 13, 16, 45, 49, 59, 65, 79,
    83, 87, 91f, 101, 107f, 130, 145, 149,
    156, 177f, 180,
Jerusalem, 23, 130, 164–71
Jesuits, 35
Jews, Jewish, 17f, 93, 107, 134, 143,
    148f, 152, 160–2, 164, 181, 191, 198,
    200f, 208, 216
Jiddah, 47, 86, 89, 138, 151
Joseph II, Habsburg emperor, 11, 68,
    210

kadi, 13, 93, 104, 117, 130f, 152, 171
kadiasker, 13
kâfir, 1
Kamieniec-Podolski, fortress of, 22
kapudan paşa (chief admiral), 83
Kara Osmanoğulları (notable family),
    63, 70, 159
Karlowitz, 64

Karlowitz/Karlofça, treaty of, 22, 58, 117, 125
Ḳaṣr-i Shīrīn, treaty of , 31, 49, 56
Kastamonu, 60
Kâtib Çelebi, 13, 179f, 194, 198–201, 205, 209, 210
'Kızılbaş', 2, 45, 48f, 60
Knights of St John see Malta, Order of
kocabaşı (Christian notable), 63
Köprülü, Fuat, 43
Korais, Adiamantos, 202, 210, 216
Kosovo, 64
Küçük Kaynarca, treaty of, 22, 31, 68, 153
Kumame, see Church of the Holy Sepulchre,

Lajos II, king of Hungary, 37, 76
legitimacy, legitimization, 8, 29, 52, 59, 69, 80, 84, 93, 96, 101, 114, 117, 160
legitimacy, loss of, 116
legitimization of outside intervention in Ottoman affairs, 61
Lepanto/İnebahtı, battle of, 38, 91
Leopold I, Habsburg emperor, 9, 58, 64
Leopold II, Habsburg emperor, 210
Levant Company, 148, 154
'line borders', 21
London, 15, 17, 201
Long War, the, 105, 112
Louis XIV, king of France, 9f, 73, 132, 145, 155, 167
Louis XV, king of France, 70, 147, 188
Louis XVI, king of France, 108
Lucaris, Cyrillos, 7, 42, 46
Lupu, Vasile, 50, 94, 217
luxury/ies luxury goods, 14f, 17, 140, 142, 156, 158

Mahmud I, sultan, 193
Mahmud II, sultan, 23, 78, 219
malikâneci see lifetime tax farmers
Malta, Order of; Knights of St John, 8, 40, 123, 125, 132f, 145f
Manisa, 70
Maria Theresa, Habsburg empress, 11, 68
Maronites, 168, 172

Marseilles, 63, 132, 139, 145–7, 155, 180
Marsigli, Luigi Fernando de, 25f, 104, 125
Martelli, Claudio Angelo de, 125, 127, 130, 134f
Matrakçı Nasuh, 187, 196f
Matthias Corvinus, king of Hungary, 21
Maundrell, Henry, 167f, 170f
Mavrocordato, Alexander, 217
Mecca(n), 1, 15, 41, 47, 59f, 72, 80–2, 85f, 88, 89, 96, 130, 133, 146, 161, 163f
mediation, 211, 213
mediation, mediators, between locals and foreigners, 173–5
Medina, 41, 72, 81f, 84, 85f, 89
Mediterranean, 2, 16, 33, 37f, 51, 53f, 62, 80, 82, 89f, 96, 119, 122, 124, 132, 145, 147f, 150, 152–5, 173, 183, 191, 195, 198f, 211
Mehmed II, sultan, 21
Mehmed III, sultan, 9, 52
Mehmed IV, sultan, 57f, 117, 140
Mehmed Ali Paşa/Muhammad 'Ali, 70
Mehmed Aşık, 196
Mehmed Efendi, Yirmisekiz, 6, 29, 182, 188
Mehmed Emni Beyefendi, 192–4, 209
Mehmed Paşa, Baltacı, 56
Mehmed Paşa, envoy to Vienna, 187
Mehmed Paşa, Sokollu, 37, 133, 174
mercenaries, 111f, 157, 181
merchants,
    Armenian, 139, 143, 152, 181
    Circassian, 152
    Dutch, 147, 150
    English, 62, 141, 145, 148f, 158, 161
    foreign, 212
    French, 62f, 70, 139, 141, 144–7, 153, 155, 158f, 161
    Greek, 152f, 181
    Indian, 158f
    Iranian, 161
    Iranian Muslim, 139
    Jewish, 143, 152, 181
    Muslim, 145, 181
    non-Muslim, 216

of Dubrovnik, 90, 131
Orthodox, 173
Ottoman, 180
Ottoman, Muslim, 100, 143, 151
Ottoman, non-Muslim, 62, 151, 153
Polish, 144
Tatar, 93, 152
Venetian, 141f
Militärgrenze (military frontier), 38, 112
'military reformation', 116
missionaries, 160, 162, 171–4, 213
Mohács, battle of, 76
mohair, 147, 150f, 158
Moldavia(n), 2, 12, 20, 37, 42, 50, 56, 76–8, 81f, 91–5, 113, 143, 176, 215
monasteries, Orthodox, 93
monks, Orthodox, 46
monopoly, of the Marseilles trading houses, 147
Montagu, Lady Mary Wortley, 162, 177
Montecuccoli, Habsburg commander, 111
Mora, Morea see Peloponnese, Peloponnesian
'morality', in trade, 155f
Mouradgea d'Ohsson (Muradcan Tosunyan), 174, 216
Mughul(s), 2, 11
Murad III, sultan, 9, 85, 91, 133, 198
Murad IV, sultan, 9, 29, 49
Mustafa II, sultan, 9, 57f, 117
Mustafa Âlî, 25, 114
Mustafa Paşa, grand vizier to Mustafa II, 57
Mustafa Paşa, Kara, 31, 57f, 74, 127
Mustafa Paşa, Lala, 4, 21, 48

Nādir Shah, shah of Iran, 56
Napoleon Bonaparte, 10, 31
narh (administratively determined price), 107
nations, 212
nation, French, 146, 155
Netherlands, the / Dutch, 3, 14, 22, 28–30, 32, 37, 52f, 141, 145, 147, 151, 154, 160, 181, 195, 200–2, 204, 206f

'neutrality' of Dubrovnik, 90f
New Djulfa, 10, 54, 60, 139, 148
notable, Christian see *kocabaşı*
notables, Muslim see *ayan*

Orthodox Church, 7, 35, 42f, 46–8, 56, 62, 64f, 78, 80, 82, 92, 116, 131, 165–8, 170f, 173, 202
Osman II, sultan, 9, 50
Osman Ağa of Temeşvar/Timisoara, 126, 133

'*pacta sunt servanda*' principle, 122
padişah, 2
Palerne, Jean, 165, 168
Palestine, 165
Papa Synadinos, 49
Passarowitz/Pasarofça, treaty of, 31, 56, 58f
patriarchate, oecumenical, 46
pax ottomana, 15
Peloponnese, Peloponnesian, 22, 31, 33, 58f, 62f, 65, 115f, 149
perceptions of 'the other', 18
Peter I, Russian tsar, 56f, 61, 65, 67, 92, 94, 96, 186
Petrovich, Moise, 64
Petru, Stamatis, 202
Phanariots, 92, 95
Philip II, king of Spain, 33, 37f, 47, 52, 103
pilgrimage accounts, 166, 168
pilgrims, pilgrimage, 160–71
pirates, 122–5, 137, 153, 173
Piri Re'is, 180, 183, 195, 197f
Pius II, pope, 4
Poland-Lithuania, Polish, 2, 7, 14, 20f, 32, 44, 50, 67f, 78, 82, 91, 96, 101, 103, 113, 123, 139, 142f
Portugal, Portuguese, 47f, 85, 138, 163, 183, 198f
power magnates, provincial, 69f, 72, 79
pragmatism, pragmatic, 3f, 28
prisoner(s) of war see captive(s)
'protection' of non-Muslims by European ambassadors, 61
protégés, 61f, 65, 148
Protestant(s), 17, 42, 80, 165, 191, 202

ransom, ransoming, 124–6, 131, 134f, 211f
Rauwolff, Leonhart, 129, 165, 167–9, 172
rebellion see eşkiya, eşkiyalık, 106
Red Sea, 47f, 79, 82, 89, 138, 151, 195
Rosales, Davidoğlı, 134f
Rumelia, 12
Russia(n), 11f, 23, 28f, 40, 46, 56, 61, 65, 67–9, 73, 95, 101, 103, 110, 113, 115–8, 123, 140, 153, 157, 161, 182, 185, 191–4, 208–10, 214
Russian tsar, 11, 16, 48, 56f, 61, 65, 67, 69, 92, 94, 96, 115f, 123, 186, 192
Rüstem Paşa, 101

Safavid(s), 2, 9, 27, 31, 34, 36, 41, 45f, 50, 55f, 60, 79, 99, 139, 149, 158, 183–7, 196, 215
Said, Edward, 23
Salonica, 107, 113, 148f
Sarmatian style, 143
Schweigger, Samuel, 165, 167f
security of routes, 59
Selim I, sultan, 34, 60, 77, 84f, 138
Selim II, sultan, 21, 38, 48, 92, 103, 142, 198
Selim III, sultan, 23, 65, 158, 188
self-ransoming, of slaves, 131
sentencing, to the galleys, 127
separation, of reaya and askeri, 106
Serbia(n), Serbs, 31, 62, 64f, 130, 152, 153
şeriat see Islamic religious law
şeyhülislam, 13
Seyyidî ʿAli Reʾîs, 12, 183–5, 193, 195, 198, 203, 209, 216
Sheik Ismāʿīl see Ismāʿīl I, shah of Iran
sherif(s) of Mecca, 47, 77, 79, 84–9
Shiʾites, 1f, 138, 161–3, 168, 176, 185, 217
silk, raw, from Iran, 149
silver, 138, 148, 157–9
    Ottoman need for, 14, 53f
Sinai, 165f
Sinan the architect, Mimar Sinan, 24f, 48
Sivas, 45

slave(s), 18f, 40, 46, 60, 84, 92, 94, 100f, 121, 125, 127, 129, 131f, 135, 152, 170, 176f, 207, 212
slaves, on galley, in case the vessel was captured, 127
slavery, 113
Sobieski, Jan, king of Poland-Lithuania, 57
Sofroni, bishop of Vratsa, 69
Spain, Spanish, Spaniards, 4, 14, 22, 32f, 38, 44, 51f, 54, 82, 90, 107, 117, 121, 133, 141, 144, 152f, 191f, 198f
Spalato, Split, 51, 90
Spanish viceroys, 123
St Catherine in the Sinai, monastery of, 166
St Gotthard at the Raab, battle of, 187
St James, Armenian church in Jerusalem, 166f
subsidies, paid to the sherifs, 86f
Süleyman the Magnificent, Kanuni Süleyman, sultan, 5, 9, 21, 24, 33f, 36–8, 40, 45, 48, 58, 60, 76f, 85, 91, 101, 103, 138, 144, 183–5, 197
Sulṭān Ḥusayn, shah of Iran, 55, 186
Sultan Yahya, 52f
Sunni, 2, 41, 49, 162, 168, 176, 185
Sweden, Swedish, 44
'symbolic appropriation' of foreign territory, 23f
Syria(n), 18, 71f, 77f, 80f, 87, 96, 141, 154, 168

Tabrīz, 31, 55f
Ṭahmāsp I, shah of Iran, 41
Ṭahmāsp II, shah of Iran, 55
take-over, of duties earlier performed by non-Muslims, on the part of Muslim officials, 219
Tatars, Crimean, 40, 50, 52, 68, 76f, 82, 93, 100, 103, 112f, 123, 140, 152, 176, 204–6
tax-exemptions, 61
tax farmers, lifetime, 30, 105
tax farming, tax farmers, 59, 105f, 116, 146, 160, 213
textiles,
    domestic trade in, 16

exported from the Ottoman Empire, 14

imported into the Ottoman Empire, 14f

Thévet, André, 23

Thirty Years War, 5, 51, 207

Thököly, Imre, 57

timar, 104f, 111

timar-holders, 87, 104f, 111

Tokat, 45, 71

trade, French, reorganized by Colbert, 145

transfer, of tax monies to Istanbul by foreign merchants, 70

transition, to directly administrated provinces, 75, 78

Transylvania(n), Erdel, 2, 12, 22, 76–8, 93f, 113, 188, 199, 215

tribute, 2, 89, 95, 215

Tripolis, 81–3, 121, 125, 131, 145f

Tunis(ian), 15, 79, 81–3, 121, 125, 131, 145f

Turgut Re'is, 40

Ukraine, 21

ulema, 13, 30

Uniates, 172f

upswing, 'economic', in the 18th century, 71

Uskoks, 112, 122f, 137

Uzbek, 2

Valensi, Lucette, 24

Vasıf Efendi, 191f, 194, 217

Vasvar, treaty of, 57

Venice, Venetian, 3–8, 10, 14f, 17, 20, 22, 25, 27f, 31–4, 38, 40, 51–3, 58, 62, 76–8, 90f, 98, 103, 111, 115–7, 121–3, 126, 129, 137, 140f, 144f, 148f, 151f, 154f, 161, 174, 180–2, 187, 203, 214

Vidin, 59

Vienna, Viennese, 10, 20, 22–4, 31f, 38, 57, 102, 111, 116f, 125, 133, 152, 179, 187f, 207, 216

vilayet, 78, 80, 89

Villeneuve, marquis de , 146f, 155

voyvoda of Moldavia, 37, 77, 91

Walachia(n), 2, 12, 31, 42, 50, 68f, 73, 76–8, 93–5, 113, 143, 215

Wallerstein, Immanuel, 55

war, preparedness for, 8f, 98, 101

'war and society', as a research topic, 111, 117, 120

'warfare state', 8, 99, 137

Wild, Hans, 130, 170f, 177f

woollens, from Salonica, 107, 148f

'world economy', European, 204, 214

'world economy', Ottoman, 14–6, 55, 156, 215

Yemen(i), 5, 14f, 47f, 79, 85f, 89, 98, 138, 151, 180

Zamosc, Simeon of, 166f

zeamet, 104

Zenta, battle of, 57

Zygomalas, Theodosios, 166